The Doctors Mayo

Since it was first published, this book has been acclaimed as one of the finest biographies ever written.

"The chronicle of one of the great success stories of America . . . a saga of absorbing interest, for the tale of the Mayos' rise to fame and power has everything."

—*Book-of-the-Month Club News*

"If you want to *enjoy* history, if you want to create, renew, or deepen your faith in men, in their power to live and work for democratic ends, do not miss *The Doctors Mayo.*"

—*Christian Register*

"Almost amazing is the manner in which the author has traced surgical progress as a portion of the lives of the Mayos and made it understandable."

-*Journal of the American Medical Association*

"A record that should make every American proud to know that the story it unfolds is part of his national heritage."

—*Hartford Times*

The Doctors Mayo was published originally by the University of Minnesota Press.

THE
DOCTORS
MAYO

by

Helen Clapesattle

PUBLISHED BY POCKET BOOKS NEW YORK

THE DOCTORS MAYO

University of Minnesota edition published December, 1941

A Pocket Book edition

1st printing........January, 1956
4th printing.......December, 1968

The Doctors Mayo has been translated
into German, Spanish, Portuguese, Urdu,
Arabic, Greek, Burmese, Thai, Japanese,
Singhalese and Tamil.

Table of Contents

TABLE OF CONTENTS

Foreword

IN HIS FOREWORD to the first edition of *The Doctors Mayo* Guy Stanton Ford, then president of the University of Minnesota, told how this story of the Mayo brothers and their father came to be written.

After the brothers had achieved world-wide fame and their name had become virtually a household word in the United States, they were approached by many writers who wanted the privilege of telling the story of their lives. But their experience with the products of professional writers in magazines and newspapers and with the effects of such publicity in medical circles had been a most unhappy one, and they persistently and summarily refused to grant permission to anyone to write a book-length biography.

Then one weekend in October 1936 President Lotus D. Coffman of the University of Minnesota and Guy Stanton Ford, dean of the university's graduate school, were among the Mayos' guests on board the *North Star* for a cruise down the Mississippi. Cornering their hosts for a few quiet minutes, the university officials told the brothers that their story did not belong to them alone, or even just to the medical profession. It belonged to all men everywhere. It had become a part of history—the history of America, the history of surgery, the history of medical practice, science, and education. As such, it was bound to be written by someone someday, and they owed it to future generations to see that the story was told as it actually happened, not as legend or fiction might distort it.

President Coffman and Dean Ford went on to suggest that, to ensure an honest, objective telling of the tale, the Mayos entrust the task and the responsibility to the University of Minnesota.

After thinking over this suggestion, Dr. Will and Dr. Charlie decided to accept the university's offer. They agreed to make available to the author chosen by the university all the necessary information, but they made it clear that beyond this they wanted no part in the project. The university must take sole responsibility for the final product.

These terms were scrupulously observed. The two brothers during the remaining years of their lives, their families, and their Clinic colleagues were generosity itself in giving time for interviews and in opening all their records and files to the author. But no one of them ever read, or asked to read, a page of the narrative until the book appeared in print on publication day.

Covering a century of tremendous activity in medicine and surgery and recounting the doings of a large cast of characters, *The Doctors Mayo* was a very long story full of many facts. It is pleasant to report that nonetheless it was bought and read by many thousands of persons throughout the world and the first edition had to be reprinted again and again. But the suggestion was repeatedly made to the university and to me that this story of truly great Americans and their peculiarly American achievement would be even more widely read if it could be made available in shorter form.

We have therefore prepared this second edition, condensed for quicker reading. The story is the same. It has not been rewritten. It has merely been streamlined—stripped of details that served to authenticate and underscore, but not to alter, the essential narrative.

The book is a biography of the Mayo brothers and their father, and as such it comes to an end with the end of the brothers' lives in 1939. I have made no attempt to add the story of the Mayo Clinic and the Mayo Foundation beyond that date.

When the Clinic board of governors gave the university

permission for me to interview the members of the Clinic staff, they requested that, in conformity with the medical code of ethics, members of the staff still active in practice be excluded from the story. Respecting the reason for this request, the university granted it—with the reservation, however, that the author's judgment must determine where historical accuracy required the factual introduction of living men. In later chapters of the book I exercised that judgment, feeling that the biography of the Mayo brothers would be pointless without the story of the Clinic, and that the story of the Clinic told solely in the names of its founders would be a historical distortion. But these reasons would not justify my extending, in this second edition, the account of the Clinic and the Foundation beyond the lives of the Mayo brothers.

The many sources—human, manuscript, and printed—from which I assembled the story of the Mayos were listed at considerable length in the first edition, for the information and aid of historians. There has seemed no good reason to repeat those notes of documentation and acknowledgment in this second edition, and students of history, amateur and professional, who wish to assure themselves of the authenticity of the narrative are referred to copies of the first edition on library shelves.

HELEN CLAPESATTLE

Minneapolis
August 1954

The Doctors Mayo

1. The Paradox of Rochester

IF YOU take a bus from Minneapolis to Rochester, Minnesota, you ride southward for ninety miles through a rolling country-side that in summer is a patchwork quilt in the greens of corn, small grains, clover, and alfalfa. The black and white of grazing cattle and the recurring pattern of hip-roofed barn flanked by the tall pillar of a silo tell you that this is a dairy land.

The towns that interrupt at every ten or fifteen miles are small, some of them just a few stores and houses grouped around a filling station at a crossroads, others large enough to boast a bank, a hotel above one of the cafés, perhaps a cheese factory or a cannery, and a furniture store that is also the undertaker's establishment. They might all be called, as one of them is, Farmington, for they exist solely as service stations for the farmers.

And then suddenly from the crest of a hill you see the metropolitan skyline of Rochester. Among the dairy farms and market villages you have come upon a city of great hospitals and crowded hotels; a city with hundreds of acres of parks and playgrounds, with fine stores and specialty shops; a city that is a crossroads of airlines, railroads, and national high-ways.

Here in the rural calm of southern Minnesota, without a scenic wonder or historic shrine in sight, is a city of thirty thousand inhabitants that has an annual transient population of ten times that number. For here, in this "little town on the edge of nowhere," is one of the world's greatest medical centers, to which men come from the ends of the earth for treatment and instruction.

1

That is the paradox of Rochester.

It was William James and Charles Horace Mayo who turned a pin point on the charts of commerce into a starred capital on the map of medicine. When the famous brothers died, in 1939, one of their fellow surgeons in England paid them this tribute: "And now death breaks the David and Jonathan partnership which for forty years has exerted a more profound influence on American medicine, and probably on world medicine, than any other single factor in modern times."

The Mayos were great surgeons. But there were other great surgeons of their day, some greater perhaps than they. What was it, then, that transformed *their* surgical partnership into the Mayo Clinic and the Mayo Foundation?

The answer is a story of unique achievement that is part of the inspiring heritage of every doctor and every American.

The paradox of Rochester has teased the minds of observers for many decades, but all most of them could find to explain it was the old quotation about the beaten path to the better mousetrap.

Dr. W. J. Mayo suggested a better explanation when he said to a visitor, "Yes, to be frank about it, we have accomplished much, my brother and I. But we should have done great things; we were given the opportunity. We were born at the right time and to the right parents. Perhaps no one will ever again have the opportunity to accomplish as much. That day is gone, unless for some genius. We were not geniuses. We were only hard workers. We were reared in medicine as a farmer boy is reared in farming. We learned from our father."

In Mayo Park in Rochester stands the statue of a man whom the inscription identifies as "William Worrall Mayo—Pioneer, Physician, Citizen—A Man of Hope and Forward-Looking Mind." The sculptor has portrayed him in a lifelike pose. Wearing a long black coat but hatless, he is pausing in the midst of a speech. In one hand he holds the roll of manu-

script he has abandoned, in the other eyeglasses he has just
removed in the intensity of his effort. You might think him
to be addressing some gathering of his medical fellows, but
those who knew him can hear him urging them to some
political reform or civic improvement.

This was the father of the Mayo brothers. As an old
man he was often congratulated upon the brilliant work of
his famous sons. To one well-meaning gentleman he snapped
in reply, "Why don't you congratulate *me?* I started all this."

That was the irritable answer of an active mind that resented being relegated to the past, but it was the truth. He
laid the foundation upon which his sons built. He gave them
the precepts and principles by which they worked. The phrase
"Our father taught us . . ." was forever on their lips.

So with him the story begins.

2. *The Way Westward*

THE levee in Galena, Illinois, on the Mississippi River, was
humming with activity and excitement in July 1854. Immigrants bound for Minnesota Territory had been arriving in
great numbers since the opening of navigation, and the men
of Galena were certain the rush would be stimulated by the
gala excursion with which the Chicago and Rock Island
Railroad had just celebrated the completion of its tracks from
Chicago to the Mississippi.

By invitation some twelve hundred of the nation's notables
had traveled over the new line to Rock Island and then up
the Mississippi to St. Paul in a flotilla of steamboats. They
had been given a gay time, and the reports from the well-
known journalists among them served notice to thousands that

Minnesota Territory was now within thirty hours' reach of Chicago.

Mingling with the crowds on the levee to join in the endless discussion of plans and prospects was a young man just arrived from Indiana. He was a small man, short and slight of build, but his straight carriage and decisive manner more than made up for his scant five feet four inches. The piercing glance of his dark eyes commanded attention even among these strangers.

This was Dr. William Worrall Mayo. He was then thirty-five years old, and was in search of a new place to live. Behind him lay a long way westward undertaken in fitful stages.

So little, even in old age, was he given to reminiscence that he left little knowledge of his parents or his youth. A faded inscription in an old family prayer book records his birth in the English village of Salford, near Manchester, on May 31, 1819, as the third child and second son of James and Anne Mayo.

Anne was the daughter of John Bonselle and his wife Tenneson, whose name before her marriage had been Worrall. *Tenneson* and *Bonselle* both crossed to England with the Huguenots fleeing from France, and the Worralls were a family of prominence in Manchester. All else about Anne Mayo is obscure.

James Mayo made his living as a skilled artisan, a joiner. His ancestry is established only by tradition and William was taught that the history of his family goes back to the early sixteenth century, when a group of Flemish Protestants migrated from the Low Countries to escape religious persecution. In England they multiplied and prospered, making *Mayo*, in all its spellings from *Mao* to *Mayhowe*, a familiar and respected name. Many of these English Mayos were physicians and several of them achieved distinction in that profession.

James Mayo died when William was seven years old, but the widowed Anne was able somehow to give the boy a good education. At a time when three quarters of the children in England got no schooling at all, William studied Latin and Greek with a French tutor, attended a college in Manchester, and took private lessons from the famous scientist John Dalton, from whom he caught an enthusiasm for chemistry that he never lost.

Perhaps under Dalton's tutelage, young Mayo began his study of medicine in Manchester and was among the medical apprentices who walked the wards of the city's infirmary. Later he went to study in the hospitals of London and Glasgow, but in neither city did he stay long enough to complete his training and receive a license to practice. He was too restless, too eager to see more of the world.

The call of America was strong in Great Britain then, ringing in the ears of any young man adventure-minded or ambitious to better his chances in life. William Mayo was both of these, and in 1845, when he was twenty-six, he decided to try his luck across the Atlantic.

His mind made up, he went straight to the nearest seaport and boarded ship for America. He asked no permissions and said no good-byes. Not that he was being secretive about his going, or that there was any ill feeling between him and his mother. Taking unceremonious leave was just his impetuous, independent way.

His first work in the New World was as a chemist in the drug department of Bellevue Hospital in New York City. Hair-raising still are descriptions of the plight of the sick poor sent to Bellevue in those years, and William could not long tolerate the conditions produced by a combination of political corruption and medical mismanagement. He soon moved on to Buffalo, and then wandered westward along the shores of Lake Erie and southward into the valley of the Wabash.

Midsummer of 1848 found him in Lafayette, Indiana, joined with two tailors in the operation of a pretentious establishment called the Hall of Fashion. This venture prospered, but for Mayo it was only a stopgap, and a year later he sold out his interest and resumed his study of medicine.

He spent the summer of 1849 working with Dr. Elizur Deming, Lafayette's foremost doctor, as his preceptor, and when fall came, he journeyed north with Deming through the valley of the Tippecanoe and across the Kankakee marshes to the little city of La Porte. There he enrolled for a course at the Indiana Medical College, of which Deming was an owner and a faculty member.

William Mayo could scarcely fail to recognize that the medical education he was now undertaking differed radically from what had been required of students in Europe. The training of doctors in western America was cut to the pattern of frontier needs and frontier conditions.

The quality of medical education had been good in colonial America, but as population spread itself thin across the mountains and along the rivers, the demand for doctors outran the supply of well-trained men and small proprietary medical schools, owned and managed by their faculties, arose in the rural areas of the eastern states. They offered short courses of a few months a year for two or three years, fitting their fees to the pocketbooks of the farm boys and their schedules to the leisure months between harvest and seedtime. Their graduates went west with the pioneers, and soon schools of the same kind were opened in the newer communities—a few at first in Kentucky and Ohio, then dozens in Indiana, Illinois, Michigan, and the states west.

These schools were only supplementary, however, for the backbone of medical education then was preceptorship, the American form of Europe's apprentice system. The student kept his preceptor's office clean, compounded his powders and salves, and looked after his horses, in return for the use of his library and the privilege of watching him at the task of examining and prescribing.

Three years of such study with a preceptor and two sessions of lectures at a medical school earned the student his degree of doctor of medicine. But the degree was not required for practice. Anyone at any stage of preparation could dub himself "doctor" and hang out his shingle; there was no one with either legal or professional authority to stop him.

The Indiana Medical College, to which chance and Dr. Deming had brought William Mayo, was a proprietary school of the usual sort, but it had such an excellent reputation that its hundred students a year were drawn from many states, some as distant as Vermont and North Carolina, and Rush Medical College of Chicago had proposed consolidation to rid itself of a dangerous rival. Yet a description makes it sound less than impressive.

It had no stated requirements for admission, its annual session was only four months long, its course was ungraded. The teaching consisted almost entirely of lectures, with virtually no clinical instruction, for La Porte had no hospital and the college had no ambulatory clinic. Anatomy was learned chiefly from lectures and textbooks. An optional course in dissection was offered, but many students were prevented from taking it by the extra fee charged.

Perhaps this financial hurdle was placed in the way deliberately, for it was difficult in those days to keep the dissecting room supplied with fresh cadavers. No legal provisions having yet been made for this necessity, a midnight excursion with sack and shovel to some new grave in a nearby churchyard was not an unusual experience for medical students.

But woe unto the body-snatchers if any resident of the community caught them prematurely resurrecting the dead. The public was sensitive on the subject of grave-robbing, and more than one pioneer medical school had its career cut short by the violent action taken against such despoilers.

To the half-dozen subjects that made up the usual medical curriculum, the Indiana Medical College added a course in pathology and physiology, and more remarkable still, it provided a microscope, imported from England "at great expense." (The microscope was not available to medical students at Harvard until 1869-70, and even twenty years later the refresher classes at the Johns Hopkins Medical School were filled with practicing physicians who had never seen a microscope.)

One microscope for a hundred students! But it was enough to arouse in William Mayo an extraordinary interest in microscopy, which endured and deepened and later played a part in the education of his two sons.

The year at Indiana Medical College cost Mayo a hundred dollars in fees and another fifty dollars for sixteen weeks' board and room. He was excused from extended preceptorship and a second year of lectures because of his previous study in Europe, and having prepared an acceptable thesis and passed an oral examination, he was given his degree on February 14, 1850.

When he returned to Lafayette as Dr. Mayo, he found an opening ready for him. The young physician employed in Daniel Hart's drugstore to serve patrons in need of medical advice had suddenly felt an urge to try his luck in the booming California gold fields, and "Dr. W. W. Mayo, Physician and Surgeon" succeeded to his place and the substantial salary of seventy-five dollars a month.

It was just a year later that friends discovered one day that William was missing from his office in the drugstore, and in a few days they read in the newspaper of his marriage to Louise Abigail Wright at Galene Woods, Michigan, on February 2, 1851. He was being impulsive and independent as always.

When he returned with his bride, his friends found her a buxom young woman, slightly taller than her husband, with energy and determination quite equal to his. She had been born in the village of Jordan, near Syracuse, New York, on December 23, 1825. Her father was a Scotsman, a mechanic with an inventive turn of mind, and her mother was the granddaughter of an English officer named Totten, who is said to have commanded a battleship during the American Revolution.

When she was eighteen, Louise Wright had gone alone, by canal barge and prairie schooner, to the home of relatives in

Michigan, later moving with one of them to La Porte, where she met her future husband during his year in medical school. Her youth had been one of hard work, with little time for formal schooling, but she was an avid reader and remembered well what she read, so that she impressed everyone she met as an educated woman of keen intelligence.

In spite of his new obligations as the head of a household, Dr. Mayo gave up his position at the drugstore the following May. Mr. Hart had proved to be less generous in payment than in promises, and the young doctor decided to accept an invitation to partnership with his former preceptor, Dr. Deming.

He had now joined the benevolent tribe of doctors on horseback. His daily local rounds might be made comfortably in a carriage, but many a call into the countryside had to be answered on horseback, with medical and surgical supplies stowed in the saddlebags.

For all the youth and hardihood of the pioneers who settled Indiana, there was plenty of sickness among them. To chronic aches and pains, and to the cholera that plagued the community during the early 1850s, were added frightful epidemics of scarlet fever, typhoid, malignant forms of dysentery and malaria, and the mysterious "milk sickness" that killed cattle and men alike, quickly desolating any area in which it took hold.

Malaria was the great scourge. The fertile bottom lands, lowlying, humid, and often flooded, upon which the prosperity of the Wabash Valley depended made that valley one of the worst malarial districts in Indiana. The agent of infection was unrecognized, so the common guess laid the disease at the door of "marsh miasma," a vaporous substance thought to rise from stagnant water to float in the air like a poisonous gas, especially at night.

From midsummer to early fall was the annual sickly season. It was usual then for more persons to be sick than well, sallow faces and listless manners were the rule, and spells of the "shakes" were too prevalent to cause remark. Sessions of court were recessed while the judge lay on a bench in the corner to chatter through his chill, and schoolroom drills were interrupted while teacher and pupils had their shake together. There was nothing strange in the experience of the farmer who came upon his neighbor sitting on a log with a gun across his knees.

"Hello, John, what are you doing here?" he asked.

Pointing with a jerking finger toward a tree, the neighbor answered, "I'm waiting for this damn shake to go off, so I can shoot that squirrel up there."

Even the doctors sometimes arrived at their patient's home so weakened by the alternating chills and fever that they had to lie down a bit before they could do the work for which they had come. Dr. Mayo himself fell victim to the disease.

All this sickness did not mean so much business for the doctors as might be supposed, because the laymen chose to act as their own doctors. They carried buckeyes or wore bags of asafetida to ward off illness, and bled themselves every spring to get rid of the bad blood and make room for a purer product. When illness came in spite of them, they dosed themselves with cathartics, emetics, and various home-brewed bitters, and yielded to glowing testimonials for quack nostrums warranted to cure everything from itch to consumption. Only as a last resort did they send for the doctor.

Perhaps this was because they knew that all too often he would be able only to purge and puke and bleed them a little more, or pull out his spatula and bottles to mix up a powder he *hoped* might help.

In the 1850s medical science had as yet contributed little to medical practice. Few scientific procedures or instruments of precision were yet available to aid in diagnosis. Even the simplest chemical analyses of urine were too new to be in general use. The stethoscope was still novel and the clinical thermometer had not been invented.

Few diseases had been sufficiently differentiated to be easily described and recognized, and for fewer still were the causes and the pathological processes known. General symptomatic designations such as "lung disease," "fever," "liver complaint," "inflammation of the bowels," and "kidney trouble" were still the terms of diagnosis.

Consequently the doctor face to face with an illness had to proceed empirically, treating the symptoms in the hope that he would reach the cause, prescribing a remedy that had *seemed* to work in what had *seemed* to be a similar case. He had to rely upon what William Osler later called "a pop-gun pharmacy, hitting now the malady and again the patient, the doctor himself not knowing which." It was not unreasonable to remark of a patient's recovery "that whether it came about from the lapsing of a sufficient number of days, the remedies employed, the nature of the disease, or the grandmother's prayers, one could hardly say."

And surgery?

The use of anesthetics was only a few years old, still a matter for wonder and controversy among doctors and laymen alike. Only the more advanced surgeons used chloroform regularly; only the most courageous patients would submit to it. Even progressive physicians were content when a patient was "nearly insensible to pain" and pleased when enough chloroform had been used to make him shout and sing during the operation.

Resort to the knife was in all cases an emergency measure, not an accepted therapeutic method. Cutting into the cavities of the body was an unwarrantedly rash procedure when operations even on the surfaces and extremities were so commonly followed by fatal infection. Suppuration of the incision wound was thought to be a natural postoperative development and the "laudable pus" a necessary adjunct of the healing process.

All the same, despite meager schooling and scant science, some pioneer doctors really learned the ways of sickness and of healing and made original contributions to medical and surgical practice. Their very lack of formal training seemed to free them from accepted notions of what could not be done, especially in surgery.

That no one had ever cut out an ovarian tumor did not prevent Dr. Ephraim McDowell of Danville, Kentucky, from doing it—while his more cautious colleagues stood on a street corner and decided that when his patient died, as she surely would, he should be charged with manslaughter rather than malpractice. That the gallbladder had never been opened and gallstones removed did not deter Dr. John Bobbs of Indianapolis from a first performance of the operation.

The crudities of frontier life, the lack of convenient aids and tools, demanded great resourcefulness. Often traditional procedures could not be followed and new ways of doing things had to be devised. And this kind of necessity fostered a practical audacity that advanced the practice of medicine.

But it did not much increase dependence on physicians among the pioneers. In general, public faith in doctors remained at low ebb.

So, although Dr. Mayo's practice in Lafayette covered a good-sized territory, it was not remunerative.

Since the Mayos' first child, a son, had died at the age of six weeks, Mrs. Mayo was free to devote her abundant energies to supplementing her husband's income. Renting a room in Lafayette's business section, she opened a millinery shop, and when she began sending to New York for buckram frames, braids, and plumes, she found herself doing a wholesale business with her less enterprising competitors.

The "New York Millinery" flourished, even moving into larger quarters from time to time. When a daughter, Gertrude, was born in July 1853, Mrs. Mayo merely took in a partner to relieve her of the need for constant personal attendance at the shop.

Meanwhile Dr. Mayo tried several ventures into medical sidelines in the hope of increasing his earnings. None of these was conspicuously successful, and when Dr. Deming was elected to the faculty of the Medical Department of the University of Missouri and left for St. Louis in the fall of 1853, Dr. Mayo went with him and spent the winter working as an unofficial assistant to the professor of anatomy. The following spring he applied for and was granted an *ad eundem* degree, that is, another M.D.

He did not stay long among the Hoosiers after his return from St. Louis. He and Mrs. Mayo had both weathered an attack of cholera without undue irritation, but the debilitating chills and fever of malaria every summer were too much for the Doctor's patience. One hour you were so hot you couldn't get cool; the next you were so cold you couldn't get warm. He loathed the recurrent misery and the languor it left behind. "Hell," he insisted, "is a place where people have malaria."

So one day in the summer of 1854 in the midst of a chill he stamped out to the barn, hitched up horse and buggy, and shouted to his startled wife as he drove off westward, "Goodbye, Louise. I'm going to keep on driving until I get well or die."

3. *On the Minnesota Frontier*

A MONTH of leisurely driving brought the Doctor to the Galena levee and its buzzing speculation about the future of Minnesota Territory.

Until recently most people had known that north country only vaguely, as a remote wilderness frequented by fur traders, missionaries to the Indians, explorers, and a few adventurous travelers. They had been told it was a land that produced only furs and lumber, where fruit would not grow and grain would not ripen, a chill land of ice and snow and interminable win-

ters, where the temperature was often too low for the thermometer to record it.

But now letters and newspapers from the Territory had
begun to tell a different tale, of a beautiful country with lakes
and rivers thick with fish, forests full of game, and fertile
acres on which farms would flourish.

Always these reports praised the Minnesota climate: It was
without an equal in healthfulness. Its cold, clear air made the
diseased lungs of the consumptive whole again, brought color
to sallow cheeks and vigor to weakened bodies.

"There has not been one case of sickness in the whole of
Hennepin County for several weeks past," boasted one writer.
"What do you think of that, you who are shaking yourselves
to pieces with the ague?"

They thought it too good to be true, and so they wrote letters of inquiry to the Minnesota editors. "Will we have to
bring two physicians for each family of four persons?" asked
a man from Indiana. "I am going to emigrate west if I can
find a region where there is no chills and fever," said one from
Kentucky.

A land without chills and fever was what Dr. Mayo too was
looking for. So, leaving his horse and rig in a Galena livery
stable, he took passage on one of the daily packets to St. Paul.

The population of St. Paul was then approaching four thousand. It was not entirely a raw frontier town. Among its dwellings were some of brick and a number of neat white cottages
with green shutters and white picket fences, and its business
places included such urban establishments as a bookstore, a
bakery, and a crockery shop that sold sets of fine china imported from Europe.

On the other side of the river was Mendota, district headquarters of the American Fur Company, and a little farther
upstream stood old Fort Snelling. To the east lay some scattered farms and beyond them the town of Stillwater, the "log
and lumber metropolis" for the rich pineries of the St. Croix
Valley. Ten miles up the Mississippi was St. Anthony, second

to St. Paul in size and growing mightily with its wealth of water power for the milling of lumber and flour. Across from St. Anthony the village of Minneapolis was waiting until the government should relinquish title to its site, and nearby was a beauty spot all visitors to the Territory rode out to see: Minnehaha Falls, the girlhood home of Laughing Water, gentle wife of Hiawatha.

But to the north and west of that knot of settlement there was only a vast, still wilderness of forest and prairie, sprinkled with lakes and threaded by streams and faint Indian trails. This was the homeland of the Chippewa, and they were its only tenants except for a few traders, trappers, and missionaries, and the colony of half-breeds at far-off Pembina on the Red River near the Canadian border.

To the south of St. Paul lay the eastern end of the "Suland," millions of acres of forest and grassland that the Sioux had been persuaded to cede to the white man three years before. The tribes had left their homeland reluctantly but they were gone now, gone to the shoestring tract reserved for them along the upper Minnesota River to the west.

Into the lands they had vacated the immigrants were pouring, to stake out claims, clear off the timber, and lay out a thin network of roads for stagecoach and wagon. Scores of towns on paper and dozens in fact were being platted on sites along the Mississippi and Minnesota rivers and in the fat triangle of land between them.

The prevailing temper of mind was exuberant optimism. Everyone was sure the next two or three years would bring ample immigration to people those unoccupied acres and plenty of capital to vein them with railroads and dot them with mills and factories. The air was electric with anticipation.

"Fence in a prairie fire! Dam up Niagara! Bail out Lake Superior! Tame a wolf! Civilize Indians! Attempt any practical thing; but not to set metes and bounds to the progress of St. Paul!" That was the spirit, in the words of a St. Paul newspaperman.

It was a spirit Dr. Mayo could not resist, and after a few
weeks' enjoyment of it he went back to Indiana to get his wife
and daughter.

Mrs. Mayo was reluctant to make the move; she did not
want to give up her flourishing millinery business. But why
give it up? Why not just move it to St. Paul? In that booming
town a milliner should do well.

So Dr. Mayo took his wife's stock of goods to Chicago,
where they were packed for shipment. He ordered a quantity
of new braids, mourning crapes, linen collars, and bandboxes
to be sent with them, and then went all the way to New York
to order still more from the dealers there. When he returned
to Indiana, the Mayos piled their household effects into a
wagon and started for St. Paul.

Arriving in October 1854, Mrs. Mayo established herself
in a shop on Third Street and immediately prospered. Spring
and fall thereafter she made the long trip to New York to
order new supplies and the latest styles in bonnets and trim-
mings. In time she added dressmaking to her activities, as well
as the retailing of fur sets, including "mantle, muff, and wrist-
lets."

But the Doctor was not so easily settled. He seems to have
made little or no attempt to practice medicine in St. Paul. Perhaps he thought it was no use; the town was overrun with
doctors, some twenty to thirty of them being in residence in
the latter months of 1854. There was not enough business to
support so many, and the doctors, like all frontiersmen, had to
become jacks-of-all-trades; they taught school, dabbled in real
estate, ran for public office, or managed a drugstore.

Dr. Mayo preferred to indulge his desire to see more of
Minnesota Territory. "I was perfectly charmed with the new
country," he said, "and I was anxious to see it in all its wild
beauty and to tread where the foot of man had never trod
before, unless it be that of the Indian."

The area he chose to explore was the head and northern
shores of Lake Superior, some hundred and thirty miles north-

ward from St. Paul. Although a few men from Superior, Wisconsin, had moved across the lake to stake out claims on the Minnesota side, the region was almost entirely unknown, and the possible routes to it from St. Paul did not promise easy traveling. The two by water were full of dangerous rapids and difficult portages, and each of the three by land included long stretches through dense woods, where the trail would be faint to inexperienced eyes.

None of this daunted Dr. Mayo, and for the next nine months he was as much at Lake Superior as in St. Paul. His frequent trips back and forth did not go unremarked, and in the spring he was appointed to take a census in the new lake counties and to act as commissioner for one of them. These tasks, plus a job inspecting copper claims for the Northwest Exploring Company, kept him at Lake Superior without a break from May to August 1855.

He probably never enjoyed anything quite so much. He expressed something of his pleasure in a description he wrote later:

> Before this time I had done considerable camping out. I had made my way on foot three times from Saint Paul to Lake Superior. Once I had trod the Indian trail alone for three days without seeing the face of man or beast. Once again in a birch bark canoe I had paddled the length of the Saint Croix from [its] commencement . . . as a small creek, rushing over its sand bars, shooting down its rapids, and again gliding leisurely along past tall pine trees or watching the bright eyes of the deer as they paused for a moment before taking those beautiful bounds for which the animal is noted.
>
> [I made my bed] on the bottom of the canoe, swung to sleep by the light, rippling waves, while the boat was tied to the banks waiting for the morning's light to pursue the journey. . . . [I carried] the canoe around the great falls by the Indian portage and launched it again

just above the dalles, passing through the narrow chan-
nels, arresting the boat's progress at every short distance
to wonder and speculate upon the time taken for the
water to cut through that rock dike and at the same
time admire the picturesque beauty of the rocks.

Thus three days passed, floating through wild scenes,
viewing nature in all her wildness and grandeur of
stillness. . . . These scenes had given me a taste for
trips in solitude. To notice a small rabbit cross my
tracks . . . to be glared at by wolves through the day
and to be regaled by their wild concert of howling during the night, had for me a real pleasure.

He rejoiced too in the opportunity the job of inspecting copper claims gave him to sample the scenery of Minnesota's
now famous North Shore. Foot travel along the length of
rocky, heavily wooded shore was impossible, so the journey
had to be made by water and Dr. Mayo set out in a Mackinaw
boat manned by three French-Canadian *voyageurs.*

Their first trip, early in July, was short, just up to Knife
River and back, but the second, begun late in the same month,
covered the entire shore line from Minnesota Point to within
a mile or two of Pigeon River on the Canadian border.

Sailing when the wind permitted, at other times rowing, the
men cruised slowly along the lonely coast. They would land
on the shore of a bay or a river's mouth, visit any cabins in
sight, and then cut their way into the interior as far as there
were any signs of men or claims. Then after cooking breakfast
or dinner on the beach, they would take to the boat again and
move on to the next dot of habitation.

The trip took a month—for Dr. Mayo a month of living
close to the solitary wilds he liked so well.

Late in August he returned to the head of the lake and
started back to St. Paul, traveling once again by canoe down
the St. Croix waterway. He reached town in time to join Mrs.
Mayo on her fall trip to New York, where he helped her select

the seasonal additions to her millinery stock. So easily did he turn from copper to milady's bonnet!

Dr. Mayo did not linger long in St. Paul. "He was a pioneer in the true sense of the word," once said his elder son. He had the curiosity of the true wanderer, who cannot resist the enticement of a highway passing his door, stretching away into the unknown distance. "I fain would see what lies beyond," Minnesota's motto, was the Doctor's too.

This time he wandered south along the course of the Minnesota River, which twists and turns from St. Paul for nearly a hundred miles, then rounds a sweeping curve and lengthens on northwestward to its source. Moving from village to village on its banks—Shakopee, Chaska, Belle Plaine, Henderson— he stopped off finally at the home of the Dunhams, a family lately come from Indiana like himself.

Their farm was one of a scattered group that made up the neighborhood known as Cronan's Precinct. It lay just within the wide belt of magnificent hardwood forest the early settlers called the Big Woods. Here and there the deep shade of the trees gave way to patches of open meadowland, bright in spring and summer with wild flowers and berries, yellow and purple and crimson. Not far to the west began the rolling, treeless hills of the prairies—a boundless white in snowtime, a gentler vista of rippling green under the summer sun.

There was beauty and wildness enough here to satisfy even Dr. Mayo, but it was less stark than Lake Superior and neighbors were more numerous.

Four miles from Dunhams', across the river and a little downstream, was the nearest town, Le Sueur, cozily settled on one of the largest and fairest woodland meadows. Not far upstream was Traverse des Sioux, grown up at the spot where an old Indian trail crossed the river, and a stone's throw beyond lay the newer and livelier village of St. Peter. Still farther upstream, at the bend of the river, was Mankato, and a few miles around the curve a colony of German immigrants were

building New Ulm. Then came the military outpost at Fort
Ridgely and the beginning of the Sioux Reservation.

These were the milestones along the river, and strung between were a score of smaller settlements or single homesteads.
Axes were clearing farms and townsites in the Big Woods back
from the river, and the immigrant wagons had already begun
to strike boldly across the prairies, cutting tracks through the
tall grass to unclaimed plots in the interior.

Dr. Mayo could make a home here. He took over an abandoned farm near the Dunham place and a few months later
Mrs. Mayo, having sold out her business in St. Paul, came
with their daughter Gertrude to join him.

In Cronan's Precinct Dr. Mayo resumed the practice of
medicine, but only slowly, because the calls for his services
were few at first. He faced the competition of doctors already
established, as well as that of the midwives, herbalists, and
bonesetters who willingly obliged the neighbors unfortunate
enough to need their services.

There were no malaria and no annual sickly season in the
Minnesota Valley, but there was plenty of sickness nonetheless. Improper food, drafty houses, exposure to cold and snow
and high waters, lack of adequate sanitation, ignorance, and
superstition nourished a bountiful crop of ills.

Stone slabs rose one after another in the churchyard as
whole families were wiped out by typhoid fever, scarlet fever,
or the increasingly prevalent diphtheria, then commonly called
putrid, or malignant, sore throat. Waves of smallpox inspired
terror and uncovered ugly depths of inhumanity in men. Children were so cold day after day, in spite of heavy wool-knit
clothing, that their little hands were too blue-numb to hold a
spoon for eating. Sickly babies cried and cried.

Infant mortality was frightful, so usual in fact that when a
child was born its parents only *hoped* it might live; they did
not assume that it would.

There was need enough for doctors. But just as in Indiana,
knowing how to care for the family's ailments was part of

mother's job, and when the illness was too acute for her skill, she called in some community grandmother wiser still in the ways of plasters, teas, and poultices. Calling the doctor was postponed as long as possible.

A few calls a week made up Dr. Mayo's practice for many months. When he was sent for, he set off with his little medical bag, walking along the narrow trails through the woods, lighting his way at night with a whale-oil lantern.

If the distance was too great for walking, the little doctor made sure his saddlebags were full and rode his pony, sometimes taking hours for the trip. He had no carriage; there were no roads for one. To reach a patient across the river he traveled by canoe or ferry boat; there were no bridges.

At the end of the journey he was likely to find his patient in a one-room log cabin or sod hut, heated by a fireplace and lighted by a lard lamp or homemade candles. Family and friends might be assembled in stifling proximity to the sick person, or he might be alone in the cabin. Sometimes Dr. Mayo stayed a day or two to act as nurse, even on occasion splitting wood to step up the fire and stirring up a nourishing gruel to help restore strength.

This practice did not return much in money. Most of the people were poor, struggling to get a start, probably deep in debt for their land and stock. If they could give the Doctor a dollar for his trouble, he accepted it as graciously as though it were adequate recompense. If they could spare him a side of bacon to carry home, it was welcome.

To supplement his income Dr. Mayo did whatever he could find to do. He was farming, of course, and at one time had eight head of cattle to look after. He also practiced veterinary medicine when called upon to do so. He was elected justice of the peace for Cronan's Precinct. And he ran a ferry boat to and from Le Sueur. But the living he made was a lean one, through little fault of his.

Prospects had been bright in the Minnesota Valley when the Mayos moved there in the spring of 1856. One of the arrivals that same spring was a young man from Indiana, Edward Eggleston by name, who had moved to Minnesota in the hope that its climate would cure his sick lungs. In one of the novels he wrote later, *The Mystery of Metropolisville*, he described the frenzy of speculation in land that was taking place.

It was a time, he said, "when money was worth five and six per cent a month on bond and mortgage, when corner lots doubled in value over night, when everybody was striving frantically to swindle everybody else." Men infected with the fever put every cent they had into the first payment on a piece of land, hoping to sell out at an increase before the second payment fell due.

But the dream of quick success vanished overnight when the failure of a New York life insurance company in August 1857 precipitated a nationwide panic. Eastern creditors called in their loans, draining the western territory of cash, and the boom collapsed.

Commodity prices fell, business came almost to a standstill, lots once quoted at hundreds of dollars could not be given away, towns that had been zooming toward city size, on paper, relapsed into wilderness, speculators quietly folded their maps and stole away.

Awakening gradually from the daze induced by the sudden disaster, the men and women who had gone to the Territory to make homes on the land pulled in their belts and settled down to work their way out of the hard times.

The most urgent need was for cash, and when an alert St. Peter man discovered that there was a ready market for the man-shaped ginseng root that grew in profusion throughout the Big Woods, the community went wild. Carpenters left the houses they were building, barkeeps closed their saloons, and merchants quit their counters to set out for the woods with sack and hoe. The trade in ginseng grew to amazing proportions. In 1859 the town of Henderson listed in its business directory one doctor, one butcher, one baker, and *seven* ginseng dealers.

This eased things a little, but it did not dispel "the blue haze of hard times." Newspaper editors pleaded with their subscribers to pay up—in wood, pumpkins, potatoes, anything useful. Ministers were kept going by "donation festivals," parties to which their parishioners brought what clothing and foodstuffs they could spare. Edward Eggleston, then serving as the pastor of churches in Traverse des Sioux and St. Peter, supplemented such uncertain bounty by working as a surveyor, by pasturing sheep, and by peddling a recipe for soap from door to door.

The doctors were hard hit. Although they were willing to accept any kind of produce in payment of their accounts, they could not get enough of it for their needs, and at last some of them, worthy men all, announced that their services must be paid for in advance. They apologized for resorting to such a stipulation but said that justice to their families demanded it.

In such circumstances it is little wonder that Dr. Mayo could not support his family by the practice of his profession alone. He seems to have done as well as most, and better than many.

Life was not easy for Mrs. Mayo either. She was not cut to the pattern of a pioneer Martha and did not wear the role happily. With the opportunities and social sanction of a later day she would have been a career woman, devoting her talents to a business or a profession and leaving the dusting and cooking to someone more suited to it. Housekeeping was not her forte.

But she buckled down to it. She had two children now and for a time three. In June 1856, shortly after she moved to the farm, a second daughter, Phoebe Louise, was born, and in March 1859 came a third, Sarah Frances, who lived little more than a year. Keeping her family clothed and fed and the house respectably clean was a hard, full-time job. She had to bake the bread, cure the meat, dry the beans, corn, and peas, spin, weave, knit, mold the candles, and make the soap by leaching lye from the winter's ashes and adding cracklings or lard.

One day as she bent over a kettle of soap on the stove, she suffered a severe hemorrhage from the lungs. Little Gertrude, badly frightened by the blood, ran screaming for her father.

Mrs. Mayo recovered after a brief spell of rest, and her family never knew that she feared a recurrence. But thereafter she kept out of doors as much as possible. She directed her reading to the woods and the sky and became a good amateur botanist and astronomer.

She had need of great courage. She and the children were often alone on the farm, and she must have been mindful of the possible presence of wolves, wildcats, and bears. There were always Indians around too. She never knew when she might look up to see one flattening his nose against the windowpane to peer inside, or when several of them might appear at the door to beg for food and liquor. They did not seem unfriendly, but she knew they could turn nasty if they were crossed.

Trachoma was prevalent among the Indians at that time, and it spread to the whites of the Valley and Mrs. Mayo caught it. For several years she was almost blind, and she suffered from "wild hairs" on her eyelids, which her children often helped her to pull out. Eventually her sight was restored, but her eyelids were left lashless.

Looking back in later years, Louise Mayo could only say of the Minnesota Valley, "It was a hard country."

One of its hardships came of the fact that the Minnesota River and its tributaries were given to frequent and heavy floods. Suddenly would come a freshet and the waters would swirl over the banks and across the prairies, sweeping along anything lying loose or lightly anchored—haystacks, fences, even livestock.

One such flood, unusually widespread and protracted, occurred in the spring of 1859. For weeks the river communities above Henderson were almost entirely cut off from the towns downstream and from communication with each other. The residents of Cronan's Precinct were virtually marooned in their homes. The trails they used were mostly under water, and the ferries were all out of order.

Once again Dr. Mayo had had enough. He did not choose to risk another such experience and decided to move across the river to Le Sueur. He bought a lot and he and his brother James (a confirmed world wanderer who turned up now and then to visit William for a few weeks or months) spent the following summer building a house and barn on it. When the house was ready the Mayos moved to town.

The house was not pretentious, just a small, two-story, gabled cottage. The largest room was the kitchen, which served also as a dining room, and upstairs under the gables, in a room so low ceiled as to give away the small stature of its builder, Dr. Mayo arranged his medical books, his massive roll-top desk, overlarge for the space, and his equipment for mixing medicines. This was his office.

In that house on June 29, 1861, a son was born to the Mayos. They named him William James, after the father and his brother. With an Englishman's feeling for family, Dr. Mayo rejoiced in the birth of a son, though he of course could not foresee what cause countless others would have to rejoice with him.

The removal to Le Sueur did not mean that the Doctor had to build up a new practice. He remained within frontier reach of his former patients and had merely enlarged the circle of possible new ones.

The first call came quickly. While he was still roofing the cottage, a man rode up and introduced himself as J. L. Drake, a farmer living near town. Neither he nor any member of his family was in need of a doctor, he said, but he had a pretty sick horse that wanted attention. Would the Doctor come and look at him?

Dr. Mayo's reply was unequivocal. "Sure I'll come. I'll look at a horse or any other damn thing you've got."

According to the story, a legend in Le Sueur, he treated the horse successfully and made a favorable impression on his new neighbors.

His coming caused some uneasiness in the mind of Dr. Otis Ayer, Le Sueur's other practitioner, a man of Dr. Mayo's own age, but dour and difficult. When Dr. Mayo did him the professional courtesy of calling on him, Ayer bluntly observed that Le Sueur was not big enough to support two physicians.

Dr. Mayo was innocently surprised. "Why, Doctor, were you thinking of leaving?"

He knew that Dr. Ayer was right, though, and that he still had to find other work to supplement his income, so during the spring and summer of 1860 he tried his hand at steamboating.

The Minnesota was a tricky stream to navigate. It fairly squirmed its way through the Valley, and its channel was full of growing sandbars. In the spring floodtime these were not serious obstacles, but by summer's coming it was more than the larger boats could do to scrape their bottoms over the bars. Then it was necessary to break the trip from St. Paul at Belle Plaine or St. Peter and transfer passengers and freight to smaller vessels of shallower draft for the rest of the journey upstream.

It was on one of these small vessels that Dr. Mayo served. By some accounts he was the captain, by others a clerk or purser. Whichever it was, Dr. Mayo had a good time that summer, for he loved the rough life on the river and the bustle and excitement that greeted the boat at every stop.

One acquaintance he made was a young man by the name of James J. Hill, who was a clerk on one of the lower river boats. Many years afterward, when Dr. Mayo was the famous father of his famous sons and Hill was one of the great railroad men of the nation, Dr. Mayo attended a reception at the Hill home in St. Paul. When he arrived, he exclaimed jovially, "Why, it's Jim Hill, coming up the river!"

"And you're the little doctor coming down the river!"

Then the two excused themselves and went off to Hill's study for a long talk about old times.

Less successful was the Doctor's venture as a newspaper publisher. He got into this through a renewed acquaintance with Harry H. Young, a newspaperman he had known in Lafayette. When Young, having moved to Minnesota for his health, turned up in Le Sueur, the result was a newspaper, the *Le Sueur Courier*, published by Dr. Mayo and edited by Young. The first issue appeared early in January 1861 and the last some three months later.

This was about par for the life expectancy of newspapers in those days. Important as they were to the growing communities, it was almost impossible to make them pay, and the editors' wail about their unfortunate lot was so constant and general that Dr. Mayo could not have started the *Courier* with any expectation of its making money for him.

He left the *Courier's* news and politics to editor Young, but he kept the agricultural department for himself. He prepared a weekly article on some phase of farming or farm homemaking, and he did not let the briefness of his own experience or its indifferent success deter him from telling the farmers and their wives how to shear sheep, tend apple trees, make good butter, and concoct substitutes for coffee out of rye, carrots, or peas.

It is a likely guess that the unmistakably Democratic *Courier* went down on the rock of politics. The year was 1861 and political passions were rising high, with the line drawn sharply between "Black Republicans" and "Slavery Democrats."

But "it was a time for the searching of hearts in politics," and newspapers, editors, and plain men were shifting their allegiance to the Republican party in great numbers, principally because of its stand on the Union question but also because of local opposition to the well-oiled Democratic machine with headquarters in St. Paul.

Dr. Mayo had apparently given his friends reason to believe that he was among those who had turned their political coats, for they were greatly puzzled by *his* publishing a Democratic paper. At last the inquiries were so many that Dr. Mayo was impelled to make a public confession of his political faith.

He denied all responsibility for the political tone of the *Courier;* that was the business of its editor, he said. On the question of slavery he himself was clearly for peace at almost any price. He hoped Mr. Lincoln would champion neither the abstract right of the Negro nor the real right of the slaveowners, but would arrange some compromise. Give time a chance and within another generation the South would acknowledge "the right of human freedom from servile bondage."

More Democrats than Republicans would have said amen to these views, but the tone of Dr. Mayo's communication, which was columns long, leaves no doubt that he considered himself a Republican, one of those who had joined the new party more for the purpose of breaking up the graft of the Democrats than from acceptance of Republican doctrines.

At any rate, within a year Dr. Mayo was actively at work in Republican ranks. He served as the chairman of the Republican district convention in 1862 and was elected to the district committee of the party for the succeeding year. His career in politics had begun.

All these divergent activities were not such deviations from the Doctor's professional path as they might appear; they helped immeasurably to spread his name and acquaintance up and down the Minnesota Valley.

The term *Minnesota Valley* is not merely a verbal abstraction used for convenience; the Valley was a geographic unit and in a very real sense a social unit too. Dependence on the river for transportation and communication made close neighbors of the families and towns scattered along its banks. Although Henderson, Le Sueur, St. Peter, and the rest were often bitterly jealous rivals, they nevertheless formed a single community within which persons and news moved easily.

When Mr. Hathaway of Belle Plaine wished to complain of the injustice of a Le Sueur editor, it was quite natural for him to do so in a Mankato newspaper. A ball at St. Peter, a dramatic performance by the Thespian Club of Mankato, an Independence Day picnic on Le Sueur Prairie, were all social occasions that drew attendance from the full length of the Valley.

To extend his acquaintance throughout this neighborhood Dr. Mayo could not have chosen his activities better. At his ferry converged the folk of two counties who wished to cross the river to do business in Le Sueur or to catch the stage for St. Paul. When the river was highway, railroad, telephone, and telegraph all in one, when "every farmhouse on the bank was a steamboat landing," and when the day's main event was the boat's arrival, no one was more widely known than the boat's captain or clerk.

The *Le Sueur Courier,* short-lived as it was, and the Doctor's subsequent political activity brought him into contact with the editors, lawyers, and businessmen who were the leaders in Valley life and would shortly become leaders in the state at large. These men found Dr. Mayo an intelligent gentleman, a good talker, serious, energetic, forthrightly honest. When they became his patients, as numbers of them did, they also found him professionally able. And they said so.

In remarkably few years Dr. Mayo had emerged as one of the outstanding citizens of the Valley, well toward the top in its medical profession. His regular practice covered most of three counties, and he was occasionally called farther afield upstream. His professional card was running in the papers of Henderson, Belle Plaine, and St. Peter as well as Le Sueur, and those papers habitually referred to him simply as "Dr. Mayo," with no initials, no place of residence, no identification of any kind. Just "Dr. Mayo," whom the readers might be expected to know. The practice of medicine alone could not have given him so wide a reputation.

When Fort Sumter fell on April 12, 1861, Governor Alexander Ramsey of Minnesota was in Washington. Knowing that now the battle must be joined, he went at once to the secretary of war and offered a thousand men from the youngest of the states for the defense of the Union. His offer was accepted, and the call for volunteers was sounded in Minnesota.

The response was good for a time, but by the summer of 1862 the pace of volunteering had slackened and President Lincoln on August 4 proclaimed a draft of three hundred thousand men. A commissioner and a surgeon were appointed in each county to act on applications for exemption, and Dr. Mayo became the examining surgeon for Le Sueur County. At once he set about recording the halt and the blind of the county according to specifications issued from Washington.

Before this task was well begun it was forgotten, for suddenly the citizens of the Valley found themselves fighting for their lives on their own doorstep. The Minnesota Sioux had taken the warpath.

The outbreak came suddenly but not without warning. In the spring of 1862 the tribes had gathered at the agencies to receive their annuity payments in foodstuffs and cash. The winter had been hard, provisions were gone, and they were hungry. But Agent Galbraith told them they must wait awhile for their payment; he had the food on hand but the money had not yet arrived, and he refused to distribute the food until the money came, simply because checking the rolls twice would be too much trouble.

With a sensible incomprehension, the Indians could not see why they had to go hungry while their flour and sugar and pork stayed locked up in the agency warehouses.

All through the summer they waited, teased along by occasional doles of just enough food to keep them from starving. On August 15 they came to parley once more with the agent and the traders. Chief Little Crow spoke for them. If the white man did not give them food they would take it, he said. "When men are hungry they help themselves."

Alarmed by this threat, Galbraith turned to the traders. Would they let the Indians have food on credit until the payment money arrived?

One Andrew J. Myrick answered for the group: "As far as I am concerned, if they are hungry let them eat grass."

The interpreter repeated the insolent words.

There was a moment's silence, then with whoops of fury the Indians strode away.

That was on Friday. At midday on Sunday a band of four Indians, drunk on anger if not on firewater, killed five whites on a lonely farm in Meeker County. Their escapade, reported to their tribes, was a match to the ready fuse, and early Monday morning a large band of Sioux braves arrayed for war attacked the Redwood agency, shot all the men they could find, then looted and plundered the stores.

Myrick the trader was one of the first to fall, and into his dead mouth the Indians stuffed a handful of the grass he had told them to eat.

Meanwhile other bands were working havoc in the countryside adjacent to the reservation. Taking the settlers unaware, they moved from farm to farm, killing the men, making captives of the women and children, gorging themselves with food, and setting fire to the barns and haystacks.

Survivors and a few friendly Christian Indians managed to warn some of the settlers, who fled downstream, spreading the alarm as they went.

The news came to the lower Valley in the night. Some courageous Paul Revere from New Ulm, galloping hard under cover of darkness, brought word of the outbreak and an urgent appeal for help. From house to house he rode, rousing the citizens of St. Peter, then spurring on through the night to spread the alarm in Traverse des Sioux and Le Sueur.

Dr. Mayo was wakened at daybreak and joined his excited neighbors in a discussion of what was to be done. It was agreed that every able-bodied man left in the town must go to the aid of New Ulm. Hastily they collected what guns they could find, molded lead into bullets, and filled their pouches and powder horns. By eleven o'clock they were ready, and set off under the command of the sheriff.

At St. Peter they joined with the company of "Frontier Guards" hurriedly organized and armed that morning like themselves, and the troop, numbering one hundred and twenty-five, began their march to New Ulm at one o'clock.

They made a motley, straggly column. A few of them rode in buggies, some were on horseback, but most of them walked. Dr. Ayer of Le Sueur and Dr. Asa W. Daniels of St. Peter took the bags of medical and surgical supplies in one of the buggies, but Dr. Mayo marched with the ranks.

Wet to the skin from a rainstorm in the late afternoon, they arrived at the ferry crossing to New Ulm just as night was falling. Two persons in the town had been killed and several wounded and half a dozen houses on the outskirts had been fired in a skirmish with the Indians that afternoon. The towns-folk were panic-stricken.

Guards were immediately posted all around the town, and hospital quarters were appointed for the doctors' use. Dr. Mayo was established with Dr. W. R. McMahon of Mankato in a front room of the Dacotah House, and Drs. Ayer and Daniels in the basement of a drygoods store across the street. They were all busy for several hours ministering to the cas-ualties of the afternoon's battle and to some of the Sioux's victims who had been brought in from the country still alive.

Friday was quiet in New Ulm but early Saturday morning the sleepy town was startled to attention by shouts from the guards, "The Indians are coming! The Indians are coming!"

The defenders prepared swiftly for battle. The women and children were hurried into the cellars of stores and houses within the barricades, and the companies were formed and marched out to their appointed positions on a low ridge about half a mile south of town.

The Sioux leaders deployed their forces at the foot of the bluff in the distance, and as they advanced slowly across the sloping prairie, their red bodies and brilliant feather headgear made a splendid spectacle in the sunlight. Suddenly as they got within rifleshot they raised a terrific yell and "came down like the wind" upon the citizen soldiers, shooting as they came.

The quick change of pace and the chilling war whoop were too much for the nerves of the inexperienced settlers. They fled precipitately toward the rear, not stopping until they were inside the barricades. The Indians could have followed them over the barriers in the scramble, but they preferred to seek cover for fighting according to their custom.

From then on the whites fought Indian-fashion too, every man or small group of men on its own. Some adventurous souls crept out to occupy the windmill or the post office or some other structure strategic for defense, while others set fire to the nearer buildings to deprive the Sioux of cover close at hand.

With the crackling of flames, the Indian yells, the cries of frightened women and children, and all the shooting, the town was a bedlam. Sharp skirmishes were in progress here and there, men were racing back to headquarters near the Dacotah House to replenish their ammunition and receive instructions, everything was wild confusion.

Not all the men were brave enough to take it, and some sought refuge in the cellars with the women. Dr. Mayo went after them, thrust pitchforks into their hands, and stationed them behind the barricades. When the frightened fellows asked what they should do if the Indians came, Dr. Mayo swore. "Run your pitchforks through them, of course."

In the first hour and a half of battle ten were killed and fifty wounded. The latter were carried to the hospital rooms on doors ripped from their hinges to serve as stretchers.

The doctors had their hands full, but Dr. Mayo managed to keep an eye on what was happening outside. Looking up once when he was amputating a man's leg, he saw two men who were supposed to be on guard at the barricades sneaking past the window. In a trice he was out the door, shouting and brandishing his bloody knife. The men returned to their posts in a hurry.

As twilight came on, the fighting slackened and men were

sent out to burn the buildings still standing outside the barricades. The flames lighted up the area sufficiently throughout
the night to prevent the Indians' advancing in a surprise attack.

In the morning the red men, after a few casual shots at long
range, gave up the attack and withdrew in the direction from
which they had come.

That afternoon the officers met to discuss the situation. The
town was a shambles inside the defenses and smoking ruins
without, provisions and ammunition were running low, and
two thousand mortals crowded into cellars and storerooms
like cattle in a boxcar were an invitation to disease. They decided to evacuate New Ulm.

The dead were hastily buried in the streets or in the garden
near the Dacotah House, the barricades were broken up, and
the wagons were moved into line to serve as conveyances for
the wounded. The merchants threw open their stores and told
the defenders to help themselves, but according to a story current at the time, they left behind several conspicuously open
barrels of whisky, brown sugar, and flour which had been lib-
erally dosed with strychnine.

Early Monday morning the wagons filed slowly out onto
the road for Mankato followed closely by a column of march-
ers more than two miles long.

News of their coming caused a flurry in Mankato. Accommodations there were already overtaxed by the refugees who
had sought shelter in the town during the past week, but the
generous citizens did their best. The wounded were received at
the American House, where the Ladies Aid Society had fitted
up rooms for them, and the others were bedded down as comfortably as possible in private homes, churches, the school,
the public hall, even in the newspaper office, where the fonts
of type got so pied in the crush that the editor complained
about it for weeks afterward.

When most of the caravan moved on toward St. Peter the
next morning, in order to put as great a distance as possible
between themselves and the "red devils," Drs. Daniels and

Ayer went with them. But Dr. Mayo stayed in Mankato a
week longer to help Dr. McMahon take care of those too seriously wounded to travel farther.

Long afterward a man from Montana, returning to his home
after a serious operation at the Mayo Clinic, received the felici-
tations of his friends on his recovery.

"Yes," he agreed, "the Mayo brothers are remarkable men.
But so was their father. He saved my life in the Sioux Outbreak when I was eleven years old. I was hurt in one of the
battles and they took me to the hospital behind the lines,
where a kindly little man dressed my wounds and praised me
for my courage. He was the Old Doctor Mayo. Everybody on
the frontier called him the 'little doctor'."

In the midst of the turmoil and alarm Mrs. Mayo was alone
with her three small children, as were most of the women of
Le Sueur. The story is that when a rumor spread that Indians
were closing in on the town, Mrs. Mayo rose to the occasion.
She called the women together and told them to put on men's
clothing and arm themselves with hoes, pitchforks, broom
handles, anything the general size and shape of a gun. Then
to the ends of the handles they tied knives or spoons to reflect
the sun and look like the bayonets on army rifles.

Thus garbed and armed the women marched in formation
up and down the streets of Le Sueur at stated periods each
day, hoping to make the Indians believe the steamboat had
landed a defense force from Fort Snelling. Their ruse was
successful and Le Sueur was not attacked.

That is the legendary story as it has been told again and
again. The core of truth from which it may have grown appears in Mrs. Mayo's own version of her experiences as
phrased by a reporter to whom she told it.

Will was a baby in arms and safe enough, and I scared
the other two children into staying indoors. When it was
necessary for me to go to the barn or the well, I'd put
on a pair of overalls and tuck my hair under one of the

Doctor's old hats. . . . With a gun in my hand what a
figure I must have cut in those overalls! I often think
of it. So brave and manly; and my heart in my mouth!

But she did her part to care for the refugees. Eleven families
took shelter in the house and barn, and beds were set up or
blankets spread out in every room. Mrs. Mayo and little Gertrude worked hard to feed their guests, and in one day baked
an entire barrel of flour into bread for them.

To Mrs. Mayo's fear for her own and her children's safety
was added anxiety about her husband. She often went out to
stand at the gate as refugees straggled by and asked the injured, "Who dressed your wounds?" When some of them
answered, "The little doctor," she knew that her husband was
still alive.

At last, two hectic weeks after his departure, Dr. Mayo
came home again and his wife relaxed.

Meanwhile Governor Ramsey had assembled some companies of drafted men and volunteers and sent them to the Minnesota front under the command of Henry H. Sibley, a man
well acquainted with the Indians and their ways. After a few
indecisive skirmishes Sibley engaged the redskins in battle and
put them to rout. Their white prisoners were recovered and
some two thousand Sioux were themselves taken captive.

After a trial before a military commission, three hundred
and seven warriors were condemned to death. When President
Lincoln, feeling the fundamental unfairness of the procedure,
as he said, "down to my boots," postponed the execution of
the sentence, the people of Minnesota threatened to lynch the
prisoners if they were pardoned.

But Lincoln delayed his decision long enough for the hot-
test passions to cool a little. Then he ordered the hanging of
thirty-nine Indians whom the evidence showed to have com-
mitted rape and wanton murder; the others he found guilty
only of waging war.

When the condemned Sioux were hanged at Mankato on

December 26, 1862, the bodies were placed two deep in a long trench dug in the sand of the riverbank, but they did not stay there long. So many unmourned dead were a windfall when subjects for dissection were hard to get. In the crowd of spectators were many medical men, including Dr. Mayo, and under cover of darkness the grave was hastily opened and the bodies removed and distributed.

To Dr. Mayo's lot fell the body of Cut Nose, a hideously ugly brave whom the little doctor had once bested in a struggle for his horse during a lonely ride to a patient's bedside. By all accounts this giant Sioux had been a fiend incarnate during the outbreak, the ringleader in all the most brutal outrages. Carted to Le Sueur, his body was dissected by Dr. Mayo in the presence of other doctors and the skeleton was cleaned and articulated for the Doctor's permanent use.

4. *Rochester Then*

THE Sioux Outbreak was a local whirlwind that did not disturb the nation's preoccupation with the Civil War.

Under the Enrolment Act passed by Congress in March 1863, the federal government took over the responsibility for administering enlistment and conscription, which were to be carried on in each congressional district by an enrolment board consisting of a provost marshal, a commissioner of enrolment, and an examining surgeon.

In April Dr. Mayo was named the examining surgeon of the enrolment board for the first Minnesota district, which comprised the entire southern half of the state. And for its headquarters the board selected Rochester, the seat of government in Olmsted County. So in mid-May 1863, Dr. Mayo

once again said good-bye to his wife and children and journeyed to Rochester to take up his new duties.

For more than a year and a half the office of the enrolment
board in Rochester was the busiest place in the state. Dr. Mayo
worked long hours every day, examining volunteers after each
new call, drafted men after each drawing, and between times
the "droves" who hoped to have their names taken from the
conscription rolls.

It was not an easy job. If a surgeon exempted too many
drafted men, he was likely to receive an official reprimand, yet
if he accepted too many recruits and cluttered the army with
unfit men, he was liable to discharge and financial penalties.

To this dilemma were added strong local pressures. The
people considered the need for a draft a disgrace to the community—with reason, since the method of procedure made
the draft a penalty for deficiency in enlistments. Consequently
every county and town offered bounties for volunteers, and
the citizens did not look with favor upon the surgeon who
examined their recruits too carefully.

Then too, the surgeon had to be on his toes to detect attempts to deceive him. The volunteers tried to conceal their
ailments, whereas those claiming exemption from the draft
often feigned theirs, and tricks of one sort or another were
so common that Washington was soon sending circulars to the
surgeons describing elaborate methods by which they could
detect fraud.

If a man claimed exemption for defective vision, for instance, the doctor was to lead him on a regular steeplechase,
a rapid run over a route marked with unexpected stairways,
boxes, barrels, and overturned chairs. If a man got over them
all without stumbling, his eyesight was good enough for the
army, but what was to be done if he could not take the hurdles
and suffered injury in the attempt was not set forth.

On the whole, Dr. Mayo and his assistant, Dr. Hector Galloway of Oronoco, steered a successful path among the pit-
falls. Visitors coming to Rochester to watch the enrolment

board at work remarked on the dispatch and fairness with which the examinations were conducted. Dr. Mayo, they said, was at the same time the most blessed and the most cursed man in southern Minnesota. Certainly he became one of the most widely known.

But he did not escape disaster.

Toward the end of 1864 a demand arose for the enrolment board to leave its berth in Rochester and travel around the district, so that more applicants for exemption could appear before it. The board complied, announcing that on certain dates in January and February 1865 it would hold sessions in Preston to the east and in St. Peter and Faribault to the west.

The sitting at Preston passed off without reported incident, but in St. Peter several thousands were awaiting the board. Around the door of the office surged the throng, jostling and shoving to be first, and the guard soon collected a tidy sum for expediting the passage of those in a hurry.

On the streets the lawyers and doctors who had assembled to profit from the board's session were doing a land-office business—the lawyers preparing the affidavits required to prove nonresidence and over-age, while the doctors filled out certificates of physical disability. Within limits these were legitimate activities, but some of the operators ignored those limits, charging what the traffic would bear instead of the five-dollar fee allowed by law and claiming to have special influence with the board which they would use for fifty, a hundred, or two hundred dollars.

Inside the office the board, faced with the herculean task of acting on five or six hundred cases a day, was making its examinations and decisions at the rate of one a minute!

Among the observers of these doings was a farmer from Ottawa in Le Sueur County. The swindle worked by the outsiders made him angry, and when he talked to a man with lung disease who had been refused exemption and to another, able-bodied, who had been granted it, he decided that the government doctor was in collusion with the swindlers. The "shameful, disloyal traffic" made his blood boil, and he wrote a lengthy letter about it to the *St. Paul Daily Press,* which published it over the signature "Radical Republican."

"Truth" and "Justice" quickly wrote to support "Radical Republican" with more examples of unfair exemptions and seeming corruption on the part of the officials. Then several others came stoutly to the defense of the board, among them a lawyer and a newspaperman of eminence in the Minnesota Valley.

They could testify, they said, that Dr. Mayo examined every candidate impartially, regardless of the certificate presented. His examinations were hurried and perhaps he made mistakes, but what on earth was the poor man to do with such a horde waiting outside the door? Besides, how did "Radical Republican" know whether a man was physically fit or not? Surely Dr. Mayo's opinion was worth more than that of an Ottawa farmer!

This discussion was in progress when the enrolment board began its session in Faribault, and the editor of the newspaper there paid special attention to the question of connivance by the enrolment board. He reported that in the several hours each day he had spent in the examining rooms he had seen nothing but the most impartial consideration of claims. But his suspicion was aroused by the fact that Dr. Mayo gave private examinations in his rooms after hours and charged five-dollar fees for them, and then exempted most of the men he had examined when they appeared before the board.

By that time, if the uproar in the newspapers is a reliable sign, the entire state was talking about the scandal, and the question most hotly argued was whether or not Dr. Mayo was involved.

Colonel John T. Averill, then acting as assistant provost marshal general for Minnesota, was moved to investigate the charges. He put a summary end to the session at Faribault and ordered the provost marshal of the board and Dr. Mayo to report to St. Paul.

In his hearing before Colonel Averill, Dr. Mayo frankly acknowledged that he had made private examinations. Some men could ill afford, or did not wish, to spend several days needlessly waiting in line. These he examined at night to inform them whether or not they were entitled to exemption. If he thought they were, they stayed for the examination in the presence of the board. If he thought not, they went home without waiting longer. What was dishonest about that?

He maintained that there was nothing at all like a bribe in the fees he collected. He had a right to charge something for his extra trouble and time, and the law permitted doctors to collect a five-dollar fee for such examinations. Besides, if he was willing to be bribed, he didn't have to stop at five dollars; he could get hundreds.

But Colonel Averill did not agree. He ordered Dr. Mayo to report at Rochester under arrest and sent an account of the affair to the authorities in Washington.

The War Department at once dismissed Dr. Mayo from the army service "for receiving fees for private examinations" and a week later revoked the appointments of the provost marshal and the commissioner. A new board was immediately appointed, with Dr. Edwin C. Cross of Rochester as the examining surgeon, and in less than a month the newspapers were printing sensational stories accusing Dr. Cross of venality and incompetence.

When allowance has been made for rumor and suspicion exaggerated by indignation, it seems clear that the worst to be said of Dr. Mayo in this episode is that he was unwise. And the public verdict at the time, as expressed in the newspapers, is an impressive testimonial to the reputation he had established. The overwhelming majority refused to believe that he could be guilty of anything dishonorable, and the *Mankato Union* was sure that "No one who is acquainted with Dr. Mayo will for a moment question his honesty and good intentions. He supposed from a reading of the law that he had a perfect right to give a private examination and charge a fee of five dollars. The authorities at Washington construed the law differently, and his official head has paid the forfeit."

There was no question of Dr. Mayo's returning to the Minnesota Valley to practice. More than a year before, in January 1864, he had decided that he wanted to live in Rochester and had bought two lots on Franklin Street, built a cottage on one of them, and moved his family over from Le Sueur.

In the bedroom of that cottage, almost exactly on the spot where more than half a century later the fountain bubbled in the lobby of the Mayo Clinic building, the Mayos' second son was born on July 19, 1865. They named him Charles Horace, Charles because that had been a favorite name in Dr. Mayo's family and Horace because it had been the name of the baby that died.

Now that Dr. Mayo was out of his job as examining surgeon, he bought a small piece of ground on downtown Third Street, built a snug little office, decorated it with a plaster bust of President Lincoln, and invited private patients with a newspaper card that was bold by virtue of its uncommonly few words and big type. No one could miss it, it stood out so among its fine-print fellows:

DR. MAYO
Office on Third Street
Rochester, Minn.

What Rochester was then is an essential factor in the story of what it has become. Although it was only ten years old, with fewer than three thousand residents, it was already the political, economic, and social capital of a rich agricultural district several hundred miles square and was rapidly developing into one of the largest primary wheat markets in the world.

The previous fall the railroad that had been moving slowly westward from Winona on the Mississippi had finally reached Rochester. An elevator was built alongside the tracks, and the inland city became the grain depot for most of south central Minnesota, the funnel into which hundreds of thousands of bushels of wheat poured from all sides each year, and then poured out again along the railroad eastward.

In harvesttime the roads into town were lined with farmers on the way to dump their loads of grain into the wide-mouthed hoppers of the elevator. Wheat buyers, many of them agents for dealers in Milwaukee and Chicago, gathered at every entrance to town and as the wagons passed them called out their bids.

The farmers went wheat mad. They claimed more land, bought more machines, planted more wheat, more, and more. Never mind that being without capital they must finance the expansion on credit. If nature was kind a few good crops would pay off the debts. Here and there a wise man warned of danger in "this eternal wheat-raising," but his warning went unheeded. Wheat production spiraled dizzily upward.

Where the farmers sold they bought. When father took the wheat to market mother and daughter went along "to trade a little" at the stores. Business boomed and Rochester soon became a thriving distribution center for furniture, clothing, "Yankee notions," hardware, and farm machinery.

It became also a center of social life. When men made a trip to the county seat to appear in district court or to pay their taxes, they took time for conviviality in the saloons, billiard rooms, or "ball alleys." On holidays the population of the countryside drained into town for the mass entertainments arranged by the merchants—a parade, a band concert, speeches, and fireworks on the Fourth of July, balls and banquets on Christmas and New Year's Day.

Not content with the drawing power of their annual county fair, the Rochester men provided grounds, buildings, and arguments enough to win the state fair away from the Twin Cities several times. On such occasions the crowds numbered thousands, and visitors paid well for the privilege of sleeping on pallets of straw in churches or barns.

Word soon spread that Rochester was a paradise for show-men, and all sorts of troupers added it to their circuit—musicians and magicians, circuses and minstrel shows. People came from as far away as Winona to hear concerts by performers like the Black Swan, a popular Negro contralto, and Ole Bull, the celebrated Norwegian violinist.

Rochester was also a favorite rendezvous for the horse-racing fraternity, for it possessed the best race track in the state. A wealthy local businessman established a brood farm and racing stables, and his horses, especially the oft-winning stallion Star of the West, became one of the prides of Rochester. The racing crowd were often rough and rowdy, but many of them had money and spent it freely, so Rochester did not complain but made them welcome.

With characteristic energy Dr. Mayo accepted the invitation to leadership offered by Rochester's possibilities, and he was soon a force to be reckoned with in community life.

He took the initiative in establishing a city library and stocking it with books. As an elected member of the school board for three years, he prodded the city fathers into building a new school that the state superintendent of education pronounced "the largest and most costly" in Minnesota. And he helped to plan annual lecture courses that brought to town such celebrities as Wendell Phillips, Horace Greeley, and Anna E. Dickinson, "the best and ablest representative of the rapidly increasing class of women known as the strong-minded." It was the strong-minded woman who drew the biggest crowd.

Unfortunately Dr. Mayo was not a man who could do all this without arousing enmity.

When the Republicans nominated him for election to the school board again in the spring of 1870, a disgruntled faction led by John Edgar, a zealous church member and temperance leader, labeled him an infidel and a friend to Demon Rum and bolted to the Democrats, thereby accomplishing the defeat of the entire Republican ticket.

Since the successful Democratic candidate was no more a

teetotaler or churchgoer than Dr. Mayo, the charge that Edgar and his friends acted from personal spite rather than moral principle seems justified. Yet there was credible support for their attacks on the Doctor.

He had become an ardent follower of Darwin, Thomas Huxley, and Herbert Spencer. Their materialism might shock pious souls who took some creed seriously and the Bible literally, but their ideas delighted him. He added their books to his library as fast as they appeared, read Huxley's essays aloud to his friends, and discussed and defended Darwinism by the hour.

The theory of evolution gave no wrench to his spiritual moorings, for he had been bent toward science by the training of his youth and had never yielded more than a superficial allegiance to any church or creed.

"He was an Episcopalian, but he didn't work very hard at it," was the way his elder son summarized his father's religion. Dr. Mayo himself defined his position by quoting Bismarck, "I never felt the need of any religious faith, and therefore never had any," and adding an echo of Huxley's humanitarian creed, "My own religion has been to do all the good I could to my fellow men, and as little harm as possible."

Freethinker and confessed unbeliever though he was, Dr. Mayo felt sincere respect for simple, honest faith always, and he did not care what church inspired it. He got on as well with Catholics as with Protestants. Easily and comfortably he stood with the parish priests at the bedsides of his many Catholic patients, and he and the fathers became fast friends.

His attitude toward social mores was equally unorthodox. He cast no stones at the prostitutes of New York or at the drunkards of Rochester. Toward the weaknesses of such persons he was tolerant, but he could feel no charity at all toward the carping busybodies who tried to run the brewers and cigar-makers out of business in order to keep men from drinking and smoking, who talked the town into an uproar because the young folk dared to dance at a public sociable, who, in short, tried to force their prejudices and proscriptions upon the entire community.

He did not himself smoke but he saw no reason why others should not do so if they wished. He liked a nip of whisky on occasion, and thought a tankard of porter or ale often the best possible medicine for what ailed folk's spirits. Teach temperance, yes; legislate prohibition, no, a positive and uncompromising no.

This attitude, exaggerated by his opponents into an all-out defense of the saloon and the whisky ring, was made an issue against him in many political campaigns.

The first of these campaigns on the county and district level came in the fall of 1870.

When the Republicans made their nomination for congressman in fulfillment of a political bargain, Dr. Mayo, "unwilling to yield servile submission to a packed convention," promptly set out to enlist support for an independent candidate. One Republican leader after another declared his approval of the project and Dr. Mayo felt sure the bolt would be a success.

But when it came time to make a public stand, the Doctor's supposed allies dropped away one by one and left him entirely alone. So he joined the Democrats, took an active part in their convention, and devoted all his energies to electing their county ticket.

This brought him again into alliance with Harry Young, his Hoosier friend who had edited the *Le Sueur Courier*. During the Civil War Young had acted as war correspondent in Virginia for the *New York Times* and the *New York World*. Then the trouble with his lungs that had sent him to Minnesota in the first place came back and, desperately ill, he headed once more for Dr. Mayo, in whose skill he had absolute confidence. The Doctor sent him west to Lake Traverse for a winter in the wilds, and now, restored to health, he was back in Rochester editing the Democratic *Federal Union*.

Young and the Doctor virtually took over the Democrats' campaign that fall, and Olmsted County never got a more thorough stumping than they gave it. Dr. Mayo was scheduled to speak almost every night in some town hall or crossroads schoolhouse.

Their efforts were rewarded with success. Olmsted County, one of the strongest Republican counties in a consistently Republican state, went to the Democrats. Jubilant at the victory, they staged a big celebration in Rochester—while the disconsolate editor of the Republican *Post* made public lament that his party had thrown away enough brains to set the Democrats up in business.

In truth, though, economic conditions were as important as personalities in determining the outcome of that election.

For several seasons bad weather had worked havoc with the local wheat crop, and striving frantically each time to stave off ruin until a good season next year should relieve the stringency, many farmers had borrowed heavily at whatever rates of interest were asked of them. Some had mortgaged everything they possessed, down to the plow in the field and the next year's crop, and many a farmer and his wife went about their work with grim faces in the tense summer of 1869. If the wheat crop should fail this year . . .

But nature smiled and the yield was bountiful.

Too bountiful. The price of wheat, which had been trending gradually downward from the peak of two dollars and more a bushel in the palmy days just after the war, now dropped sharply, to sixty cents, fifty cents, forty cents a bushel.

Forty cents, when it cost the farmer from sixty to eighty cents to raise and harvest it!

Creditors hurriedly took legal action to recover their investments and panic resulted. The lien and mortgage foreclosures listed in the Rochester newspapers mounted to more than fifty a week.

The national economic forces contributing to their plight were beyond the horizon of most of the losers, so they fastened upon grievances nearer home, of which the chief was the strangle hold of the railroad and the "wheat ring."

Being the only carrier out of Rochester, the Winona and St. Peter Railroad raised its freight rates there to compensate for losses at points where it had to meet competition, and by refusing to handle the shipments of independent warehousemen, it had secured a monopoly for its own elevator, which was charged with resorting to unfair grading practices to increase its profits. The farmer could store, sell, and ship his grain on monopoly terms, or he could let it rot in the field. He was at the mercy of the railroad and the wheat ring, and he found no mercy in them.

In the spring of 1870 the price of wheat again neared seventy-five cents, and the farmers who had been able to hold out for such an eventuality rushed to sell. Whereupon the railroad upped the freight rate from eight to fifteen cents a bushel!

The farmers swore "oaths loud and deep" and gathered in angry, excited knots on the street corners and called public indignation meetings. Slowly came the realization that although individually they were helpless, collectively they could be strong. They had the power of the ballot and must unite to elect legislators and executives who would represent them instead of the "soulless corporations."

This was the beginning in the Rochester vicinity of the social phenomenon historians call "the agrarian crusade," and for more than two decades Dr. Mayo was an outstanding local leader in that crusade.

The despair and destitution he met at close hand on his daily rounds called into full play the quick, flooding sympathy that put him always on the side of the underdog. For him the man on top was *ipso facto* in the wrong. He was naturally, therefore, the champion of "the people" in their attempts to challenge the monopoly practices of the railroads, elevator companies, and wheat dealers. But his efforts and the farmers' made headway slowly.

Meanwhile Rochester was suffering grievously from the slump in wheat. Some of its business firms went into bankruptcy, others moved away, and the main street was lined with vacant storerooms. Houses stood empty too, and prairie schooners were once again a familiar sight, but now they were going, not coming. Family after family left to make new homes in Dakota Territory.

The decline was reflected on all sides. One constant reminder of it was the Cook House. Ambitious citizens, dissatisfied with the crude little boardinghouses that passed for hotels, had clamored for a new hostelry to impress visitors with the prosperity and importance of Rochester. Finally John R. Cook, the banker, began the erection of a new business block to house storerooms on the first floor and a hotel on the three above.

With complacent pride the citizens watched the structure rise, knowing it would be the finest and largest hotel in southern Minnesota. No one dreamed it might be too big for the town. But there it stood now, empty except for a few stores and offices because Mr. Cook could find no one with temerity enough to undertake its management.

All in all, remembering happier times, Rochester was sunk in gloom.

But Dr. Mayo was stoutheartedly sure that if the citizens would only bestir themselves to develop new lines of activity good times would come again. So he became a sort of Io's oxfly in municipal affairs. He would not let the city fathers rest, but was always urging them to make some improvement or expansion.

When, after more than a decade out of public office, his penalty for having put himself on the wrong side of the political fence in Republican Rochester, he was elected mayor in 1882 as the candidate of the Democrats and also of a "People's Anti-Monopoly Convention," he was sure that now he would get things done.

But Dr. Mayo was entirely lacking in the qualities of compromise and patience necessary for success as an executive. He was suited more to command than to persuade. So throughout his term he and the council majority were continually at loggerheads and nothing of moment was accomplished. He was not reelected.

In 1885, however, he was elected alderman from his ward and for four years carried on his agitation for civic improvements from within the council.

For instance, he thought Rochester ought to have a waterworks to provide the citizens with a steady supply of good water, and for months he talked and argued the matter against strong opposition. Finally the council granted a franchise to a private company and Dr. Mayo was content. But some folk remained hostile to the idea of any water system at all, and they called it an act of God when an epidemic of sunstroke broke out among the workmen who were digging the new wells.

Why they thought the Almighty would object so vigorously to the provision of a city water supply is beyond explaining, but Dr. Mayo ordered that a cupful of oatmeal be added to each bucket of drinking water for the workmen, and, whether as a direct result or not, the sunstrokes stopped.

He waged similar battles for a system of sewers, a gas works, an electric light plant, and a city park.

The park project was his special pet. He wanted the city to build up the roadbed of College Street so as to dam Bear Creek, one of the tributaries of the Zumbro River. This, he thought, would not only save the cost of repairing College Street every time the Zumbro developed a freshet but it would turn the flats along Bear Creek into a pretty lake whose shores could be made into a park. At present the flats, almost in the center of town, were good for nothing but a rubbish dump and a cow pasture.

In time he saw all these projects carried out and heard people give him credit for them. But in the beginning each proposal encountered bitter opposition.

Affairs in Rochester did not in the least exhaust Dr. Mayo's energies; he continued to participate in county and district politics all the while, working usually with the Democrats but always actively in support of any coalition with the ephemeral reform groups that flickered across the screen at election times.

No literate person in Olmsted County could have been unaware of Dr. Mayo's position on any public question. He was forever addressing some group on something: the holiday crowds at Fourth of July or Memorial Day exercises; the German citizens when they staged a parade and bonfire to celebrate the victory of their fatherland in the war with France; the Irishmen when they met to express their indignation at the plight of Ireland; all sorts of workingmen's, farmers', and citizens' rallies, many of which he himself called together. In addition he made a speaking tour of the county in almost every fall campaign, and sometimes covered the district too.

Many of his speeches were published, and together with his frequent letters to the editor and reports to the city council and the board of trade, they fill an astonishing number of columns of fine print on an equally astonishing array of subjects.

So whenever Dr. Mayo was the candidate of the Democrats for state representative or state senator in the latter eighties, the *Federal Union* was at a loss for something to say about him. Everybody knew Dr. Mayo; everybody knew what he stood for. People agreed with him and would vote for him, or they did not and would not.

More and more of them did so agree and so vote. In 1886 he lost the election by just two hundred votes, and in 1888 by a single vote.

In the fall of 1889 the Farmers' Alliance entered the political field as a third party, and the following spring Dr. Mayo joined the local Alliance unit. He considered himself entirely eligible, for he was again a farmer. In 1875 he had bought a farm on the outskirts of Rochester and the next year moved his family out there to live, at least during the summer months.

A reporter for the *Rochester Post* described the Mayos' new home:

> The Doctor's farm embraces thirty-five acres . . .
>
> On a gentle eminence some twenty rods from the street are the buildings which are approached by a pleasant driveway lined on either side with young thrifty Lombardy poplars. From this site, a beautiful and magnificent view of the city, Zumbro valley, and the towering bluffs, together with portions of the far-stretching prairie, is had.
>
> The Doctor is putting up a large and elegant two-story addition to his residence, which, when completed, will be one of the most convenient and imposing residences in the city. Among the desirable features of the new building are two large bay windows and a tower some forty feet in height with an observatory at the top [for Mrs. Mayo's study of astronomy].
>
> Dr. Mayo has an eye to good stock, [such] as blooded cows and some choice breeds of hogs, while his large flock of English pigeons, with their beautiful plumage and constant chattering and cooing, are very pretty to look upon and listen to.

Dr. Mayo took his avocation seriously. Although he hired a man to supervise the actual work, he managed the farm himself and became very much interested in improvements in farm machinery and in livestock breeding.

In August 1890 the district Farmers' Alliance nominated Dr. Mayo for a four-year term in the state senate, and two months later the Democrats endorsed the Alliance candidates. And this time the Doctor won the election.

He did not make any phenomenal record as state senator. He learned that it is easier to say what ought to be done in legislative halls than to do it when one gets there. He served on several important committees and secured the passage of some special bills for the benefit of his constituents, but none of his major bills became law.

It did give him great satisfaction, though, to share in the enactment of a law that eventually eliminated the unfair grain-grading practices of which the farmers had complained so long.

Dr. Mayo ended his active career in politics when he retired from the state senate, at the age of seventy-four. But for more than ten years longer he was an honored adviser in district Democratic councils. He kept well abreast of political developments and was never without positive convictions on any issue or any candidate.

5. *Horse-and-Buggy Doctor*

ONLY at times during major campaigns did Dr. Mayo neglect his professional duties for the sake of politics. With a manifestation of energy in his wiry little body that moved his friends to head-shaking wonder, he carried on the two main phases of his life side by side, each influencing his progress in the other.

When he began to practice in Rochester he got no such discouraging reception as Dr. Ayer had given him in Le Sueur; there were enough patients here to keep several doctors busy. Where men transact their business and find their amusements they are quite likely also to seek their doctors, so Rochester was already the medical capital of a good-sized country district.

It even boasted what might be called a kind of clinic: the Rochester Infirmary, owned by two brothers, Drs. Edwin C. and Elisha W. Cross.

The older brother, Edwin, with an excellent medical education and ten years' experience in practice, had wandered west-

ward from Vermont in 1858, seeking a promising spot in
which to settle. He found it in Rochester, and within two years
was so busy that he sent for his younger brother, Elisha, also
well trained and experienced, to help him. Three years more
and Rochester was claiming for the Cross brothers the largest
medical practice in southern Minnesota.

By that time they had bought an old grocery store, remodeled it into an infirmary, and equipped it with all the
necessary apparatus for the practice of homeopathic and hy-
dropathic medicine. They had facilities for "Shower Baths,
Full Baths, Half Baths, Sitz Baths, Douches, Plunges, and all
other Baths necessary for the treatment of diseases." They were
also prepared to dispense, singly or in assortments for the
family medicine shelf, the thirty-four kinds of white pellets
that constituted the homeopath's weapons against disease.

In their profuse advertising the Drs. Cross solicited especially the patronage of "patients from a distance," and the
sick came to them from all over Olmsted and adjoining counties. When a broken leg or a fractured skull did not mend
under a local doctor's treatment, the sufferer was taken to the
Drs. Cross.

Edwin Cross was a man of great bulk, with heavy dark
brows above a forbidding face. As he rode his powerful black
horse through the streets of Rochester, he carried his huge
shoulders hunched close to his head, so the youngsters called
him "Monkey Cross." He was rough and gruff and patients
feared him, especially women in confinement, but they employed him.

Elisha, to the end of his days known as "young Dr. Cross,"
had equal physical proportions and probably equal ability as
a doctor, but he was less impressive, being more amiable and
less obviously aggressive.

The systems of medical practice to which the Cross brothers
adhered did not in the least prejudice their standing in the
community, for only in the minds of doctors themselves was
there any clear distinction among the various medical sects.

To the lay public a doctor was a doctor, and his abilities and personality rather than his school of medical thought determined his status. Indeed, reacting against regular medicine's copious bloodletting and heroic dosage with emetics and purgatives, patients were inclined to welcome the gentle medication of the homeopath and the pleasant water cure of the hydropathist.

In 1866, however, Dr. Elisha Cross refused to continue under the sign of homeopath and dissolved the partnership with his brother. A few years later Edwin also returned to the fold of the regular profession and soon became a leader in the local and state medical societies. Thereafter the two brothers resumed their partnership at intervals and, working jointly or alone, continued to be Rochester's busiest and wealthiest doctors throughout the first half of the 1870s.

With the kindly Elisha Dr. Mayo got on very well, but he and Edwin never more than tolerated each other. From the first they took opposite sides of almost every civic and political question. To a man like Dr. Cross, Mayo seemed an impecunious, impractical idealist whom one could comfortably ignore except when he made a confounded nuisance of himself with his radical ideas, and Dr. Mayo thought E. C. Cross more concerned with money-making than any man, let alone a doctor, had a right to be.

More to Dr. Mayo's liking was Dr. Hector Galloway, his former assistant surgeon on the enrolment board. He was a man of great girth, ponderous in movement and slow in thought. Once when Mrs. Mayo was taken ill while Dr. Mayo was away, she called Dr. Galloway to prescribe for her. He sat by her bedside and pondered. She might have this. Or perhaps that. Maybe a little of this medicine would help her. Or, on second thought, another kind might be better.

Mrs. Mayo lost patience. "Dr. Galloway, you're just like my old rag bag. There's a lot in it, but it takes a devil of a time to find it!"

Later she confided to a friend that Dr. Mayo would have

had a sick person "in medicine" in the time it took Dr. Galloway to decide how to begin the examination. But he was sound and sure, and when Dr. Mayo wanted a consultative opinion on a local case he usually called in Dr. Galloway.

The resident doctors did not have the care of Rochester's sick all to themselves. The community was a veritable honeypot for the itinerant quacks who journeyed from town to town, staying at each for a few days or weeks and leaving behind a trail of useless nostrums, worthless advice, and disappointed hopes.

In Christmas week of 1868 three of these men were simultaneously laying siege to the pocketbooks of Rochester and the surrounding countryside: Dr. Ballou, a spiritualist healer; Dr. Duvall, a "natural healer"; and Dr. Jones, an oculist and aurist from Chicago.

Dr. Ballou and Dr. Jones were unlucky to be competing with the sensational Dr. William P. Duvall "of the Western Healing Institute," a man who used no instruments or medicines to work his cures, just the natural healing power manifest in him since his tenth year. The patient had only to sit in his presence for a few minutes and all pains and ailments would pass away—though it might of course take several weeks for these beneficial effects to appear.

When such well-known sufferers as the village dressmaker and the proprietor of the Bradley House announced the miracles Dr. Duvall had wrought within them, Rochester was convinced and opened its heart and its purse. Anyone could see what a saintly man this healer was, with his flowing locks, his soulful eyes, and that warm, soothing voice.

After several weeks of land-office business Dr. Duvall moved on to serve other communities, but Rochester citizens avidly followed his doings as chronicled in the local paper. Soon there was word that he had taken to himself a lovely young wife, but six weeks later came the sad news that Mrs. Duvall was dead. The *poor* man!

Then came the facts in quick succession. Mrs. Duvall's

death was mysterious, an autopsy revealed a lethal dose of strychnine, and the doctor was under suspicion. Nor was he Dr. Duvall. He was just plain William Pott of Newark, New Jersey, and all of his three previous wives had died under similarly suspicious circumstances.

When Pott was found guilty of murder and sentenced to life imprisonment, the Rochester editors turned indignant. What a rogue! To think of the way he had "fleeced . . . credulous people out of their hard-earned dollars" by his "senseless mummery."

Striking is the unanimity with which men like Duvall emphasized *chronic* diseases. Their power was always chiefly displayed in, or their attention especially given to, ailments of long standing—precisely those in which the knowledge and skill of honest doctors were as yet ineffectual. The quacks were quick to see a potentially rich harvest in the vast accumulation of sick folk who wearily made the rounds of the doctors' offices without securing benefit. These made up the backlog of patients to whom the Mayo brothers brought the effective techniques of a new surgery a few years later.

Though courteous, kindly, and often a sympathetic confidant, Dr. Mayo was not a man to offer or invite familiarity. Men might call him Mayo and a very few William, but no one called him Will or Bill, not even his wife.

An outward sign of this inner inhibition was a strict code of professional conduct extending even to dress. He seldom appeared in public except in a long-tailed, double-breasted coat and tall top hat. These were the badge of a calling of which he was proud.

Dr. Mayo thus garbed and "going somewhere in a hurry" became one of the familiar sights of Rochester. In town he always made his calls on foot; for country trips he kept four or five horses of his own and sometimes had to rent others from a livery stable, for his daily rounds soon covered most of the roads radiating from Rochester. He would drive out one road, come back, change horses, drive out another, and so on, until the necessary calls had been made. And always he drove like mad.

One bitingly cold winter day Burt W. Eaton, a rising young Rochester lawyer, found it necessary to get to a neighboring town in a hurry. He hired a cutter with driver from one of the stables, muffled himself in furs, and started off. They were making good time when suddenly they heard hoofbeats and a faint halloo behind. The next thing Eaton knew he was sitting in his cutter in a snowbank beside the road, while Dr. Mayo dashed by with a wave of thanks.

As he and his driver dug and pulled to get the cutter free, Mr. Eaton fumed. Wasn't he as good as the Doctor? And wasn't he in a hurry too? But the driver explained that Rochester liverymen always gave Dr. Mayo the right of way; *he* was making a sick call. They all knew the sound of his voice, and whenever they heard him shout they pulled over to let him pass.

Dr. Mayo's maxim was "Don't spare the horses when a human life is at stake." But he *never* spared his. He enjoyed driving and he loved good horses. Not for him the easy-paced nag that would stand without hitching. He wanted an animal with spirit and speed, so he always bought the runaways no one else could handle; he knew they had "guts" and could go, he said, and he could usually manage them. Usually, but not always.

One of his worst smashups occurred one morning as he was starting on a trip to High Forest. The team was skittish, he was careless, and soon they began to run. Seeing that they were getting out of control, he guided them toward a clump of trees, thinking the obstacle would stop them, but they simply straddled a tree and kept on going. The violent collision of carriage with tree threw Dr. Mayo against the dashboard, stunning him for a few minutes.

When he regained consciousness his nose was bleeding hard but he seemed otherwise unhurt, and some men working near by helped him get the horses and the wrecked carriage back to the farm. Stopping only long enough to clean the blood from his face, he hitched the team to another buggy and started again for High Forest. When he returned sometime after noon, he examined his nose, found the bone was broken, set it himself, and went on about his business.

He never lacked grit. When a sore appeared on his lower lip he watched it carefully for some three months, then decided it was cancerous and must come off. Assembling instruments and needles, he took a stiff shot of whisky, seated himself in front of a mirror, and directed an assistant in the swift excision of a triangular piece of the lip.

Little Charlie, who was looking on, remembered that "of course he hollered," but he stanched the flow of blood and stitched the lip together himself.

He was just as decisive with patients. On a professional visit to the Granger farm one day he noticed little George hovering all ears among the grownups and addressed a pleasant question to him. When the child answered, Dr. Mayo snapped to attention.

"Why, that child is tongue-tied," he exclaimed. "Come here, George," reaching into his pocket as he spoke.

Unsuspecting, the boy climbed onto the Doctor's knee and obediently opened his mouth. In an instant Dr. Mayo snipped the membrane under his tongue with the little pair of scissors he carried in his pocket case, and when the tongue healed George Granger could speak like other children. He grew up to be a lawyer, a judge, and legal adviser to the Mayos.

The case histories Dr. Mayo elicited from patients were not of the kind that occupy the present-day intern. In later life he scoffed at what he considered a tendency to lose important diagnostic symptoms in a fog of minutiae. He wanted to know it if the patient passed blood from the bowels, for instance, but he did not think it necessary to ask what the man's great-grandmother had died of.

The idea of accumulating case records as a valuable source for the statistical study of disease had not yet penetrated to the rank and file of the profession. A notation of the patient's name, his disorder, and the fee charged made up the customary entry. But Dr. Mayo sometimes felt an urge to review a case at length in writing.

He must have resolved on New Year's Day, 1866, to keep a record of his major cases from that time forward. Convenient to his hand lay the old ledger in which Mrs. Mayo had kept her millinery accounts. A short time before, the Doctor had punched holes through the used sheets, tied them carefully out of the way with a piece of pink tape, and started to use the ledger as a scrapbook, copying into it excerpts from things he read.

Among some bits from Hall's *Journal of Health* was one on the beauty of gray eyes and another entitled "School Rooms Should Be Attractive" taken from the report of the school in Duxbury, Massachusetts. Immediately following a series of paragraphs on agriculture by Edward Everett, Dr. Mayo began his case stories.

That first resolution of 1866 lasted until January 14, but on January 1, 1867, he firmly began again and kept going until January 18. In 1868 he wrote nothing, because he was busy with a new venture as coproprietor of one of Rochester's biggest drugstores, and a year later he was equally busy dissolving the partnership. So his resolutions produced only about a dozen case records from his own pen.

These bear little resemblance to the clipped, stripped models of the present day. He wrote them as little stories, in which he recounted everything the patient said and the doctor answered, even to the anecdotes they exchanged.

Little Octavia Gray fell from a horse in October. After three months of home treatment she was brought to Dr. Mayo to see what he could do about the paralysis on one side of her face. He ordered her parents to use the Galvanic battery and come back if that didn't work. In the ledger he admitted that he was puzzled. "Querie, where is the injury?" he wrote, and then reviewed and rejected all the likely possibilities.

Next came a series of entries tracing the day-by-day progress of tubercular meningitis in a child of nine years. When in spite of Dr. Mayo's best efforts the patient died, he wrote a long review of the case and the treatment. What might he have done differently, and more successfully?

Also puzzling was the case of Mr. Johnson of Rock Dell, who had been suffering from retention of urine for three days. Confidently the Doctor introduced a catheter. With no effect. Was the instrument clogged? No. Then what was the matter?

It took suction of considerable force to start the flow of thick, clotted pus that had been causing the stoppage. When more than four ounces of this had been removed and then a quart of heavy red urine, the patient was much relieved and Dr. Mayo returned home.

To the old ledger he confided his bewilderment. Where did the pus come from? Where was the abscess, and what was the cause of it? "The people were Norwegian, understood little of English, the patient no English. All I could gather about the history of the case was that the man had been sick about eight weeks."

He argued the possibilities at length but could come to no satisfactory conclusion. So he ended the record, "Left open for further thought and research."

"Left open for further thought and research." There spoke a mind in league with the future.

Dr. Mayo was necessarily an empiric of the old school. He used the clinical thermometer and the crude wooden stethoscope, the only instruments of precision yet available, and he had made urinalysis an unfailing part of his examination routine. Over a lamp or a candle by the bedside he would boil a bit of urine in a teaspoon, testing it for sugar and for albumen with reagents that he always carried in his bag. More elaborate analyses he made later at the office.

Aside from these meager scientific aids, he and his fellows still had to depend on their own five senses to tell them what was wrong with the patient, and the height to which they had developed the art of clinical observation and diagnosis is the glory of their tribe. Practice trained their senses to recognize and their minds to interpret with astonishing accuracy the clues a deranged physiology left in the eyes, the tongue, or the skin of the sick man.

The difficulty was that many of them could not see any need for improvement, any possibility of something better. To that number Dr. Mayo did not belong. He was a friend of progress in medical science as much as in transportation, communication, or farming.

He checked his diagnoses by postmortem examinations whenever he could get permission from authorities or relatives, and he examined pathological specimens under the microscope. His model was an old, low-powered one, rapidly becoming obsolete, but just the attempt to study diseased tissues removed at operation or postmortem was enough to set him apart among Minnesota practitioners.

So too was his unabated enthusiasm for chemical analysis; he always had a laboratory in one corner of his office or in an adjoining back room.

With this slant of mind, Dr. Mayo joined eagerly in the attempt of some St. Paul men in 1869 to revive the dormant state medical society. He attended the meeting they called and participated in the organization of a new Minnesota State Medical Society, which has remained a vital force in Minnesota medicine ever since. For more than ten years Dr. Mayo was among its active leaders and for another ten among its advisory elder statesmen.

Membership was not required of the state's doctors and it carried no special privileges or premiums in practice, so only the most alert members of the profession found time and energy for participation. Dr. Mayo made some interesting friends among them.

One was Dr. Franklin R. Staples, beloved dean of Winona doctors. He was president of the state society in 1871, vice-president of the American Medical Association in 1877, president of the state board of health for fifteen years, and for five years a member of the examining faculty of medicine set up by the first effective medical practice act in Minnesota.

Probably the ablest man in the group, and certainly the most scientific-minded, was Dr. Charles N. Hewitt of Red Wing. Sober, earnest, wholeheartedly devoted to medicine, he sacrificed his career as a surgeon in order to establish a proper program and agency for public health in Minnesota.

Foremost in direct influence on Dr. Mayo was the affable Dr. Alexander J. Stone of Stillwater, later of St. Paul. A congenital pioneer, he established the first medical journal in Minnesota and the first medical school in St. Paul, and later attained distinction as a medical editor and educator. His fellow doctors liked him personally, but in the early years of the medical society many of them shook their heads over his unseemly enthusiasm for new methods and theories in the treatment of diseases of women.

Participating in the "collision of intellect" among such men gave Dr. Mayo a periodic renewal of the perspective a man is likely to lose in the daily grind. His professional consciousness deepened, his pride in medicine grew, and with it his concern for the good name of the medical profession.

At this time malpractice suits were a real problem. In spite of the best care a doctor could give, fractures sometimes left deformities and limbs had to be amputated. In such cases the patient could always find a lawyer willing to sue the doctor for malpractice, and nine times in ten the jury, looking only at the deformity or the stump and not at the conditions that might have made it unavoidable, would award the damages.

And why not? pointed out the leaders of the society, when doctors themselves appeared on the witness stand to support the charges of negligence, implying that nothing of the sort ever happened in *their* cases. Doctors had better stick together on this matter if they did not want to pay separately.

Dr. Mayo took these discussions to heart and acted upon them in the next malpractice case that crossed his path.

Dr. E. C. Cross was the defendant. It was charged that in taking care of a broken arm for the plaintiff he had made the bandages and splints so tight they had obstructed circulation, causing mortification and necessitating eventual amputation of the injured limb.

Dr. Mayo suggested the theory on which the defense was chiefly based, that the artery had been injured and the blood supply shut off when the arm was broken and not when the splints were applied. He supported this theory on the witness stand and in company with several other prominent doctors, including Dr. Staples of Winona, made it so plausible that Dr. Cross won the verdict in both the district and the state supreme court.

That Dr. Mayo should show such wit and spirit in the defense of a man he was known to detest caused so much speculation in Rochester that one man finally ventured to ask him why he had done it.

"I did it for the profession, not for him, damn him."

6. *Pioneer in Surgery*

DR. MAYO was a general practitioner, as all American doctors were then, but surgery was what he wanted most to do; he liked the sense of tangible accomplishment he got from a successful operation. But up to the seventies he had not done any unusual amount of operating.

Surgery was still, as it had been in his medical school days, mostly a matter of repair work on the surfaces and extremities of the body, and accidents provided the chief need for it. Industrial hazards, in mine and mill and foundry, were lacking in Rochester, but farming had plenty of dangers of its own.

Farmers and their wives seem to have been slow to learn that moving mechanisms will not yield to human flesh. The whirring knives of the new reapers did not stop when fingers and toes got in their way, and the revolving knuckles of the tumbling rod in the threshing machine took twisting hold of any loose garment that ballooned near them. In harvesttime observers reported that those maimed and mangled in accidents with the new farm machinery were keeping the surgeons of Rochester busy day and night.

There lay one opportunity for specializing in surgery. Another was developing in the special field of practice that so interested his friend Dr. Stone.

The number of sufferers from disorders of the female reproductive organs was in that day greatly increased by the crudities of ignorant and unskilled midwifery, and the treatment of the diseases of women made up a large share of every doctor's practice.

But there was really little as yet the doctors could do about them. They applied blisters and poultices externally, dosed with morphine or ergot internally, or tried to reduce a swollen cervix by drawing blood with leeches. In severe cases of ulceration they resorted to the use of caustics, including the baneful silver nitrate stick that caused more damage than it repaired.

Many "female complaints," often severe enough to make the woman a bedridden invalid, were caused by displacement of the uterus. It was advanced practice then to treat this by pushing the organ back into place and attempting to keep it there by packing the vaginal cavity with tampons of gauze or by inserting a mechanical support called a pessary.

Such methods were seldom effective, and in every community a growing number of ailing women wandered restlessly from doctor to doctor and quack to quack, hoping to find someone who could give them relief.

Cultivation of the field by qualified practitioners was beginning in the 1860s. Two decades before, James Marion Sims of Alabama had learned how to repair vesicovaginal fistula, an accident of childbirth that made the women who suffered it truly pitiable. In a fine instance of frontier ingenuity, he fashioned from a pewter teaspoon the duckbill speculum that made the body parts accessible to surgery and from a half-dollar piece the silver-wire suture that made the surgical technique effective.

The doctors could not believe the reports of Sims' success, so he moved to New York and showed them, not only that he could do it but how to do it themselves. During the sixties and seventies he and his assistants and successors devised and disseminated, through the printed page and their trained disciples, one new method after another for the successful treatment of the diseases peculiar to women.

Dr. Mayo was aware of these developments through his reading, and he was venturing to perform a few of the operations he read about. On August 25, 1866, the *Rochester Post* reported "An Important Surgical Operation":

Dr. Mayo performed an operation a few days ago upon Mrs. Titus of Mantorville.

Mrs. Titus had been suffering for several months from the growth of a tumor in the abdomen; its size had become so great as to render her perfectly helpless and endanger her life. Before the operation she measured 54 inches over the tumor.

The operation was performed by making an opening in the abdomen about an inch long and deep enough to reach the sac of the tumor. There was discharged from the opening nearly five gallons of thick, gluey substance.

When the doctor left, the patient was feeling very comfortable and much relieved by the removal of the enormous burden. Dr. Mayo was assisted in the operation by Dr. Dearborn of Wasioja, who has charge of the patient.

We understand that Dr. Mayo gives special attention to this class of Female diseases.

Tapping an ovarian tumor when it required an abdominal incision, even so small a one, was more than other Rochester doctors were yet daring. But Dr. Stone, who had spent a year as an assistant in a Boston hospital, was full of tales about more remarkable things men in the East were doing, and Dr. Mayo grew restless in the knowledge that he might do better work if he knew how.

Consequently in the fall of 1869 he announced to his wife that he was going to New York for several months to study general surgery and gynecology.

He spent much of his time at Bellevue Hospital. It had undergone many reforms since his service there in the forties, and though New Yorkers were complaining loudly about the infection rampant in its surgical wards and its high mortality rate, conditions were probably no worse there than in most of the hospitals of Europe and America in those days before the advent of Listerism.

In fact the first ambulance corps in the world had just been established at Bellevue, and Dr. Mayo was much impressed by the wonder of it. "When an accident occurs in any part of the city," he said in a letter to the editor of the *Rochester Post,* "there is a dispatch sent from police headquarters . . . and the ambulance is on the ground in a few minutes after. The injured are picked up, and at once taken to the hospital. Truly this is quite as astonishing as any of the fairy tales, and a perfect realization of the Eastern story of Aladdin and his wonderful lamp."

Of course the insatiable little doctor did not limit his experience of New York to hospitals and study. He made the rounds of the churches to compare the eloquence of their preachers and the seraphic voices of their choirs. He went to the opera and the theater, on one occasion to see Edwin Booth play Hamlet. He attended inquests, and wandered for an hour or two from slab to slab in the city morgue musing on the characters and fortunes that had brought these men to their common end, "dead on admission." He walked slowly down Fifth Avenue, delighting in the palatial residences and the fine horses and carriages.

On his way home from New York Dr. Mayo stopped off at Philadelphia and went out to Lancaster to visit the Atlee brothers, the great apostles of ovariotomy. This operation for the removal of ovarian tumor had first been performed by Ephraim McDowell on the Kentucky frontier in 1809, but after his death it fell into disuse; it was too seldom successful in other hands.

John and Washington Atlee revived the procedure about 1845 and set about demonstrating its practicability for saving lives. When Dr. Mayo arrived, Washington Lemuel, the younger and abler of the brothers, was nearing his three hundredth ovariotomy, with an average mortality of slightly over thirty per cent.

In spite of the Atlees' success, the main body of the medical profession condemned the operation as foolhardy. Any abdominal operation was a method of the executioner that no wise and humane surgeon would use. Ovariotomists were "belly rippers who ought not to be at large."

The attitude is vividly illustrated by the story of the general practitioner in Jericho, Vermont, who took one of his patients to the Woman's Hospital in New York, having heard that the doctors there could do something to cure ovarian tumors. After seeing his patient settled in bed for a day's rest before the operation, the old Yankee sauntered into the staff room to ask how the surgeons would go about getting "the darned thing out."

An intern explained, and the man from Jericho listened in horror.

"What?" he shouted. "Do you mean to tell me you've got to cut her wide open?" When the intern nodded, he hurried upstairs to tell his patient he had made a mistake; she must not let these men operate on her. But she had more courage than he.

He watched the operation next day, and at its end addressed the surgeon. "Do you expect the woman to come out of that alive?"

"Of course," said the surgeon.

"Well, I don't," snapped the old doctor. And the next word the hospital had from him was a telegram sent from some point on his way home, telling them what to do with his patient's remains. Fortunately the instructions were not needed.

That occurred about 1875, and in spite of the New York surgeons' nonchalance in the presence of the man from Jericho, they were not taking ovariotomy at all as a matter of course. Every such operation was an event that attracted doctors from all over the city to watch the performance and note the outcome.

Dr. Mayo's visit to the Atlees did not give him the courage immediately to attempt ovariotomy himself. When a few months after his return to Rochester he was faced with a case of ovarian tumor that had got beyond treatment by tapping, he called Dr. William H. Byford from Chicago to see the patient. Byford had become that city's outstanding authority in the new gynecology and he performed ovariotomy on occasion, but in this instance he decided the risk was unjustified.

While Byford was in Rochester, Dr. Mayo asked him to look at another puzzling case. Three years before, a woman had come to him complaining of headache, backache, and a host of other symptoms from which she had suffered for fourteen years. The doctors she had gone to said she had "falling of the womb" and fitted one pessary after another without noticeable benefit.

Dr. Mayo decided the trouble was caused by a good-sized rectocele, a hernial protrusion of a part of the vagina. His first attempt to correct the difficulty was a failure, party because of trouble with the anesthetic, but in a second attempt he used an ingenious method of his own devising and was greatly pleased with himself when it proved successful.

For two years he heard nothing more of the case and assumed the woman was well. Then one day as he was passing her house she called out, "Oh, Doctor, come here a minute. I want to see you. That thing is coming out again."

Sure enough, the rectocele was as large and troublesome as ever. "Well, Mrs. H., I will try again. I will make another effort for you."

When the effort failed the Doctor was stumped, but Mrs. H. was cheerfully sure he would succeed eventually and was quite willing to submit to anything he suggested.

"As there was but little danger of her seeking other aid," said Dr. Mayo, "I took time to look up the literature on the subject more carefully."

In accordance with surgical practice at that time, all his efforts had been in the direction of returning the protruded parts to their proper place and fashioning a thick wall of tissue, an artificial perineum, to hold them there. Now as he read and studied, he asked himself why he could not make sure of a cure by radical removal of the rectocele. He worked out a plan of procedure that seemed feasible, but he hesitated to try it on his judgment alone.

When he told Byford about his idea, the Chicago man was dubious. He had never heard of any such operation, and he would be afraid of fatal hemorrhage. He suggested a more conservative procedure.

Dr. Mayo gladly tried this, but it didn't work.

Then he screwed his courage to the sticking point and in May 1871 performed the radical operation he had planned. With the patient under ether and the hernial bag emptied of its contents, he fastened a clamp behind it to shut off the circulation, carefully put in the necessary sutures, and cut off the rectocele close to the clamp. Quickly he seared the cut surfaces with an iron he had heating in the flame of a spirit lamp near by. The bleeding was very slight.

The patient rallied nicely, the wound healed rapidly, and from the fourth day forward the woman was up and about, cured at last.

This result of his audacity contributed greatly to Dr. Mayo's confidence in his own surgical judgment. But he still was not ready to risk his hand at ovariotomy. That had to wait a few more years.

In reporting the case of the returning rectocele at the next session of the Minnesota State Medical Society, Dr. Mayo interrupted his characteristically circumstantial narrative to say, "At this point I wish to make public acknowledgement to Miss Harriet Preston, M.D., a graduate of Women's Medical College of Philadelphia, for her very able assistance to me while performing this and other operations on women . . ."

This was an unmistakable rebuke to his listeners, for they had been voting regularly for three years past against admitting Dr. Preston of Rochester to membership in the society. She was one of the small vanguard of women who, unwilling to be forced into a life of teaching or making hats, were seeking to enter the practice of medicine, and the Minnesota profession was receiving her with something less than open arms.

Although Dr. Mayo held no brief for the emancipation of woman in the mass, he championed Dr. Preston's cause from the start. She was a competent practitioner and he believed her worthy of membership in the profession.

He talked in vain. At first the doctors based their refusal to recognize Dr. Preston on various pretexts, but at one of the annual debates on the matter they came out with the truth. Dr. Mattocks of St. Paul did not want a woman around because then the men couldn't say everything they wanted to, and Dr. Blood of Owatonna "had observed that women who stepped aside from the usual course of obtaining a living adopted by their sex were strong-minded women with whom it was desirable to have nothing to do."

Although Dr. Mayo did not get far with the men by his stand on the question, he did with Dr. Preston. That being a painfully modest age—medical students were taught to keep their eyes fixed on the ceiling while they fumbled through a manual examination of well-draped women patients—she built up a very large practice among the women of the Rochester community, and she referred her major cases and those requiring surgery to Dr. Mayo. This was no mean aid to the development of his practice in gynecology.

In 1872 Dr. Mayo was elected the third president of the state medical society, and almost immediately some of his doctor friends began urging him to leave Rochester. That small town could not offer sufficient scope for the development of his abilities, they argued. Why don't you come to St. Paul? Here are hospitals and a medical school and stimulating professional companionship. Here are more patients and a chance for specialization. You're foolish to waste yourself down there in the sticks.

Dr. Mayo's vanity was flattered. The idea seemed good, and the arguments reasonable. Surely St. Paul would offer greater opportunities, especially in view of the depression into which Rochester had fallen. Moreover, Dr. Charles Hill of Pine Island, not far from Rochester, was moving to St. Paul. He was a congenial person and a good doctor, and he was looking for a partner.

So in April 1873 the Rochester newspapers announced that Dr. Mayo was going to St. Paul to establish himself in partnership with Dr. Hill.

The public expressions of regret sound more than perfunctory. Even the Republican newspaper called the Doctor's going "a public loss" and when the day of his departure came, a host of friends "attended him to the cars."

Since Mrs. Mayo and the children remained in Rochester, the Doctor returned every month or two to see them and to visit some of his old patients.

He was never more his headstrong, foolhardy self than on one of those trips. He stopped off at Kasson, eighteen miles from Rochester, to see a patient, and was overtaken by one of the raging blizzards the Upper Midwest occasionally suffers. Whirling madly before the wind, the fury of snow piled itself high on everything, and there was nothing anyone could do but wait until nature had calmed herself and the tracks could be cleared.

Dr. Mayo waited from Friday night till Monday morning. Then his fund of patience, never large, was exhausted and he announced his intention of proceeding to Rochester on foot. His snowbound companions were amazed. On foot? Through eighteen miles of trackless drifts? Why, the man was mad!

But he would not be dissuaded. And he got through. He reached Rochester, attended to his business, and was ready to return to St. Paul by the time the trains were moving again.

In St. Paul the new partners rented a handsome downtown office, announced themselves available to patients, and received a cordial welcome from the city press. They immediately joined the Ramsey County Medical Society, and at its next election Dr. Mayo was made vice-president.

Three months later he resigned the office and returned to Rochester to stay.

Why? The records do not say.

To Rochester friends he had reported that his prospects in St. Paul were good, but perhaps they remained only prospects. Perhaps he discovered that if there were more patients in St. Paul there were also more doctors to claim them. This is a likely guess, since Dr. Hill also returned to his former place of practice. Or the two men may have found the formalities of city practice too impersonal for their liking.

Upon his return to Rochester Dr. Mayo rented an office above Geisinger and Newton's drugstore and took up where he had left off the year before. His old patients were glad to have him back, and he was soon as busy as though he had never been away.

From this time on much can be learned about the develop-

ment of his practice from the stories of his cases that were
published in the newspapers.

These newspaper accounts, which continued to appear well
beyond 1900, have been cited as evidence that the Mayos
indulged in unethical advertising. This view of them is unhis-
torical, for it applies the taboos of today to an age that did
not share them. The publication of such items was then sanc-
tioned by custom, and every doctor in the community enjoyed
the "advertising" if his cases had news value.

It was the editors, not the doctors, who took the initiative
in this practice, for case histories were the sort of news their
readers liked. In Rochester the *Record and Union* editor made
the rounds each week to ask what casualties the doctors could
report, and he also went directly to the family or friends of
the patients or picked up the information in the market place,
so that he sometimes had to publish an apology for having
assigned a case to the wrong doctor, saying "the parties who
informed us misspoke the name."

One might think the patients would have objected to having
the intimate details about their cancers and ruptures, their mis-
shapen limbs, their bloating and bleeding, broadcast impartially to friend and foe. But apparently they did not. People
have resorted to stranger ways of getting their names in the
newspapers.

The newspaper accounts do not provide a rounded picture
of Dr. Mayo's practice, for the editor was not interested in the
common ailments that made up the bulk of it. He reported
epidemics and an occasional serious case of illness, but for the
most part he gave space only to the accidental injuries and
other ills that necessitated surgery.

A few samples from these hundreds of press items may
demonstrate their interest and value.

John Dolan, who lives on the High Forest road, made
a brutal assault on his wife on Thursday morning of last
week. John is a confirmed inebriate and while under

the influence of liquor is no better than a brute. On the day mentioned he was drunk. . . . Becoming enraged he threw a tumbler at his wife which struck her on the forehead, making a severe gash and severing the temporal artery. Dr. Mayo was called, and he had great difficulty in stopping the flow of blood and preventing Mrs. Dolan from bleeding to death. Some one ought to enter a complaint again Dolan and have him dealt with as he deserves to be.

Mr. G. Sampson, of Salem, got within kicking distance of a horse last Saturday evening, and when he got away, it was with two teeth and part of his jaw bone imbedded in his tongue. Dr. Mayo attended the injured man.

Saturday morning last, Dr. W. W. Mayo, assisted by Dr. E. W. Cross, performed a surgical operation on Miss Clara Higbee, at Hadley Valley, cutting off her right leg six inches above the knee. Some six years ago Miss Higbee was riding and a storm coming up, she caught cold in the limb. Inflammation set in, the limb swelled and the bone above the knee became affected and at last rotten, so that large sores formed and pieces of bone came out. She has been confined to her bed all these years and her suffering has been severe. She bore the operation with great fortitude, and is getting along very nicely.

James Stevenson, who lives on the Marion road, near the city, met with a severe accident last Friday. He was threshing at Mr. Rafferty's place, and part of the thresher becoming covered with straw he stepped upon the feed-board to remove it. He slipped and his foot got caught in the cylinder and was completely crushed. Dr. Mayo was called, who found it necessary to amputate the leg below the knee. The muscles were pulled out up to the calf of the leg.

Amputate, amputate. For everything from the bite of a cat

to the misdirection of a woodsman's ax. Persons with missing extremities must have been commonplace in the community.

If a limb is diseased cut it off, was one of the oldest principles in surgery, and improvement had occurred only in the direction of greater neatness and dispatch. The technique was the thing, the surgeon most honored being the one who could dismember a limb in the fewest seconds. The coming of anesthesia had removed any excuse for this standard of competence, but it lingered on.

A saner idea had been slowly gaining ground, however, since the time of the great James Syme of Edinburgh. He had preached the obvious but revolutionary principle that it is better for a man to have a stiff leg or arm than to have none at all, better for the surgeon to excise a diseased piece of bone than to cut off the entire limb, even though it takes a little longer.

Dr. Mayo had acquired this principle and applied it to the limit of his knowledge and skill. There were plenty of severed members in his record, but there also appeared with growing frequency instances like these:

Dr. W. W. Mayo, assisted by Dr. E. W. Cross, performed the operation of exsection of the bone of a man's arm, named Ole Syvertson from Grand Meadow, who had had that member broken last September by the tumbling rod of a threshing machine. The arm had been set, but the bone did not grow together, and portions of it rotted and crumbled, making great running sores. The process was what is called Esmark's bloodless operation. About four inches of bone were taken out, the ends brought together and a union will take place. The operation was performed Wednesday and was very successful.

A son of J. C. Patton, of Rock Dell, has just passed through a very trying operation for a disease of the leg bone. The leg was cut open from knee to ankle, and two-thirds of the bone cut and chiseled out. The bone was dead, apparently, and of course was doing damage. Dr. Mayo performed the operation.

Dr. Mayo was ahead of his Rochester fellows on this point and he sometimes disagreed sharply with them as to the need for amputation. He and Dr. E. C. Cross were once called together to see a young man with a badly injured hand. Dr. Cross said it must come off, but Dr. Mayo said no and he won, assuming responsibility for the outcome. When the man died half a century later, he still had his hand.

Modesty forbade the publication of details about Dr. Mayo's gynecological operations, but there were enough of them by the mid-1870s to rank him high among the half-dozen Minnesota men who could be called gynecologists. Since 1871 the state society had maintained a standing committee on gynecology, and in 1874 Dr. Mayo was named its chairman.

Up to that time only five attempts at ovariotomy had been made in the entire state, and all five patients had died. In reporting his case to the society, Dr. Stone of St. Paul declared that he was not in the least ashamed to admit failure in a procedure that was still stigmatized in the best surgical circles of the world as an "American audacity."

Little wonder then that when in 1875 Dr. Warner of Mankato realized that a patient of his was threatened with death from an ovarian tumor, he decided to take no chances with a Minnesota surgeon and called Dr. Washington L. Atlee from Pennsylvania to perform the operation.

Dr. Atlee never forgot his trip to Good Thunder, Minnesota. It occurred in March and Minnesota again produced a blizzard. Dr. Atlee's train being stalled, he learned that he could keep his appointment on time only by driving twenty-five miles across the open prairie. Old settlers warned him against attempting the trip in such a storm, but he found a driver willing to risk it and started out across the white waste.

They lost their way, the sleigh hit a submerged fence post

and overturned, and the driver wanted to give up. But Dr. Atlee insisted upon continuing the journey, finally reached the patient's home, and was rewarded by success in the operation.

The first successful ovariotomy by a Minnesota doctor was performed the next year by a young St. Paul surgeon. Then came three more failures, and that constituted the reported record in 1880.

Early in January of that year Dr. Mayo was called to see Mrs. Jacob Waggoner, a young matron who lived just across the alley from him in Rochester. The swelling in her side proved to be an ovarian tumor, but it was still too small to justify such a last resort as operation.

Mrs. Waggoner then became pregnant and in May suffered a miscarriage. A bad case of pelvic infection followed, and thereafter the tumor grew rapidly, until by October it was interfering with respiration. Dr. Mayo recommended removal, but Mrs. Waggoner refused it, so he tapped the growth, draining off its fluid contents. It quickly refilled and continued to grow.

The woman grew thin and weak, and could not eat. She was facing death and the operation could mean no worse, so she gave her consent.

Carefully Dr. Mayo planned. Under his instructions the patient's husband, who was a blacksmith, forged the instruments, among them some clamps fitted with hooks made from the teeth of an old mowing machine.

On December 14 the operating force assembled at the Waggoner home. Dr. J. E. Bowers, superintendent of the Rochester State Hospital for the Insane, was on hand to give the anesthetic, and to render other assistance there were Mrs. Mayo and Dr. David Berkman, the young veterinarian whom Gertrude Mayo had married in 1877.

Young Will and Charlie were there too, "peeking through the door."

With the patient under chloroform, Dr. Mayo made the incision, plunged a trocar into the tumor, and drained its contents into a tub ready for the purpose. Then he applied the homemade clamps, which had been heating in a little charcoal furnace such as solderers used, and began to pull the tumor out bit by bit. It was a large one, weighing some twenty pounds.

All went well until a big pelvic abscess lying behind the growth broke and spilled its contents into the abdominal cavity. This was bad, but Dr. Mayo sponged out the pus as thoroughly as he could, inserted a drainage tube, and stitched up the incision.

The operation took nearly an hour and the patient showed signs of severe shock, but she rallied and regained consciousness.

Three days later the newspaper concluded a notice of the event with the statement that "the lady is doing well," and in the next week's issue it reported that she was out of danger. "We are personally glad this is so," commented the editor, "for it is not much to the credit of a state like Minnesota to have to send all patients who require difficult and dangerous surgical operations to Chicago for treatment. The citizens of Rochester must feel equally glad with us that there is one amongst us (Dr. Mayo) who has the nerve and courage to undertake to relieve suffering humanity from this dangerous disease."

Mrs. Waggoner's operation was the favorite topic of conversation for weeks, and the lady herself was one of the wonders of the town. Dr. Mayo had "cut her wide open," and she lived!

That operation was the first of a series. Its successful outcome led to enough others like it during the next decade to make Dr. Mayo the foremost ovariotomist in Minnesota by a good margin.

Obviously, Dr. Mayo did not operate in a well-ordered world of men in white. His was "kitchen surgery," attended with all the informality and makeshift that term implies.

The theater was usually the patient's home, the operating

table one from the kitchen, or the parlor sofa, or even a door taken from its hinges and laid across two sawhorses. The room was seldom large enough, and Dr. Mayo refused to permit the presence of anyone but those who were helping him or other doctors who had come to watch. But the friends and neighbors who had gathered to support the patient's family through the ordeal milled around the doorway or in the yard outside, excited and curious.

Modern men, accustomed to strict asepsis in operative routine and surroundings, can scarcely credit the stories of pre-antiseptic methods, stories of men who operated in whatever coat or shirt they happened to be wearing, covering it perhaps with a linen duster or an apron stiff with the stains of previous operations; who stropped their knives on the soles of their shoes before they began and while using one knife held another ready between their teeth, its blade nestling among their whiskers; who economized on the water that must be carried in from the well by squeezing the blood from the sponge instead of washing it out; who washed their hands after, not before, the operation.

Being fastidious in dress and person, Dr. Mayo may have kept his few instruments fairly clean, free at least of dried blood between operations, but they were certainly not sterile. Some of them he carried in a little case or even loose in his vest pocket, where he could reach them easily to lance a boil or clip the ragged edges of a minor wound.

He may have removed his long black coat when he operated, to allow himself greater freedom of movement or to save the garment from soiling. But perhaps he shared that peculiar sense of values which made it a matter of pride for the surgeon to perform an amputation or other major operation without spotting the whiteness of shirt cuff or front.

It is said that Dr. Henry J. Bigelow of Boston, one of the nation's ablest surgeons at the time, always operated in a "well-valeted dark blue Prince Albert coat with a rose in the buttonhole," and that he always gave his appearance a critical once-over in the mirror before entering the surgical amphi-theater of the Massachusetts General Hospital.

Like all his fellows Dr. Mayo expected infection to develop in the incision or stump, but he had got far enough to know that this was not the ideal, for he congratulated himself when the wound healed "almost entirely by primary intention," that is, almost entirely without complications from postoperative infections.

Such was the professional development that combined with Dr. Mayo's crusade for reform in government to make him known "nearly everywhere in the state." Men who listened to the little doctor discuss their problems at some campaign rally in October were likely to think of him when little Mary got diphtheria in December. As his reputation spread from family to family and neighborhood to neighborhood, his practice grew to an enormous size.

To his own patients was added an extensive consultation practice. As word of his conspicuous successes passed from person to person, the village and country doctors roundabout who had been calling the Drs. Cross of Rochester or Dr. Hewitt of Red Wing or Dr. Staples of Winona—or even Dr. Atlee of Pennsylvania—began to summon Dr. Mayo of Rochester.

For dozens of doctors in south central Minnesota it became habitual to send their surgical cases to Dr. Mayo and to con-sult him in medical cases that baffled them.

Even his own neighbors began to realize he was one of the best doctors in the state; the awakening of Dr. Elisha Cross is more or less typical. He was called upon to treat a young woman for purpura hemorrhagica, or land scurvy, a disease that manifests itself in great purple blotches on the skin caused by internal bleeding. Purpura as severe as hers was then almost invariably fatal.

Dr. Cross summoned Dr. Staples to his aid, but the patient got rapidly worse and her parents changed to Dr. Mayo. By regulating her diet and dosing her with turpentine he cured her, though it took him a year to do it. After that whenever Dr. Cross got a case he did not feel able to handle alone, he called in Dr. Mayo, and for a year and a half he and Dr. Mayo shared an office as partners.

By 1883 Dr. Mayo had one of the three largest practices, perhaps the largest, in southern Minnesota. Only Dr. Hewitt and Dr. Staples might have matched him.

In handling so many calls, Dr. Mayo had help from time to time from the medical students for whom he was acting as preceptor, but unfortunately, little more is known of them than their names. What he could do for a young man, though, appears in the story of the prescription clerk in the drugstore below his office.

The young man's name was Henry Wellcome. Dr. Mayo took an interest in him, and was soon giving him lessons in chemistry and physics and urging him not to be content with the life of a poorly trained, small-town druggist, but to go away to school and fit himself for a real professional career.

Henry was a lad with ears to hear and, given practical assistance by Dr. Mayo, he took a thorough course in pharmacy at colleges in Chicago and Philadelphia and then went abroad for further study. In London he secured a position with a manufacturing chemist by the name of Burroughs, and soon he was married to his employer's daughter and the firm was Burroughs and Wellcome—a name well known in the world of medicine and pharmacy today.

When Henry Wellcome left the United States the manufacture of medicines in tablet form had just begun, and it had not yet started in England. Burroughs and Wellcome introduced it there. Tablets of standardized size and content were much easier to prescribe than the old powders and homemade pills, and they were much more easily carried to those far places of the world that Englishmen were exploring and colonizing. So the firm was phenomenally successful and its proprietors became men of great wealth.

Wellcome devoted his money to encouraging research in science. The work of the Wellcome Bureau of Scientific Research is known to scientists throughout the world, and for it the founder was knighted by the king of England.

Henry Wellcome often returned to the United States and to Rochester, always finding occasion to speak with gratitude of the part Dr. Mayo had played in his career.

For many years Dr. Mayo's best assistant was his wife. Applying her ability for self-education to her husband's books and journals, Mrs. Mayo acquired a knowledge of medicine that some friends of the family considered very nearly equal to the Doctor's own. He did not scruple to ask her opinion on a puzzling case, and she frequently went with him to see a patient. She helped too in his operations, and was so often present to assist in reducing fractures and applying splints that she acquired the knack of doing it herself.

Her younger son once described another phase of her helpfulness: "Patients used to call at the house for father . . . and if mother knew he was out in the country she would keep the patients interested, discussing their troubles and problems, until he returned, even if she had to prepare a meal for them.

"Often the neighbors and the country people came to talk to her about their families, their troubles, the children, and the babies, with as much satisfaction from a social standpoint as they got from consulting my father when sickness descended on them. When father was taking special studies in the East, or in Europe, patients came to mother to talk about illness, and she told them of the simple remedies, which would tide them through the most common illness. Mother was a real good doctor herself."

Mrs. Mayo made a good confidante, for she was a wise woman. She had a strong sense of humor too, and a witty, pleasantly sharp tongue. According to one neighbor, she made "thousands of friends" in Rochester, many of them through her active participation in the doings of the Episcopal Church. But domestic duties sometimes stalked her even at divine worship. Rochester folk long chuckled about the time she almost disrupted the Sunday morning service. In the midst of it she suddenly jumped to her feet, cried aloud, "Godalmighty, I left my bread in the oven!" and went streaking up the aisle toward the door.

Dr. and Mrs. Mayo, both forceful personalities, did not always pull smoothly in double harness. It was well known to their close friends that for long periods of time they spoke to each other no more than necessary to keep the affairs of the household going.

They agreed on most fundamentals. Mrs. Mayo joined willingly in her husband's impulsive generosity, though it often meant added burdens for her shoulders. One day he brought her four children to care for, ranging in age from six to twelve. Their mother, a patient of his, had just died and they had no place else to go. Other homes were later found for the two younger girls, but the two older ones lived with the Mayos until they married.

A few years later one of the colonizing schemes of the day brought to the Rochester area a party of some sixty young Englishmen, second and third sons of impoverished aristocrats who thought to better their fortunes in the New World. The idea of the promoter was to hire them out as farm hands until they learned the ways of American agriculture, but the boys, blithe and unaware, had come fully equipped with dress suits, guns, and fishing tackle. Some of them found farm life and the rigors of a Minnesota winter more than they could take.

Dr. Mayo was indignant about the whole affair and felt himself morally responsible for the boys. They kept coming to his office for help and advice, and before the winter was over he had taken no fewer than eight of them home for Mrs. Mayo to look after until they could find more suitable work or could arrange for passage back to England.

Such demands upon her good nature Mrs. Mayo met with

equanimity and sympathy. It was Dr. Mayo's championship of the underdog in the mass that she could not approve.

Her judgment was more balanced than his, her tolerant understanding deeper and inclusive enough to take in the banker as well as the widow and orphans. She knew that some of the economic distress that sent her husband into a tirade against the wheat rings and the railroads was quite as much the fault of individual shiftlessness and bad management as of general conditions or the cussedness of the wealthy.

Then too, since she had to keep the family clothed and fed on the Doctor's income, she was understandably cross when he went off for two weeks at a time on political campaigns and neglected the work that provided this income.

She had a good business head and knew the Doctor's big practice could keep the family in comfort without strain. When Dr. Mayo set off for New York in the fall of 1869 he gave her his account books, saying she could collect enough of what his patients owed him to support the family while he was away. She undertook the job with alacrity, and never had the Mayos lived so well and so easily as they did that winter. Knowing this, Mrs. Mayo was exasperated when she had to struggle to make ends meet.

The stories of Dr. Mayo's houses in town and on the farm, of his trips, books, horses, carriages, his relatively generous contributions to civic projects, and his readiness to invest money in one venture or another do not give the impression of insufficient funds.

Never a year passed without the paper's reporting some improvement that Dr. Mayo was making on one of his properties, and sometimes the improvement was extensive and costly. He did not always go to the conventions of the American Medical Association as a delegate with expenses paid, and in the summer of 1876, just after buying the farm, he spent three months in Europe. Nor did his sons have to work their way through medical college, as some doctors did and do.

Yet Will and Charlie could not remember that their father

ever had any ready money. The Mayos always had to practice the strictest economy in their daily living, and Dr. Mayo himself said that his profession enabled him only to hang onto the world by the skin of his teeth. His activities were often financed on credit, and although he always paid his bills, the horse might be dead before he got it paid for.

One trouble was that Dr. Mayo was as impulsive in spending money as in everything else, and he had a marked inclination to sacrifice the bread and butter of life for its jam. In a rush of enthusiasm he would hire an engineer to plan the water system he was urging for Rochester, set off on a trip, or have a fancy new gig built to order at the carriage shop— and let the old suit or carpet or churn serve for another year.

Unwise? Improvident? Perhaps, though there is a view of living that counts the grasshopper wiser than the ant, the feast worth the famine.

But this does not entirely explain why in spite of his large practice Dr. Mayo was never listed with the Drs. Cross and Galloway among Rochester's rich men whose incomes were large enough to be taxable. For that his haphazard, easygoing business methods were chiefly to blame. Posting his books was a task he did not like, so he put it off as long as he could.

Mrs. Granger, living on a farm some miles from Rochester, was confined to her bed for something over a year and a half and required almost daily visits from Dr. Mayo for most of the period. Her husband did not want the bill to mount beyond his ability to pay it, so after the first few months he told the Doctor he wanted to pay what he owed.

"I haven't got my books up to date and I don't know how much it is," replied the Doctor.

Mr. Granger insisted.

"Well, then, give me fifty dollars."

A few months later Granger raised the same question, got the same answer, and paid another fifty dollars. Then shortly after his wife had recovered sufficiently to dispense with the

Doctor's services, he stopped by to settle the bill in full. Dr. Mayo still did not know the amount of it. "But give me fifty dollars and we'll call it square." And that was the end of it.

At last his daughter Phoebe and later Gertrude's husband took over the bookkeeping and brought a measure of system into it. But they could not put system into the charges and collections. The Doctor hated to set a fee and detested asking for money. He would have preferred the old way of the honorarium: I'll do the best job I can and you give me what it's worth to you. Not until he was himself being pressed by some urgent need would he send out bills.

To this habit he added an incurable softheartedness; he could not put down a charge for poor folks. Whether his social and political views were right or wrong they were sincere, and he lived according to them. He would not take money from a struggling widow or a farmer bent low under a load of debt. Accept a mortgage in payment? Sue to collect an account? Not Dr. Mayo. He simply could not do it.

Tuesday, May 31, 1881, was Dr. Mayo's sixty-second birthday. His sentiment not being of the kind that makes much of birthdays, he went quietly about his ordinary routine.

In the pleasant early evening, however, he was glad to oblige a friend who had asked him to take her riding for a breath of air after supper. As the fast-stepping grays were speeding the carriage back toward town, his companion decided she would like to stop for a chat with Mrs. Mayo before going home. So Dr. Mayo turned in at his own gate.

The place was ablaze with the light of torches and a crowd of several hundred persons filled the yard and the porch. As the carriage drew abreast of them, there was a fanfare from a band and a rush toward the buggy.

Dr. Mayo's Rochester friends and patients had gathered to surprise him. And he *was* surprised.

After a round of greetings and handshaking, one of the men stepped forward, called for silence, then addressed the Doctor:

"I have been requested to assure you that . . . our mission to your beautiful home this evening is one of love and respect for you. . . . The great majority of those present have at some period of their lives been your patients, and we wish now to thank you for your kindness and devotion . . . and for your skill. . . . For nearly a quarter of a century you have been our friend and physician. . . . By night as well as by day, through darkness and storms, you have visited the poor and destitute sick, from whom you never expected to receive any pecuniary remuneration, as freely and as promptly as you have visited those who were able to pay for your services. Through all these years . . . you have never hesitated in the performance of the responsible duties of your profession.

"We thought this, the anniversary of your birth, the most fitting occasion to make some acknowledgment of the great service you have rendered this entire community. I, therefore, in the name and in behalf of those present, present to you these books as a token of our high regard for you as a kind and obliging neighbor, a faithful friend, and a trusted physician."

The books were five beautiful volumes, bound in morocco and gilt-edged, comprising a de luxe edition of Wilson and Bonaparte's *Natural History of the Birds of the United States*. (The newspaper revealed next day that they had cost one hundred and ten dollars.)

The little doctor was completely overcome. He tried to reply but could not speak for the emotion that choked him, and half the crowd were likewise moved to tears. Finally he managed a few words. "I have endeavored to do my duty as a physician in a manner satisfactory to myself and to the public, and never thought my efforts were so far appreciated by the community as to bring out a public expression of this character."

Present to share in the Doctor's happiness that evening were his entire family: Mrs. Mayo; Gertrude, now Mrs. Berkman, direct, positive, outspoken, very like her father in manner and temperament; Phoebe, gentle and winning, for the past five years an invalid as the result of an injury to the spleen suffered when she was thrown from a carriage as it made the sharp turn into the farm driveway; *and* the two boys.

Will had just arrived from medical school on the six o'clock train, having come home for the summer a day early in order to be present for the occasion. Charlie, a lad of seventeen, was still in high school.

What thoughts stirred in their minds as they listened and watched that night? Pleasure, pride, excitement, of course. But perhaps also a determination to earn such a tribute for themselves someday.

7. The Mayo Boys

"FROM the very beginning Charlie and I always went together. We were known as the Mayo boys. Anyone that picked on one of us had the two to contend with."

Imagination can picture the childhood partners: Will, a slender boy, with fair hair and blue eyes, a little lonely, wanting companionship and love; he is the older brother, slight but strong, spirited, able. And with him almost constantly, in play and at their chores, is Charlie, short, stocky, with thick dark hair and big brown eyes, an affectionate boy, needing oversight and protection, for he is the little brother and not very strong.

In some such relationship was formed the infrangible brotherhood that was to be the wonder of all who witnessed it and on the strength of which both men were to reach the heights.

The boys spent long hours together, reading, shooting marbles, fishing at Oronoco or Zumbro Falls, or hunting arrowheads in the old Indian burial grounds atop the bluffs surrounding Rochester. They loved to go to the circus and seldom missed any animal show that came to town.

In spring "pigeon days" they sometimes hitched Will's pony to a buggy and drove over to the roost about twelve miles from town to club a bagful of the young birds from the trees. This was then good sport for youngsters and grownups alike, because the passenger pigeons ate up the farmers' grain and there were such thousands of them they darkened the sun in their flight.

To his family Charlie seemed quieter, more serious and studious than Will. "He was always reading or writing or making things," his sister recalled. They were all proud of him, for he had a skill with things mechanical that astonished them all. If the stove or pump or churn didn't work, Charlie would fix it. If a gadget was wanted for some purpose in house or barn, Charlie would contrive it.

When the two brothers were in their early teens, Charlie persuaded their father to buy them a little steam engine that would turn wheels to do the family washing, cut wood, and work the well pump. When the engine came, and forever thereafter, its working was an unfathomable mystery to Will. He would push and pull and pry, turn this screw and that one. To no avail. "I could never make the cussed thing go."

Then Charlie would come and with a simple twist or two set it chugging. When repairs were needed, he took the engine apart, found and fixed the trouble, and put all the pieces back in their proper place. "Absolutely magical" this seemed to Will.

There is a family tradition that Charlie at fourteen, with no instruction other than the pictures and descriptions he had seen, rigged up a telephone from his father's office to the family farm home. And the instrument is said to have worked so well that the telephone company threatened suit for infringement of patent when they heard of it.

Whatever the truth of the tradition, it is a fact that in 1879, when Charlie was fourteen, the first telephone in Rochester was put in to connect Dr. Mayo's office with the farmhouse.

Both the boys went to school at Rochester Central, that "model of magnificence and elegance" the school board had built across the street from their home. They were neither precociously brilliant students nor teacher's pets. Will was lively, so full of teasing tricks to torment the girls that they did not like to play with him. He got on easily enough with his lessons, except in arithmetic, which he could never master and therefore always heartily disliked.

Will Mayo could never have endured wearing the dunce cap; he was too proud and too sensitive to ridicule. He reacted violently and without humor to anything that turned the joke on him and made him feel a fool.

On one occasion he went to a show given by a playmate, Jimmy Ells, the son of a Rochester druggist. The admission was ten pins, and the theater a barn. As part of the entertainment Jimmy was to demonstrate his prowess in sleight of hand by finding two eggs under someone's hat. He chose Will's hat, and the eggs were rotten.

When Will got the egg out of his eyes, he grabbed a hatchet and started for Jimmy. By his own admission, if someone had not tripped him on the way he would have done his first surgery then and there.

Another time, when he was riding on the tailboard of a grocer's wagon and did not heed a command to get off, the driver flicked him with the tip of the whip, then laughed to see him jump. Will's temper flared, more at the laugh than at the sting of the whip. He snatched up a handful of stones and hurled them in a fury at the driver, with a string of words that were neither gentle nor genteel.

Will Mayo's barriers against intrusion were up early. Withdrawal, protective pride, independence, all were there, creating an inability to be one of the gang, an incapacity for easy intimacy and informality. He could never express his feelings of boyish affection and comradeship in playful hair-pulling or in throwing an arm across another's shoulders. Playmates would do that to Charlie, but not to Will. And he would not have liked it if they had.

His choice of pastimes was in keeping with his disposition. One of the familiar sights of Rochester for those whose school days fell with his was that of "Will Mayo dashing spiritedly around the streets on his little bay pony." Dr. Mayo had got him the pony as soon as he was old enough to ride, and it was his pride and pleasure for several years, until he had to relinquish it for his sister Gertrude to ride to and from the school near town in which she was teaching. Then Will fell heir to a horse from his father's stable.

He learned to ride well and without fear. Once when he was watching a circus parade from on horseback, his mount was frightened by the elephants and in its terrified cavorting jumped over a hitching rail and back again, causing a commotion in the crowd. "But Will never batted an eye."

On an earlier occasion the wills of master and mount collided and Will rode toward a tree to get a switch, but the pony acted first. Will's left arm struck a rock and was broken just below the elbow. Someone near by helped him to remount, and the child, just eight years old, rode home alone, a mile and a half. The story of that mishap to "Willie Mayo, son of Dr. Mayo" was the first of his many appearances in the newspapers.

The next year, in a trial of horsemanship for boys under eighteen at the county fair, Willie placed second in a field of four. In after years the local graybeards, recalling this early achievement of their most successful neighbor, ended with a chuckle, "That was the only time Will Mayo ever came out second best."

When Charlie started to school in the "baby room" at Central, he did not like it, and often played hooky. But each time he ran away his mother took him firmly back to school until the lesson was learned and the habit broken.

At recess he would run across the street to mother for a piece of bread and brown sugar. Sometimes he had to sprint to get back in time, and then the old janitor would call "Hurry!" and keep on ringing the bell until the boy could get up the stairs and into his seat.

"Which proves that it's just as good to stand in with the janitor as with the superintendent," remarked Charlie some years later.

He always stood well toward the top of his class, but he also stood well up in mischief. He was so often the ringleader in the fun that Charlie Mayo and his chum, Albert Younglove, were the teacher's chief suspects when anything was amiss in the classroom.

At last the black marks against him were too many and he was summoned before the principal. That gentleman intended a birching and twirled a sturdy stick in his fingers as he read the culprit a homily on the advantages of being a good boy. Then he asked Charlie whether he had anything to say.

"Yes, please, if you could wait until this afternoon, I'd like to get my other pair of pants."

The schoolmaster struggled to stay severe, then surrendered to a laugh. "And that was the end of that."

Unusual in its day, Rochester Central included a high school, and although its single course of study offered too little of science and languages and too much of mathematics to suit Dr. Mayo, he sent Will to it for two or three years.

These were followed by nine months' study of Latin, French, and German in "Miss Finch's select school" and then a year's course in the new Rochester Training School, a private academy that paid special attention to "fitting for college."

Physical training was not in the course at the academy, but "Prof. Sam Manchester" conducted a "Rochester Gymnasium" near by, and at two public exhibitions given by his pupils Willie Mayo was among those who demonstrated their prowess in "leaping the horizontal bar, whirling, tumbling, parallel bars, ladder, dumb bells, club swinging, handsprings, and somersaults; all exercises requiring both activity and strength."

Charlie was not one of Manchester's pupils, perhaps because

his strength was not up to gymnastics, but otherwise he followed Will's course, transferring to the Rochester Training School after two years of high school and a spell of private study with a Mrs. McMahon.

On the whole then, in a day when schooling often stopped with three or four years of random attendance in an ungraded class and at best seldom included more than eight years of rudimentary graded work, Will and Charlie Mayo were fortunate in the preparatory education their parents secured for them.

In some respects, though, the results were not conspicuously good. Charlie in particular was always an indifferent speller, impatient with insistence on anything more than a phonetic approximation. As he once told a secretary, any damn fool would know that *bellie* meant belly, and *phisicks* physics. And Dr. Will never found his French and German adequate for understanding the foreign medical journals he wanted to read.

"The Doctor had one weakness," said Mrs. Mayo of her husband. "It was for the book agents. He knew and loved good books. Oh, many a time I planned to buy a dress for Trude or something for the boys or the house, only to have a book agent come to town and tip over my bucket of milk."

The Doctor's library was the living room, walled with well-filled shelves from floor to ceiling, and Will remembered that living room to the end of his days: "I can see Father now, standing on a wooden chair, reaching up to take books down, or, with one book under his arm, another held between his knees, looking into the pages of a third."

Among the books were a great many novels, which Will and Charlie were encouraged to read: some by Scott, many by Dickens, and the Leatherstocking Tales of James Fenimore Cooper, which moved Dr. and Mrs. Mayo to reminiscences of their own experiences with the Indians. For the boys the tales of the Sioux Outbreak were so thoroughly mixed with *The Deerslayer* and *The Last of the Mohicans* that the Minnesota

Valley was always for them the real scene of Cooper's stories of romance and adventure.

Into the mixture of fact and fiction would come sooner or later the name of Cut Nose, the wild Sioux whose bones were lying in that big iron kettle in the Doctor's office.

See, here they are. Look how small his head was. But he was very tall. Here's the femur, see how long it is. Thus began the boys' first lessons in anatomy, for they learned their osteology from the skeleton of the Indian warrior.

They were introduced to other sciences in the same casual way. Mrs. Mayo taught them botany while they worked together in the garden or rambled in the fields and woods along Bear Creek. Astronomy too they absorbed with enthusiasm under their mother's guidance, with books from the shelves to explain what they saw through the four-foot telescope Mrs. Mayo had mounted on a tripod in the observatory that topped the Mayo farmhouse.

Long hours of looking made the heavens ever after wear a friendly face for Will, and when he was himself rich enough to gratify any whim in building his house, he asked only that it have a tower like his mother's.

The boys picked up physics and chemistry from their father, who talked to them often about his early teacher, the great John Dalton. "When my brother and I were small boys, he told us much about this tall, gaunt, awkward scholar, the keenness of his intelligence, his modesty, and how little it was realized in his day that the atomic theory was more than the vagary of a scientist."

From casual chats like these, carried on over test tube and burner in the crude little laboratory in a back room off the Doctor's office, Will and Charlie learned something of the methods of scientists. But they met the principles of science full face during their high school days, when their father set them to reading Darwin, Huxley, Haeckel, and Spencer. The freethinking Doctor did not consider those writers at all unsuitable for teen-age boys, and the brothers in turn found them fascinating.

From the time they were old enough to be of any help, Will and Charlie were expected to work as well as to study and play. "Father wanted us to be handy." He believed in useful children and did not allow his sons to acquire the art of loafing.

Even as little fellows they had chores to do. They drove the family cows in the morning to the pasture lot half a mile from home and fetched them back at night, and since Mrs. Mayo had no hired help, they were expected to assist in doing the washing and weeding the garden. They carried water in from the well and kept the woodbox filled, usually with Charlie handling the saw and Will the ax.

Mrs. Mayo made her own butter at that time, so the boys served many a turn at the tiresome task of moving the handle of the old dash churn up and down till the butter came. And if it was too long in coming, they knew a way to hurry it up— just sneak in a little hot water when mother wasn't looking. But be careful, for if the water was too hot or if you added too much, the butter would be a mess, and then how you'd catch it!

After Dr. Mayo bought the farm, there was plenty of work to keep the boys busy. They and their sisters had to help Jay Neville, a young Irishman who had recently attached himself to the Mayo household and was in charge of the farming. "I picked potato bugs, and raked hay with a jug of beer under the hay rake," said Charlie later. "They used to have big umbrellas over open buggies, so I put one on the rake. I thought I did most of the work on the farm."

Charlie acquired a love of farming then that resulted in his making a hobby of it later. But Will would have none of it. He loathed every operation connected with it, and one noon he came in from the field and firmly announced that he was through. He was going into town to get a job.

He found a place in Geisinger and Newton's drugstore below his father's office, beginning with menial tasks like sweeping out, washing bottles, and scrubbing the mortars and pestles. The hours were long, from seven in the morning to six and sometimes nine o'clock in the evening, and the pay was only four dollars a week.

With his first month's salary Will did a favor for Charlie. Clothes were handed down in the Mayo family, so that whenever Dr. Mayo's Prince Albert coat got shiny, Mrs. Mayo cut it down for one of the boys. "Charlie looked so funny in that coat, long-waisted, and with little tails. So I bought him a new suit, a store suit, and he was so happy." Neither of the brothers ever forgot the pleasure they shared in that suit.

Will soon advanced to the position of prescription clerk, and when Charlie finished school, he went to work in the drugstore too. "Will had and I wanted to." For a while he worked alone as prescription clerk, but the volume of business finally forced the owners to hire an assistant for him and the responsibility made him very proud.

Against such a background of being useful, the cardinal fact of the Mayo boys' childhood and youth appears inevitable: They helped their father in his work as they helped their mother in hers, and so they were learning the practice of medicine almost from their cradle days.

They began by cleaning the office, taking care of the horses, and driving their father on his rounds. Will could remember having the responsibility for the horses when he was so small he had to climb up in the manger to throw the bridle onto the neck of one high-headed horse called Frank. He enjoyed the duty and took pride in the horses his father raised, keeping a record of them in the family Bible.

The boys were expected to sweep and dust the office before they went to school. "As soon as school closed each day, father had me come to the office," said Charlie. "If he was delayed, I had to clean up some room in the office and then I drove the horse on the round of calls, taking up this work as my

brother dropped it. Father said it saved him much time hitching and unhitching the horse."

When Dr. Mayo left the boy sitting outside the house, some
of the calls seemed interminably long, "especially in marble-
playing time." It was more fun in cold weather when he took
the youngster into the house to see the patient with him.
Eagerly the boy watched and listened and then, on the way
to the next call, asked his father the meaning of what he had
seen and heard.

Neither Dr. Mayo nor his patients saw anything undignified
in his pressing his sons into service, or his wife or even his
daughters if the emergency was great. Will and Charlie progressed from washing windows and sweeping floors to rolling
bandages, applying them and the plasters and poultices used
under them, helping to put on plaster casts, and similar jobs
that would be done today by a hospital intern or an office
nurse.

Will often told the story of a young man who came to deliver produce of some kind to the house. While he was there
Dr. Mayo came into the kitchen, noticed a boil on the boy's
neck, and whipped out a knife and lanced the boil almost before the young man was aware of his intentions. Then the
Doctor went on about other business, calling over his shoulder,
"Will, come dress Bill's neck for him, will you?"

Transfer this episode to the office, where the Doctor, busy
with a queue of patients, would need help of the same sort,
and it becomes clear how the Mayo boys acquired the minor
skills of a doctor.

Of even more importance was what their eyes and ears took
in while the work was going on. Again and again they heard
the significant questions to be asked in taking a case history,
saw the points to be looked into in a thorough physical examination, listened to the diagnosis and prescription that followed from the findings. From frequent repetition they learned
many of Dr. Mayo's tested principles of diagnosis and prog-

nosis, which he often put in succinct, homely sayings they long remembered.

Dr. Mayo was still at the business of "further thought and research" while his sons were working with him, and he returned from many a trip to St. Paul, the East, or Europe with something new to describe to the boys.

On one occasion that Will remembered he came home with a dramatic story to illustrate the new principle that anesthesia had made possible for surgery. He had attended a clinic in New York at which James R. Wood and John McCormick both operated. Wood, noted for his speed in operating, completed an amputation at the thigh in two minutes, and the crowded amphitheater echoed with applause. Then McCormick, an English surgeon, performed an equally difficult operation carefully and without haste, turning when he had finished to say quietly, "Not how quickly but how well."

From another trip to New York came an impetus to Dr. Mayo's use of the microscope. His model was out of date, and on this trip he was much impressed with some of the new, higher powered ones he saw on exhibition.

He returned home on a train that reached Rochester early in the morning, and Will and Charlie and their sister Gertrude drove down to meet him. In preparation for his coming the boys had made the office spick-and-span and so were pleased when he said he would like to go to the office before driving home for breakfast. After commending them for the clean windows and floors, he picked up his little old microscope and took it along out to the house.

At the breakfast table he distributed the presents he had brought and then, placing the microscope on the table, pulled from his pocket a circular describing a new model, the present he'd like to have for himself. It would do wonderful things, he said, but it cost six hundred dollars, and there was no money left after his trip. To buy the instrument he would have to put a mortgage on the house.

Mrs. Mayo's Scottish prudence balked a little. Four children, and the times so hard. Would they ever get a mortgage paid off? But finally she said, "Well, William, if you could do better by the people with this new microscope and you really think you need it, we'll do it."

They did it, and legend says it took the Doctor ten years to pay off the mortgage. But Will was sure the circumstances under which the new microscope was bought helped to give him and Charlie an especially keen interest in its use.

Dr. Mayo taught the boys to fix in alcohol the tissues he removed at operations and to cut and mount sections, technical procedures which at that time took several days. Following these steps with eager study of the results through the microscope, they got an introduction to microscopic pathology in the embryonic stages of that science.

They were already acquainted with the rudiments of gross pathology, for Dr. Mayo frequently took them along to his autopsies. He began taking Will when the boy was so small he could not see if he stood on the floor; so Dr. Mayo set him up on the head of the table, where he could lean forward and hang onto the hair of the corpse to steady himself while he watched.

As in other phases of the work, watching grew into assisting. For Will the climax of this training came just a few months before he set out for medical school. One of his father's patients died and the Doctor decided to do a postmortem.

The night was gusty with storm winds; the way led across the river to the Bradley House, an abandoned hotel in which the patient had lived alone as a sort of caretaker; and the work had to be done by the light of a lantern. Dr. Mayo had received a call just as they set out, so when the examination of the body was finished, about ten o'clock, he left Will to close the abdomen and take the specimens to the office.

The boy would not let his father know he was afraid, but "I can feel yet," he wrote many years later, "the weird atmosphere of that squeaky old house, with its long shadowy corridors, and I remember the struggle I had to complete the job and force myself to walk slowly to the front door. The creaking of the old hotel signboard swinging above the entrance as I stepped out was the last straw, and I made good speed down the street."

The dissecting room at medical school could hold no terrors after that.

Always the boys' practical experience was complemented by a good deal of reading urged upon them by their father. Again and again he would answer a question or end a discussion by taking from his shelves such stand-bys as Gray's *Anatomy,* Holden's *Anatomical Landmarks,* and Paget's *Lectures on Surgical Pathology,* insisting that Will and Charlie must learn their contents.

It was Paget's book that introduced Will as a schoolboy to John Hunter, the great eighteenth-century student of gross pathology. In a day when the pathologist had to be a practitioner pursuing mammon as well as science, Hunter refused to let what he called "the eternal chase after the damned guinea" keep him from making systematic studies of disease. Rising at four o'clock every morning to work with his specimens before beginning the day's practice at the office, he founded the science of experimental and surgical pathology. The thirteen thousand specimens that he assembled, prepared, and labeled neatly in black with his own hands constituted the museum collection of the Royal College of Surgeons, on which Paget based his book.

John Hunter became a hero to Will Mayo, providing inspiration that seemingly never lapsed. The place of honor in his office at the Mayo Clinic, on the wall directly across from his desk where he could see it whenever he raised his eyes, was always reserved for Joshua Reynolds's portrait of John Hunter.

Used to helping their father in any way they could, Will and Charlie naturally grew into assisting him at his operations, and there were always a number of important odd jobs they could do.

For tying off the blood vessels and closing the wound Dr. Mayo used silk and linen thread, and it was the task of one of the boys to cut hanks of this into the desired lengths, coat them with wax, and then twist the strands into ligatures and sutures. With these he would thread an assortment of needles, stick them through the lapel of his coat, and stand where his father could reach for the ones he wanted. In between times the boy might be called on to heat the instruments in the fire or to handle the sponges.

It was on one such occasion that the accident occurred which resulted in Charlie's becoming his father's anesthetist. The operation was to remove an ovarian tumor, and Will was acting as the Doctor's first assistant.

Since anesthesia was still new enough for the layman to fear it, it was the custom to have some physician of established reputation give the anesthetic, and on this occasion Dr. Mayo's anesthetist was a doctor well known in Rochester. He was a surgeon and had served as coroner for Olmsted County, but obviously he was not accustomed to major operations on a breathing, pulsing body.

Dr. Mayo made a small incision and drained the fluid contents of the tumor into a tub. Then by means of clamps worked by thumbscrews he began to pull the tissue of the growth out through the incision. The base of the tumor was pulled back and forth in the process, producing a peculiar sucking noise like that made "by a cow's foot in the mud." This was too much for the nerves of the anesthetist and he fainted.

After a quick survey of the possibilities, Dr. Mayo kicked over a cracker box at the end of the sofa and said, "Here, Charlie, you stand on this and give the anesthetic."

"He did it well, with perfect composure," said Will, but Charlie added a few details: "When she stopped wiggling Father would tell me to stop, and when she started again I would drop some more. I did fine, but like doctors called in to help another, I was looking at the operation and paying no attention to the patient."

This was an oft-told tale among the Mayos, and their memories placed it when Charlie was about ten years old. But documentary evidence based on the identity of the anesthetist and the patient makes him eighteen at the time. In any case Charlie took over the work of anesthetist at so early an age that some patients were afraid he was too young for the responsibility.

The office and country rounds, the sickroom and autopsy table, the library of medical books and journals, osteology, pathology, chemistry—all these were for the Mayo boys familiar sights and occupations. Medicine was not a thing apart, a series of laborious lessons to be learned, or a means only as good as any other for earning a living; it was the very stuff of living. "We were reared in medicine as a farmer boy is reared in farming."

This would not be possible now. Surgery has moved into the hospitals, the postmortem into autopsy rooms, and that the practitioner's sons should be underfoot in either is unthinkable.

The doctor's office has been spruced up, and his manners formalized along with it. Businesslike methods, up-to-the-minute records, and a trimly efficient nurse as receptionist have replaced the top hat and Prince Albert coat as the badge of professional dignity. Amid such order curious children would be out of place.

And what would patients say today if their doctor's sons came along to watch procedures at the bedside!

The roots of more than the Mayo brothers' practical facility in medicine can be found in their boyhood. The Doctor introduced the boys also to the principles and ethics of the physician.

He took them, even when they were little tykes, along to the meetings of the local and district medical societies, and there they listened to the exchange of ideas among the colleagues on many important problems of the profession. There too, as well as in their home, they met their father's friends, among them some fine examples of the pioneer physician at his best.

It was at a meeting of the Minnesota Valley Medical Association that Will met Dr. Asa W. Daniels of St. Peter, Dr. Mayo's associate in the days of the Sioux Outbreak and one of the grand old men of the Valley.

"So you're going to study medicine," said Dr. Daniels. "Well, it's the most satisfactory of all the professions; it is doing for others. Let me advise you that when you go into the practice of medicine and begin to go about the country seeing patients, be careful what you eat. I have found it wise to ask for something that has been boiled and is still hot." This was experiential wisdom, in the days before Pasteur.

Another of the men Will and Charlie came to know was Dr. N. S. Tefft of Plainview. He was a surgeon of exceptional skill and a vigorous freethinker like their father. But what the Mayo boys chiefly remembered was his pluck in carrying on his professional duties.

He was a man "with dangling lower extremities, crippled by infantile paralysis, carrying his heavy body around on crutches, doing country practice, but nothing was allowed to interfere with his work. He would start off through the snow in winter, and if he did not return at a certain time, the livery man would take a team and go to find him. Perhaps he would be in a snow drift, hardly able to blanket his horse, and waiting down under the robes for rescue."

It was good for the two brothers to know such men in the early youth that is "a period of generous self-surrender to ideals." They grew up in a tradition that the life of a doctor must be one of service, that his profession demanded of him a response to every call, whether there was pecuniary reward in it or not.

They were present on more than one occasion when a call from the country came in late at night or in the midst of a heavy snowstorm and Jay Neville tried to persuade Dr. Mayo not to answer it. "They won't pay you anything. You know they won't."

"But, Jay, you don't understand. Those people are sick, and they need a doctor." And the Doctor would drive away, while Jay muttered after him, "But they never pay."

It was while the boys were helping in the office, marking up the ledger after the patients had gone, that they heard their father say, as Charlie remembered so well, "Now, those folks are poor. Don't put them down in the book."

It is a pregnant fact that the Mayo boys grew up during a period of depression and hard times. The dreams of a happy prosperous future with which the pioneers had come to the new land had faded for many of them into the bitter reality of drought and debt, bad crops, low prices, and lost homes. Will and Charlie saw the situation and its causes through their father's eyes, and they learned his principle of *noblesse oblige*.

"Our father believed that a man with unusual physical strength or with unusual intellectual capacity or opportunities owed something to the people. He should do for others in proportion as he had the strength to do." Time and again the brothers offered this as sufficient explanation for things they did that won them the plaudits of the world.

But wise friends of the family, sure that Will and Charlie did not get all their ability and ideas from their father, have left a caution to biographers, "Don't forget the mother." Unfortunately there is scant record of what Mrs. Mayo believed and taught. But there does remain the tone of wonder in which her sons spoke of her tolerance, her understanding, and her charitable spirit. "She accepted what good there was in folks and did not criticize the bad. I never knew her to say a hateful word about anyone," said Dr. Will.

All in all, Dr. Charlie probably erred only in degree when he told a group of Rochester folk assembled to do him honor, "The biggest thing Will and I ever did was to pick the father and mother we had."

8. At Medical School

THERE was no question about the choice of career for the Mayo brothers. "It never occurred to us that we could be anything but doctors," said Will. When he was ready to begin his professional schooling, the only decision to be made was where he should go.

The schools, all too plentiful, were on the whole a sorry lot, little changed since the Doctor's days at Indiana Medical College. And the preceptorship that had saved the situation in that earlier day had become only nominal, many a student seeing nothing of his preceptor from the time he registered as an apprentice until he returned with his degree.

So ten or twelve months was the total time many a doctor gave to his training. As the advocates of reform pointed out, it took longer than this to learn the trade of a machinist, a printer, or a river-boat pilot.

Teaching in the schools was still of the "windy, wordy" kind under which students "heard much, saw little, and did nothing." They heard elaborate word pictures of disease, saw little of patients or illness at first hand, and did nothing themselves at the bedside or in the laboratory. Most students received the degree in medicine without ever having felt a sick man's pulse, listened to the sounds of lung and heart, or stood at the side of a woman in labor.

Leaders of the medical profession were well aware of the shocking state of the schools, and they were loud in their protest and denunciation, but the waves of words spent themselves without effect against the wall of the proprietary system. The teacher-owners of the schools were not inclined to make changes, however desirable, when these were certain to in-

106

crease expenses or lessen the number of fee-paying students.

So reform waited, while the proprietary schools multiplied beyond belief and here and there appeared the notorious diploma mills, which did not bother to give any courses at all but sold the degree in medicine to all applicants at fifty or a hundred dollars per sheepskin.

In the words of William Osler, the American system of medical education had become a byword among the nations.

Dr. Mayo knew all about this problem. As a member of the committee on medical education of the Minnesota State Medical Society he had helped to prepare a lengthy report setting it forth and commending the example of Harvard College, which had led the way in reform by adopting entrance requirements, a three-year graded course, and an annual session nine months long. So the Doctor knew what to look for in choosing a school for Will.

Minnesota offered no real possibility in 1880. It had only the St. Paul Medical College, more a hope than an actuality. Dr. A. J. Stone was its dean and its janitor as well as the teacher of every subject in its curriculum except chemistry. Dr. Mayo did not let his friendship with Stone blind him to the fact that the St. Paul school was not the place to send Will.

In 1880 the medical school of the University of Michigan moved into the first class by following Harvard's example and stiffening its requirements all along the line. Its faculty was good and it stressed clinical teaching and instruction in the medical sciences. Without exaggeration it could claim to have the biggest and best chemistry laboratory available to medical students in the United States.

And as the capstone of Michigan's excellence the first real university hospital in the country had been built in Ann Arbor in 1877. A wooden building of the pavilion type developed during the Civil War, this hospital provided accommodations for one hundred and fifty patients and a surgical amphitheater for clinical demonstration.

All this sounded good to the Mayos. So on September 16,

1880, Will took the noon train from Rochester to the East to begin his medical studies at the University of Michigan.

He was then nineteen years old, slender and not very tall, but straight and strong. This was his first trip away from home alone. How he felt he never said, but to his teachers he seemed just "a green Western boy."

Little is known of his daily life at Michigan, and even the official record of his courses and grades has been lost in the shuffle of the years. His only extracurricular activity seems to have been boxing, in which he won the university championship in the 133-pound class.

One of his friends was Franklin Paine Mall, a frail lad from Iowa who tried to harden himself physically by defying the winter cold without an overcoat. "A choice spirit," Will found him, first and last a student even then. He became one of the distinguished anatomists of his time and a power for reform in medical education.

Another chap that Will Mayo knew well was Woods Hutchinson, nephew of the learned London doctor remembered in Hutchinson's teeth, the notched incisors considered a sign of congenital syphilis. The nephew was a tall man with a long face, red hair, and a mind full of facts about all things medical, but he lacked the talents of a successful mixer, made few friends in college, and was only moderately successful later in practice.

Dr. Will never gave a name to a third classmate he described. The boy was the most promising member of the group and won all the honors at graduation. Everyone predicted a great career for him. And the first reports after graduation showed that he had quickly built up a flourishing practice.

Then with details from his own lips came suspicion. Where did he find so many movable kidneys to be fastened and so many diseased ovaries that ought to come out?

For Dr. Will disillusionment was complete when he heard the man boasting one day that there had never been a post-mortem on a patient he had lost. "We all make mistakes," he said, "but I take mighty good care that nobody knows about mine."

Among the professors Dr. Will remembered was Alonzo B. Palmer, dean of the medical school and professor of the practice of medicine. He was a kindly old man nearing his three-score years and ten, with a devotion to the Presbyterian church so intense that when a student failed Palmer's quiz on Saturday he tried to offset the failure by letting the dean see him entering church on Sunday.

Palmer was a clinician of the old school, not too receptive to the new ideas in medicine. He loved to teach and would forgo a consultation any time for the chance of another hour before his class, but it was lecturing, not clinical teaching, he rejoiced in.

The two men whose forte was clinical demonstration were George E. Frothingham, professor of ophthalmology, and Donald Maclean, professor of surgery. Young, able, dramatic, these two were the idols of the student body, though they were suspect to most of their colleagues because of their unorthodox religious beliefs.

Frothingham was perhaps the most brilliant man on the staff. He had carved his own niche by concentrating on diseases of the eye and ear when that field was almost entirely neglected by the regular profession, and the school officials found that his spectacular results in making the blind see and the deaf hear were good arguments to lay before the legislature when seeking an appropriation.

But not even Frothingham could always keep control of the class. Medical students then were usually a rough lot, "lusty, bearded adults" who talked, clapped, stamped, and jeered at will, making no outward sign of any respect they felt for the professor, who suffered their lack of manners with Job-like patience. The playfulness often took the form of seizing some boy in one of the front seats and passing him up from row to row of the amphitheater until the top row received him and set him on his feet again.

Such a prank disturbed Frothingham's clinic one day during Will Mayo's freshman year. One of the seniors asked to be excused from the next clinic to go into Detroit to hear a lecture by the noted agnostic, Bob Ingersoll. Before giving his permission Frothingham began a little lecture on the bad taste of calling a distinguished man like Ingersoll by the nickname Bob.

He got no further. A red-haired, red-whiskered medical missionary of forty years jumped to his feet, protesting with vigorous voice and gesture against such atheistic teaching.

His seat was in the second row, and in an instant he was on his way up from hand to hand. The boys at the top failed to stop him and he went head foremost through a window and into a lilac bush, where he added some bruises to his bad temper.

The sequel was a furor of publicity that rocked the university community. It smeared Maclean as well as Frothingham, put into their mouths words they had never uttered, and pictured the medical school as a veritable hotbed of atheism, a menace to the morals of youth. Whereupon the orthodox members of the faculty turned against their two brethren and stirred up a storm within the school that threatened to wreck it.

Some of the freshmen were greatly upset by the fuss and fury. They knew Frothingham had not said the things ascribed to him, nor Maclean either, and they did their best to establish the truth.

A small group of them, including Will Mayo, continued their discussions throughout the next year, extending them to include a consideration of the weaknesses of their future profession. It needed higher scholarship, better teaching, and more loyalty among its members, they thought, something to make doctors unite against common foes instead of fighting each other.

Toward achieving these ends the students finally decided to organize Nu Sigma Nu fraternity, which received its charter and adopted its constitution on March 2, 1882. Will Mayo had prepared most of the statement of aims and ideals to which the boys subscribed.

By fall the group had ten members, and they rented a house, lived together, and shared expenses throughout their senior year. They elected to honorary membership their two idols, Frothingham and Maclean, who took a lively interest in the enterprise.

Within a few years alumni of the Michigan fraternity were asking permission to organize branch chapters in the communities to which they had gone, and the practice spread until today Nu Sigma Nu is recognized as one of the great American professional fraternities. It numbers some forty chapters and ten thousand members, including some of the most able men of medicine in the world.

The clinics at Michigan were of the prevailing sort, a parade of patients at a distance. Though much was made in the school's catalogues of the new hospital wards, these were not as yet used for bedside teaching. They merely provided more cases for the demonstration clinics.

These clinics were held in the low-ceiled amphitheater of the hospital, which was reached by outside stairs leading up from the campus. The front seats were officially reserved for the senior class and the juniors enforced their unofficial right to those next highest, so the freshmen sat at the top, where the least of what happened below could be seen. But even at the freshman heights Will was thrilled.

"I can visualize my freshman class sitting on the back seats," he wrote, "too far away to see the technic of the operation, but inspired by the fact that operations were going on; by seeing the assistants as they performed their duties; by seeing the members of the senior class called down to be quizzed on diagnosis and permitted to take some minor part in the operations."

The experience was for him a stirring call to ambition, and

when he reached the right to a senior seat he did not need it, for he was among the chosen, an assistant to Dr. Maclean at the operating table.

Canadian born, Donald Maclean was a graduate of Queen's University, Kingston, Ontario, and of the medical department of the University of Edinburgh, Scotland. In the course of his training he had served as house surgeon and assistant for the great Scottish surgeon James Syme, and he had been called to the chair of surgery at Michigan from a similar post at his alma mater in Ontario. He quickly won the devotion and confidence of Michigan physicians and surgeons, many of whom would have the advice of no other consultant when they struck a perplexing case.

But the important question is where Maclean stood on Listerism when Will Mayo was his student, for surgery was then poised between two eras: before Lister and after Lister.

As Joseph Lister walked through his wards at the Glasgow Infirmary he was often discouraged. There in long rows lay his surgical patients. He had brought them through the operations successfully, but there they lay, tossing restlessly in high fever, their stumps or wounds honeycombed with cavities that dripped foul, yellow pus. There they lay, fighting for their lives against a seemingly inevitable and commonly fatal septic infection.

Under such circumstances every advance that invited the surgeon to attempt more operations, even anesthesia, was as much a curse as a boon to mankind. Sepsis must be eliminated. But how?

By prolonged observation and thought Lister had come to the conclusion that inflammation and suppuration were the result of putrefaction, which in turn was produced by something in the air. But what that something was he had no idea.

Then one day a chemist in Glasgow suggested that he read the published findings of Louis Pasteur. This young French chemist had demonstrated conclusively that fermentation and putrefaction were wrought by microorganisms, bacteria.

Lister seized upon this clue eagerly. Here was hope! If bacteria were the cause of infection and they could be excluded from wounds, healing would take place without fever, inflammation, or suppuration. Since the organisms might lodge on any solid, on hands, instruments, dressings, even on dust particles in the air, everything must be kept clean—not just aesthetically clean, but antiseptically clean. Even the air must be made sterile if possible.

On that principle Lister developed a new surgical method, in which he used carbolic acid as an antiseptic: in solutions for cleansing hands and instruments, in plasters and putties for sterile dressings, and in a steam spray for purifying the air.

There were as yet no tests to tell Lister whether his procedures achieved the sterile surroundings he desired, but empirically he knew they did, for his wards no longer stank of decaying flesh, were no longer hopeless hells of fever and inflammation. His patients made uneventful recoveries, their wounds healing without disturbance in the natural processes of repair.

He had shown that sepsis could be prevented, and how it could be done. He had cleared the road to surgical horizons unseen.

In 1864 Lister read Pasteur, in 1865 he first applied lint soaked in carbolic acid to an open wound, in 1867 he announced his method and its amazing results.

Awareness of his work dawned slowly on the medical world. Surgeons from Continental Europe came to his clinic, gasped at the operations he dared to perform, and marveled at how quickly his patients recovered. They went home to try antisepsis in their own clinics.

Volkmann of Halle, who was about to close his hospital because pyemia was taking an insupportably heavy toll in its wards, and Nussbaum of Munich, who was being driven to the same step by the ravages of erysipelas, applied Lister's methods as a last resort. The infections died out, the hospitals were saved, and the clinics of Volkmann and Nussbaum became important Continental schools of the new antiseptic surgery.

By 1875 appreciation was widespread enough in Germany to turn Lister's tour of that nation's medical centers into a triumphal march, and in 1879 an international medical congress in Paris literally went wild when he appeared before it.

Surely, one might think, with such international acclaim for Lister in 1879, American medical students would be learning Listerian methods and principles by 1883. Not at all. Listerism took hold slowly in the United States, and "first Listerian operations" were still dotting the American surgical scene throughout the eighties.

All the descriptions by participants in those operations show the same general conditions and attitudes. Interns and assistants, since trained nurses were not yet on hand, spent days of preparation beforehand, boiling the necessary gallons of water, scrubbing the operating table, soaking the sponges and instruments in antiseptic solutions, carbolizing the dressings, sutures, and ligatures.

Then comes the operation itself, an ovariotomy perhaps, since that, being the major operation of the day, will provide a real test of the method.

All the important medical men of the community have gathered to watch the great experiment. Everyone is nervous and flurried lest some detail of commission or omission nullify the elaborate preparations, but though the surgeon and first assistant may be wearing aprons of rubber or oiled silk or, in extreme affectation, linen dusters or black dissecting-room gowns, all the others are in ordinary street clothes.

The steam atomizers are started, some from wall brackets and others in the hands of assistants who aim them directly onto the field of operation. By the time the patient has been anesthetized and wheeled in, the room is dimly gray in a fine mist of antiseptic. The gallery moves in close to see through the haze, the incision is made, and the task of removing the tumor is begun.

When the operation is finished and the incision has been swathed in the prescribed eight layers of carbolized gauze topped with a layer of mackintosh and another of gauze, the hands of the surgeon and his assistants are numb from the acid and everyone is wet to the skin with the spray.

And the patient? With fear and fervor her progress is noted. No rise in temperature after so large an abdominal wound? What about the dressings? Normally they would be changed at least once a day, but Lister says to let them alone as long as there is no fever and no hemorrhage. Still, perhaps one had better look. So the surgeon nervously lifts the edges of the dressings, with the carbolic spray playing over the wound and gauze all the while. The flesh is dry and cool; no pus and no inflammation!

As the days go on without disaster confidence mounts, and on the tenth day, according to Lister's instructions, the dressings are removed and the stitches drawn out, again in the dripping presence of the spray. The incision is still dry and without pus; it has healed by primary intention, probably the first instance of such healing either surgeons or assistants have ever seen.

Every such experience made converts for the new deal in surgery, but they were long a minority. The body of the profession remained unconvinced. Some scoffed at the belief in anything so fantastic as microbes, and others, ready to believe but not understanding the ways of bacteria, argued that while Listerism might be needed in crowded cities and in old, "tainted" hospitals, it was superfluous in the pure air of the country or the bracing ozone of a healthful climate.

Missing the point that vigilance against contamination at every step was the end to be sought, an astonishing number of doctors thought that by an "indiscriminate squirting of carbolic acid" or by the mere application of carbolized dressings they were practicing Listerism.

It took time to develop the antiseptic conscience in men unaccustomed to so strict a discipline. It was not easy for

the older surgeons to break the habits of years, to remember
that once they had washed their hands in antiseptic they
could not move a chair, scratch their noses, or shake the
unwashed hands of a visiting colleague without having to
observe the cleansing rite all over again.

It took time too to educate men to realize the difference
between aesthetic and antiseptic cleanliness. They were not
quick to understand that though a marine sponge was rinsed
clean enough to satisfy a New England housewife, it might
still be filthy with microbes, and that even if a surgeon's hands
were free of surface dirt, deadly bacteria might still lie deep
in the pores of his skin or under his fingernails.

Because of such deficiencies in understanding, many men
of the eighties who tried what they thought was Listerism
did not obtain the results claimed for it, and so quite sincerely they scorned the practice of antisepsis as a fashion or,
worse still, a reprehensible form of self-advertisement.

The consequent battle waged with words was spirited, and
medical journals bristled with the pros and cons. In the
meantime only a relatively few leaders, chiefly the younger
ones, practiced the new surgery without reservation, a few
more toyed with it halfheartedly, and the majority continued
contentedly in the good old way.

The students at Michigan should have had an unusual
advantage in this matter, for Donald Maclean had worked
with Joseph Lister when the two were house surgeons for
Syme in Edinburgh. Their association had ended before Lister
read Pasteur, but having known Lister, Maclean might be
expected to give ear to his ideas with more sympathy than
most.

And apparently Maclean was early in his attempts to give
Listerism a trial, for Victor Vaughan, later dean of the Michigan school, recalled "the old days in the seventies, when, as
Maclean's assistant, [he] had spent hours drenched in the
poisonous sprays of carbolic acid." During Will Mayo's junior
year in surgery, Maclean was still, or again, "trying out the

merits of the carbolic acid spray." Unfortunately he was one in whom absorption of the acid produced a toxic condition, so that he had to discontinue its use, and when Will became the surgeon's assistant he was spared Vaughan's unpleasant experience with the saturating mist of the spray.

On the whole, it is safe to say that Will Mayo finished his course at Ann Arbor with only an elementary knowledge of the revolutionary theory that was to create his own great opportunity.

Both Will and his friend Frank Mall were "underdemonstrators" (laboratory assistants in the terminology of today) for Corydon L. Ford, the professor of anatomy, during their junior and senior years. Together they spent long extra hours in the dissecting room, which like all such rooms then was a dirty, noisy, foul-smelling place. Modern methods of embalming and of refrigerated storage for bodies were not known, and unless the weather was very cold, painstaking dissection was a nauseating job.

Nor did the habits of the students help matters; while they worked or watched, they smoked and chewed and spat, contributing much to the general unpleasantness.

Under those associations Will Mayo conceived a distaste for smoking that lasted throughout his life. Mall hated it too, and when he came to take charge of the dissecting rooms at the Johns Hopkins Medical School, he forbade smoking on the premises. In fact, he instituted a general house cleaning in manners and methods, developing the means of preserving and storing bodies that are in general use in medical schools today.

Only one incident survives to indicate Will's student experiences in the newer medical sciences.

A chair in physiology was established in 1880-81, and Dr. Henry Sewall, who became one of the country's great clinical physiologists, was named its incumbent. It was not possible to start laboratory work at once, so he relied upon lectures and demonstrations for the remainder of the year. When examination time arrived, he wondered how much physiology he might reasonably expect the students to have absorbed and decided to try an informal conference with a few of the best students to see how much they had learned.

William Mayo, Franklin Mall, and Walter Courtney were chosen. Sewall did not expect much of them, but he got even less. In disgust he told them, and Professor Vaughan too, that not one of those three would ever succeed in medicine, either in science or in practice.

When all three had achieved national prominence in their respective fields, Sewall's pronouncement became a favorite story.

Judged by the standards of today, the medical course at Michigan was not impressive. But except at Harvard, possibly one or two of the New York hospital schools, and the great European centers, it was the best available at the time.

In any event, on June 28, 1883, in the presence of his sister Phoebe, who came on from Rochester to represent the family at the ceremonies, "Will James Mayo" received his sheepskin and the right to call himself a doctor.

The preceding June the American Medical Association had held its annual convention in St. Paul, and Will Mayo, home from Ann Arbor for the summer, went with his father to attend the sessions. He was excited by the presence of the great men of the profession, men whose writings he studied in school or read in the journals.

Among them was Dr. John Light Atlee, the elder of the two Atlee brothers of Pennsylvania. Washington, the younger and greater of the brothers, had died, and in the course of the session the president of the section on women's diseases paid high tribute to his memory. When the venerable, white-haired older brother rose to acknowledge the tribute, he described his long and cherished companionship with his brother and the struggles, failures, and successes they had gone through together.

A little later Dr. Atlee was unanimously elected the association's president for the coming year, and in a few moving words he accepted the honor—but not only for himself: "I accept it also with gratitude as a tribute to the memory of a dear brother, who were he now living, would more deservedly occupy this position."

Those words have a familiar ring to anyone who heard William J. Mayo accept any of the honors that later came to him.

It cannot be stated as fact that the Atlee episode awakened or encouraged in young Will's mind dreams of what he and Charlie might be able to accomplish in their turn working together, but more than forty years later he described the incident vividly and accurately, bearing witness to the impression made upon him by the story of the Atlee brothers.

Certain it is that three years later, when Charlie was ready to enter medical school, the Mayos were thinking of him and Will as partners in practice. In a family council they decided that Charlie should go to the Chicago Medical College, "because there he would get a different viewpoint."

By this time the Chicago Medical College, nominally affiliated with Northwestern University but entirely independent in location and administration, had made its three-year course compulsory and was offering a fourth year of instruction to those who desired it, though the annual session was still only six months long. There were excellent men on its faculty, and it too was beginning to boast of laboratories and science courses. And the student in Chicago was not limited to one college staff and one hospital; he could visit the clinics of outstanding surgeons like Christian Fenger, Nicholas Senn, and Edmund Andrews.

So in the fall of 1885 Charles Mayo set off for Chicago, accompanied by his father, who went along to make a round of the clinics and see for himself what the city had to offer.

After completing his registration, Charlie stood waiting on the steps of the college building for a few minutes, not quite certain what to do next. Soon another lad emerged from the building who was also alone. Charlie introduced himself and learned that the other was Harry C. Whiting of Mount Pleasant, Iowa.

"We talked together for a few minutes," recalled Dr. Whiting, "then he asked me if I had secured a room. On my answer that I had just arrived and had made no effort to find one he asked me if I would not like to go in with him. We agreed not to discuss politics, since he was a Democrat and I was a Republican, nor religion, an agreement we kept for the two years we bunked together."

The room they found "was on the third floor, back, up a winding stair. It had a mantel bed, which was shut up in the day time and let down at night. On the mantel we arranged our medical books. We had a study table with a student light, three chairs, and a large closet in which we kept our trunks, clothes, and junk. We took our meals at Mrs. Henry's Boarding House, on the corner of Twenty-fourth and Cottage Grove avenues."

Whiting and Mayo soon made the acquaintance of another pair, Edward C. Morton of Wyoming Territory and James Morgan of Chicago, and the four remained inseparable friends throughout their college years. They even dressed alike, in heavy mouse-colored corduroy trousers because they were inexpensive. Charlie wore his dark hair pompadour, but it was generally hidden under an old shapeless cap. Most of his friends thought him indifferent to clothes.

They found him friendly and pleasant always, though inclined to be somewhat retiring, with little to say about himself. "He was companionable, but not aggressively so."

As a student Charlie was only average. "He was not conspicuous in any way, neither brilliant nor dumb—just one of us," according to one of his classmates. And the official record still extant in the files of the Northwestern University Medical School bears him out by listing neither failures nor honors for Charles Mayo.

On the numerical rating from one to ten then in use, he was graded 8.5 in descriptive and practical anatomy, 8.0 in surgical anatomy. He received the full 10.0 in dermatology— and in "punctuality"! His lowest grade was 7.0, which he got, strangely enough, in the principles and practice of surgery.

Charlie's school-day friends recalled almost as with one mind his uncanny ability to locate the operations he wanted to see and his absorbed interest in them. Night after night he would greet his roommate with the same story, "I saw Dr. Senn [or Dr. Andrews, or Dr. Fenger] do a fine operation today," and then he would proceed to describe every move the surgeon had made.

Surely he carried over something extra from those occasions to his classwork in surgery, but perhaps it was too much of the "practice" and too little of the "principles" to impress the professors.

Clinical instruction was given for two hours a day, either at Mercy Hospital, located within a block of the college and under the exclusive control of its faculty, or at the South Side Dispensary, maintained by the college in its own building chiefly to supply teaching material. In small groups of six or seven, the second- and third-year students alternated between hospital and dispensary for their clinical classwork, spending a week at a time in each.

At the hospital, clinics were sometimes held in the wards at the bedside, and then the students were allowed to examine the patients for themselves, and in their third year they were permitted to observe the progress of obstetrical cases under the care of the house physician. However inadequate, this was an advance.

Most of the surgeons whose methods Charles Mayo studied were converts to Listerism and insisted on antiseptic precautions, and in Chicago hospitals was appearing a nobly useful aid, the trained nurse, to facilitate the practice of Lister's routine in all its details. So it is likely that the younger Mayo brother graduated with a fair understanding of the new method and its advantages.

He concluded his formal training with the third year. One of the requirements for the degree was a certificate of age and character, which his father supplied with admirable succinctness: "To whom it may concern, This is to certify that Chas. H. Mayo is over 21 years of age and is of good moral character. W. W. Mayo."

When Dr. Mayo penned that brief note he did not suspect that it would someday be framed and cherished as part of the historical records of the Northwestern University Medical School.

The degree in medicine was conferred on Charles Mayo on March 27, 1888, and this time the father represented the family at the exercises.

9. *From Father to Sons*

A DOCTOR'S practice is a mortal thing. With a human being at its core, it may dissolve with an expelled breath. The product of a life-time's labor in medical practice will perish with its creator unless there is a successor to whom he may transfer, while he is still active and his practice intact, the mantle of custom and confidence he has woven.

For Dr. Mayo his two sons were such successors, and they were ready in time.

For them the opportunity was golden. They were heirs to one of the largest practices in the Upper Midwest, and allowing for the brief period necessary for the mantle to settle securely on their shoulders, they could begin at a point it had taken a lifetime to attain.

Continuity from father to sons was a fundamental factor in the rapid growth of the Mayo practice.

In their efforts to convince patients that the young Dr. Will was as able as the Old Doctor, the Mayos got a measure of help from the official seal of the state.

In 1883 the state legislature moved to exclude the unfit from practice in Minnesota by making the university faculty of medicine a state examining board with the power to certify acceptable applicants. Those who had a diploma from a good medical college were to receive certificates without further question, but others must pass an examination.

Although the law exempted from its provisions all who had been practicing within the state for five years or more, Dr. W. W. Mayo refused to take advantage of the exemption. Father and son together presented their diplomas, paid their one-dollar fees, and received their certificates on November 12, 1883.

The equality of father and son before the law was all very well, but it was a tussle to make the sick folks believe they were equal in healing skill.

A call would come in from the country and the Old Doctor would send his son, but the farmer would send him back, saying that by "Dr. Mayo" he meant W. W. Mayo. If the father thought he could do so without alienating his patient altogether, he would send the boy back to try again. In one instance he sent Dr. Will four times before the patient finally gave in, saying with a grin that if in Dr. Mayo's opinion this stripling was a doctor it was all right with him because Dr. Mayo's opinion was what he wanted.

When the young doctor was given the chance he proved himself worthy of confidence by his own merit.

The lawyer, Burt W. Eaton, called the Drs. Mayo to attend his mother when she was taken ill late in May 1884. Dr. Will arrived alone, explaining that his father had gone to Washington to attend a meeting of the American Medical Association. He pronounced Mrs. Eaton very ill indeed, outlined his proposed plan of treatment, and set to work on it, all without question or ado.

But Mr. Eaton was uneasy. Finally he said, "Look here, Will, you're a young man and a new hand at this game. My mother means everything to me, and I'd like to call in old Dr. Cross."

Will swallowed hard but he agreed, and Dr. Cross was summoned. He assured Mr. Eaton that the young doctor was entirely right in his diagnosis and was doing all anyone could do. Then he left and the case was Dr. Will's, the first serious one he had faced alone.

Throughout the day and evening he stayed with the patient, never leaving her bedside. About three o'clock the next morning he came out of the bedroom, white and weary but smiling. "She'll be all right now," he said. And she was. The Eatons did not ever again insist upon having the Old Doctor.

The story of a less successful case is best told in Dr. Will's own words: "An old Irishman, a friend of father's, had lumbago. In that day salicylic acid was supposed to be good for rheumatism and I gave him some. He came in ten days later and in a loud voice told father about it . . . said that he had been in desperate agony, that Will had given him this medicine, and now he was all right. He congratulated father on his wonderful son. I was feeling pretty good.

"About an hour afterward I went downstairs to the street, and there directly in front of the building was a traveling medicine wagon, for Wizard Oil, with a ballyhoo man and a Negro to pass out samples of the oil and to take up money. On the wagon, in the seat given to patients, was my old Irishman, telling loudly that he had been to all the doctors for his rheumatism, that none could help him, but that he had used Wizard Oil and now was cured."

Some who knew Dr. W. J. Mayo in later years found it hard to imagine him driving a horse on country rounds, but that is the way he began, facing as a matter of course the floods and washouts, heat and dust, snow and freezing cold of the turning seasons.

One blustery day in January 1885 he made a long drive to

answer a call in Mower County. It was getting dark when he approached his destination, and the snow had drifted across the road so high that he decided to leave his team and cut through the woods about a mile afoot. He had no sooner entered the timber than he became aware of two wolves watching him from very near by. With chills chasing up and down his back he took to his heels, flourishing his medicine bag at the beasts to scare them off, but they followed him to the very door of his patient's cottage.

Like nearly all their brethren, the Mayos were still "physicians and surgeons" and handled their share of the community's childbirths, indigestion, kidney trouble, and typhoid fever, measles, whooping cough, and the dread diphtheria. But it was surgery they wanted, and surgery they got in increasing proportion.

The bulk of their operating continued to be repair work after accidental injury, but the number of more radical procedures slowly increased. During the decade of the eighties Dr. W. W. Mayo piled up a record of thirty-six ovariotomies, with twenty-seven recoveries and nine deaths.

A mortality of twenty-five per cent would be disastrously high today, but it was not so when a tabulation of ovariotomies throughout the United States showed a mortality of 20.93 in 86 cases in hospital practice and 30.4 in 311 cases in private practice. In Minnesota Dr. Mayo's record was unique, unequaled as far as the reports show either in total number or in number of successes.

Twenty-seven successful ovariotomies. To reveal the full import of that fact imagination must bring the figures to life by reading into them the individual human experiences they so coldly conceal. Twenty-seven times something like the following must have happened.

A circle of friends and relatives fearfully watched a woman get weaker and weaker while her belly swelled steadily toward the point they knew meant death. Despairingly they turned to their doctor. Could he do nothing to help? He plunged a trocar into the mass and drew off a quart or two of fluid, bringing some relief, but only temporarily. Soon the tumor refilled and went on growing relentlessly. Perhaps the doctor tapped it a second, even a third, time before he admitted that he had done all he could.

But, he said, maybe Dr. Mayo over in Rochester could do something more. In some cases like this he had cut the abdomen open and removed the tumor at its roots. Of course this was a drastic measure and might mean the end at once.

The agonizing choice was made, and one day the family and friends watched the woman lie down upon her kitchen table to submit to chloroform and Dr. Mayo's knife. An hour or two later they watched her awake again and as the days passed saw her recover health and strength, her size restored to normal, her life so seemingly near its end prolonged for many years.

They had a story to tell, those who watched from close at hand or from next door, a dramatic tale that made a choice morsel for tongues set free over a piece of needlework or a cup of coffee. From mouth to mouth, home to home, neighborhood to neighborhood it passed.

And with it spread the name of Dr. Mayo of Rochester, the worker of the miracle. There were women still living in the 1940s who remembered having first heard his name when as girls they listened to just such a story told in their homes.

Only by similar reconstruction against the contemporary background can the effect of news stories like the following be adequately gauged:

[In November 1884:] Thos. Mahony of Rochester had his arm terribly mutilated in the gearing to a threshing machine. . . . His coat sleeve was caught and drew his arm into the gear, and took the skin from it from the wrist to the shoulder. It was a frightful looking spectacle, large patches of the skin being torn completely away, leaving the naked flesh and muscles exposed to sight.

Irwin Tolbert brought him into the city and the Doctors Mayo dressed the wound. It is doubtful if he ever recovers the full use of the arm.

[In December:] Young Mahony has so far recovered from his injury as to be able to come into the city last Saturday to have his arm dressed. He says his arm pains him but little now, and he is hopeful of having a good arm yet. He can move it and it has commenced healing. The Doctor has commenced to skin-graft it, as there was so much of the skin destroyed that it would hardly heal over without the assistance of skin-grafting.

[The following April:] Young Mahony of Rochester was in the city last Saturday. His arm that was so terribly lacerated in the gearing of a threshing machine last fall, has entirely healed, and he has the use of it as well as ever.

The repeated telling of such stories was widening the area of the Mayo practice and so was the movement of people. Immigration to the new land of promise in Dakota Territory was at high tide in the eighties and brought two new states into the Union in 1889. Little boys in the sod-house homes of northwestern Minnesota could while away the hours watching the lumbering prairie schooners, forty or fifty each day, roll slowly along the old Pembina trail into the newer West.

Into this stream flowing toward the Dakota settlements the southeastern counties of Minnesota continued to spill their share of restless men. A Rochester merchant returned from a tour of Dakota in 1885 to tell his associates on the board of trade it was no wonder the city's population had declined; not a Dakota town could you enter without finding men from Olmsted County.

The new communities were not isolated from the old, for the railroads were strong bridges. Over the tracks of the Chicago and Northwestern men could and did move easily between Rochester and Dakota. In season ten or a dozen newspaper items a week announced the visits of Dakota sons and daughters to relatives in Rochester.

The Dakota doctors, few, scattered, and untried, might do for minor complaints, had to do for acute illness, but when a chronic malady allowed time, former residents of Rochester journeyed back to the doctor who had always taken care of them and their parents. And they recommended him to their new neighbors.

A Mrs. Vail of Dakota, nearly blind from "wild hairs" in her eyes, traveled to Rochester for a series of operations by the Drs. Mayo which gradually restored her sight.

David Dyson of Dakota, son of Robert Dyson of Rochester, was ill with a disease of the spinal column which so crippled him that he could not stand erect and finally could not work or even walk. He was taken to the Drs. Mayo, who found and drained an abscess that was causing the trouble and then applied a plaster cast and a supporting iron rod to his back. He was soon straight again, three inches taller, able to walk and to return to his work.

Such dramatic successes brought many patients from Dakota to the Drs. Mayo.

There was no hospital in Rochester as yet and for out-of-town residents the Mayos usually took rooms in the old Norton Hotel on the banks of the Zumbro River, but it was a problem to provide suitable aftercare there, especially for a patient unaccompanied by friends or relatives.

There were a few women in town who would act as practical nurses, and one of the best of these was a Mrs. Carpenter who lived in a large square house in north Rochester, near the later site of the Samaritan Hospital. She had room enough to accommodate eight or nine patients and was willing to make her house into a nursing home, so the Mayos began taking more and more of their surgical cases there. They had no separate operating room but used a little portable table and operating outfit which they moved from room to room.

Often a number of their fellow doctors gathered to watch a

major operation. They were welcome, and to make it easier
for them to attend, the Mayos soon began to schedule their
more important operations for Sunday mornings at Mrs. Carpenter's. When a case of unusual interest was on the docket
they tried to let the men in the nearby towns know so they
could drive over if they wished. At such times Dr. Mayo
talked informally as he worked, answering questions from the
onlookers and explaining what he was doing and why.

In all this activity, insofar as the patients would permit,
young Dr. Will was sharing equally within a year after his
graduation from medical school—in all, that is, except ovariotomy.

The senior Dr. Mayo had great confidence in his son's surgical ability. On the way home from the first operation he saw
Dr. Will perform he bubbled with admiration. He talked of
nothing else to the young priest who had been present at the
bedside and who was riding back to Rochester in the Old Doctor's buggy.

"Yes sir," he told Father Lawler, "that boy will make a
great surgeon; he's going to make his mark in the world."

But his confidence was not quite enough for him to allow
the boy to remove an ovarian tumor; that was too hazardous
an operation for anyone but a man of experience and proven
skill.

Dr. Will did not at once challenge his father's opinion. Instead he set out to develop a specialty of his own. Diseases
of the eye were a field exploited in and around Rochester only
by itinerant "eye specialists," most of whom were quacks, and
there, Will decided, was his opportunity. He would concentrate on the surgery of the eye and add another string to the
Mayos' bow. But he must know more about the pathology
and anatomy of the eye before he ventured to operate.

Dr. Charlie once said of Will that he was "filled with the
genius of finding opportunities." On the outskirts of Rochester
was a slaughterhouse berated by the city officials as a menace
to the health of the community, and to that unlikely place Dr.

Will went for the knowledge he needed. He spent many hours practicing his dissections and operations on the eyes of slaughtered pigs and sheep.

Then, sure of his knowledge, he sought a chance to demonstrate his new skill, and again he "found" an opportunity. At the county poorhouse were three inmates blind with senile cataracts. Dr. Will volunteered to remove them and in two cases got perfect results, failing in the third only because beneath the cataract was an atrophied optic nerve.

One of the cured patients was an elderly woman who, in Dr. Will's words, "had sufficient strength to stump the county for me, exhibiting the cure," and soon the papers were telling of paying patients from whose eyes Dr. W. J. Mayo had removed cataracts.

There is no understanding the young Will Mayo without giving full account to the driving urge to excel that possessed him. Again and again in story or sentence its strength is manifest.

Just after he had graduated from medical school he was talking one night with Judge Start, an old friend of his father's. What did he plan to do? the judge asked. After a year or two in his father's office, what then? Would he be moving to St. Paul or Chicago?

The questions were casual, but the reply was not. It fairly took the judge's breath, it was so direct, so sure. "I expect to remain in Rochester and become the greatest surgeon in the world."

That was William James Mayo at twenty-two.

Two years later he experienced a moment of doubt. He went to Washington to attend, as a spectator, a meeting of the recently organized American Surgical Association. This was an exclusive body of the surgical elite of the nation, and as he sat in a rear seat listening to the papers and discussions Dr. Will felt, in his own words, "like a hungry, penniless boy in front of a bake-shop window."

In momentary despair he wondered, "Is it possible for a

small-town man to get into the company of these giants, and sit with the mighty?" Then his eye fell upon Dr. Jacob Rowland Weist sitting on the platform. Dr. Weist was a fellow of the association and its secretary, and he came, not from New York or Boston, but from Richmond, Indiana. There was Will's answer.

It was his determination to get to the top of the ladder that dictated the program of continuing education on which he embarked, with the support and encouragement of his father.

One of the Old Doctor's valuable contributions to his sons' career was his insistence that no matter how busy they might be they must give at least an hour a day to reading and study. Quick to see the value of this, Dr. Will formed a habit in these early years of practice that he never broke. To the end of his life he kept scrupulous account of his reading time, carefully setting down all unavoidable debits to be paid in full later, though he never bothered to record any credits he earned in advance.

But reading was not enough. He wanted further training in the more practical aspects and the newer developments of his profession. Toward achieving this he was aided by the circumstance that the first two postgraduate schools in the country had just been organized in New York.

Graduate work in medicine did not yet exist. One might earn an advanced degree in physiology, chemistry, or anatomy, but nowhere could one find systematic, organized training in clinical medicine or surgery leading to a degree beyond the M.D. That phase of medical education was to come many years later and was to originate with William and Charles Mayo and the University of Minnesota.

Postgraduate work, however, was not new. American medical schools being what they were, intelligent and ambitious graduates had long sought to repair the deficiencies in their training by study abroad. Berlin, Munich, Vienna, Paris, Edinburgh, Glasgow, London, and Liverpool provided the postgraduate schools for American doctors.

For those who could not afford such a trip the United States had offered little. There was good work to be seen in New York hospitals, but their faculties were not organized for postgraduate instruction. Their clinics and courses were intended for undergraduates.

In 1882, however, both the New York Polyclinic and the New York Postgraduate School opened their doors. Both were for practitioners only and both gave instruction only in clinical and laboratory subjects. Not one didactic lecture did they offer. They were frankly "undergraduate repair shops" aiming to teach the young doctor in the quickest manner possible the practical technique his alma mater had failed to impart.

For his first course Dr. Will chose the Postgraduate School, which he attended from late September to early November 1884. And from one experience he had there an interesting and significant sequence of events can be traced.

After learning his way about among the New York hospitals, he settled upon the surgical clinics of Dr. Henry B. Sands as his favorites. Sands was then the outstanding surgeon in New York, and his surgical service at Roosevelt Hospital was the largest and best managed in the United States. At that time he was especially interested in the malady known as perityphlitis, or perityphlitic abscess.

This was not at all a new disease. It had been known to the ancients, who called it colic or iliac passion, but it was known only as a group of symptoms: sudden severe pain in the right lower quadrant of the torso accompanied by fever, nausea, and constipation and followed, if death did not immediately occur, by the formation of an abscess that caused fatal general peritonitis if it ruptured into the peritoneal cavity.

A long series of studies had shown the trouble to result from inflammation, but exactly where in the body that inflammation originated was still a matter for dispute. A few thought it began with a foreign body or catarrhal discharge in the appendix but most of those who were acquainted with the disease thought the point of origin was the cecum and general region at the head of the colon.

While pathologists were arguing about the etiology of the ailment, a few daring surgeons had made some progress in treating it. First and foremost in America was Willard Parker, who in 1867 announced that he had opened the abdomen and drained the perityphlitic abscess with success in three out of four cases.

Henry Sands was Parker's student and learned from him how to diagnose perityphlitis and when and how to open the abscess. Since then Sands had performed this operation nearly a hundred times.

Sands' clinics were held in the afternoons beginning at two o'clock, and day after day Dr. Will was on hand at one o'clock to secure a front seat in the amphitheater, from which he watched the operations with absorbed interest until the very end, sometimes until six-thirty or seven in the evening, long after the other spectators had gone.

Late one night, as Dr. Sands was finishing the day's operations, an orderly brought him word that an emergency case had just arrived in the surgical ward. As he turned back toward the table Sands looked up into the amphitheater and saw its one remaining occupant. "I see you sitting here through every clinic. They tell me there is an interesting case out in the surgical ward. Perhaps you would like to go with me."

Dr. Will welcomed the chance.

In the ward they found the man very ill, vomiting and feverish. Dr. Sands motioned his young companion to feel the swelling in the right iliac region and said, "I believe we have here a perityphlitic abscess described by my old teacher, Willard Parker. We will give the patient a little chloroform and open the abscess here in the ward."

As he worked he explained the operation to his keen-eyed companion. Finally he asked Dr. Will whether he had ever seen such an abscess before.

Yes, he thought perhaps he had, said Dr. Will. He had just

been thinking of a case he had seen when he was his father's office boy. The patient had inflammation of the bowels and was thought to be dying. Father introduced an exploring needle into the iliac region, found pus, and leaving the needle in as a guide, incised an abscess and drew off about a quart of foul fluid.

Dr. Sands chuckled his approval of leaving the needle in as a guide to the collection of pus. It had taken him a long time to learn that trick, he said, and he had been humiliated more than once by not being able to find the abscess again when he was ready to open it.

This experience gave Dr. Will food for thought. His father had many cases of abdominal pain with fever and vomiting that he called inflammation of the bowels, and they often ended fatally. How many of them were actually this perityphlitis in which evacuation of an abscess might bring recovery?

Within a week or two of his return to Rochester a young Swede was brought in from the country with what looked to the young doctor very much like the perityphlitic abscess he had examined at Roosevelt Hospital with Dr. Sands. His father being away, the responsibility was Dr. Will's. With the grooved needle he probed for pus, he found it, cut down into the abscess, and drained its contents. And the young Swede quickly recovered.

Dr. Will had other cases that he considered perityphlitis but his father could not always accept the new diagnosis. When a young schoolteacher who lived near Rochester was taken suddenly ill, the Old Doctor said she had inflammation of the bowels but Dr. Will insisted the trouble was perityphlitic abscess, which an incision and drainage would relieve.

The girl's parents refused to permit an operation and she died. Then Dr. Will secured permission to do a postmortem and by it clearly demonstrated the accuracy of his own diagnosis.

In telling of this case later he said he had found the trouble to be appendicitis. But was his use of that term merely the retroactive application of later knowledge, or did he at the time actually locate the seat of the disease in the appendix?

The question is of interest because the episode occurred in August 1885, and not until the following June did Reginald Fitz read his famous paper on "Perforating Inflammation of the Vermiform Appendix" before the Association of American Physicians. It was that paper which made it convincingly clear to everyone that virtually all cases of perityphlitis actually originated in the appendix and ought therefore to be called appendicitis.

Fitz did a classic job of marshaling and presenting his evidence, and he stated his positive conviction that if the symptoms did not subside within twenty-four hours after their appearance the surgeon should remove the appendix.

But Fitz was a pathologist, and the surgeons did not immediately follow his advice. Not until 1889, when Dr. Charles McBurney, Sands' successor at Roosevelt Hospital, described the famous McBurney's point in the abdomen at which pressure would reveal a diseased appendix and came out firmly in favor of early removal did appendectomy begin its march to general use.

Dr. Will was no quicker than others to adopt the radical measures Fitz recommended. He read Fitz's paper soon after it appeared, but it merely made him more sure in diagnosis and less hesitant about opening the abscess when it had formed. Only gradually did he come to practice removal of the appendix, and then not until other therapeutic measures had failed to bring recovery.

By the spring of 1888 Dr. Will felt that his experience with appendicitis was worth reporting, and he prepared a paper on the subject which he read before the surgical section at the annual meeting of the Minnesota State Medical Society.

Conservative though its conclusions were, Dr. Will's paper made his listeners sit up in surprise at its thorough survey of the subject and the amount of personal experience it revealed.

Ordinarily one or two cases of an uncommon malady were enough to occasion a report to the state society, and on peri-typhlitis, as it was still generally called, only two such reports of three cases had been made previously. But this mere lad from Rochester had illustrated his points with nine case histories, and some of these he said were typical of several others of the same sort. He must have treated a score or more altogether!

The impression Dr. Will's paper made on the group may be guessed from the fact that they, the assembled surgeons of the state, promptly elected this young man, twenty-seven years old and only five years out of medical school, the chairman of their surgical section for the following year.

There, in one sequence which it has been possible to reconstruct in fairly complete detail, is an almost perfect miniature of the pattern of action and circumstance that made the Mayo brothers world-famous surgeons.

At the dawn of modern surgery they went forth to learn the latest developments from others. With sound judgment they adopted what was good, and with consummate skill they applied and refined it. Around them, in southern Minnesota and adjacent states, a virgin growth of illness waited to be brought under control. Because they were the first there to apply the new surgery they stood forth in a wide area as men who could heal where others failed. More and more sick folk sought them, and they gained more and more experience and skill. Then with unprecedented numbers to add to unusual results they made reports to their professional colleagues that startled these men into incredulous, then admiring, attention.

In part, that pattern had appeared in the Old Doctor's achievements in ovariotomy. Complete, it appeared again and again, on a larger and larger scale, at a faster and faster tempo —in stomach surgery, gallbladder surgery, thyroid surgery. And in the end it carried the name of Mayo to the farthest corner of the surgical world and made it known to more persons of the lay world than would recognize the name of any other medical man alive or dead.

The chairman of the state's surgeons could not admit that any operation performed by others was beyond him. In November 1888 Dr. Will was called to Kasson to examine a woman for what proved to be an ovarian tumor. Normally slight, she was now huge. To examine her Dr. Will had her lie down on the parlor sofa, and as she attempted to turn onto her side at his request, the weight of the tumor upset her balance and she fell onto the floor. Dr. Will had to call for help to get her up again.

When he heard his son's report, the Old Doctor set the operation for the following Sunday morning and sent word of it to the doctors roundabout. Then he received a note from Dr. A. J. Stone asking him to come up to St. Paul for consultation on a case there, and he left, planning to be back by Saturday night. But he did not come. Nor did he arrive on the first train Sunday morning.

By the hour set for the operation, some fifteen doctors had gathered at Mrs. Carpenter's, the patient was waiting, and with her several relatives who had left small children alone at home. Taking his courage in his hands, Dr. Will told the woman *he* would do the operation if she was willing. She was, and Dr. Will removed the tumor. It was enormous, completely filling the washtub they put it in, and the watching doctors were greatly impressed.

Although everything had gone well, Dr. Will spent the day wondering what his father would say. A little fearfully he went down to meet the evening train, which brought Dr. Mayo and with him Dr. Stone. Dr. Mayo had stayed over in St. Paul to assist at Dr. Stone's operation and had brought that gentleman back to watch his own, which he was planning to do the next morning. He was in high spirits, gloating a little, Will thought, over the fine gynecologic case he had to show his St. Paul friend.

Hesitantly Will told them he had done the operation that morning.

His father was speechless. And Dr. Stone sat down on the station steps, beat his hat against the platform's edge, and laughed till the tears came at the thought of the boy's stealing his father's big case.

Dr. Will always felt it was then that his father fully realized for the first time that his son had become a thoroughly competent surgeon in his own right.

Not the least of the young man's competence by this time was his wholehearted practice of antiseptic surgery. He had come home from medical school to find his father defiantly anti-Listerism in opinion and practice, and he heard little in the discussions at state medical society meetings to incline him otherwise. Only a few of the younger Minnesota surgeons who had seen the new system in use in Europe were advocating it.

Then Dr. Will, in 1885, went to New York for his second postgraduate course, this time at the Polyclinic, and there from Dr. Arpad Gerster he got his first real understanding of antisepsis and learned how to use it.

Gerster was of European birth and training, a Hungarian who had learned the new surgery in Volkmann's clinic at Halle when he stopped off there on the way to America in 1874. So thoroughly had the antiseptic discipline become a part of him that he would not operate among the crowded audiences and trooping assistants of the Polyclinic but took his small private classes to Mt. Sinai Hospital, where he could keep conditions under better control.

Gerster's teaching made a deep impression on Dr. Will. "It was a happy day for me when I came under his influence, and I shall always have for him reverence and respect."

His influence on young Mayo's mastery of the antiseptic method was exercised as much through his book, *The Rules of Aseptic and Antiseptic Surgery*, published in 1887, as through personal contact. Dr. Will said he practically learned the book by heart. It ran quickly through three large editions, was the most talked-of book of its time in medical circles, and may well have been the strongest single factor in spreading the practice of antisepsis.

In it Gerster stated simply and clearly the case for a discipline that might seem irksome until it had been mastered, and more important still, he described in concrete detail all the steps in the "handicraft of asepticism." *

He told the country doctor exactly what equipment he would need and how he should use it to turn a farmhouse kitchen or bedroom into an aseptic operating room—how many and what size tin dishpans or enamel basins he would need and how he could nest them for convenience in transportation, how to suspend the syringe full of antiseptic solution from the bedpost or the chandelier above the table, how to fold and arrange towels as a trough to carry the fluid from the wound into buckets placed on the floor below, and so on.

The writing of this eminently practical little book was begun and some of the photographs to illustrate it were taken during the month of October 1885, when Dr. Will was attending Gerster's clinics, and it always pleased him that he was to be seen among the bystanders in one of the pictures.

Surgical skill was not W. J. Mayo's only ability to show itself in these beginning years. When he came home from medical school his parents were in debt, in part for the microscope bought years before and for a horse already dead and perhaps in part for the costs of Will's own schooling. The young man soon put an end to the financial stringency.

He was as willing as his father to give his services without fee when it was necessary, but he was methodical in charges and collections and felt no qualms about insisting on payment

* The present precise differentiation of asepsis from antisepsis did not develop until after the coming of steam sterilization, rubber gloves, gowns, masks, and all the other appurtenances of modern aseptic surgery. In the eighties the two terms were commonly used as synonyms.

if the patient could afford it. Moreover, money did not slip so easily and unproductively through his fingers as it had through his father's, and of course as the double practice grew there was more and more money coming in.

Improvements in the offices followed each other in rapid succession. Rooms more easily accessible to patients were taken on the first floor of the Cook Block, and repainting, refurnishing, and recarpeting kept the community agog. Gas lighting and running water were put in, and heat was piped in from the new boilers of the Cook House next door.

Life at home was easier and more pleasant too. The Mayos entertained more often, and the Old Doctor began the frequent and extensive travels that filled much of his later years. From 1884 on he seems not to have missed a single convention of the American Medical Association, no matter where it was held. His wife began to get away too, to spend a winter in Florida or to visit relatives in Michigan.

Dr. Will allowed himself little time for recreation. He sometimes went on a camping trip to Lake Elysian, took a wintertime jaunt to the gay ice carnival in St. Paul, or spent a day with young friends "ruralizing" around the lake at Oronoco. And occasionally he joined Charlie and his friends when they chipped together and rented a gig and a boat to give their best girls an outing.

Dr. Will's best girl was the chubby, red-cheeked, dark-haired daughter of Eleazer Damon, pioneer resident of Rochester, the town's jeweler, and at intervals one of its aldermen. Quiet, even shy, good-natured, and content with home and its duties, Hattie Damon agreed happily to Will Mayo's proposal of marriage, and the wedding took place on the young doctor's return from New York in 1884. It was a major social event described at length and with flourish in the newspaper.

The young couple bought themselves an "elegant cherry bedroom set" and moved into the old Mayo house on Franklin Street.

Mingled joy and grief followed. In May 1885 Dr. Will's beloved sister Phoebe died from the splenic disorder that had made her an invalid for seven years, and it became a source of keen regret to him that he did not know then what he later learned about the spleen, for he could have saved her life by an operation. In March 1887 the young couple proudly announced the birth of a daughter, Carrie, but their joy in the coming of a son in August 1889 was cut short by the baby's death three months later.

The small cottage home did not satisfy the rising young doctor very long. He bought the property at the corner of College and Dakota streets, on the site of the later College Apartments, tore down the old brick house, and ordered the construction of a model house and barn.

When the building was finished the townsfolk were impressed with the elegance and spaciousness of the house, the three large fireplaces topped by handsome mantels, the covered driveway, the speaking tube from house to barn, the not yet common conveniences of gas light and city water. Dr. W. J. Mayo believed, as have enterprising business and professional men since the Renaissance, that investment in the appearances of success pays good returns.

By so much of accomplishment in professional and personal life was the elder of the Mayo brothers ahead of the younger when Charlie graduated from the Chicago Medical College and in his turn settled into practice at Rochester.

He fitted easily and naturally into the partnership, for he had been working in the office during summer vacations. It took a little time for the father and older brother to realize that Charlie need no longer play the role of assistant, but his surgical ability, quickly recognized by Dr. Will, soon put things right.

With the patients it was his turn to face the toe-in-the-door days that were all but over for Dr. Will, and in his case too the normal skepticism was aggravated by his youthful appearance. So for a while, as he confessed, he wore whiskers "like an old buffalo robe" to make himself look older.

Speaking of those early days, he told how the patients "would talk through a crack in the door, and I would put my foot in it so they couldn't close it, and would explain that father was busy or called away. Could I do anything for them? I would, when given the chance, give a thorough examination with all my instruments, and it would take me quite a while, whereas father could detect the trouble offhand, and consequently by the time I had finished they would remark that I had given them the best examination they had ever had."

Almost immediately Dr. Charlie took over the surgery of the eyes. He was so much better at it, according to Dr. Will, that for the good of all concerned it was turned over to him. And soon he too had a patient to stump the countryside for him.

A fighting Irishman living about three miles from Rochester engaged the Drs. Mayo to remove the cataract from one of his eyes, but he wanted it saved so he could show it to his friends. Accordingly, Dr. Charlie wrapped it up in a little piece of oiled silk for Mike's convenience in carrying it. But since Mike had not yet got his glasses, he lost the bit of tissue without knowing it and thought the oiled silk was it. He had several fights trying to make his friends believe that piece of silk was what Dr. Charlie had taken out of his eye, and was convinced of his error only in the police court.

Unfortunately Charlie had barely started his professional activities when they were halted by illness. He contracted whooping cough and could not get over it. When the racking cough had hung on for nearly six months, his parents decided that he needed a rest and a change of scene.

Judge Start was about to leave for Europe on a business trip, and it was arranged for Dr. Charlie to make the crossing with him. They set out in January 1889. Charlie went first to his father's birthplace, Salford, to visit his aged uncle and aunt, then over to Ireland for a short stay, and finally to the Continent for a tour of the hospitals there.

Lister was at work in London at the time, but for some reason Dr. Charlie missed seeing him. He did attend a lecture by Pasteur in Paris. "Of course he spoke in French and I did not understand it, but I saw this great man. He had had a mild stroke, and he came in with a little drag to his left leg. He was gray, and wore a tightly fitting skull cap. His face was covered with a short beard. The hall would seat 150, and there were about sixty students present. He sat at a desk while he lectured, and spoke from notes, and most of the time his head was bent forward and down, which greatly muffled his voice and seemed to make it difficult for those present to hear him."

In the Continental hospitals, especially those of Germany, Dr. Charlie made special note of the forms of antisepsis in use. The walls of the rooms were lined with large jars full of many different kinds of antiseptic solutions, each a different color. The operating tables, designed for the extremely wet operations then in vogue, were covered with rubber and flanked all around with drain pans to catch the boiled water, sometimes warm, sometimes cold, that was sloshed generously over everything in sight. The surgical staff all wore rubber boots.

Much emphasis was being placed on the careful scrubbing of the surgeon's hands and the cleaning of his nails, and a few men were already using gloves, white cotton ones that were boiled after each wearing. Asepsis in its present-day form was appearing.

Refreshed in mind and well again in body, Dr. Charlie returned home, to make good use of what he had seen abroad in the small hospital under construction in Rochester, as a delayed but direct result of the best known incident in the whole Mayo story.

10. *St. Mary's Hospital*

TUESDAY, August 21, 1883, was a very hot day in Rochester. Weary and restless in the stifling heat, the residents hopefully watched black storm clouds pile up in the west late in the afternoon.

About six o'clock Will and Charlie Mayo, their day's work done, hitched a fast little mare to the light buggy and started for the slaughterhouse to get a sheep's head upon which to practice eye operations that night. As they drove along the narrow road north of town they watched the rolling clouds and remarked on their peculiar formation.

When the young men reached the slaughterhouse they found the butchers starting for home. They were leaving early because of the impending storm, they said, and they advised Will and Charlie to make for their own home quickly in order to escape it.

Turning around to start back, the brothers saw the huge whirling cloud, funnel-shaped now, moving toward them, saw buildings sucked into its maw like wheat into a thresher and the pieces blown out in all directions like chaff.

In alarm they whipped the mare to a gallop across the path of the storm. And just in time, for they got barely a block past the Zumbro River bridge when it was torn from its moorings by the wind and smashed to bits. As they crossed the railroad tracks on Broadway a grain elevator toppled and cars careened crazily down the rails. The din was terrible as planks, shingles, bricks, tree limbs, everything, went flying helter-skelter in the gale.

As they passed the intersection of Broadway and Zumbro

Street the heavy cornice was ripped off the Cook House opposite and hurtled down upon the dashboard at their feet, then bounced off and broke the wheels and shafts of the buggy. The terrified horse, loosed from the carriage, bolted down Zumbro Street and into an alley, and when the brothers jumped out to follow they were literally blown along the way.

They took shelter in a blacksmith's shop just as its tin roof whirled away over their heads. They hugged the wall with the horse and watched until the wind subsided. Then they started for home, but turned back when they heard there were dead and injured in north Rochester.

As in a detective story, the time of the tornado can be fixed by a stopped clock; the whirl of wind had picked up a little desk clock in some home west of town and set it down a block away, unbroken but with its hands stopped at twenty-four minutes to seven.

Considerable damage had been done in many parts of town, but north Rochester, called Lower Town, was a shambles. Scarcely a house was left standing, and the slaughterhouse was in ruins.

The work of rescue began at once. With lanterns men searched out the dead and wounded and carried them into hotels or offices and some forty of them into the convent of the Sisters of St. Francis, where they were laid on the parlor floors until cots could be set up.

The doctors were quickly on the job, in the private homes to which they had been called, in their own offices, or in the hotels used as first-aid depots. Dr. W. W. Mayo took charge at the Buck Hotel on the edge of Lower Town, while Drs. Will and Charlie worked with those brought into the Mayo office. All night long the work went on, women helping too by preparing beds, bandages, medicine, and food.

Early the next morning Rommel's dance hall on Broadway near Center Street and the nearby lodge rooms of the German Library Association were turned into hospital quarters. Wires were strung and curtains hung to divide the floor space into rooms, beds and bedding were moved in and made up by the women who had volunteered as nurses, and then the wounded were brought in from the scattered quarters they had occupied during the night. By eleven o'clock thirty-four patients were established in the improvised hospital, and the doctors went to work on their gashes and fractures.

But before long there was friction. One of the doctors who had heard somewhere that an emetic should be given the first thing in case of accident ordered this treatment for all the injured. Dr. Mayo was outraged by the idea, and when the fellow stubbornly persisted the Old Doctor issued an ultimatum, "Either he gets out or I do." Clearly someone must be put in command, and the city council asked Dr. Mayo to take charge.

His first task was to do something about the nursing staff. The volunteers were willing enough, but they could not be depended on because they had homes and families to look after. Nurses must be found who could give their entire time to the job. Dr. Mayo thought of the teaching Sisters of St. Francis who were at home in the mother house for the summer vacation; some of them ought to be available.

When he suggested this solution to the mother superior of the convent, she agreed at once, and from then on until the hospital was closed, Sisters of St. Francis supervised the nursing.

Meanwhile the destitute were receiving attention elsewhere. A storeroom near Lower Town was made into a public mess hall, where generous housewives, grocers, and bakers provided food, and public halls downtown were turned into temporary sleeping quarters.

In response to the call sent out for relief funds, Minneapolis and St. Paul each subscribed $5000, Chicago $10,000, Winona and St. Cloud each $3000. Communities in Dakota to which Rochester had sent help when grasshoppers stripped their fields a few years before now gave benefit socials to raise funds to return the kindness. All told, the relief committee collected

$60,441.51. With this they furnished clothing for 253 families, rebuilt 119 houses, and gave to each family about seventy-eight dollars toward new furniture. Thus gradually through the fall and winter Rochester life returned to normal.

But the act of God had left an idea in the mind of the mother superior of the Sisters of St. Francis.

This order of nuns had established their convent and school in Rochester in 1877, when they were still a part of the congregation in Joliet, Illinois. A few weeks later the bishop of Chicago separated them from the Illinois mother house, and Mother Alfred with twenty-four sisters formed the new Congregation of Our Lady of Lourdes.

Though the life of postulants in pioneer sisterhoods was hard, the new congregation did not lack recruits and by 1883 it numbered nearly one hundred members and was conducting an academy and a day school in Rochester, an academy in Owatonna, and a score of other missions scattered through Minnesota, Ohio, Missouri, and Kentucky. And it was ready for new enterprises.

Shortly before the tornado the Right Reverend John Ireland, Bishop of St. Paul, in whose diocese Rochester then lay, suggested to Mother Alfred that the sisters might build a hospital in Rochester. The idea did not then appeal to her overmuch, because her sisters were trained for teaching, not nursing, but she thought better of it during the dreadful August days of 1883. Rochester needed a hospital, she decided, it would be a worthy enterprise for the sisterhood, and if it was a costly and difficult departure, so much the better perhaps; it would test their mettle.

One day soon after the temporary hospital was closed Mother Alfred paid a visit to Dr. W. W. Mayo. Did he not think it would be well to build a hospital in Rochester?

His reply was quick and positive: The city was too small to support a hospital, it would cost a great deal, and there was not much likelihood of its success.

But Mother Alfred had made up her mind. Quietly she

overruled the Old Doctor's objections and said that if he would promise to take charge of a hospital the sisters would finance it. When he insisted that it might cost as much as forty thousand dollars, she replied that they would spend that and more if necessary. Then, asking him to begin drawing up plans for the building, she went away.

It is not surprising that Dr. Mayo thought Mother Alfred a visionary to propose a hospital for Rochester. Hospitals ranked low in public favor then. Maintained almost solely for the indigent, they were usually grim and gloomy places in which care of the sick in nowise matched the personal attention of good home nursing. The records of even the best hospitals in the days before antisepsis fostered the general impression that one did not go to a hospital to get well but simply to die. Surgeons themselves in reporting their mortality rates sometimes asked allowances for "the disadvantages of a hospital atmosphere."

So hospitals were not sought as sanctuaries by patients who could pay for care; they were essentially charity asylums for the sick poor who had no place else to go and no one to look after them. They were classed with poorhouses, jails, and insane asylums.

In 1883 there were three hospitals in St. Paul, "one an achievement, one a hope, and one a promise," there were three of about the same degree of adequacy in Minneapolis, Duluth had one small one, and in Winona "an old house down in the lower part of the city, dismal, lonely, and equipped with an old corded bedstead was all that the city could show in the way of appliances to lighten the sufferings of the unfortunate."

That was the lot in Minnesota when Mother Alfred announced her plan. There was not a hospital worthy of the name, even by that day's standards, in the whole expanse of southern or western Minnesota—nor beyond in Dakota Territory, although two or three Sisters of St. Benedict were offering nursing care to the sick in a few hotel rooms in Bismarck.

As it turned out, this very fact provided a large tributary

area from which a Rochester hospital could draw its patients, but this possibility seems not to have occurred to Dr. Mayo.

For nearly four years the hospital remained just an idea, but it was not forgotten. By hard work and frugal living the Sisters of St. Francis were accumulating funds. Every cent the missions could save was sent to the mother house, and to send more they encouraged donations of food and clothing and took in extra work for pay, the sisters spending their scant leisure in giving music lessons or in crocheting and embroidering linens to be sold.

Carefully Mother Alfred counted the nickels and dimes. Not one more than necessary did she spend. The sisters wore rough, two-dollar shoes and habits of coarse cloth, and sat down always to plain, sometimes meager, fare. It is said that five pounds of round steak and a fifteen-cent soupbone were a day's supply of meat for a household of some thirty boarders and twenty sisters and postulants.

Thus, by constant labor and stint, was the building fund for St. Mary's Hospital raised.

At last there was money enough to proceed, and Dr. Mayo chose the site, nine acres just west of the city limits on Zumbro Street. On July 26, 1887, the Congregation of Our Lady of Lourdes voted to build the hospital, and four months later the property was bought for twenty-two hundred dollars in cash.

Now it was time for Dr. Mayo to present his plans for the building. He and Dr. Will made a special tour of eastern hospitals to study such matters as floor plans, lighting arrangements, and administrative organization, and from this experience they made up their instructions for the architect. And when the plans came from him they sent them back "once and twice and thrice" until they got exactly what they wanted.

Public interest rose with the building, and it became quite the thing to do of a summer evening to walk or drive out and see how the hospital was coming along. The Rochester papers also made periodic reports, lengthening as the structure approached completion into detailed descriptions of the "imposing edifice," three stories high, built of brick with window ledges of roughhewn stone and four balconies on the west and north sides.

The reporter made much of the wards and private rooms that could accommodate forty-five patients, the operating room with its bay window to catch the north light and its inclined floor to facilitate adequate scrubbing, the chapel for the sisters' devotions, and the "remarkable ventilating system" designed to prevent the usual unpleasant hospital odor.

The papers described too the pretty gaslight fixtures throughout the building, the water faucets in the halls for use in case of fire, the artistic staining of all the wainscoting, and the beautiful floors of curly maple cushioned with two layers of "deadening felt."

But a note, a little tart in tone, inserted in the manuscript Annals of St. Mary's Hospital warns the reader against these newspaper descriptions. The editor, it says, wishing "to give as favorable an account as possible of the new building . . . described as already existing some features that at the time were only hoped for."

During the last days of September 1889 the sisters began making the building ready for occupants. Three of them went over every morning, carrying their lunch, and spent the day clearing out rubbish, sweeping, dusting, and scrubbing.

They planned to begin receiving patients on October 1, but the Mayos had an operation to perform the day before and the operating room was ready, so with a fine disregard for pomp and palaver they simply began. The operation was for the removal of a cancer of the eye; Dr. Charles Mayo performed it, Dr. W. J. Mayo assisted, and Dr. W. W. Mayo gave the anesthetic.

Within a week eight patients were admitted, four sisters had been assigned to duty in the hospital, and Edith Graham, a Rochester girl graduated from the school of nursing at the

Women's Hospital in Chicago and the first trained nurse in town, was put in temporary charge of the nursing staff.

According to a policy repeatedly announced, the hospital was open to all sick persons regardless of their color, sex, financial status, or professed religion. It was to be neither solely a charity asylum nor exclusively a nursing home for the wealthy. It was sometimes referred to, even by the sisters, as a "noble charity" or a "free hospital," but in practice persons of all social classes were to be received and given care of the same quality.

This accommodation of paying and charity cases in the same institution was an innovation in hospital management. John Shaw Billings had suggested it in his plans for the Johns Hopkins Hospital, but for many years the Baltimore doctors, even those on the hospital staff, took care of their paying patients at home or in little private hospitals.

Nor was St. Mary's intended to be a hospital for Catholics only. When this question was raised, Mother Alfred made the sisters' position quite clear: "The cause of suffering humanity knows no religion and no sex; the charity of the Sisters of St. Francis is as broad as their religion."

And finally, there was no intention of reserving the facilities of the hospital for the patients of the Mayos. True, it had been understood from the beginning that Dr. W. W. Mayo was to be the physician in charge and he and his sons had planned the building and supervised its construction, but neither they nor Mother Alfred had any thought of excluding other doctors from St. Mary's Hospital. In all public announcements it was made clear that a patient could choose any doctor he wished and that the hospital doors were "open to all physicians who wish to put their patients in the institution."

But when Dr. Mayo tried to organize a staff he met with evasions and refusals. Although the doctors he approached were personally friendly to him and collectively welcomed the hospital, individually they refused to join in a venture that seemed already doomed.

Doomed because religious fanaticism was breeding antagonism to it. Increasing immigration was causing a resurgence of nativism in the United States, especially in the Middle West. The American Protective Association, successor to the Know-Nothings and forerunner of the Ku Klux Klan, had been organized at Clinton, Iowa, in 1887 and had spread into the states immediately to the north and east. Seeing the bogey man of papal imperialism behind the door of every Catholic home and institution, the A.P.A. used every means, foul or fair, to fan Protestant and nationalist bigotry to a flame.

The A.P.A. was strong in Minnesota, and the Mayos ascribed much of the early opposition to St. Mary's Hospital to its influence. Ardent Protestants would have none of an institution that was managed by black-robed nuns and in which there was a chapel set aside for the exercises of popery.

Alarmed by this threat to the success of the hospital, the Old Doctor asked his friend John Willis Baer, a prominent member of the Presbyterian church but a man above fanaticism, to become the nominal superintendent of the hospital, and for some weeks Mr. Baer made frequent and ostentatious visits of inspection to the hospital—ostentatious until he got inside, where he became very unobtrusive indeed.

But Mr. Baer's activity was not enough to persuade the Rochester doctors to accept staff positions, and it aggravated the antagonism of some of the Catholics, who thought they too had a grievance in the sisters' choice of a non-Catholic doctor to manage their hospital enterprise.

There was one Catholic practicing medicine in Rochester, a member of one of the town's most prominent Catholic families. But he was young, about the age of Dr. Will, and he made only occasional attempts at surgery. He was hardly qualified to head a hospital, and he himself felt no pique at being passed over. But his family and friends thought he should at least have been consulted in the making of plans for St. Mary's Hospital.

So the Mayos now had on their hands the whole responsibility for the success of the hospital, and this without the support of a united community. To make matters still worse, they did not have the full support of the Sisters of St. Francis either.

For the most part the sisters backed Mother Alfred's decisions loyally, but the hard work and meager living exacted by the hospital venture frayed some tempers, and a few of the sisters considered this departure from their teaching mission a sign of advancing age and lessening wisdom in their mother superior. They complained bitterly to Archbishop Ireland, as he now was, and finally, although he had encouraged the undertaking, he arbitrarily retired Mother Alfred as mother superior and appointed Sister Matilda in her place.

Uncomplaining, Mother Alfred went to take personal charge of St. Mary's Hospital, but she knew that she could not hope to guide the destinies of this creature of hers for long, and before she resigned control of the congregation she arranged for the transfer to the hospital of a young sister whose remarkable abilities were already manifest to her discerning eye. Julia Dempsey of Rochester, who had taken the habit as Sister Joseph in 1878, was recalled from her teaching at the mission in Ashland, Kentucky, to take up nursing duties at St. Mary's Hospital on November 19, 1889.

Mother Alfred remained in charge until August 1890, when she was replaced by Sister Hyacinth, who in turn gave way to Sister Joseph on September 9, 1892. And a lucky day that was for St. Mary's Hospital.

Dr. W. W. Mayo was now seventy years old. He was still alert and full of energy, and it was he in large measure who still commanded the confidence of patients. But at seventy the slope ahead, however gentle and long, is necessarily downward; the responsibility for success in the new enterprise must rest upon the shoulders of the two younger Mayos. The father became consulting physician and surgeon, and they the attending staff.

Dr. Will and Dr. Charlie were both entirely without experience in hospital management and practice; neither of them had served an internship. "We were a green crew and we knew it," declared Dr. Will in reminiscing of those days.

The little band of sisters were as untried as the doctors, and they were not at all prepared in either disposition or training for hospital service. They were used to nothing more unnerving than the pranks of children in the classroom, and for some of them the first operation they witnessed was a shock that remained a vivid memory for life.

In Sister Joseph's first major contact with the necessities of nursing, she was asked to assist at the examination of a male patient whose entire body had to be uncovered for observation. While one of the doctors and Miss Graham worked with him, the young sister stood off in the corner, her back turned, quivering with outrage and shame.

As she left the room when the task was done she protested vehemently to Miss Graham that she could never do such work, that she would ask Mother Matilda to send her back to teaching at once. But she stayed on, and quickly learned that the needs of human suffering transcend the dictates of modesty. In her subsequent management of St. Mary's she was always on guard against prudery among the sisters wherever it might lead to neglect in nursing.

To inexperience was added the further handicap of inadequate equipment because the hospital necessarily opened with the most meager furnishings.

The Mayos undertook to equip the operating room, and Dr. Charlie himself fashioned some of the instruments and built an operating table like those he had seen in European hospitals. He padded the top and covered it with oilcloth, then slanted three boards downward on the sides to carry the fluids into tin drain pans held in position by stirrups at the corners. With large "percolators" to hold the antiseptic solutions, plenty of tin basins in which to rinse instruments and sponges, and an array of syringes for squirting boiled water all around, the room was ready for antiseptic surgery as it was then practiced.

The responsibility for furnishing the wards and private rooms was the sisters', and they were hard put to it to find the bare necessities. They had about a dozen iron cots, three or four dozen unbleached muslin sheets and pillow cases, and a few rough gowns. Outer bedclothing was scarce, so that not the least pressing task in preparing for a patient's coming was to find covering for his bed. The sisters had been given a few heavy quilts of garish pattern, but for blankets they had to wait until they earned the money to buy them.

The mattresses did not fit the cots and slipped around so freely on the crude springs that the nurses had to be alert to prevent them from sliding to the floor, carrying the patient and bedclothing with them.

The eight persons admitted in the first week exhausted the number of beds set aside for patients, and the sisters had to give up their own to make room for more. After that at bedtime they dragged out some extra mattresses and made up their sleeping accommodations on the floor.

There was virtually no furniture except beds, not a commode or a dresser in the hospital, except one heavy black walnut piece sent over from the convent. The rough wooden stands that held the enamelware washbowls were fitted with oilcloth covers whose edges had been pinked by Mother Alfred herself. Odds and ends of dishes and linens were made to do for the trays at mealtime, and the knives and forks and spoons were heavy iron pieces that had to be scoured after each meal to keep them even passably presentable.

Since there was as yet no gas to fuel the pretty fixtures, the sisters carried lanterns to light their way through the hospital at night and hung one on a tree outside to guide the doctors or any others coming to the hospital after dark.

An elevator shaft had been constructed through the center of the building, but there was no elevator in it and no guards around it, so until a wooden railing could be built to enclose the opening on each floor, sisters came from the convent at night to sit on guard at the gaping holes. There was a dumb-waiter from the kitchen to the upper floors, but half the time it would not work and the sisters had to carry the trays of food up and down on foot.

Water was piped from the city main into a large reservoir in the basement, from which it was pumped by hand when needed. All the water used for cooking, cleaning, baths, and toilets had to be carried upstairs from this basement supply.

The sisters did not always have to carry out the sewage. A surface sewer in the yard behind the hospital took care of that, except when it backed up into the basement, as it did all too frequently. Then the odor summoned the sisters by day or night to come and clean up the mess, and for the next few days, until the cesspool could be put in order again, the long-suffering nuns carried out all the slops. Not until 1898 was the hospital connected with the city sewer system, and then at the sisters' expense.

The location of the hospital was an added inconvenience. Zumbro Street at that distance from Broadway was only a country road, ungraded, unpaved, and without bordering side-walks. Visitors and patients with no conveyance of their own often had to trudge the mile from town on the footpath along-side the road, for Rochester's only hack service was a large yellow wagon that shuttled between the railroad station and the Cook House. Sometimes patients were driven out by the Drs. Mayo or in their absence by Jay Neville, who had be-come the general handy man around the doctors' offices.

The sisters walked into town each day to do their marketing, usually after supper, and they carried their own parcels home, for Rochester had no free delivery service yet. It had no tele-phone system either, and if it was suddenly necessary to call the doctors, as on one well-remembered occasion when a pa-tient got hysterical beyond the nurses' ability to control him, one of the sisters had to leave her work and carry the message on foot to the Mayo office or home.

Against such odds of hardship, physical and mental, the faithful sisters worked with unflagging energy. Their day ordinarily began at three or four o'clock in the morning and continued until eleven or twelve at night, and every third or fourth morning they rose at two o'clock to get the laundry work out of the way before the regular routine of the day began. The operating-room linen had to be taken care of every day of course, so it was washed and ironed in the evening between supper and bedtime.

After the first few weeks the sisters took over all the nursing as well as the housekeeping tasks. The Mayos had employed Edith Graham to assist them in their office practice and had merely loaned her services to the hospital to get the work started, so she taught the sisters the rudiments of their new work in informal little classes and then gradually shifted the care of the patients into their hands.

Her own work as far as the hospital was concerned came to be the giving of anesthetics. The Drs. Mayo saw no reason why an intelligent nurse could not be an able anesthetist, and Dr. W. W. Mayo undertook to teach Miss Graham how to administer chloroform. She learned the trick all right, but she was still so young that nervous patients did not trust her, so to calm their fears the Old Doctor continued to stand by her side while she gave the anesthetic.

On the mornings when surgery was scheduled Miss Graham would go to St. Mary's early, see that everything was properly ready in the operating room, and then act as anesthetist and remain with the new patients throughout the day. From then on the sisters were responsible for them. At first they were nervous and a little fearful and would ask Miss Graham please to look in the next morning just to make sure that everything was all right before the Drs. Mayo made their call. But they soon got over that.

When a critical case needed special care at night the sisters took turns at staying up to give it, and since there were not enough of them for one to be spared in the daytime, a period of two days and the intervening night was not an unusual shift on duty. For the first three years there was no male orderly on St. Mary's staff, and the Mayo brothers added to their heavy practice the responsibility of nursing the male patients who needed special attention. They took turns on night duty, depending on the alarm clock to arouse them from the sleep they dared not entirely forgo.

Under such conditions the Rochester editor justifiably thought it worthy of awe that in a succession of four hundred admissions to St. Mary's Hospital there were but two deaths. The dauntless sisters deserve a goodly share of the credit; they helped to make a success of what might for all the surgeons' skill have been a failure—by unceasing toil, by determination to make good, by willingness to offer whatever sacrifice the task demanded.

And also by the inspiration of their faith, for to their labors they added prayer. Often while they worked, lighted candles in their chapel kept vigil for them. When a critical operation was to be done they sent word to the convent for prayers, and many a rosary was said to bless the surgeon's work while he was operating.

The Drs. Mayo did not share the sisters' faith, but they did not scorn it. One time when Dr. Will was leaving a seemingly hopeless case, he said to Sister Joseph, "I know she can't live, but you burn the candles and I'll pay for them." And the patient lived.

The Mayos could have kept St. Mary's filled twice over from their practice had not most of their patients shied away from hospitalization, preferring to be ill at home. Miss Graham remembered that "We almost had to lock some of the first patients in their rooms; they were so sure they were going to die if they came to a hospital."

But by cajolery, insistence, and repeated explanation of the advantages, the doctors persuaded first a few, then more and more, to enter the hospital. By the close of 1889 sixty-two persons had been served by St. Mary's, in 1890 there were three hundred more, and by the close of 1893 the grand total had passed a thousand.

To the great satisfaction of the Drs. Mayo the institution was paying its own way. When they saw that the entire responsibility was to be theirs, they determined that the hospital must be self-supporting. There was good reason to believe that the sisterhood would not be willing to make up a deficit should there be one, and the Mayos did not wish to rely on public contributions. They even asked the sisters not to set out the usual little mite boxes for gifts to the poor. They wanted the hospital to earn the money for its own charity, as they did, and to this end they adopted the policy of telling their patients to pay the sisters' bill first and theirs for professional services second.

The hospital rates were eminently reasonable: one dollar a day or six dollars a week for ward beds and from eight to ten dollars a week for private rooms. Receipts for the first eleven months were about eleven hundred dollars, and by thrifty corner-cutting on expenses this sum was made to yield a surplus, which grew larger year by year and financed all improvements.

One of the first uses to which extra money was put was to make the rooms pleasant. Good beds and bedclothing were bought, then rocking chairs, dressers, pictures, and mirrors. On September 21, 1891, the first half-dozen silver knives and forks were bought, and the event was carefully recorded in the hospital annals, along with the fact that they were wrapped up between meals for better care.

The Mayos helped too. In 1891 they donated to the hospital a complete set of glazed enamelware operating-room equipment imported from Berlin. That same year the sisters secured permission from the city fathers to set up telephone poles along Zumbro Street from the Mayo offices to the hospital, and Dr. Charlie installed the telephone with the aid of a mechanically minded neighbor boy. He and the same boy also installed the doctors' Christmas gift to the hospital, an electric annunciator by which the patients could summon the nurses when they were needed.

The amateur electricians got some of the wires crossed, and at times "the bells would start ringing and would not stop; so the sisters got to carrying shears around with them. If a bell kept on ringing, swsshsh!! would go the wires, and the next morning Dr. Charlie would have to resurrect the whole system again."

In that year too the shaft was finally fitted with an elevator. The kindhearted sisters fed a good many tramps in their kitchen, and among these one day was a traveled hobo who described to them a hydraulic elevator he had seen in Paris. Dr. Charlie decided to copy it for the hospital. With the aid of a plumber friend he excavated the necessary depth at the bottom of the shaft and screwed into the hole length after length of pipe, so as to form a sort of syringe. When the water was turned into this contrivance it pushed the elevator upward. But thrifty Dr. Charlie could not bear to see the water wasted after each trip, so he ran a pipe along one corner of the shaft into a tank on the roof. Then as the elevator descended it pumped the water up into the tank, from which it was piped into the toilets.

Just one thing was wrong with this elevator; it could be operated only from within the car, and it was sure to be standing at some other level when it was wanted. Once when Dr. Will was lame for a few weeks and had to use the elevator to get around in the hospital, one of the sisters kept watch for his coming every morning so she could "go after the elevator for him."

As the number of patients mounted, more help was a necessity and the number of nursing sisters was increased to eleven, but this was still too few for the work to be done and in desperation Sister Hyacinth tried the distrusted practice of hiring lay help. She drove into Rochester and searched out two likely girls to work as maids at a wage of six dollars a month.

The success of the hospital and its ability to support itself quieted the opposition within the sisterhood, and antagonism in the community also died away. Late in 1889 Rochester and the Sisters of St. Francis came under the jurisdiction of the newly formed diocese of Winona, of which the Right Reverend Joseph B. Cotter was named the first bishop. A man of wisdom and great tact, he did much to still the ruffled waters and secure the support of the Catholic community.

The noisy Protestant minority subsided too, and for the moment all was serene. Friends of the hospital sponsored a public ball and cleared some seventy dollars for its coffers, the Olmsted County commissioners began making a small annual appropriation to the hospital to pay for the care of the county's wards, and the three Masonic lodges in Rochester chipped together to pay one hundred and fifty dollars a year to maintain a free bed at St. Mary's for the use of their members—all pleasant signs that Rochester citizens were forgetting their distrust and suspicion.

Others less pleasant appeared. The townspeople began to show a tendency to use St. Mary's as a pesthouse upon which to dump the heavy and dangerous care of infectious diseases. And gradually some of the Rochester doctors began to use the hospital facilities for their patients. Unfortunately they still seemed to regard the hospital as a last resort and so failed to recommend hospitalization until the patient was at death's door. They probably did not aim to transfer the death from their own records to that of the hospital, but in effect that was what they were doing.

The mortality rate of St. Mary's Hospital began to rise, and the sisters, in alarm, decided upon a bold step. They ruled that no patient should be admitted to the hospital until he had been examined by one of the Drs. Mayo.

Though the purpose of the ruling was merely to make sure that the privileges of the hospital were not abused, the effect of it was to close St. Mary's to all but the Mayos and those doctors who were willing to call them in consultation or refer cases to them.

One who was not so willing was Dr. W. A. Allen, Rochester's most successful homeopathic physician. In the fall of 1892 he and his young partner, Dr. Charles T. Granger, announced that they were about to open a second hospital in Rochester. They rented a large house on the east side of town, remodeled it to suit hospital needs, and engaged a matron and a trained nurse from St. Paul to manage it. In November the Riverside Hospital began to receive patients.

This event had no noticeable effect on the patronage of St. Mary's, which by now had outgrown its original capacity and was showing symptoms of dangerous overcrowding. After much discussion and with the encouragement of Bishop Cotter, the Sisters of St. Francis ventured to begin building an addition.

And then the American Protective Association came to life again. A new wave of nativist sentiment swept through the country, reflecting faithfully the peak that immigration had reached in 1892. Feeling spread wide enough and rose high enough to put a number of A.P.A. candidates into office in the election of 1892 on a platform almost wholly aimed against Catholic institutions or policies.

As a result of all the agitation, local Protestants renewed their vociferous opposition to St. Mary's Hospital and pointed to the rival Riverside as an institution that Protestants and patriots could enter without doing outrage to their convictions.

Drs. Allen and Granger saw their chance; they made a bid for more business by announcing that "contrary to what many suppose, the [Riverside] hospital is not a homeopathic institution, for any regular physician can have the benefit of any of the advantages afforded there, and can take their patients there for operations or care."

At this juncture two important members of the Presbyterian church fell ill, and they were taken to the Riverside Hospital, and the Drs. Mayo were called to attend them.

It was a weighty decision the Mayos had to make when that call came in. To refuse it would more or less formally cement their alliance with the Catholic St. Mary's; to accept it would doubtless lead to the division of their practice between the two hospitals, for if they showed a willingness to serve patients at either institution, many would probably choose the non-Catholic hospital.

And after all, why should the Drs. Mayo not so divide their practice? It was customary for physicians in eastern cities to hold appointments and attend patients at several hospitals.

But the Mayos were wise enough to see the advantages of centralizing their practice in one hospital under one staff—especially a hospital and staff they controlled. The Riverside, small in capacity and in staff and so recently improvised from a dwelling, could not possibly offer the facilities or the quality of nursing care they had developed to their own taste at St. Mary's.

Also, the Mayos felt a strong moral obligation to the Sisters of St. Francis, who had just lately decided to put all their eggs in the Mayo basket and were even now adding to their investment. To divert a share, perhaps in time the larger share, of the Mayo practice to another hospital seemed a poor return for loyalty and confidence.

So the father and sons explicity refused to attend patients or to operate in the Riverside Hospital.

The decision brought them censure aplenty. One enraged pastor abused them publicly from his pulpit, calling them servants of the Catholics and accusing them of forgetting their sworn duty to the sick. At the instigation of another Protestant minister, some thirty women organized a Riverside Hospital Aid Society and met to sew and quilt, gave benefit socials, and made plans to endow a bed for the poor. Given generous publicity in the press, these activities made a great stir.

Through it all, the Mayos were conscious of eyes askance and ears cocked to catch any sign of their reaction. Wisely, they went quietly on their way, ignoring alike the attacks made on them and the noisy support given to their rivals.

For more than two years the Riverside Hospital prospered, and then suddenly an astonishing announcement appeared in the Rochester paper. Dr. Allen's practice had become too big for him to handle, it said, and so he had decided to give it up and move to St. Paul. The Riverside Hospital was therefore to be closed.

Whatever the true cause for Dr. Allen's departure, the closing of the Riverside marked the end of opposition to St. Mary's Hospital. For it the road ahead now lay smooth and straight, mounting with scarcely a level stretch or a detour to the heights of world-wide service and fame.

Struggling together to succeed despite inexperience, hardship, and hostility, the young doctors and the Sisters of St. Francis had learned to depend upon each other. Forced to it by circumstances, the Mayos had shown that alone they could furnish all the patients the hospital could care for, and the Sisters of St. Francis in turn had demonstrated their ability to give all the doctors could ask in the way of nursing care. The hospital had no need of other doctors; the doctors had no need of another hospital. Each made the decision to rely solely upon the other.

The result, pregnant with consequences, was to give the Mayo brothers a monopoly of the *only* hospital facilities in existence throughout a wide area and the *best* available in a still wider one.

11. *Young Doctors from the West*

THE star of surgery was now rising rapidly. Before Lister a hospital of two or three hundred beds might record four hundred operations a year, with twenty-five per cent of them amputations. After Lister a hospital of equal size might reasonably expect four or five thousand operations a year, with less than one per cent amputations.

The most striking general advance lay in lifting the taboo from the internal cavities of the body. With the risk of infection wiped away, the surgeon learned that an incision into the abdomen, the chest, or the skull need be no more dangerous than the amputation of a little finger.

The doctor faced with an abdomen ripped open by accident no longer hastily pushed the contents back into the cavity and sewed the wound shut, then waited with bated breath to see what nature would do with the mess. Now he could search for the bullet with impunity and remove it if possible, stitch up ruptured intestines, tie bleeding vessels, and in general start the repair of the damage.

With success in such emergency cases came the prospect of a surgery of expediency, of operations that would not be just a last desperate throw of the dice with death but a means of restoring health deliberately chosen in the early, curable stages of disease.

But there was much to be learned first. With the forbidden cavities of the body opened before him the surgeon looked upon an unfamiliar mass of tissues, vessels, and nerves—unfamiliar because they were pulsing with life.

Just where and how much dared he interfere without jeopardizing bodily functions? Where lay the outer limits of the reserves nature provides to safeguard life? How many feet of the intestines could be removed and still leave enough to carry on the necessary processes? How much of the stomach could the body get along without? Could the pancreas or the gall-bladder be spared?

And when the answers to such fundamental questions were known, there still remained a host of others about the most efficacious techniques. In what position should the patient be placed on the table, where should the incision be made, how should the sutures be put in? If an artificial opening was needed to detour the contents of the alimentary canal around an obstruction in the pylorus, where was the best place to make it to be sure it would function successfully?

Many such problems had to be solved by trial and error, in large measure on living patients, for animal experimentation was still young and its development was threatened by the noisy horror of antivivisectionists, who had more pity for dogs than for human beings.

Outstanding German surgeons and Lawson Tait of England boldly led the way. In some operations their results were amazingly good, in some frighteningly bad, but in almost all they were sufficient to demonstrate the possibility of success. So others took up the work of improvement, and there was a rush of progress in abdominal surgery, then in cranial, neurologic, and thoracic surgery.

Men could give their whole time to operating now; specialization in general surgery developed, and the surgeon was differentiated from the physician. In America as well as in Europe outstanding leaders developed great surgical clinics, from which poured a flood of new uses for surgery and to which patients flocked for healing and other surgeons for instruction.

Because its results were dramatic and immediate, surgery quickly took the limelight. General medicine, overwhelmed by the precocious brilliance of its latest child, lagged gaspingly behind.

This boom in surgery, at its height from about 1890 to 1910, offered medical men an unprecedented opportunity for fame and fortune. Those who could take the lead in developments would win acclaim among their colleagues for their contributions to knowledge and technique and would find many patients among laymen because of their ability to deal successfully with hitherto incurable ailments.

It was to this situation chiefly that Dr. W. J. Mayo referred in a suggestion for his biographer: "Stress the unusual opportunity that existed in the time, the place, the general setup, not to be duplicated now."

With all the more determination because of their remoteness from the centers of activity, the Mayo brothers kept eagerly abreast of developments. Keenly aware of their own inadequacies, they made time for continued study and travel and seized upon every opportunity to learn from others. They were never averse to confessing ignorance if by so doing they could learn.

Their attitude is illustrated by an incident that took place at the session of the section on surgery of the Minnesota State Medical Society in 1891. The audience was apathetic and the discussion of papers desultory. Time and again when no one else was moved to comment, one of the Mayo brothers rose to offer some criticism or a supplementary case history. Sometimes one or two others followed him briefly, but more often no one stirred.

The program droned on to a paper about "Acute Intestinal Obstruction." The speaker carefully outlined the methods of treatment he thought best: opiates to relieve the pain, leeches or blisters applied to the abdomen, enemas of warm water or olive oil. If after a fair trial these measures did not relieve the obstruction, then of course one must resort to surgery.

Surely that would touch off the fireworks!

But the audience just sat. No one rose to comment, and the

chairman was about to call for the next paper. Then Dr. Will Mayo took the floor, fire in his eye.

I would like to know what we are here for. We from the country come up here to the city. We accept the hospitality of the gentlemen who live here. We find out that they are royal good fellows, but we come up here to learn something from them. . . . We think the papers should elicit something more than the experience of one man. We want the experience of the leaders who live up here in the cities.

I think these gentlemen are not doing all of their duty. I see Dr. Ohage, and Dr. Dunn . . . Dr. Moore and Dr. Dunsmoor. I see a great many gentlemen who could enlighten us, and we would like to hear from them. The paper of Dr. Ranson is one we ought to have discussed.

Then he proceeded to take decided issue with it. He did not approve of deadening pain, the instructive danger signal, with opiates. He emphatically did not believe that surgery should be the last resort in acute intestinal obstruction. "As long as we make it the last resort, just so long will it be something that is fearful."

He sat down. The silence must have been electric.

Then the section chairman, Dr. E. C. Spencer of St. Paul, spoke: "I think most of the instruction which the society has received, outside of the papers, has been from the members from the country, and especially the two from Rochester; so I hope you gentlemen from Minneapolis and St. Paul who think you can tell anything that the Doctors Mayo, of Rochester, do not know will get up and tell them."

One after another the four men Dr. Will had named took the floor, and together they made it impossible for anyone listening to return to his practice unaware of the possible danger of treating intestinal obstruction medically.

Such hearing from others was good but seeing was better.

Whenever the brothers learned of a new operation that sounded promising, one of them set out at the earliest opportunity to see it on the spot and if it proved good, master it for use in Rochester. They established the habit of an annual "brain-dusting" to keep down the cobwebs of routine by going each year, Dr. Will usually in the fall and Dr. Charlie in the spring, to spend a month or more in intensive observation of the work of other surgeons.

They were fortunate in being two. One of them could always get away without seriously disrupting their practice. Even after other doctors had become their partners, Dr. Will and Dr. Charlie traveled together only when both were scheduled to give papers before some national group. For the most part they stuck to their rule: When patients come to Rochester they must always find a Mayo on hand to take care of them.

So the two brothers took turns at traveling, sometimes so closely on each other's heels that the trains they rode would pass in the night and at the midway station to Chicago their thoughts would cross: There comes Will. There goes Charlie.

Whether they could afford these trips was never a question; they felt they *had* to afford them. At first they were content with coach seats on the poky, smoky trains that plied between Rochester and Chicago, but as affluence came and the consciousness of appearances deepened, in the older brother at least, they indulged in the comfort of a Pullman.

Not the least part of this comfort for Dr. Charlie, so people said, lay in the fact that when he had forgotten to clean the country mud from his shoes he had only to leave them out for the porter. Part of the education the Mayos got from their travels was in social conventions; they learned how much men judge from the choice of a fork, the press of a suit, or the shine of a boot. But to the end of his life Dr. Charlie could not be persuaded to bother overmuch about the fine points of spruceness.

Unfortunately Dr. Charlie left no accounts of his experiences on those early travels, but Dr. Will talked about his often, and in his papers are many stories of the men and clinics he visited. They help to sketch a backdrop for the action at Rochester.

New York drew the brothers first. Arpad Gerster was still an outstanding leader there and the Mayos attended his clinic often, but more and more they turned to a group of younger men: Charles McBurney, Robert Abbe, William T. Bull, Robert F. Weir. These men had learned the radical operations introduced by the Germans and were using them, often against the vigorous protests of their older colleagues.

From them the Mayos picked up many a new operative procedure: for instance, from McBurney his own method of removing a gallstone impacted in one of the bile ducts, from Robert Abbe his ingenious "string-saw" operation for dilating strictures of the esophagus, from Robert Weir the symptoms and surgical treatment for perforating ulcer of the stomach and duodenum.

One of the notorious feuds of this vital period was between the conservative New Yorkers and Joseph Price of Philadelphia. Price was introducing into the United States the radical procedures of the English titan, Lawson Tait, and was reporting such amazing success in abdominal operations, one hundred in a series without a single death, that the die-hards simply refused to believe him.

When Dr. Will began to venture beyond ovariotomy in abdominal surgery, he was dissatisfied with his results. His death rate was too high, he thought, so he decided to visit Joseph Price on his next trip.

More than once the Mayo brothers acted on the advice that Dr. Will later gave to his young associates: "When you hear that a certain celebrated surgeon is a liar, and that you are not to believe what he says, go to see him. Find out whether the trouble is his goodness or his badness. Sometimes a good man is cussed more vigorously than he would be if he were bad."

"I had heard that Price was a liar," said Dr. Will. "So I went to see him."

Price was out of town when Dr. Will arrived. A second and a third time he returned, but Price was still away. Then on the fourth morning as Dr. Will sat waiting in the bare little reception room, the door opened with a rush and a tall man with cropped hair and a mustache stalked in. Seeing the visitor, he snapped, "Who are you? What do you want?"

"I am Dr. Mayo from Rochester, Minnesota. I want to see Dr. Price."

"I'm Dr. Price. What do you want?"

"I want to see you operate."

"Sorry. There are more people around here now than I can bother with." And Price turned abruptly away.

With him had come Dr. Lewis McMurtry of Louisville, Kentucky, another prominent surgeon of the day. Winking at Dr. Will, he touched Price on the shoulder and spoke a few words to him. Price turned back. "How long have you been here?"

"Four days," said Dr. Will.

"Whom have you seen?"

"No one." Then shrewdly sizing up his man, "I have been waiting to see you, but I shall go on to New York this morning."

"Don't do that. You won't learn anything there. Come on in."

The room to which he led Dr. Will was meagerly furnished. For an operating table there was only a wide board laid across two sawhorses, with a zinc washtub underneath and a small copper sterilizer near by. A splint-bottomed chair for the surgeon's use in vaginal operations completed the equipment.

Joseph Price's hospital, seemingly makeshift though it was, was his own, and he would not have it otherwise. He had begun his practice with a service at the Philadelphia Dispensary, where he became familiar with the lives and ills of a wretched people, the offscourings of a smug, corrupt, and badly governed city. To these poor souls he was tender and kind, sometimes digging deep into his own pockets to send some Negro mammy to the country to recuperate from an operation he had performed without charge.

He had to do such operations in the patient's home, usually in surroundings of unspeakable squalor, where he could succeed only by cleaning up a small circle and staying within it. To improve upon such conditions he had rigged up this tenement hospital, where he continued to do an immense amount of charity work, entirely at his own expense. He summarily refused the municipal aid proffered by Philadelphia politicians, saying he would have none of the strings he knew would be attached to their grants.

For three weeks Dr. Will watched Price at work, taking particular note of the Philadelphian's special field, the surgery of the uterus, ovaries, and fallopian tubes. Then he went home and in a few months reduced his own mortality rate in such operations to five per cent. For several years thereafter he spent a week or two each year with Price, and soon Dr. Charlie was doing likewise.

Price was a master of sarcasm and sharp repartee, and it is no wonder that those he opposed hated him intensely.

At a medical meeting in Toronto that Dr. Will attended, a New York surgeon, one of Price's pet enemies, read a long and involved paper in which he attempted to describe how a surgeon could tell from the appearance of a loop of intestine just where in the length of gut he had got hold of it. The man concluded with a caution to his hearers that this work was still in the experimental stage, that he could not really tell much about it, and that he doubted whether it had any real value.

When he sat down Joseph Price sprang to his feet and moved that the assembly give a rising vote of thanks to the gentleman for presenting the finest piece of original scientific work to come out of New York in the last twenty years.

Impressed by this description of what they had just heard,

the gathering rose to a man. Then someone saw the joke and began to laugh, and in a moment the whole crowd was roaring.

An incident Dr. Charlie witnessed shows how devastatingly cruel Price could be in his militant defense of surgery. There was in Philadelphia a practitioner who advocated electrotherapy as simpler and safer than operation for the treatment of pelvic disorders. Many honest, sincere men considered this method of real value, but not so Joseph Price. He began to follow up this competitor's work and kept on his trail for months.

Finally the electrotherapist announced his intention of making a report before the College of Physicians of Philadelphia, and Price advised Dr. Charlie, who was visiting him at the time, to attend the meeting.

Price arrived at the hall with a collection of labeled jars, which he arranged on a long table at the front of the room. He listened attentively to the speaker and each time a case history was given with the name or initials of the patient, he leaned forward to pencil a note on one of the labels.

When the invitation to discussion was given, Price arose and exhibited one by one in the jars before him the pathological specimens he had removed surgically from the patients the electrotherapist had just reported as cured. Here was a uterine tumor cut open to show the streaks of cauterization that were the electrical treatments' only effect on the growth; there was a uterus in which the electric needles had entered the wall far from the site of the tumor; and here were the tubes from a "cured" pelvic inflammation, still full of pus.

The effect was so overwhelming that the hearers were moved to sympathy for the crushed speaker of the evening, but Price had dealt a death blow to electrotherapy in Philadelphia.

Among the Chicago men who contributed to the Mayos' surgical education the first place belongs to Christian Fenger, who by common consent is called the father of modern surgery in the West.

Week after week for several years Dr. Will or Dr. Charlie, turnabout, made the journey to Chicago on Wednesday night in order to attend Fenger's clinic on Thursday, and afterward to join the smaller circle in his autopsy room. Sometimes they stayed over to meet with the little band of students Fenger entertained in his home every Thursday night, discussing medical literature and reminiscing over a stein of beer about his experiences in the clinics of Vienna, Heidelberg, and Berlin.

Such a day with Fenger, the Mayos found, stored their minds with pabulum for a week or two's chewing. "He gave me more mental indigestion than any man I ever knew," said Dr. Will.

Fenger was a native of Copenhagen and a finished product of the Danish and German schools of medicine. These northern European schools were leading the world in the application of science, especially the new pathology, to medicine, but they had the early defects of their qualities. In their intense interest in the study of *disease* they had lost sight of the *patient*. Understanding the processes of illness was their objective, and they were frankly skeptical of the power of medicine to relieve suffering. Their meticulous work would mean the discovery of remedial agents for the future, but this was small consolation for the patient of the present.

Fenger was tinged with this therapeutic nihilism. He did not teach that to recognize and classify diseases was more important than to heal them, but his interest, beyond his power to control it, lay in diagnosis more than in treatment.

From Dr. A. J. Ochsner, a disciple of Fenger's, Dr. Will heard a story that illustrates this attitude. The wife of a friend of Ochsner's was seriously ill and the young physician was worried about her, so he sent for Fenger.

After making a careful examination the Danish surgeon recommended an immediate operation.

"Will she get well?" asked Ochsner.

"No, she will die."

"But will she get well if we don't operate?"

"God only knows," was Fenger's reply. Whereupon Ochsner promptly vetoed the operation.

"Well, where is your diagnosis then?" shrugged Fenger.

On another occasion, when Dr. Will was present, Fenger made a brilliant diagnosis of a fibroid tumor of the brain and operated to remove it. While he was closing the wound the patient died.

"Dr. Fenger, the patient is dead," said the anesthetist quietly. There was no answer.

Again, "Dr. Fenger, the patient is dead." Still not a word.

Carefully the surgeon sewed up the incision and as carefully wound the bandages around it. Then he said softly, "You damned fool, to die just as you were cured."

Fenger's emphasis on exact diagnosis was salutary for young American practitioners so long as they did not carry it too far. When a doctor could do nothing about a lump in the abdomen whatever it was, it mattered little whether he was right or wrong in thinking it a tumor, but now it mattered tremendously, for if it was a tumor the surgeon could operate to remove it.

So doctors crowded around Fenger's postmortem table in the morgue of the Cook County Hospital and his operating table in the Passavant Memorial Hospital. Men who in their own theaters wielded the knife more dexterously than he came to learn from him the meaning of things they saw in the body but did not understand, or looked at but did not see.

In the group around Fenger the Mayos made the acquaintance of Nicholas Senn, Albert J. Ochsner, and John B. Murphy.

They learned much from Nicholas Senn; there were few surgeons of his day, east or west, who did not, through his writings if not by direct observation in his clinic. The West was proud of him; he was its gift to the nation.

Born in Switzerland and raised in Wisconsin, Senn had finished off his medical education with a lengthy period of study in German clinics and then under Dr. Fenger. He built up a large private practice in Milwaukee, which he gave up only when his teaching duties in Chicago became too heavy to be handled by commuting.

His endurance and capacity for work were amazing. No matter how busy he was he always found time, late at night usually, for experimental research on the animals he kept in his stable loft, or later in the laboratory built under the sidewalk in front of his Chicago home. He worked on most of the major surgical problems of the day and raised many new ones, but he solved few. His contributions were inspiring and fermentative rather than conclusive; he set the tasks for others.

He was an excellent teacher. Despite an unpleasantly strident voice, he could hold an audience engrossed and put his ideas across with clarity and force. His clinics were always crowded, and through them and his voluminous writings Senn did more than any other one man, unless it was John B. Murphy, to popularize the new surgery with the general profession. To adopt Dr. Will's figure of speech, Senn came into a land without music and soon had the populace singing.

But unfortunately his ability was equaled by his egotism, unrelieved by any saving trace of humor. He was utterly intolerant of opinions not in agreement with his own, and he could not endure the presence of a possible rival near his throne. To share the limelight for even a moment made him ill-tempered.

Albert Ochsner became Senn's chief of staff at Rush Medical College, and it was soon apparent, to Dr. Will Mayo at least, that Senn was worried by Ochsner's ability.

One day Senn was giving a clinical lecture on a patient who had a hard mass in her abdomen. Exact diagnosis was difficult and the operation was to be exploratory. After reviewing the various possible diagnoses, Senn turned to Ochsner, who was standing quietly by, and said condescendingly, "Perhaps our chief of staff can tell us what is the matter with this patient."

Ochsner said he thought the tumor was a lithopedion (a calcified fetus). Senn snorted his derision and quickly listed half a dozen reasons why it could not possibly be a lithopedion. Then he opened the abdomen and found—a lithopedion. The large audience cheered Ochsner to the echo.

Will Mayo was present on this occasion, and he said to Ochsner after the operation, "This will end you in this clinic." Ochsner, who had not yet taken Senn's measure, asked what Mayo meant. "You will find out." And he did.

But Ochsner was not long without a position. Within the year he was appointed chief surgeon of the new Augustana Hospital. It was a small hospital, only twenty beds, but under his guidance it grew to two hundred and fifty beds and became one of the surgical centers sought by visitors from abroad.

William Mayo's friendship with Ochsner ripened into what was probably the closest personal relationship Dr. Will ever had outside his family circle. "My elder brother, guide, philosopher, and friend," he called Ochsner, and many of his later journeys to medical centers were made in Ochsner's company. Neither man being jealous of his knowledge, the two shared their opinions and discoveries, each criticizing the other and helping to test and prove his theories before they were published to the profession at large.

There was nothing of the exhibitionist in Ochsner. He shunned the spectacular and refused to be daring in surgery merely for the sake of a good performance. He was a sincerely simple and kindly man. With his quiet voice, low collar, and white bow tie he could have passed for a Lutheran pastor. His modesty amazed men who had less of it, and they marveled at the reputation and influence he gained in professional circles solely by virtue of an ability too great to be hidden.

But if Ochsner filled his canvas with pastel shades, John B. Murphy splashed his with vivid color. His achievements were always spectacular; they invited reporting and he frequently made page one of the newspapers. And how his brethren of lesser stature hated him for that! They called him a liar, said he stole his ideas and his patients, and accused him of deliberately courting publicity by histrionics.

No one could deny that John B. Murphy dramatized everything he did or that he played best to the grandstand. But the records do not substantiate the charges hurled at him; they were born of jealousy and nourished by envy. Murphy's crime was the possession of an incredibly quick and brilliant mind.

When the Mayos first met him, he was waging a dramatic fight to make the nation, doctors and laymen alike, conscious of appendicitis and its dangers. And his opponents did not like the strength of his arguments.

Then came the battle over the Murphy button.

In the early nineties abdominal surgery was somewhat hung up on the problem of intestinal anastomosis, that is, of how to unite successfully two open ends of the intestinal tract—how to join the gallbladder with the duodenum, for instance, or the stomach with the jejunum, or two severed ends within the intestines themselves. Surgeons needed a method that would join the ends firmly without forming a scar to close the passage. Sewing the parts together was dangerous because the stitches did not always hold, sometimes the bowel became gangrenous at the line of suture, or it took so long to perform the operation that the patient died of shock.

Many men were interested in this fundamental problem, and a number of experiments had been made with mechanical devices that might do the job.

Murphy read everything he could find about the matter, and in the experiments of a French surgeon he saw an idea that had fallen just short of success. With feverish concentration he set to work to overcome the defects in the Frenchman's device, and one day not long afterward he ran from the workroom shouting his eureka to his wife.

What he showed her was a gadget looking something like a sleighbell. Constructed on the principle of the snap fasteners used by dressmakers, it consisted of two small metal bowls fitted with invaginating cylinders. Put a bowl in each end of the severed gut and snap the two together. What could be simpler? As the cut ends within the bowls sloughed off in the healing process the button would be released into the bowel to pass from the body, leaving an unscarred opening the exact size of the button used.

With the aid of his wife and assistants, Murphy tested the button on dogs and then on human patients, and in December 1892 he announced his invention to the profession. Here was a method of end-to-end union that was simple, safe, and quick, he said. Anastomoses that had always taken hours to perform could be done with the Murphy button in half an hour or less.

In April of the following year Dr. Charlie and his father visited Murphy's clinic and for the first time saw an operation performed with the button. Impressed, Dr. Charlie took one of the gadgets home, showed it to Dr. Will, and explained how it worked. Only a few days later the use of this button saved the life of a patient the brothers must otherwise have lost, and after that they used the Murphy button often.

There can be little doubt that Murphy's device cleared the way for advance in intestinal, gallbladder, and stomach surgery. Even the bitter opposition to it helped, for those who criticized it were moved to find something better to take its place. Eventually successful methods of suturing were developed and the button was superseded. But meanwhile it served an immensely useful purpose.

After this triumph in abdominal surgery, Murphy, on the advice of the greathearted Christian Fenger, branched out into research in one field after another—gynecology, nerve surgery, lung surgery. And in each of them he contributed something sensationally original. "His every shot hit the center of the target," as Dr. Will Mayo said.

Each time Murphy would think happily that he had at last won the acceptance by his colleagues that he craved, but then "Murphy Cures Consumption" or some such headline would appear in the papers and the doctors would be hostile again, "outwardly because their profession was being dragged through a puddle of prosaic printer's ink, inwardly because Murphy was again in the news."

The Mayos' admiration for John B. Murphy was unconcealed. They gave him a boost whenever they could and defended him stoutly against his critics. They considered him one of the greatest surgeons of his generation. "As far as one could go he could walk with Murphy" was the elder brother's eloquent tribute.

But for all his ability and originality Murphy left no school of followers to carry on when he was through, because he gave no thought to fostering the development of others. His assistants worked *for* Murphy, not *with* him, and they were not encouraged to have any higher personal ambition than to serve their chief.

Recognizing this deficiency in Murphy, and in Joseph Price and Nicholas Senn, who shared it, underscored for Dr. Will and Dr. Charlie the most pregnant precept the Old Doctor had given his sons: "No man is big enough to be independent of others."

Dr. Will saw this precept applied when in 1894 he elected Baltimore for his annual period of study. The medical news of the time was full of the new Johns Hopkins Hospital and the medical school of university stature that had been opened in conjunction with it, and Dr. Will wanted to see them both.

Reaching the hospital early one morning, he found it as quiet as the streets outside, and for a time he wandered alone through the reception rooms. Then a light, quick step behind him made him turn to face a man with dark eyes and drooping mustaches, who asked briskly but kindly, "Well, what would you like to see?"

"I'm a young doctor from the West and I have heard so much about this hospital that I should like to visit it, if I am not in the way."

"Not at all. Come with me. I am Dr. Osler."

Osler led the way to the wards and introduced the visitor

to his assistants. Then they went to work, blithely but intently, Dr. Will with the rest.

In the weeks that followed Dr. Will got a good introduction to a group of men and a spirit of camaraderie in work that have become a legend in American medicine. The Johns Hopkins Hospital had no large staff of consulting, visiting, and attending doctors, rotating in service to disrupt the organization every few months. Each of its units was under the supervision of a permanent chief who held the corresponding chair in the medical school.

The medical clinic was the charge of William Osler, the beloved physician of Canada, the United States, and England in turn; surgery was the province of William S. Halsted, a shy, unapproachable perfectionist; gynecology was that of the young surgical artist, Howard A. Kelly, whom the Mayos had met with Price in Philadelphia; and the department of pathology was directed by the genial William Welch, known affectionately to hundreds as "Popsy."

These were the famous Big Four of the well-known Sargent painting. With their assistants they formed a congenial, gay, cooperative group, for whom accomplishment of a high order was the normal business of life.

Dr. Will liked all this so much that Dr. Charlie's next journey was to Baltimore, and thereafter the two brothers were frequent visitors at the Johns Hopkins clinics.

The repeated appearance of the two young westerners, first one and then the other, caught the interest of Dr. Osler, and he showed it in characteristic fashion. From here and there on his own travels he sent a memento to the Mayos, usually a trinket or an interesting item about brothers, often brother physicians.

The Mayos spent most of their time at Johns Hopkins in the clinics of Halsted the surgeon. For most visitors it was a shock to find, in this big new hospital that was a model in so many ways, cramped surgical quarters with makeshift equipment. Because surgery was in a state of rapid change, it had been decided to wait and let the surgeons plan and furnish their own buildings when it was quite clear just what they needed. The visitor's surprise in most cases soon gave way to something akin to awe, for in that little room with its old wooden operating table Dr. Halsted maintained standards and secured results of such uniform excellence as to put most surgeons to shame.

At the time the Mayos began to visit his clinic Halsted was changing from antisepsis to the newer asepsis—from drenching the scene with chemical solutions to sterilizing everything that came in contact with the wound, either by boiling or by dry heat in an autoclave. This was a great improvement, but it did not solve the problem of human fingers. The Hopkins men had tried wearing white cotton gloves but found them unsatisfactory.

A few years before, the head nurse of the Hopkins operating room had complained that the harsh antiseptics were making her hands painfully sore, and taking an idea from the heavy coachman's gloves Dr. Welch used for performing autopsies, Halsted asked a New York manufacturer to make her a special pair of thin rubber gloves. They served her so well that the assistants took to wearing them too, and finally Halsted got some for himself. Now he was urging them upon other surgeons, having become a firm believer in their importance in the aseptic routine.

From another aspect of Halsted's surgery Dr. Will derived great comfort. Because postoperative shock was proving a dangerous complication in abdominal surgery, there had been a marked resurgence of the emphasis on speed in operating. This disturbed Dr. Will, for he felt himself to be a slow worker, and the dispatch with which men like Senn, Murphy, and Kelly did their work did not add to his peace of mind.

But in Halsted he saw a surgeon obtain results equal to theirs despite methods that were painfully deliberate. In fact, Halsted maintained that if a surgeon covered the exposed viscera to keep them from getting cold, was careful to handle the tissues gently so as not to bruise them, and took pains to tie off all bleeding vessels so as to leave the cavity dry and clean, he would have fewer cases of shock than if he operated at high speed.

Halsted did not consider surgery merely a means to more knowledge; if an operation did not contribute to the increased well-being of the sick person, it was not good. When he saw the attitude of men like Senn and Fenger at its source in the German clinics he was moved to protest. He urged American surgeons not to go too far in following the German leaders, but to take instead a stand "for conscientious surgery with some interest in the result to the patient."

To such opinions the Mayo brothers listened all the more readily because of their own inclination to moderation in audacity.

For ten years the Mayos steered clear of Boston, though it ranked with New York and Philadelphia as a surgical center. They had heard that its people were cold and inhospitable to visitors, and they shrank from the attempt to scale its ramparts.

But Dr. Will wanted badly to see the work Dr. Maurice Richardson was doing in stomach surgery, and in the fall of 1898, having got fresh haircuts and provided themselves with dress suits, so they wouldn't look "too woolly and hayseedish," Dr. Will and his friend Ochsner ventured to Boston.

Arriving at the Massachusetts General Hospital early in the morning, they asked a janitor who was sweeping the walk in front whether there were to be any operations there that morning. He started to direct them to the office, then broke off to nod down the street, "Here comes Dr. Mixter; maybe he can tell you."

Dr. Samuel Mixter was affability itself. Yes, he said, he was doing some surgery that morning and he thought Dr. Arthur Cabot and Dr. Richardson were too. Come right along. They did, and had a full and pleasant morning, staying at the hospital for lunch and on into the afternoon.

When Dr. Mixter invited them to have dinner with him they hesitated, but he urged them, "Come on. I want you or I wouldn't have asked you."

So they donned their dress suits and went to dine with half a dozen of Boston's great medical men: David Cheever, chief surgeon of the Boston City Hospital, John Honans, nationally known gynecologist, Cabot and Richardson, whom they had met that morning, and John Collins Warren, professor of surgery at Harvard Medical College.

Only four years later these same Boston men asked William J. Mayo to come all the way from Rochester to tell them how to do what he was doing in stomach surgery, but that evening he tingled with the wonder of being accepted on equal terms in such a company.

The two westerners returned to their hotel ready to admit that all they had heard about Boston men was a slander. Not until years later did the cat escape from the bag. Then at some medical convention Dr. J. C. Warren approached Dr. Will to congratulate him on a mark of honor he had just received.

"I remember the first time I heard your name," Warren said. "It was about ten years ago. Sam Mixter called me up late one afternoon and asked me to come to dinner to meet Drs. Ochsner and Mayo.

" 'Who are they?' I asked.

" 'Damned if I know,' he said. 'Just a couple of young fellows from the West. But come on anyway. They say that Boston is cold.' "

Dr. Will did not go abroad until 1900. Then, again in Ochsner's company, he went to attend the International Medical Congress in Paris. There were more than six thousand in attendance, some four hundred and fifty of them from the United States.

Taking time off from the scheduled program one hot afternoon, Dr. Mayo, Dr. Ochsner, and Dr. Harvey Cushing, the great neurosurgeon who was then working with Halsted at Johns Hopkins, sat down to rest awhile in the shade on the steps of the École de Médicine. They talked of the value of watching other men at work in their own clinics and decided it would be an excellent idea for American surgeons to form a new professional society that would occupy its sessions with observation and informal discussion over the operating table rather than with a long program of formal papers.

When they returned to the United States they mentioned their idea to other surgeons, who agreed that it was good. So the Society of Clinical Surgery was organized in 1903. Its membership was to be elective and exclusive, limited to forty practicing surgeons, who twice each year would meet with one of their number for a clinical demonstration of his work. William J. and Charles H. Mayo were two of the original members, and the fifth meeting of the society was held in Rochester.

Clearly, the Mayo brothers were no longer hungry, penniless boys, looking with longing into the bakeshop window. They were now inside, visited as well as visiting for instruction. This had come about because of what had been happening in Rochester during these same years from 1890 to 1905.

12. *The New Surgery*

THE opening of St. Mary's Hospital did not transform the Mayos overnight from general practitioners into surgeons. Throughout the early nineties their surgery remained only the graft of a special interest upon a general practice. One or two mornings a week sufficed for the operations at St. Mary's and the remainder of their long hours the Mayos spent in examining and prescribing at the office or at patients' homes.

One striking fact had impressed itself upon the brothers

early in their travels: The men whose work they found it
worth while to study had almost without exception developed
their abilities in charity service rather than in private practice.
Some busy municipal hospital, university clinic, or free dispensary provided them with the multitude of patients they
needed to give them experience and skill.

The Mayos' home town did not offer any comparable opportunities, but it did have a state hospital for the insane with
a thousand or more inmates, and ninety miles to the west in
St. Peter was another still larger. Neither of these possessed
adequate surgical service, so the two superintendents jumped
at the chance when the Mayo brothers volunteered to provide
it just for the experience.

Each Saturday night one of the brothers made the journey
to St. Peter to do on Sunday whatever operations were necessary and whatever autopsies the superintendent had saved for
his visit. They continued this service, without fees, long after
their need for experience had passed, and whenever the hospital boards insisted on voting them a token of appreciation,
they turned the sum back for the purchase of improved equipment for the operating rooms.

In applying the new surgery in their own practice, the brothers' peculiar position at St. Mary's Hospital proved an ines-
timable advantage. Medical biography is full of the frustration
suffered by young enthusiasts where the authority of inflexible
seniors was too strong. But for Dr. Will and Dr. Charlie there
were no nurses to protest that Dr. Blank had always done it
this way, no staff of elders to raise a prohibitory voice against
methods in advance of theirs, and no board of well-meaning
but ignorant lay trustees to forbid what they did not understand.

The Old Doctor might have interfered but there is no evidence that he ever did. Sometimes, fondling his little pocket
case of needles and knives, he scoffed at the number of instruments the boys thought they needed, and sometimes he as-
serted his authority by "changing the medicine" when he

thought a patient was not coming on as fast as he should, but apparently he never prevented his sons from introducing a new procedure at St. Mary's. Although he was always impatient with the fuss of the antiseptic ritual, he let the boys use it at St. Mary's from the beginning.

Dr. Will and Dr. Charlie followed the unpleasant rites of wet antisepsis for a few years, but they adopted the methods of asepsis as fast as they came in. They were among the first to buy a portable sterilizer and to wear Halsted's rubber gloves for every surgical procedure.

For the first decade the two young men did their operating as a team, each serving in his turn as the other's first assistant. Together they bent over the table, every faculty intent, one seeing what the other missed, pooling their knowledge and ingenuity to meet a crisis when it came. And afterward they talked together, over their books or a microscope slide or pathological specimen, about the why of failure or success and the ways and means of improvement.

By persistently and systematically reviewing their cases in this critical fashion, the Mayo brothers extracted the last jot of value from their own work, finding useful pointers in their successful cases as well as in their mistakes.

Both brothers must do all sorts of surgery if either was to be able to get away for study, and each seems to have tried his hand at every kind of operation on the calendar. But as the number of operations increased, Dr. Will found more and more of his time occupied with pelvic and abdominal surgery, while Dr. Charlie took over the work on the eye, ear, nose, and throat, the bones and joints, the brain, nerves, and neck.

Dr. Will always maintained that this division of labor was the result of Charlie's superiority as an operator. "I was driven to cover by a better surgeon," he said. "Charlie drove me down and down until I reached the belly."

But Dr. Will had got started on the belly before Dr. Charlie joined him, so it is more likely that the younger brother's quick skill in all kinds of operating left Dr. Will free to devote himself to the new abdominal surgery as the amount of it increased.

The increase came first of course in gynecology, where the new surgery first developed and where the Old Doctor had made a good start. During the first three and a quarter years that St. Mary's Hospital was open minor surgery accounted for 164 of the 195 gynecologic operations the Mayos performed. But in 1905 the total for the single year was 637, and nearly two thirds of these were radical operations.

When Pasteur made it possible to understand the processes of infection, Lawson Tait read in a pus-filled fallopian tube the true story of pelvic inflammation: The unclean fingers of the midwife or placental remains give rise to an infection in the uterus, from which it spreads through the tubes into the ovaries and surrounding tissues. Boldly Tait advised the removal of infected tubes and ovaries as the treatment for inflammatory diseases of the pelvis.

He was vigorously opposed, as were Joseph Price, Howard Kelly, and the others who carried his teachings to the United States. These chaps were making a great to-do over rarities, said the men of the old school, who did not consider the fallopian tubes important in the diseases of women. But the crusaders answered with platefuls of specimens and sheaves of case histories.

First only the infected tube and ovary were removed; then those on the other side too were cut out to prevent the spread of the infection; and finally the uterus, which after all was the source of the infection, was taken too.

This was possible because hysterectomy, the operation for removing the uterus, had been brought to a high state of technical perfection. For a long time the likelihood of hemorrhage had made it too dangerous for wide use. Gradually, however, the technical difficulties were overcome, the mortality rate dropped, and the operation came within the practical reach of general surgeons. They went a little wild and were inclined to find in hysterectomy a panacea for all the ills of women.

Ovariotomy, or ovariectomy, as it is called today, passed through somewhat the same phases. It was only a step from removing the ovaries for tumor to removing them for pain in menstruation, and then for various nervous symptoms that baffled physicians. From this grew the theory that mental derangement was produced by the generative organs, and ovariectomy was advocated as a treatment for insanity.

That was the "hysterical adolescence" of gynecology. Dr. Will learned the new operations from some of the Twin City surgeons and then polished up on the finer points during his visits to Joseph Price and Howard Kelly. But with the techniques he learned the debate about them, and he proceeded cautiously in applying them.

In spite of his caution, though, he was sometimes fooled by neurotic women and sometimes persuaded by the enthusiasm of fellow surgeons into unnecessary operations, and he later admitted, "It would seem to me that the genital organs of woman had suffered from an excess of operative zeal, to her detriment and our discredit."

But certainly by the use of the new operations he restored health and energy to scores of ailing women whom the medical treatment of that day had not and could not have helped.

The spotlight swung next to surgery for appendicitis. By the nineties the more progressive surgeons had accepted removal of the appendix as the treatment to be preferred. But because of the growing differentiation between physicians and surgeons, it was the general practitioner who must be trained to recognize this malady early and accept the need of surgical treatment for it.

These practitioners clung firmly to their belief in medical treatment. Look at the mortality of operation, they said to the surgeons; it's twenty-five to thirty per cent. As many die under surgical treatment as under medical therapy, so why hurry every patient off to the operating room?

They die in operation because you don't get them to us in time, retorted the surgeons. If you doctors would learn to recognize appendicitis and would call the surgeon in at once, the mortality rate would drop. And as for those patients you say you cure, follow them up and see what state of health they're in. You've just turned an acute case into a chronic one. That patient who suffers from periodic stomach and bowel upsets, so-called bilious attacks, is what you have called a medical "cure" of appendicitis. You ought to get that man to a surgeon *now*.

The physicians shrugged in disgust; the surgeons were seeing appendicitis in every case of plain bellyache. They were going mad on operation again, as they had with woman's pelvic organs. What they really wanted was the hundred and fifty dollars the poor patient gave up along with his appendix.

The argument was really bitter, one of the classic battles of medical history. It raged throughout the nineties, all over the country but especially in the Middle West, where feeling ran higher and language plainer. John B. Murphy, who was making it his mission to spread the gospel of immediate appendectomy, often attended meetings of the various state medical societies in the vicinity of Chicago, always dramatizing and exaggerating his position in order to drive his points home.

Dr. Will and Dr. Charlie took little part publicly in the controversy, but the fact that St. Mary's Hospital reported only twelve operations for appendicitis in 1895 attests the caution with which the brothers were moving.

They were willing to grant the logic of operating immediately upon diagnosis, but when they faced the cases in practice they could not stick to any such rule of thumb. Operation simply was not safe in some of the cases they saw. Although their mortality rate was not the thirty per cent admitted by some city hospitals, it was still twelve to fifteen per cent, too high to justify operation if the patient had a chance without it.

Then Dr. Ochsner took Will Mayo into his confidence. He had worked out a method of treatment that seemed to reduce the operative mortality considerably, but he wanted it thoroughly tested before he published it. The Mayo brothers tried the Ochsner treatment and almost at once their death rate dropped to less than four per cent, then with refinements in technique to one per cent and under.

The essence of Ochsner's idea was this: If a patient is seen before the appendix ruptures, the organ should be removed at once, but if the infection has already spread to the peritoneum it is not safe to operate. Instead, peristalsis should be stopped in order to aid nature in localizing the infection. Put the patient at rest and give him absolutely nothing to eat or drink, above all no cathartics. In a few days the acutely dangerous phase will pass and appendectomy will be safe.

This eventually became famous as the Ochsner starvation treatment. It was first described to the profession at the international congress in Paris that Ochsner and Mayo attended together in 1900, and thereafter it was widely acclaimed as a tremendous advance in the treatment of appendicitis.

Inevitably, hundreds of physicians, seeking to justify their own stubborn opposition to appendectomy, pounced upon the Ochsner treatment as support for their position. See, they said gleefully to their critics, the great Chicago surgeon saves most of his appendicitis cases by not operating on them!

The storm of argument eventually made everyone, the plain people and their family doctors, aware of appendicitis and its dangers. The bad appendix joined the much-publicized germs as public fright number two, and children walked in terror of the grape seed and cherry pit which if swallowed, their parents warned them solemnly, would bring a pain in the side and the dreaded operation.

Probably nowhere in the nation did the number of operations for appendicitis mount so quickly or so high as in Rochester. In 1900 the number for the year was one hundred and eighty-six. In 1905 it passed the thousand mark.

Another of the arguments precipitated by the new deal in surgery was over the exploratory incision. If the source of an abdominal disorder is obscure, said the progressive surgeons, open up the cavity and find out whether the cause is a condition you can do anything about.

Subject a patient to all the dangers of peritonitis just to find out what is wrong with him? Reckless, utterly irresponsible, said the conservatives. And besides, it's a confession of failure in diagnosis.

Exactly, replied the surgeons. We do fail in diagnosis on clinical signs, so why not admit it in the only way that promises the patient relief from his troubles?

With this position the Mayos agreed. The Old Doctor once told a carping colleague in a medical meeting: "It is the custom with me and those associated with me, where there is a seriously diseased condition of either a man or woman's abdomen, and the diagnosis cannot be made without, to open the abdomen very frequently."

This custom led to their first operation for gallstones. In December 1890 a machinist from Sleepy Eye, Minnesota, many miles to the west of Rochester, presented himself at the Mayos' offices. For years he had suffered from spells of pain in his right side and he was now having to use opiates almost constantly.

Not sure what was causing his trouble, the Mayos suggested an exploratory operation and he consented. When Dr. Will found a mass of adhesions surrounding a contracted gallbladder containing one large stone, he removed the stone and inserted a drain. In three weeks the patient was discharged, had soon gained forty pounds, and went back to work at his trade.

Diseases of the gallbladder, long known as a plague of adult mankind, were still the province of the physician. Postmortem examinations had shown that the gallbladder so often contained stones whose presence had not been suspected that it was generally believed most gallstones were "slumbering" or "innocent," that is, lying quietly in the gallbladder without causing any trouble.

The one recognized sign of active stones was the excruciating colic that any practitioner could identify at a glance. This agonizing pain, which might last for a few hours or for a week or more, was thought to be a kind of labor that occurred when the stone passed from the gallbladder through the cystic and common ducts into the bowel, and the end of the colic was taken to mean that the stone had completed this passage.

For this malady the therapeutics of the day prescribed morphine to deaden the pain, doses of ether mixed with turpentine to dissolve the stones, and the old favorite, spoonfuls of olive oil. Proudly the doctor would exhibit to the patient the stones he had passed with the aid of the olive oil, but actually the "stones" were soap balls formed by the action of the intestinal alkalies on the oil.

The futility of these measures was demonstrated by the fact that scattered through every community were men and women who had sweated through spells of colic for four, ten, even twenty years. Sometimes their gallstones slumbered for a month or two, but then something, no one knew what, woke them to new activity and the almost intolerable pain began again.

In 1890 surgeons were just beginning to advise surgery for gallstones. Removal of the gallbladder (cholecystectomy) was thought advisable only in such desperate straits as cancer, but merely opening the organ and scraping out the stones (cholecystotomy) seemed a relatively simple procedure.

The Mayos learned early that cholecystotomy would not suffice for all gallbladder ills. In April 1893 Dr. Albert Plummer of Racine, Minnesota, sent one of his patients to see them. The man was seventy-one years old and very ill. He had been having attacks of gallstone colic for two years and for the past four months had been in almost constant pain, with vomiting, emaciation, and jaundice.

The Mayos decided that a stone was obstructing the common duct. A few years earlier there would have been nothing they or anyone else could do about it, but McBurney and Abbe of New York had recently outlined a method by which the biliary ducts could be opened and impacted stones removed. And Dr. Will had learned how to do that operation.

But he struck a snag. When he got the abdomen open he found the site of obstruction in the duct so inaccessible that removal of the stone was out of the question.

There was one alternative—to cut a back door for the escape of the bile by fastening the gallbladder directly to the bowel and cutting a permanent opening between them. But the patient was in such bad condition that he could not possibly last through the long procedure of a suture anastomosis.

At this juncture Dr. Charlie remembered the gadget he and his father had brought back from Chicago a day or two before. Murphy's button was supposed to work in just such cases as this. Quickly Dr. Will made an opening in the gallbladder and another in the duodenum, fastened one half of the button in each, and snapped the two together. Then he closed the incision and got the patient back to bed.

His recovery was quick and complete. The jaundice disappeared, his strength returned, and he was able to go home. For six years he remained well and active, dying in the end from an ailment far removed from the gallbladder and its ducts.

The number of stones in a gallbladder is not of great importance; one good-sized concretion can be as troublesome as many small ones. But the Mayo cases that caught the attention of the public were those in which the gallstones numbered hundreds—or more. This was one such case:

An operation was performed at St. Mary's Hospital within the past few days that savors of the marvelous. Nearly three thousand gall stones were removed from a woman. The number is known to be about three thousand for bacteriologist T. Spillane spent all one day counting them. The woman still lives and is sure to recover. The stones ranged in size from a pin head up to a pea.

That experience would command an audience for the

woman who had it today. How much more so at a time when
major operations were novelties and in a community where
the drab drudgery of farm life was enlivened only by talking
and where there was little to talk about except the weather
and the crops and the neighbors.

So word of what the Mayos were doing got around, and the
year's total of ten gallbladder operations in 1895 became seventy-five in 1900 and three hundred and twenty-four in 1905.

By that time the -ectomy operation had been so improved
that it was almost as safe as the -otomy, and many surgeons
were saying that any gallbladder which contained stones was
obsolete and should therefore be removed.

The Mayos did not hold with this idea. It seemed better to
them to strive for earlier diagnosis, so they could operate
before complications developed. What they wanted was to get
after the gallstones that were supposed to be slumbering.

They were convinced that half of the so-called innocent
stones were no such thing; they were merely thought to be so
because the signs of their mischief were not recognized. Doctors had so long thought of colic as the one indication of gallstones that they were blind to any other symptom, but the
Mayos had found gallstones in many cases of vaguely defined
"stomach trouble" which vanished with the stones. Here was
further work for the diagnostician.

To the unhappy victims of hernia—fifteen per cent of mankind they were said to be—the medical men of the 1880s
could offer only the makeshift of a truss to hold the viscera
in place. Such abdominal supports were usually expensive,
uncomfortable, and but partially effective, providing poor defense against the ever-present danger of strangulation, which
occurs when the hernia cannot be reduced and the circulation
is shut off in the protruded parts so that they become gangrenous.

The hernia patient, used to looking after himself, usually
tried to do so when strangulation occurred, and the doctor was

seldom called until the choked tissues had begun to mortify and the patient was in an alarming condition.

What the physician could do then may be illustrated by the practice of the Old Doctor. He would freeze the protruded mass by applying salt and ice wrapped in a handkerchief, and then split the skin to allow the pus and feces to escape. If the patient recovered after this, which he sometimes did, Dr. Mayo twisted off the spur of dead tissue with clamps and threaded buttons into the fistula to close it.

In such extreme cases as this Dr. Will began his work with hernia. He could now open the abdominal cavity, relieve the stricture, remove the gangrenous portion of the bowel, and unite the severed ends. Soon he was able also to try one of the operations proposed for the so-called radical, that is, surgical, cure of hernia.

These operations were young, the first practical one dating from 1889, and their results were notoriously impermanent. The best of the few men who were using them admitted to forty or fifty per cent of relapses, and others said gloomily that seventy-five or eighty per cent would be nearer the mark.

Surgeons had a strong incentive for improving these results, because rupture through the line of incision was a likely sequel to any abdominal operation. Dr. Will found it discouraging indeed to have one and then another of the patients on whom he had operated for appendicitis or gallstones turn up a little later with a troublesome hernia.

Gradually it became evident that the skin and peritoneum could not be made into an adequate bulwark against rerupture, that the underlying muscles and tendons must be used as the retaining wall. When this principle was put into practice, the percentage of relapse in hernia operations fell to five per cent and surgical repair began slowly to replace the wearing of a truss.

Up to 1893 the Mayos attempted only thirty-nine radical cures of hernia; by 1905 they were averaging about three hundred a year.

But umbilical hernias did not immediately share in this improvement. At the navel the muscles of the abdomen lie too far apart to be brought easily and successfully together, and besides, umbilical hernia occurred most frequently in obese persons whose abdominal muscles were so flabby that they were of little use as a retaining wall. Surgeons despaired of ever being able to cure rupture at the umbilicus.

As Dr. Will saw more of such cases he noted again and again that the patients' abdominal tissues were stretched and pendulous. When the patient lay relaxed on the table he could gather the sagging flesh in his fingers and overlap it a number of inches.

Overlap it. There was an idea! Why not lap the fibrous tendons edge over edge for a couple of inches to form a wall of double strength at the critical spot? The resistance ought to be perfect.

Carefully he thought the method through, talked it over with Dr. Charlie, and perhaps tried it a time or two on the cadaver. Then he performed it on a patient and watched the results. The union was lasting and the wall held. He used the method in a second case, a third, a fourth. He explained it to a few professional friends, Dr. Ochsner among them, and their experience confirmed his own. By 1903 he and Dr. Charlie had done thirty-five such operations without a death and with but one slight relapse. They had something useful to report to the profession.

Another area of surgical development at Rochester was provided by the fact that children *will* swallow things not meant to be swallowed.

The old way of handling them in such an emergency, if the foreign body seemed to be stuck above the entrance to the stomach, was to turn the child upside down and shake him vigorously. In the consequent coughing and crying the offending object might be dislodged and fall out, but of course it might just as easily become more firmly and dangerously

stuck. If the foreign body had entered the stomach, the patient was fed quantities of mashed potato to form a mass
around it and carry it safely through the intestinal tract, but
this did not always work and obstruction was an even chance.

The newer method was to make an incision into the trachea,
esophagus, or stomach and remove the object by direct sight
or touch. The Mayo brothers dealt with a number of cases in
this way and had a goodly collection of prune pits, corn
kernels, coins, and safety pins to show for them.

Some mistakes in swallowing were not so easily handled,
however. Concentrated lye was then in common use in the
rural households of the Upper Midwest for making soap, and
the poisonous, burning stuff, looking like sugar, often sat
around the kitchen in open containers within easy reach of
unsuspecting children.

A child might survive the immediate effects of swallowing
lye, but as the severe burns in the gullet healed, contraction
occurred and scar tissue formed to obstruct the esophagus.
The little victim could seldom swallow anything but liquids,
and less and less of those as the stricture tightened.

If the doctor got hold of the case before the channel was
too nearly closed, he could dilate the stricture by the use
of bougies, slender cylindrical probes of graduated sizes. He
could force one of these through what opening remained and
by daily sounding with progressively thicker bougies he could
enlarge the opening to near-normal size.

But sometimes the obstruction was so far advanced that the
most patient efforts could not find an opening for the bougie.
Such patients, almost all of them children, came to the doctor
in pitiable condition, thin and pale, weak, pathetically hungry
but unable to swallow the milk they craved.

For them surgical treatment was now possible. Dr. Abbe of
New York had devised an ingenious operation in which several strands of string were threaded from a stomach incision
through the stricture and out the mouth. By using the string
as a saw an opening was cut in the obstructing scar tissue

sufficiently large to admit the smallest bougie for beginning the dilation process.

The Mayos had learned this "string-saw" method from Abbe and applied it in a number of cases, where the successes they won were unusually satisfying to all concerned.

For instance, in October 1892 a little girl three years old was brought to St. Mary's. She had been unable to eat solid food since swallowing lye a year before and was now regurgitating most of the liquid nourishment given her. Unable to find an opening for even the smallest bougie, Dr. Will advised operation, but the parents refused it and took the girl home again.

A few months later they brought her back, scarcely alive. Dr. Will immediately made an opening into the stomach, and for a month the child was fed through that opening. Then Dr. Charlie started the string-saw operation, and he worked for five weeks to enlarge the esophageal opening enough to admit a bougie. Two months later the child was discharged "in good general condition, able to drink milk readily and to take chopped meat and bread with little effort." A few years afterward the parents happily reported the child to be entirely well and eating normally.

The gastrotomies made in such cases to permit the manipulation of bougies and string-saws were the first incisions into the stomach cavity made by the Mayo brothers.

Stomach ailments probably brought more patients to the doctors than any other complaint, but the Mayos had been surprised to see how often "gastralgia" disappeared with the removal of an inflamed appendix, "dyspepsia" with the drainage of a diseased gallbladder, and "stomach cramps" with the repair of a ventral hernia. Stomach trouble under its various names had long been a sort of diagnostic catchall for the vague miseries of the upper abdomen.

Naturally, and often correctly, the source of stomach disorders was thought to be bad diet habits, chiefly the overeating of greasy, fried foods, hot breads, and heavy pastries. The time-honored treatment consisted of emetics, cathartics, and chemical aids to digestion like bismuth, pepsin, and hydrochloric acid. Some disorders of the stomach, however, were not chemical but mechanical in nature, and these were logically the province of surgery.

But stomach surgery was in disrepute because of the frightful mortality attending it. Billroth, the German surgeon who was the first to practice operation in desperate cases of gastric disorder, had been wry about his own results. "All the patients left the operating room in shock, from which some of them recovered," he said. More than half of them had died.

Even by the nineties stomach surgery had progressed little beyond the stage of use in emergencies to avert imminent death; much was still to be done to make it safe enough for the relief of disability.

The Mayos soon learned to spot the symptoms that made one type of stomach disorder virtually unmistakable. Its victims told a story of chronic gastric distress lasting over a number of years, sometimes as many as fifteen or twenty. In the last year or two their food would not digest properly; it just lay heavy and sour in the stomach, causing them great discomfort until they brought it up again by vomiting or by washing it out with the stomach tube. Some of them were reduced to a liquid diet; all had lost weight.

Theirs was chronic starvation caused by obstruction of the pylorus, the narrow outlet from the stomach into the duodenum. The obstruction was thought to result from a chronic lesion of the pylorus, which in its repeated healing, reopening, and healing again had formed a mass of scar tissue that closed the channel. This was the sort of mechanical difficulty medicine could not touch.

When Dr. Will in 1894 turned his attention to the possibilities of surgical relief for this ailment, he found that Wölfler of Germany had originated a method of making an opening from the stomach directly into the small bowel to serve as a substitute for the blocked pyloric passageway. This operation (gastroenterostomy) was an admirable solution of the problem, but with suture anastomosis its death rate had been fifty per cent or over.

Accustomed to use the Murphy button in other operations, Dr. Will began with it in this one, and together with other refinements of technique, the button lowered the mortality from gastroenterostomy enough to make this the procedure of choice in the Mayos' treatment of pyloric obstruction.

This obstruction was not always benign in nature. In fact, cancer was thought to be the commoner cause of it, but early in his experience Dr. Will had occasion to perform a postmortem in a case where the certified cause of death was "cancer of the pylorus" but in which he found the stricture to be benign, and this gave him a jolt. The man had died of starvation due to a condition that surgery could have cured. How often was this mistake made?

Obviously there was need for some means of differential diagnosis between these two kinds of obstruction, and the Mayos combed their case histories looking for significant signs of one or the other, but they could find none that proved reliable. Forced to admit that they could tell the difference only by direct observation at the operating table (and not always even there), they took the position that an exploratory incision was imperative in all cases of pyloric stricture. If it revealed a benign condition, curative surgery could be performed.

And if it revealed cancer? Surgeons had tried cutting out the cancerous portion and even removing the entire stomach, but the immediate mortality had proved prohibitive. Even if the patient did survive the operation, the recurrence of the disease was so certain and quick that the brief respite did not seem worth the ordeal of the operation.

Dr. Will rejected so gloomy a view. He took a look at the patients on whom resections for gastric cancer were done and saw that all of them were in the last stages of the disease, some of them near death from hemorrhage and exhaustion, before they came to operation. It was a wonder any of them survived. If surgery could be applied earlier the results would be better.

Here again the stumbling block was the difficulty of diagnosis, and again the Mayos accepted the need for exploration upon suspicion. Their maxim was, if the cause of the trouble may be cancer and is not quickly found to be something else, operate. They always told the patient just what they proposed to do, and seldom did he hesitate. It was more often his attending physician who counseled delay—because most medical men did not believe that stomach cancer was curable even by early removal.

By 1906 the Mayo brothers were able to report one hundred stomach resections for cancer, with a mortality and a record of permanent cure that compared favorably with results in cancer of other parts of the body where the value of surgery was generally accepted. Since medical men had absolutely no hope to offer in this disease, the surgeons had proved their right to try operation.

Inevitably, experience with benign pyloric obstruction led the Mayos and their fellows to ask: What about the ulcer that produces this condition? Must we let it go its way to this result? Can't we interrupt these years of suffering at some earlier point?

Ulcer of the stomach was a medical disease. Only when it hemorrhaged or perforated was the surgeon called, in his customary role of the last resort, to stop the bleeding and patch up the hole.

It was the same old story, told before in appendicitis and then in gallbladder disease. The exacerbations of chronic ulcer were being treated as acute ulcer, and the subsidence of the attack was being mistaken for a cure. But a condition of ten or fifteen years' standing is not acute, nor has it been cured.

What could surgery do about it? It seemed logical that if the ulcer area was put at rest with no gastric juices or food passing over it to irritate it, it would heal and remain healed. On that supposition the artificial passage from the stomach into the bowel that relieved pyloric obstruction ought also to work for open ulcers.

In 1900 Dr. Will first performed gastroenterostomy in two cases of chronic ulcer, and in both the results were all he could ask for. So he recommended surgical treatment for chronic ulcer with rapidly increasing frequency.

The Mayos noticed that a surprising number of the chronic ulcers they saw occurred in the duodenum—surprising because duodenal ulcer was then thought to be rare and relatively unimportant.

Once his eyes were opened to duodenal ulcers, Dr. Will found that many pyloric obstructions he had thought due to gastric ulcer were really extensions of the lesion upward from the duodenum, and that cases that had baffled him when he tried to find the trouble in the gallbladder were actually chronic ulcer of the duodenum.

Early in his experience with surgery for ulcers Dr. Will was pulled up short by performing operations on some persons with typical ulcer symptoms in whom he could find no lesion, search as he would. He then reviewed their histories and found them to be what the Old Doctor would have called "nervous dyspeptics." This was Dr. Will's introduction to the kind of neurosis that simulates with baffling precision the symptoms of chronic ulcer.

When word spread of Dr. Will's work on ulcers, seldom a week went by without several neurotic women appearing to ask for a stomach operation. A little wearily Dr. Will warned his fellow surgeons against this "vast army of neurasthenics. . . . Many have already had their movable organs fixed (kidneys and uterus) and the removable ones removed (ovaries and appendix) and now are anxious to secure relief by a further resort to the knife."

If contemporary estimates were correct, medicine was failing to cure in more than seventy-five per cent of chronic ulcer cases, and since this had been true for years, there was a goodly accumulation of sufferers to welcome the surgeon. The trend toward operation was just getting under way in 1905, and in that year Dr. W. J. Mayo, by then the foremost American authority on stomach surgery, performed two hundred and seventeen operations on the stomach and duodenum.

That in brief is the story of the Mayos' advance into differential diagnosis and surgical treatment of diseases of the pelvis and upper abdomen. A similar story might be told for other abdominal organs—the kidneys, the pancreas, the intestines. But the record given must suffice to explain the steady rise in the number of abdominal operations at St. Mary's Hospital, from 54 in the first three and a quarter years to 612 in 1900 and 2,157 in 1905.

The expanded usefulness of surgery was the fruit of a steady improvement in operative techniques that reduced the death rate and made permanent results more certain, but this is a long story that can only be suggested by some highlights in the evolution of gastroenterostomy, which came into general use in the United States largely through the work of the Mayos.

Dr. Will quickly appreciated the usefulness of this operation for short-circuiting the current of digestion, but he trod warily in the use of it because of the tricks it was said to play.

The practice then was to join the stomach to the jejunum (the section of the small bowel that follows the duodenum), and in order to do this the jejunum had to be pulled around the membranous mesocolon that separates it from the stomach. A loop of jejunum was thus left hanging unused after the operation, and this loop caused most of the trouble in gastroenterostomy. Most frequent among the possible difficulties was the kinking of the loop at the site of union so that the bile and pancreatic juices flowed into the stomach.

When such kinking occurred immediately after the operation, the constant vomiting of bile so exhausted the already weakened patient that death was probable. Known to doctors as "the vicious circle," this complication was so often the sequel to gastroenterostomy that surgeons hesitated to use the operation at all.

The vicious circle plagued Dr. Will in his first fourteen operations, but then he began cutting the new opening as low on the stomach wall as possible, so that the weight of the dependent bowel would pull the baglike stomach into the shape of a funnel. In his next three hundred gastroenterostomies there was only one case of vicious circle.

But he found that elimination of the vicious circle did not eliminate bile regurgitation. The angulation of the jejunum that caused it could usually be corrected in a second operation to join the two limbs of the loop of bowel so as to make a channel for the bile at a level below the opening into the stomach, but having to do this second operation was a mark of failure.

In 1903 the German surgeon Mikulicz, probably the leading stomach surgeon in Continental Europe, visited Rochester and showed the brothers how to do a no-loop operation. The results with this were good though not phenomenal—four deaths and four cases of secondary operation in a total of forty-three cases—but the Mayos were a little afraid of the procedure because it required a crosswise incision of the bowel, which permitted so small an outlet from the stomach as almost to court difficulty. If this no-loop operation could be done with the usual lengthwise incision it would be ideal.

In October 1903 Dr. Charlie had occasion to do two gastroenterostomies while Dr. Will was away, and he boldly attempted the lengthwise incision. He accomplished it successfully, but found it difficult to prevent leakage of the bowel contents during the operation.

In the meantime Dr. Will had turned to a trial of the method demonstrated to him by Berkeley Moynihan of Leeds during a visit to Rochester in the summer of 1903. His was a loop operation, but it was done with clamps he had devised to simplify the technique. In fifty-three gastroenterostomies by this method Dr. Will found the primary results good, only three deaths, but within the year seven patients had to have a second operation for regurgitant bile.

On January 1, 1905, Dr. Will, seeing that with Moynihan's clamps the lengthwise incision would be easily possible, returned to the no-loop operation as done by Dr. Charlie in 1903. In the succeeding six months he performed fifty-six gastroenterostomies with only one death, but there were still two cases of secondary operation.

Determined to get rid of even this much failure, Dr. Will studied once more the anatomy and physiology of the parts involved. As a result he made a slight shift in the angle at which the jejunum was joined to the stomach, and during the second six months of 1905 he performed sixty-five gastroenterostomies with no deaths and no secondary operations.

The problem was solved!

Meanwhile Dr. Charlie's versatile fingers were standing the team in good stead. With apparent ease and gratifying success he could turn from the fine work on the eye to the broader motions of an excision of the knee joint, or from the tricky manipulation of a cranial nerve to the removal of a bunion. The stories of only a few of the fields in which he worked must serve to illustrate how the usefulness of surgery expanded in all of them.

To improved and extended eye surgery Dr. Charlie soon added the newer specialty of ear, nose, and throat, where the development of chief importance, in number of cases at least, was in surgery of the tonsils and adenoids.

Operations on the tonsils had been used since the days of ancient Greece, but only for bad cases of tonsillar abscess and quinsy. Mere enlargement and mild tonsillitis, however often an attack laid the patient low, were not thought to call for surgery.

The removal of adenoids did not come into use until the last quarter of the nineteenth century. If swabbing and spraying the throat and snuffing powders into the nose failed to correct difficulties in breathing, the doctors comforted themselves and the patient's parents with the knowledge that such difficulties vanished as adolescence passed.

When throat specialists began to urge removal of the adenoids in many cases of deafness, annoying noises in the head, and easy susceptibility to colds, another conflict between the general practitioner and the specialist was on.

The removal operations were as yet imperfect, did not always bring relief, and sometimes proved dangerous because of hemorrhage. Pointing to these facts, physicians asked why they should recommend surgery for a condition the child would outgrow anyway. The specialist answered that the child might outgrow the abnormal enlargements but not the defects they had caused.

The Mayo brothers seemingly sided with the specialists in this argument, because Dr. Charlie cut out an increasing number of tonsils and adenoids. He devised his own instruments for the procedure, crude ones perhaps, not conducive to painless operating, but as serviceable as any then on the market and certainly to be preferred to the fingernails, which the progressive William Osler was still recommending in 1892 as the instrument of choice for scraping out the adenoids.

The use of tonsillectomy received a tremendous push after the turn of the century from the theory of focal infection, the idea that infection in the tonsils or the teeth may be a focus from which the bacteria pass to other parts of the body. In time the tonsils were blamed for everything from rheumatism to pneumonia, and they were shelled out on a breath of suspicion. This fad passed, but as late as 1940 tonsillectomies were still numbering one third of all operations performed.

In comparison with that record, the round hundred tonsil removals that Dr. Charlie was doing annually by 1905 were a bagatelle, but they were a noteworthy increase over the five or ten he had been doing in 1890.

He scored one of his earliest triumphs when he was called to see a patient with acute suppuration of the knee joint. It

was too late for mild measures; the patient was already showing all the constitutional signs of dangerously active infection. Yet Dr. Charlie hesitated. He hated to amputate. If only
he could get at the inner cavities of the joint, to clean them
out and drain them thoroughly.

Well, why not lay the knee joint wide open by a sweeping
transverse incision so he *could* get at them freely? Of course
the motion of the joint would be gone, but a stiff leg would be
better than no leg at all. So he made the incision, drained all
the recesses of the joint, and packed it full of antiseptic gauze.

The effect was astonishing. In a few hours the symptoms of
active inflammation subsided and the patient was obviously
on the road to recovery. Then Dr. Charlie put the joint in
position and allowed the parts to unite. Soon the patient was
up and about again, his leg stiff but useful and his own.

Feeling that this outcome was no lucky accident, Dr. Charlie wrote a report of the case for publication in the *Annals
of Surgery*. And a few months later he was delighted to read
in that same journal a communication from Dr. Arpad Gerster
calling attention to this "Mayo operation" and testifying from
his own experience to its worth.

Another such "Mayo operation" contributed to the treatment of varicose veins, which were frequent among the hard-
working farmers of the Rochester community. Often they
caused no discomfort or so little that it was not thought worth
complaining about in this vale of woes, and the condition
dragged on for years before the doctor's help was sought.

Dr. Charlie once told how casually these patients came to
him. Sometimes, in the spring of the year perhaps, a farmer
would drop into the office, apologizing for his appearance.
"I've just put in my crop," he would say. "I've been following
the drag and I'm all dirty, but I don't like the looks of this old
ulcer." Then he would pull off the faded bandana he had
wrapped around his leg and Dr. Charlie would see a varicose
ulcer, as big as the palm of his hand sometimes, raw and ugly.

If the condition was not too old or too extensive, rest in

bed and strapping the legs with elastic bandages, with antiseptic salves and dressings for the ulcer, would work the healing. Otherwise operation was necessary.

German surgeons had devised practicable procedures for removing the offending saphenous vein through an incision stretching from the thigh to several inches below the knee, but the operation was tedious because of the time it took to close the long incision, the scar was almost certain to break open later at the knee through motion of the leg, and the extensive exposure was risky because of the peculiar susceptibility of the veins to infection.

Putting his mechanical bent to work, Dr. Charlie designed some long-handled forceps that formed a ring at the end when closed. Inserted through a short crosswise incision and closed around the vein, these forceps were pushed along for several inches underneath the skin, stripping the vein from its sheath and cutting off its lateral feeders as they went. When the end of their length was reached, another crosswise incision was made and the forceps were reintroduced and pushed on as before.

By this method the entire length of vein could be removed with from three to five incisions which it took only a short time to close.

In 1904 Dr. Archibald MacLaren of St. Paul told the state medical society he had seen Dr. Mayo use his new method and "The next day I saw another surgeon do the same operation, where he himself and four assistants, all at work, did about the same amount of work in four times the length of time, using the old method."

Where the varicose ulcer was extremely large or persistently refused to heal, it had to be cut out and new skin grafted onto the wound. This too was practicable because of a recent development.

Skin-grafting was first tried in 1854 but the grafts used were tiny and could be applied only one at a time, so that it might take three or four thousand grafts and from six months to three years to cover a scalp or a thigh with new skin.

Karl Thiersch of Munich proposed a new procedure in the middle seventies, but it was not generally adopted until after he described it a second time in 1886. By his method an area twenty-four inches square could be covered with new skin at one operation, with healing in from ten days to two weeks. Dr. Charlie was using the Thiersch technique frequently by 1893.

Among the uses for skin-grafting was the covering of the large denuded area left by the new radical operation for breast cancer.

Surgeons had been cutting out such a cancer when they found it, but to no avail. A quick and fatal recurrence was apparently inevitable. Then in 1888 Halsted announced his conviction that not just the growth itself but the entire breast must be removed. This complete amputation left such an enormous wound that surgeons as well as laymen shuddered away from the mutilation. But by 1894 Halsted could report that in fifty such operations there had been only three recurrences, and since it was surely better for a woman to live with one breast gone than to die intact, the use of the radical operation spread.

The Mayos adopted it promptly, having learned it firsthand by watching Halsted himself perform it, and the number of their breast operations increased from eleven in 1895 to fifty-nine in 1905, all but five of the latter being amputations by the Halsted method.

The Mayos' work in thyroid surgery began on the day in 1890 when Mr. Strain, a brawny Scotsman of some sixty years, walked into their office. Large goiters were no rarity in the Rochester vicinity, but the brothers had never seen such an enormous growth as this man had. It hung far down onto his chest and forced his head up and back as far as it could go. He had come to them because the tumor was interfering seriously with his breathing.

What could they do? Dr. Will remembered having heard

that injecting iodine into these thyroid tumors would make them shrink, so he tried it in several places. But the skin had literally had the life stretched out of it, and it broke open at the points of puncture, discharging large amounts of pus and blood.

The brothers talked over the possibilities and decided that whatever happened, that goiter had to come out; the man's condition was desperate.

They knew one big danger in removing it would be that of hemorrhage, and remembering that their father always used turpentine to check bleeding, they saturated a big sponge with turpentine and put it in a bowl handy to the operating table. Then they got Mr. Strain onto the table, gave him a little anesthetic—he could not take much—incised the skin and superficial tissues freely, and quickly scooped the tumor out with their hands.

The bleeding was terrific, for they could take time to tie off only the largest vessels. The minute the goiter was out they stuffed the sponge filled with turpentine into the cavity, sewed the skin and flesh together across it, and bandaged the wound as tightly as they dared.

They had no real hope that the man would live, but he fooled them. He recovered slowly, but he recovered. Why, only nature knew.

In a few days they reopened the incision and removed the sponge, and a couple of months later Mr. Strain was able to return to his farm, where he lived for many years, a willing witness to what those Mayos could do.

That was the beginning and the end of Dr. Will's work in the goiter field, but it was only the beginning of Dr. Charlie's. The case awakened his interest in that mysterious little body, the thyroid gland, and he began learning what he could about it and about goiters.

Mr. Strain's tumor was what is called simple goiter, an enlargement of the thyroid gland that at that time was thought to be only an inconvenience and disfigurement, unless it grew large enough to press upon the trachea and cause distress in breathing.

Theodor Kocher, the pupil of Billroth at work in Switzerland, where goiter was endemic, began to remove enlarged thyroid glands in 1878, and by the 1890s the treatment of this kind of goiter, where necessary, was recognized as a job for the surgeon.

Not that the operation was simple or safe. There was first the difficulty of controlling hemorrhage and second the vexing problem of removing just enough of the gland. If the surgeon cut away too little of it the goiter might grow again; if he took away too much the patient suffered a grievous change. She (it was most often a woman) swelled in bulk, her features coarsened, her skin got dry and rough, her hair thin and brittle, and mentally and physically she slowed down.

This condition was known as myxedema, and its developing after total thyroidectomy helped doctors reach the conclusion that it was somehow the result of atrophy or loss of the thyroid. An analogous disease called cretinism was known to occur among children, making itself evident in a marked retardation of mental and physical development.

Administering thyroid extract made from the glands of sheep to overcome the insufficiency in myxedema and cretinism was first tried in 1891, and before long it was being used in Rochester. On June 9, 1897, a little boy was brought to the Mayo offices. He was five years old but he could neither walk nor talk and he had the heavy, short body, broad, flat nose, thick lips, and moronic expression characteristic of the cretin. Thyroid extract was prescribed and the effects were swift and amazing. The boy brightened up, learned to say a few words and to walk a little, and his body thinned out and lengthened.

Then bad weather set in and the parents could not get to Rochester for more medicine, and, disappointingly, the child relapsed to his former state. But with spring and more of the pills, growth began again and continued steadily and rapidly until the boy had caught up with his years. The happy mother fumbled for words: "John was always so bloated; now he is like other children."

Adequate knowledge of the functions and diseases of the thyroid was still years away, but meanwhile the surgical treatment of goiter groped forward empirically, with Dr. Halsted, Dr. George Crile of Cleveland, and Dr. C. H. Mayo leading the way in the United States. The major problems of thyroidectomy were solved and use of the procedure increased slowly until by 1904 Dr. Mayo could report a total of sixty-eight operations for simple goiter, with only two deaths among them.

Yet he was doing only a score of such operations a year, in spite of the fact that there were plenty of goiters roundabout, since Rochester lay well within the principal American goiter belt, which stretched roughly from southeast to northwest across the Middle West. Persons afflicted with the terribly disfiguring "big neck" were familiar sights throughout the area.

The explanation for the slow pickup in surgery may be that the people and the doctors had to be educated to accept operation for what seemed more a humiliation than a danger. Or, more probably, they did not distinguish between the operative results in simple goiter and those in exophthalmic goiter.

The latter disorder, known to doctors also as Graves' disease or Basedow's disease, is characterized by a number of severe symptoms: great nervousness, rapid pulse, quick and extreme changes of mood, vomiting, diarrhea, and the two from which it was named, a goiter and protruding eyeballs (exophthalmos). The goiter was then considered merely one of many symptoms, and the disease was not associated primarily with the thyroid gland.

Writing in 1892, William Osler said that no theory proposed thus far could account for all the diverse symptoms of Graves' disease and added that in his experience rest in bed with the occasional application of an ice bag over the heart had proved the most satisfactory remedy. Operating on the thyroid gland had been tried but was not successful, he said.

A decade later some progress had been made, but real success in the treatment of exophthalmic goiter was still to be achieved.

Repetition in disease after disease emphasizes the essence of this story of the Mayo brothers' use of the new surgery: The omissions and errors of medicine had accumulated a vast reservoir of uncured illness of long standing, to which the new surgery made it possible for qualified practitioners to bring relief. And the Mayo brothers began practice at just the right moment to be the first to tap the reservoir in a wide area surrounding Rochester.

Understanding the basic importance of this circumstance in their achievement, Dr. Will once musingly remarked to a friend, "As I look back over those early years, I am impressed with the fact that much of our success, if not most of it, was due to the time at which we entered medicine."

The time *and* the place—plus, of course, the brothers' ability to grasp the exceptional opportunity these presented.

13.   *The Radius Lengthens*

THE Mayo brothers were working on the frontiers of medicine from 1890 to 1905, and the new life-saving, health-giving operations were miracles to those to whom they brought hope and happiness. For the purposes of medical science the patient might be only a set of initials identifying a group of anatomic and physiologic facts, but "H. W., male, white, aged 46" was a husband and father, a brother, a friend, a member of the community. Without this fact there is no explaining the amazing increase in the Mayos' surgical practice.

Something of all this is distilled in the recollection of a Nebraska doctor who was born and raised in the vicinity of Rochester, where a certain Irishman was one of the sights of the little community. Natives would point him out: "There is Pat Glynn," they would say. "Will Mayo cut a piece out of his stomach, and he lived!"

A deep and comforting faith in the marvelous powers of the brother surgeons in Rochester spread through the countryside like fingers of water in thirsty sand.

True, when Dr. Will first began to do major surgery, to remove the appendix or the dead portion of the bowel in strangulated hernia, the bewhiskered elder physicians of the neighboring villages shook their heads and said something ought to be done about that rash young man; it was malpractice to cut up a patient like that. But they, too, soon saw that "he lived," and their disapproval turned to incredulity, then to admiration and confidence.

Gradually a few of them learned to do for themselves some of the less radical operations, especially those of an emergency nature, but for anything really serious they continued to rely upon the Mayos.

In this matter of referred cases St. Mary's was of signal importance because it was the only hospital in the district. If a doctor had a patient who must be hospitalized there was only St. Mary's in Rochester to take him to, and if he was to enter St. Mary's he must be referred to the Mayos.

After a while other hospitals were built in the towns roundabout, often with the success of St. Mary's as the spur to action. The editor of the *Owatonna Journal* pointed out that the fares paid by Owatonnans going to the hospital at Rochester over a period of five years would build a hospital of their own. But when Owatonna got its hospital it learned, as had Winona and other towns before it, that such facilities at home could no longer keep patients from going to Rochester. Operations were new and frightening, and if the ailing man could afford it, he preferred to go over to Rochester to the surgeons of whose prowess he had heard so many tales.

The patient did not always go to Rochester; frequently his doctor summoned one of the Mayos to come to him. And time and again the operation that Dr. Will or Dr. Charlie performed on such an occasion was the first instance of major surgery in that community. In 1893 a physician from Faribault, a town of eight thousand inhabitants to the northwest of Rochester, defended himself for not using surgery in appendicitis by saying there had never been an operation in his town and he could not induce anyone to submit to one!

When someone in such a neighborhood got desperate enough to say call a surgeon, the operation was an event. The doctors for miles around assembled to witness the visitor's performance and afterward perhaps to break bread with him in the local doctor's home. Each success in such circumstances meant return calls and more patients referred to Rochester.

But this journeyman surgery was time-consuming and wearying. Dr. Will long remembered one day he had of it.

Early in the morning he started out for Plainview to the east to operate on the wife of the president of the bank for what the local physician, Dr. Slocum, diagnosed as extra-uterine pregnancy. This accident of nature, in which the development of the impregnated ovum occurs outside the uterus, usually in the fallopian tube, was one of the medical mysteries Lawson Tait cleared up, and Dr. Will had learned the surgical handling of it from Joseph Price.

When Dr. Will arrived at the patient's home he found some fifteen doctors assembled, at Dr. Slocum's invitation. The rug had been taken up and the curtains down, the floor and the walls had been scrubbed, and a quantity of hot water and clean towels were at hand. Everything was ready and waiting for the surgeon.

But when Dr. Will examined the patient he found that she had merely a lateral pregnancy, in one horn of the uterus, and he refused to operate.

It was a twelve-mile drive to the nearest railroad station, and Dr. Will got back to Rochester about noon—and found a call waiting for him to come over to Aurora to do an appendectomy. He took the next train west, but it was early evening when he reached Aurora, only to learn that the patient lived in Blooming Prairie, some ten miles farther on. It was nearly eight o'clock when he reached the bedside.

Again he found a group of doctors waiting and a room in readiness. This time the diagnosis was correct, but the patient was in no condition for surgery. Her father insisted that they had called Dr. Mayo to operate and he ought to go ahead, but Dr. Will flatly refused.

As he turned to go he felt tired and discouraged; such a futile, wasted day!

Then a neighbor standing near by spoke to him. "Doctor, you have an old friend here in town who would like to see you. Do you remember the girl from Blooming Prairie you operated on a year or two ago?"

When he gave the name, Dr. Will did remember. She was the patient a German doctor had brought to Rochester, a little girl eight or nine years old, "the thinnest creature you ever saw, about half an inch thick." Yes, Dr. Will remembered her very well, for she was one of the first persons he had operated on for stomach ulcer. He remembered how frightened she was, how her father hung onto her while she took the anesthetic, and how her mother stood outside in the corridor crying loudly while he did the operation.

He drove over with the neighbor and was welcomed without reserve. The father hugged him, the mother kissed him, and the little girl, healthy and robust-looking now, kissed him too. Then they got out a bottle of wine to celebrate his visit.

Dr. Will was deeply touched, and felt a warmth that was not of wine. The day had been hard and disappointing, but this was reward enough.

Sometimes, of course, a case was referred to the Mayos reluctantly and the referring doctor was not happy when they did what he could not do, especially if the remedy was a simple one requiring ingenuity rather than surgical skill. But the Mayos handled referred cases tactfully and never showed up a local doctor's mistakes or incompetence if they could help it.

In one instance, a man in a town not far from Rochester injured his hand badly and called in the family doctor, whose name may be Smith, a fine old man, one of the pioneer doctors of Minnesota, and a highly respected practitioner in the community. Dr. Smith prepared to amputate the hand. But the injured man's brother interfered. He was going to take his brother over to the hospital in Rochester.

When the Mayos examined the hand they saw there was no need for amputation; it was already getting better. But they gave a thought to old Dr. Smith. Redressing the wounded member, they told the patient that since Dr. Smith had seen the hand the previous day they would have to call him in for his opinion. So Dr. Smith was credited with having helped to save the hand and he was pathetically grateful to Dr. Will and Dr. Charlie, saying they had saved him from ruin in his community.

The brothers' policy in such instances was determined partly by their realization that keeping the friendship and confidence of their colleagues was to their own advantage but mostly by the lesson in professional solidarity they had learned from their father: "I did it for the profession, not for him."

Professional solidarity suffered somewhat in this period from the practice of fee-splitting, which grew up with specialization, when the general practitioner began sending his patients, not to the most competent specialist he knew, but to the man who paid him the biggest commission.

In 1900 two members of the Chicago Medical Society, wishing to expose the extent of this racket in their city, sent to all its leading surgeons a letter that purported to come from a country doctor and asked what share of his fee the specialist would give for a patient. When the answers, with names attached, were published in the newspapers, the scandal shook the city.

The society's members were particularly annoyed because John B. Murphy, whom they were accusing of all the unethical practices in the medical calendar, was among those who had peremptorily refused to make any proposition. In the end the society, to its discredit, disciplined the two men who had concocted the hoax and let those who had revealed themselves as fee-splitters go scot-free.

This episode brought the problem into the open throughout the country, and it got a thorough airing at the annual session of the Minnesota State Medical Society that year. Who was to blame for the pernicious practice? The general practitioner said it was the fault of the specialist, who charged so much that the patient had no money left to pay the family doctor. The specialist retorted that it was the other way round; the local doctor bled his patient white without doing him any good, so that the specialist had to give his services free of charge. The younger men blamed the older for setting a bad example, and the older men accused the younger of splitting fees because they were unwilling to work up a practice slowly, as their elders had done.

Finally Dr. A. S. Adams of Rochester got the floor. He was bewildered by all this argument that took the existence of fee-splitting for granted. He had practiced medicine next door to surgical specialists for fifteen years, he said, and never once had they so much as intimated that they would give him a commission of any sort for placing a patient in their hands.

Dr. Adams was speaking of the Mayos. They considered the barter in sick men a damnable business and never hesitated to say so, but Dr. Will once pointed out that they could not claim uncommon virtue for this. They had never lacked patients, had never been forced to struggle with competitors for enough cases to get started on, and so "were never tempted into unfair practices that competitive medicine sometimes appears to force on very excellent men."

The practitioners in Olmsted and adjoining counties who had formed the habit of going to Rochester to watch Dr. Mayo operate when the Old Doctor began his work in surgery kept it up after the sons took over the operating, and they were always made welcome. At first the brothers sent out postcards to the doctors roundabout whenever some operation of unusual interest was scheduled, but soon the doctors began dropping in whenever they wanted to, and items like these became frequent in the Rochester papers:

Drs. Dixon and Holoran of Chatfield and Dr. Bigelow of Dodge Center were in the city yesterday to attend a clinic at St. Mary's Hospital.

Doctors Wright of Kasson, Adams of Elgin, Chamberlain of St. Charles, and Dugan of Eyota attended a clinic at St. Mary's Hospital yesterday.

When the Mayos were ready for expansion beyond the radius of team-and-wagon travel, the rails were ready to carry the surgeons out and the patients in.

Until late in the century there was only one railroad through Rochester, the Winona and St. Peter division of the Chicago and Northwestern Railroad, but that ran in the right direction, east and west through southern Minnesota into the Dakotas, with extensive branches south into Iowa. The train connections left something to be desired, and the feeder lines could hardly be said to form a network in the hinterland, but "the cars" to Rochester were within reasonable reach of anyone willing to juggle timetables and spend a few tedious hours between trains at the junctions.

Providing care for injured employees and passengers had been no great problem for railroads in the well-populated East, but when the rails plunged into the wide open West the companies found themselves faced with the task of providing their own medical services. So they equipped each train with an emergency chest of medical supplies and taught their trainmen the rudiments of first aid. And they named a railway surgeon at each station to whom accident victims could be taken or who could be summoned to the scene of a disaster, district surgeons to be called for serious cases on each division, and a full-time chief surgeon to keep a supervisory eye on the entire network.

The companies built their own hospitals where necessary, but they preferred to pay for accommodations in existing institutions wherever there were such. The building of St. Mary's Hospital quickly brought to Dr. W. J. Mayo an appointment as local surgeon for the Chicago and Northwestern road. He was required by his contract to provide a competent substitute whenever he was not available, and where could William James find a better substitute for himself than Charles Horace?

The fees allowed for the work were low but the appointment carried the valuable perquisite of an annual pass on any company line. This greatly reduced the costs of the brothers' trips for professional study and gave them free transportation in their daily practice, on passenger train, freight car, or caboose, whichever was going their way first.

While the Mayos remained local surgeons, the railroad work was an unimportant element of their practice. Only once in three years did a serious accident occur near Rochester.

On a night in September 1892 a Chicago and Northwestern train struck a carriage in which two women were riding, one of them a visitor from New York state, Mrs. William Bennett. She was badly injured, unconscious, suffering from shock, and bleeding freely from the nose, mouth, and ear. The conductor got her on board at once and headed at full speed for Rochester, where she was taken to St. Mary's Hospital.

Both of the Mayo brothers were on the job immediately, but the injury was obviously to the skull and brain, so Dr. Charlie took charge. He opened the line of fissure in the skull, exposed the severed meningeal artery, and tied it. The bleeding ceased at once, and Mrs. Bennett soon regained consciousness and began to mend.

But back in Buffalo, New York, Mr. William Bennett was horrified when he received word of the accident. His wife seriously injured in a hick western town and at the mercy of god-knew-what kind of a doctor! As soon as the trains could get him there Mr. Bennett arrived in Rochester.

What he found there set his mind at rest, and before he left to take his wife home, he wrote a letter to the Rochester paper. It semed a miracle that his wife had recovered, he said, and nothing "but the most skillful surgery" could have saved her, he knew. So he expressed special gratitude to the train conductor "for his discriminating judgment in bringing her to this city and to St. Mary's Hospital, for I feel assured that had not such been done she would not have been spared to me."

The earlier trickle of Dakotans back to their Rochester doctors became a stream in the nineties, fed at the beginning of the decade by hard times in the Dakotas, when the boom of the eighties that populated the territory collapsed. Once again those who had trekked westward with high hopes saw their dreams in ruin at their feet.

With famine rode pestilence and with destitution came worry and illness. More and more of those who were ill remembered the Mayos back in Rochester and made every effort to get to them for treatment. So many and so insistent were they that the railroad officials wondered what manner of men these Mayos were, that sick folk should want to travel hundreds of miles to consult them and should be so certain that if they could just get back to Rochester Dr. Will and Dr. Charlie would take care of them whether they could pay the fees or not.

Alexander C. Johnson, the special agent who was managing the company's philanthropies, authorized free transportation and food on the way for those who wanted to go to Rochester but could not scrape together the price of a ticket. And often he added a few dollars from his own pocket to see them through.

The hard times passed, but going to the Mayos had become a habit, particularly with those needing surgery. When the superintendent of the Dakota division of the Chicago and Northwestern road felt ill, he boarded his private car and ordered the engineer to take him to Rochester, where his appendix was removed. When the son of South Dakota's governor developed appendicitis Pierre doctors sent for one of the Mayos to perform the operation.

Meanwhile Dr. Will had become district surgeon for the Minnesota division of the railroad, and two years later for the Dakota division as well. He, or his brother substitute, was called to the scene of any major accident along the line in either district, and though such occasions were not numerous they were dramatic.

The message would come in: *Tornado derailed passenger train at Owatonna; five killed and twenty injured. Dr. Mayo at once.* And away he would go, on a special train or riding in the cab of a detached engine, with all tracks cleared for him.

Special trains and the right-of-way were soon given him and Dr. Charlie for any emergency trip, whether on a company case or not. Just as the liverymen used to turn aside into snowdrifts to clear the road for the Old Doctor, so now passenger trains waited in the station and freights took to the sidings to keep the tracks clear for the sons on their errands of healing.

When Mr. Johnson finished his work in South Dakota he became the company's general agent at Winona, and when his wife was seized with acute appendicitis he too wanted Dr. Mayo. Since the next train was not due at Winona for several hours, he wired an engineer and a fireman at Dodge Center to detach the engine from a special train standing there, proceed with all speed to Rochester, pick up Dr. Mayo, and bring him to Winona.

Dr. Will was waiting at the station when the locomotive

with caboose attached pulled in. He swung aboard, and "At 11:04 p.m. the train plunged out into the night, wound its way down among the hills and arrived in Winona at ten minutes past the hour of midnight, having made the entire run of fifty miles over heavy grades and around sharp curves in just one hour and four [*sic*] minutes. This is twenty-six minutes faster than the quickest time made by the lightflyer, the fastest train on the line."

That made a story for the trainmen to tell in the yards or at home when the day's run was over.

There were many such: the time they carried to Rochester the young woman who shot her little brother by accident and then turned the gun on herself in remorse; or that helpless paralytic, Sister Martha, who came on a cot all the way from Ironton, Ohio, where not even the Cincinnati doctors had been able to find out what was wrong with her, though the Mayos located her trouble and had her getting better within a week; or that nine-year-old John Lewis from Butte, Montana, who couldn't swallow even milk and was so thin and sick they had to carry him on a pillow, but who was running about as lively as a cricket when they took him home a year later.

And there was the time a young mother in Mountain Lake, one of the German Mennonites from Russia who settled there, put her little boy on the train and asked the trainmen to take him to Rochester. The little fellow was almost blind, only six years old, and couldn't speak a word of English. His mother couldn't afford to go with him, but she fixed him a basket of food, and across his front she pinned a big sign, "Take me to St. Mary's Hospital."

When the conductor set him off at Rochester, the people at the depot couldn't believe he'd come all that distance alone. A hackman took care of him, and drove him right out to the hospital.

With incidents like these for the trainmen to talk about, it was not mere coincidence that there soon began to appear on the Mayo records patients identified as "engineer from

Omaha," "railroad man from La Crosse," "dispatcher at Dubuque."

Nor were trainmen the only ones from beyond the state. As early as 1893 St. Mary's was admitting patients from Illinois, Kansas, Missouri, Nebraska, New York, and Ohio as well as the nearer Iowa, Wisconsin, Dakota, and Montana. Those from the more distant states at this early date were mostly members of the nationwide Catholic church or relatives and friends of pleased Minnesota patients.

The Mayo brothers were willing to treat the poor without charge, but it was not by so doing that they were able to expand their facilities and activities. There had also to be men and women who could afford to pay the surgeons' fees as well as the costs of the trip and the expenses of residence and hospitalization. If agriculture in the Middle West had not got out of the doldrums it was in during the 1870s and 1880s, the development at Rochester could not possibly have occurred on the scale it did.

Solutions of the farmers' problems took time, but they were under way in the southeastern counties of Minnesota by 1890. At Rochester blooded livestock was rapidly taking the place of primary importance, which wheat had surrendered. The breeding of stock, especially of fine horses, became the leading enterprise of Olmsted County, and Rochester became the port of call for buyers from Chicago and eastern centers. It was called "the Lexington of the Northwest," and Mr. Blickle, the town jeweler, designed for sale to visitors a souvenir spoon on which was engraved a horse's head within a horseshoe.

The panic of 1893 and the subsequent depression only interrupted the general improvement in economic conditions, and by 1900 the hard times were entirely forgotten. In that year Rochester was jubilant about its need for more laborers, about its many new stores and busy old ones, and its lack of vacant storerooms.

The Mayo practice was already large enough to be responsible for some of this activity, but not for all of it. It was

largely a reflection of improving economic conditions in the
country roundabout. The census of 1900 showed Olmsted
County to be one of the richest agricultural counties in the
United States, flourishing on its production of cattle, pigs,
sheep, butter, flax, and small grains.

This was a remarkable change from the conditions that had
aroused the wrath and sympathy of the Old Doctor a few
decades before. The developments responsible for it were oc-
curring in varying degrees throughout the Middle West. The
western farmer was entering upon a period of prosperity.

In Minnesota itself the timber counties to the north were
still basking in the glow of lumbering's golden age, and the
lumbermen were going exuberantly about their stripping,
slashing business, excusing the destruction they wrought by
pointing to the taxes and wages they paid, the market they
provided for agriculture and industry, and the useful boxes and
barrels, houses and barns their lumber built.

In the north also the richest iron ore deposits of the American continent were being uncovered, to pour wealth into the
coffers of eastern financiers but in the process to bring new
communities into being with phenomenal rapidity. Towns
sprang up on the iron ranges like mushrooms, and the entire
northeast of Minnesota was turned from wilderness into settled
territory almost overnight. The population of Duluth jumped
from three thousand to thirty-three thousand in a single
decade.

In Minneapolis and St. Paul commercial, industrial, and
financial activity was humming. As the result of a revolution
in milling machinery and methods and of the quantity of excellent hard spring wheat at its door, Minneapolis was attain-
ing preeminence as the flour milling center of the world, from
which Pillsbury's Best and Gold Medal flours were being advertised into every kitchen and the slogan "Eventually—Why
Not Now?" was being added to the parlance of the nation.

Only at first glance do such developments seem far from

the story of two doctors in a small town in the southeastern corner of the state. For it was these developments that enabled thrifty farmers, laborers, and professional men to build better homes, buy better furniture and clothes, send their sons to high school and the state university—and finance a trip to Rochester for expedient physical repairs.

All these factors—the new surgery, railway transportation, economic betterment in the surrounding community—help to explain how the Mayos developed at Rochester a second center of surgery in Minnesota. But it was a *second* center, for patients from all over the state went or were sent to consultants in the Twin Cities too.

Why then was it not one or two Twin City surgeons who developed an international reputation? Why was it not Minneapolis or St. Paul that drew the nation's doctors and the nation's sick to Minnesota? Why did Rochester become America's surgical mecca?

Individual ability is not the whole answer, for there were men of commanding intellect and skill in Minneapolis and St. Paul too. Perhaps they lacked the drive, the unwearying energy, the single-minded application to the task of the moment that went hand in hand with ability in the Mayo brothers, but certain other differences mattered quite as much.

Each of those men worked alone. If he had a partner it was only for the convenience of sharing an office; his practice remained his own. The partnership was never a close-knit working team in which each member was an alter ego, a second brain and pair of hands, an equally able and acceptable substitute for the other.

Also, the patients going to the Twin Cities were distributed among many practitioners who were competing among themselves, in friendly fashion perhaps, but competing nonetheless. No one of the surgeons, no two of them, stood out on the horizon as the one sheltering tree on a broad, level landscape.

Then too, the hospitals at which those men worked were public institutions maintained by the city, a church, or a medical school, and many of the patients came to the institution rather than to some one doctor. Each man shared its work and the direction of its policies with others and enjoyed its privileges on sufferance.

Almost all the good Twin City men were teachers as well as practitioners, and though teaching might help to keep them alert to developments in surgery, it took their time and divided their interests. There were always lectures to prepare and classes to meet.

So the Mayos came abreast of them and then pulled ahead. No longer did Dr. Will rise in medical meetings to ask the men of the metropolis to instruct him out of their greater learning and experience; no longer did he apologize because Rochester had nothing comparable to offer. Instead, Dr. James E. Moore of Minneapolis admitted that whereas Will Mayo used to come to him for pointers, now he went to Dr. Mayo, and Dr. Dunsmoor confessed that he felt complimented when a patient from the country came to him instead of going to Rochester.

Working together and without nearby competitors, the Mayos piled up an experience of hundreds, for some operations thousands, of cases while each of their Twin City colleagues was accumulating scores or a few hundreds. And it was the volume of their work that enabled the Mayos, even forced them, to secure assistance and expand their activities; it was the volume of their experience, given their unexcelled use of it, that sent them soaring into worldwide prominence.

14. The Partnership

THE nearly four thousand operations Dr. Will and Dr. Charlie performed at St. Mary's Hospital in 1905 represented the surgical culmination of some ten or eleven thousand office examinations. Obviously they did not handle all of these alone.

Their need for assistance first made itself felt in the early nineties. Dr. W. W. Mayo was then too concerned with his political and civic activities to give dependable assistance to his sons, and they felt he had earned the freedom to come and go as he liked.

But whom should they ask to take his place?

They rejected the customary solution of taking into the office some fledgling just out of medical school, because it was not a lackey they wanted, not just a medical odd-job man, but a responsible partner who could contribute positively to the practice.

For some time they had remarked that they were seldom called to see a patient in the vicinity of Eyota and Dover except by the local doctor himself. Apparently Dr. Stinchfield was able to satisfy his patients and retain their confidence. And that was the sort of man the Mayos were looking for.

Early in 1892 they asked Dr. Stinchfield to become their partner and he accepted.

Dr. Augustus W. Stinchfield was then fifty years old, a man of short, spare figure, with the courtly manner and distinctive costume of the practitioner of the old school. Born in Maine and graduated from Bowdoin College in 1868, he had gone west to practice, opening an office in southern Missouri first, then in Dundas, Minnesota, and finally in Eyota, where he had

been living for eighteen years. He had built up a large local
practice and a reputation throughout Olmsted County second
only to that of the Mayos.

In preparation for his coming the Mayos enlarged their
offices in the Cook Block, building a stairway to the second
floor and renting additional space there.

Edith Graham was still serving the Mayos as anesthetist,
office nurse, and general bookkeeper and secretary. She was a
small, sprightly young woman, so attractive that the doctor
to whom she was assigned on her first case in Chicago refused
to accept her because she was too young and beautiful for a
nurse. Dr. Charlie found her a good and gay companion outside as well as in the office and gradually came to spend most
of his leisure hours in her company.

His favorite pastime at the moment was bicycling, so Edith
Graham learned to ride too, and part of their courtship took
place on bicycle trips for two.

They were married in April 1893 in a simple ceremony at
the Graham home south of Rochester. Hurrying out to the
house on foot, Dr. Charlie tried to leap across a rivulet in
his path and fell into it, so the ceremony had to wait until
his clothes were dried out.

Mrs. Mayo joined happily and intelligently in her husband's
professional activities. Their wedding trip was a round of
eastern medical centers, and often thereafter Mrs. Mayo accompanied her husband to conventions and on his observation
jaunts. She went with him to visit hospitals and clinics, met
his doctor friends, and quickly made them hers as well.

At the time of his marriage Dr. Charlie was living with Dr.
Will and his wife in their home on College Street, and he and
Edith now bought the property next door, tore down the old
house on the lot, and built themselves a fine new one, the one
so long known affectionately to Rochester as "the red house."

Enthusiastically the brothers planned to take advantage of
the adjacency of their homes. The architect was told to draw
up plans for a covered passageway connecting the two houses

and broadening into a one-room building halfway between, which they could use for a joint study and library.

But the two wives united firmly against this idea. Will and Charlie spent all their days together and if they had a joint workroom they would spend all their evenings together too. So the brothers contented themselves with a speaking tube between their houses. When either was ready to start out in the morning, he whistled through to the house next door and the two went off together.

To replace Edith Graham as anesthetist, the brothers chose Alice Magaw, a friend of Edith's who had taken a course in nursing at the Women's Hospital in Chicago. Dinah Graham, Edith's sister, was taken on to do the office work.

There were thirteen children in the Graham family. The parents, both English born, had come from Cortland County, New York, to pioneer in Minnesota in 1856. Mrs. Graham had long been one of the community's favorite midwives and had brought two hundred and forty children into the world without losing one of them.

Christopher Graham, one of the sons, was now thirty-seven, but he had yet to find a niche that fitted him. When he was twenty-six he decided he did not want to be a farmer and went to study at the state university, where he received a bachelor of science degree in 1887. Two years of academy teaching convinced him that he did not want to be a schoolmaster either, so he entered the school of veterinary medicine at the University of Pennsylvania and received his degree in 1892.

At the time of his sister's marriage to Charles Mayo he was teaching veterinary science in the school of agriculture at the University of Minnesota. But he was not happy, for the course in physiology at the University of Pennsylvania had made him sure that he wanted to be a doctor of human medicine.

The Mayos told "Kit" that if he would go back to Pennsylvania and take the additional year of work needed for the medical degree, he could work with them when he was through. He jumped at the chance, spent the summer studying bacteriology in Dr. Hewitt's laboratory at Red Wing, re-entered the University of Pennsylvania in the fall, and was graduated the following June a full-fledged doctor of medicine.

Dr. Will and Dr. Charlie pushed him into the practice as their father had pushed them, because the time had come for them to resign the country calls to other hands. Their days were full with the work at St. Mary's Hospital, at the offices, and on calls for consultation, so as rapidly as their patients would permit they turned the local daily ride over to Drs. Stinchfield and Graham.

Most of the pregnancy cases fell to Graham, and he liked them; given his choice, he would have become a specialist in obstetrics, but developments turned him into a specialist in differential diagnosis instead.

The Mayo brothers had long appreciated the fundamental importance of diagnosis in medical practice; this was one of the lessons their father had taught them, and it was being driven home hard at every step of their advance into surgery. So often they had to grope and explore because they could not tell from examination exactly what was wrong with a patient.

How, *how*, could they distinguish between inflammation of the gallbladder and duodenal ulcer, cancer of the stomach and ulcer of the stomach, appendicitis and typhoid fever in the beginning phases?

Promising instruments and laboratory procedures for better diagnosis were beginning to appear, and the Mayos felt they must try them in Rochester. Christopher Graham had learned some of the new laboratory techniques in his medical courses, and when he was taken formally into the Mayo partnership in August 1895, he began at once to apply them—in a new laboratory that had been fitted up alongside his examining room on the second floor of the Mayo offices.

He took over the work in urinalysis and began to make a few simple blood analyses too. But the most important beginning he undertook was in gastric analysis.

By numerous experiments medical scientists had determined the chemical state to which a normal digestion will reduce a prescribed amount of food in a specified number of hours, and certain variations from that normal state were supposed to have diagnostic significance. The presence of free hydrochloric acid, for instance, was said to mean ulcer and the absence of it cancer, and this was a differential diagnosis that Dr. Will wanted especially to be able to make.

So patients with serious stomach symptoms were sent to Dr. Graham, and he fed them the prescribed rolls and water after a night of fasting, then in a few hours gave them a tube to swallow and pumped out their stomach contents for analysis.

Eagerly at first he and Dr. Will compared the results with the clinical and surgical findings, but as the number of such examinations mounted to a thousand and beyond, Dr. Will's hope waned. The acid sign was not dependable. It seemed to increase in value with the progress of the disease and to become most reliable when the case was hopeless.

Dr. Graham continued the work in gastric analysis, hoping that more precise determinations could be developed, but Dr. Will turned back to reliance on his clinical hunches and the exploratory incision.

Those were the meager beginnings of clinical pathology in the Mayo practice. Since the laboratory work was necessarily incidental in Dr. Graham's day, he never became expert at it and in a few years resigned it to other hands. But he had started it.

The most useful of all aids to diagnosis made its appearance in the world at about this same time. In December 1895 Wilhelm Conrad Roentgen, a German physicist, announced to his scientific brethren "a new kind of ray" that he had discovered by accident a month before. He knew so little about it that he called it the X ray, but he did know it could penetrate clothes and flesh and sensitize a photographic plate to make a picture of the internal structures of the body.

The news of Roentgen's discovery spread rapidly and the

people responded to it with indignant alarm. Morality brigades were organized for militant defense against this threat to decency and privacy; an English manufacturer made a quick fortune from the sale of x-ray-proof underwear; New York state considered legislation against "the use of X rays in opera-glasses in theaters." And in Rochester the public was warned that salesmen and merchants would soon be using x-rays to pry out the minds and habits of prospective customers.

Gradually, with some measure of disappointment, people learned the limitations of the x-ray, and although for years the new device attracted unbelievably long queues at fairs and exhibitions, the practical use of it was left to the physician and the surgeon.

Two months after Roentgen's announcement Dr. J. Grosvenor Cross, the son of E. C. Cross, bought an x-ray machine for his office, and before long the Mayo brothers had an occasion to test it out.

A little boy who had swallowed a vest buckle was brought to the office. It would help in deciding how best to remove it if they could know just where in the esophagus it was lodged and in what position it was lying, so they went over to see whether Cross's x-ray machine could tell them.

The x-ray picture showed the buckle in remarkably clear outline, with the prongs pointing upward, and Dr. Charlie therefore made an incision into the esophagus and pulled the buckle out blunt end first.

During the next three years Dr. Cross did a considerable amount of x-ray diagnosis for the Mayos, but in 1900 the brothers bought a machine for themselves.

The latest model, it was an imposing apparatus fitted with a number of connections that served no purpose except to flash lights and throw off sparks to impress the patient. Such theatrical "hooey," as he called it, filled Dr. Will with contempt, and after he and Dr. Charlie had experimented to find out what was essential and what was added merely for dramatic action, they called in an electrician to replace the latter with wooden plugs.

As the number of operations mounted, it became an impracticable expenditure of time and ability for Dr. Will and Dr. Charlie to serve as each other's assistant. So they combined their efforts in fewer and fewer instances, until finally the separation of their operating schedules was virtually complete.

That it was Sister Joseph the *nurse* who became the surgeons' first regular assistant bespeaks the informal atmosphere that prevailed. But why should she not? She was an exceptional woman, highly intelligent, and possessed of executive ability of an unusual order, as she was demonstrating in her management of the hospital. She soon acquired a remarkable understanding of surgical procedures and could often guess the surgeon's intentions before he voiced them. Her fingers were nimble, their touch light, and her hands were so tiny that she could sometimes get them into parts of the body the surgeon could not reach.

Dr. Will never hesitated to credit Sister Joseph with a substantial share in his success. He always ranked her an easy first among his assistants, though he later had many good ones with medical degrees.

In the summer of 1897 the Mayos hired T. R. Spillane, formerly the head of the male nursing staff at the state hospital for the insane, to relieve them of some of the routine tasks in pathology—such as counting gallstones!—and a few months later Dr. Charlie chose Dr. Gertrude Booker, a recent graduate of the University of Minnesota, to help him at the office. He taught her himself how to test eyes and fit glasses, and she soon took off his hands all the work of refracting.

By this time, too, orderlies and flitting summertime interns were no longer help enough in the hospital; someone was needed in permanent residence, and the right man might also take over the work of gastric analysis to relieve Dr. Graham.

The right man proved to be Melvin C. Millet, a school-

teacher turned doctor with a degree from the University of
Minnesota, who had practiced for several years at Dover and
was now at Le Roy. In both locations he had called the Mayos
to do his surgery and they knew he was interested in physiological chemistry and well versed in the techniques of gastric
analysis.

Dr. Millet took up residence at St. Mary's Hospital in
November 1898 and made himself generally useful, relieving
the Mayos of the need to answer night calls and acting as
Dr. Charlie's assistant in the operating room. After a laboratory had been fitted up for him in the basement of the hospital, he also took charge of gastric analysis. And he was soon
deep in the mysteries of urinary disease.

Dr. Will was doing the partners' surgery of the kidneys and
ureters and knew their work was weak in that field. The possibilities of exact diagnosis in renal disease had been greatly
increased by several inventions, chief among them the cystoscope, an instrument that enables the physician to see into the
urinary bladder and even to do some kinds of direct treatment through its tube. Though it had been available since
1877, the cystoscope was not widely used because most practitioners had neither the time nor the occasion to become skilled
in handling it.

At Dr. Will's suggestion, Dr. Millet turned his attention to
this undeveloped field. He mastered the use of the cystoscope,
and even made some important improvements in it. He learned
other new techniques of diagnosis, such as the "separation of
the urines," by which the secretion of each kidney was examined separately to determine which organ was diseased.

The Mayos gave him every encouragement, even sending
him to London for a year's study of methods in use there. And
they were rewarded by seeing diseases of the kidney climb
gradually into place alongside gastric ulcer, gallstones, and
goiter as a field in which the Rochester doctors were known
to be especially proficient.

Dr. Millet remained in charge of gastric analysis, but he

asked to be released from his work in the operating room. He wanted to give up residence at the hospital too, because he was planning to be married. Consequently he was promoted from resident physician to attending physician, and his place at the hospital was taken by the first regular intern. Thereafter two or more interns were appointed each year, to serve as Dr. Charlie's assistants among other duties, while Sister Joseph continued to work with Dr. Will.

Dr. Charlie needed his own anesthetist too, and the brothers thought the same person might take charge of the work in pathology, which was in danger of being neglected in the rush. For this combination of duties Dr. Ochsner recommended a young woman who had made a special study of anesthesia in his operating room the year before, and Dr. Isabella Herb took up her duties in Rochester in November 1899.

The next addition to the staff, in 1901, came about as a result of a call for consultation from Dr. Albert Plummer of Racine, Minnesota. When Dr. Will arrived he found Dr. Plummer in bed with a cold and unable to keep the appointment. But Henry would go with Dr. Mayo to see the patient, said Dr. Plummer, referring to his son, who was in practice with him.

Soon Henry appeared, with a microscope in his hand, and he and Dr. Will started on the hour's drive to the patient's house.

"A slender, eager boy, dreamy appearing, full of ideas and ideals, his thought rushing ahead of his language, which one or two sentences behind, was attempting to keep up." So Henry Plummer seemed to Dr. Will that day.

He had known the boy before, for Plummer had spent several summer vacations at St. Mary's Hospital during his school days, first at the University of Minnesota and then at the Northwestern University Medical School, from which he had graduated in 1898. But not until that day did Dr. Mayo learn what young Plummer was really like.

The patient they were going to see was suffering from leukemia, and during the ride they discussed the chemistry and physiology of the blood. Later, at the bedside, the young man took a drop of blood from the ear of the patient and another from the ear of the hired man and demonstrated to Dr. Will the microscopic differences between them. On the way home he continued to talk about the blood.

"I was overcome that this gangling boy should know so much about the blood, and I so little," confessed Dr. Will.

When he got home that night he said to Dr. Charlie, "That son of Dr. Plummer's is an extraordinary young man. I believe we ought to get him up here to take charge of our laboratories; he would do us a lot of good."

Dr. Charlie agreed, and a few weeks later Henry Plummer joined the staff in the Masonic Temple offices.

That event must be red-starred in any history of the Mayo Clinic. Dr. Will Mayo himself said the hiring of Henry Plummer was the best day's work he ever did for the Clinic. There was genius in the man, with the eccentricity that often accompanies it, and both contributed mightily to the development at Rochester.

Dr. Plummer took over the supervision of the clinical laboratories and quickly brought their methods and apparatus up to date. He also took charge of x-ray diagnosis and built it solidly into the structure of the practice. But he steadfastly refused to let anyone think of him in the slightest degree as an x-ray or laboratory technician. He considered the whole of medicine his province, and he would not content himself with just a *piece* of it.

Another medical student who haunted the operating rooms of St. Mary's during the summers was Edward Starr Judd, the son of a Rochester businessman who had got his start as a grain dealer in the heyday of wheat. Starr, as he was called, had begun to work at the hospital during his high school days, doing odd jobs for the sisters. He made the acquaintance of surgery, fell in love with it, and took Dr. W. J. Mayo for his hero.

Talking over the events of the day with his mother, he would say, "Why, I'd rather be a Dr. Will than be president of the United States."

When Starr graduated from the University of Minnesota medical school in 1902, he was appointed to an internship at St. Mary's and quickly attracted Dr. Charlie's special notice. He was a quiet chap, but he was an untiring worker, utterly absorbed in surgery. And he had the gift. One showing was all he needed to learn any procedure, and he would be doing it with great skill in an amazingly short time. With training and experience he would make a superb surgical craftsman.

Up to this time the Mayos had chosen partners and assistants who could relieve them of the nonsurgical phases of the practice, while they kept the operating entirely in their own hands. But they knew they would shortly face the necessity of employing an associate surgeon. Young Judd seemed a possibility. If he continued to work with Dr. Charlie he would be able to take over a share of the operating a few years hence when the need arose.

So when his year's internship ended, Dr. Judd was made a member of the staff, serving as Dr. Charlie's first assistant in the mornings and helping at the offices in the afternoons. He developed according to their expectations and the next year was encouraged with the title of junior surgeon, though he continued to act principally as Dr. Charlie's assistant for several years longer.

Dr. Judd's appointment as junior surgeon coincided with a further enlargement of St. Mary's Hospital.

In 1897 the Sisters of St. Francis had added a four-story unit to the west of the original building to raise the capacity to one hundred and thirty-four beds, thinking this would surely take care of all demands for some time to come. But before the carpenters had gone, the new rooms were nearly filled.

Now the overcrowding had again become insupportable. Patients sometimes had to wait days for their operations be-

cause there was no hospital bed available for them. So the
Sisters of St. Francis once more called in the architect and
the contractor, and the third addition to the hospital was completed in 1904.

The new four-story east wing brought the capacity up to
one hundred and seventy-five beds and provided spacious new
quarters for the surgeons: two operating rooms connected by
a small dressing and sterilizing room, and near them a comfortable lounge for visiting physicians.

Meanwhile Dr. Will and Dr. Charlie had paused to take
stock of their position and make some decisions for the future.

The two men had only one bank account between them. All
they earned went into it, and whatever either wanted—for
travel, homebuilding, clothes, food, fun, everything—he took
from it without any accounting to the other. What was left
over at the end of the year they divided equally.

This single pocketbook supplied them well. Their homes
were among the largest and most comfortably appointed in
Rochester, jointly a center of the community's social life. The
two men and their wives had become members of a sociable
crowd, and they went out often for dinner and an evening
of dancing or card-playing. But the brothers were finding this
a drain on their time and strength, conflicting with the demands of their work. If they were to have any home life at
all, something had to be given up. And it could not be their
work.

Their wives agreeing, reluctantly perhaps, the Mayos withdrew from the social round that occupied their friends.

"We knew they wouldn't mind much," said Mrs. C. H.
Mayo. "We were so often late for their dinners or had to
leave in the middle of an evening, because Charlie would get
a call. And Charlie never cared much about playing cards. He
wasn't as bad a player as he let on, but he wouldn't bother
to put his mind to it."

The Mayos continued to entertain in lavish style, with parties that were the highlights of the Rochester social season. Two or three times a year one or the other of the two houses was thrown open to seventy-five, a hundred, or even three hundred guests, for a reception, a musicale, or an evening of dancing. Those were the formal occasions; a "dinner for fifty intimate friends" was informal.

For recreation at home there was a well-equipped game room in each house. Dr. Charlie, having injured his arm one season in a fall from a bicycle, gave up cycling as too dangerous for a surgeon, but he found a new plaything in the horseless carriage. He bought the first one, steam-driven, and the second one, gasoline-powered, to appear in town. Dr. Will still preferred the horse and buggy and treated himself to the finest that money could buy.

Summers found the Mayos at their lake cottages near Oronoco, but the men drove back and forth to Rochester every day. On the lake they had a sailboat named *Ariel,* a steam launch, and a motorboat—for Dr. Charlie to tinker with and Dr. Will to ride in, for the elder brother was already feeling some of the need for motion while resting that was characteristic of him in later years.

Their families were coming along too. Dr. and Mrs. W. J. Mayo had lost several babies, two boys among them, but they had two daughters, the elder soon to enter finishing school at Bryn Mawr and then go on to Wellesley College. Dr. Charlie's family numbered two girls and a boy and was still growing.

The Mayos had done well for themselves. They had all their idea of abundant living demanded and they had started a substantial life insurance program to take care of the future. Yet they had a sizable surplus on hand and their income was increasing rapidly. They wondered what they ought to do about it?

Their father had so filled them with the idea that no man has a right to great wealth while others are in poverty that they regarded their growing bank balance with uneasy minds.

The size of their income was due to the volume of their business, not to exorbitant charges, for they kept to the schedule of fees customary among their colleagues. They were always willing to adjust these fees for any patient who could not afford to pay them, even to the point of making no charge at all. As they went through the day collecting from the patients they saw, they merely stuffed the money into their pockets, and when they came to the bedside of a person worried about making ends meet, they dipped into those pockets to leave a bill or two in his hand or under his pillow.

If they were convinced of a man's need they were as likely as not to give *him* the amount of their fee, or more, and they lost surprisingly little money that way, they found, for what they gave came back after a while; men would come in to repay them long after they had forgotten the giving The tales of their generosity spread through the countryside, multiplying with the years.

But if the Mayos were not shylocks, they were certainly not suckers either. They saw no reason why a man who could afford it should not pay a reasonable amount for their serv· ices. Surely his life and health were worth as much to him as a new horse or an extra suit or a hunting trip' That the doctor should sell his services cheaply was not to the advantage of the profession, nor in the long run of the patient either The doctor must earn enough to pay for good equipment and finance study and travel if he was to give the patient the best medical care available.

The brothers talked about this problem a great deal for almost a year, sometime between 1898 and 1900 And from their talking emerged certain policies, not new, most of them. but crystallized and definite

They would make no charge to other doctors, nurses, ministers, and missionaries, or to educators or state employees whose salaries were small. They would collect the usual fee from those who could pay it and from others in accordance with their ability to pay, but never would they knowingly let their bill become an economic burden to any patient. They would never sue to collect a fee or accept in payment a note or a mortgage or money raised by a mortgage.

Above all, they would never let financial considerations influence the degree or kind of care they gave. A man's income should determine only what he paid; it should have nothing whatever to do with the quality of the medicine and surgery he got.

In the use of their earnings they would always put the improvement of facilities and personnel first. The professional men who worked with them, either as partners or as employees, would be generously paid, and there would be enough of them to allow each man time for self-improvement. They would finance observation journeys for the others as well as for themselves, because it was a necessary investment in the betterment of the practice.

As to their growing personal income, solemnly they vowed to set aside one half of it that year and as much each year thereafter as they could. One half or less would suffice for themselves and their families; of the remainder they would consider themselves only the trustees. They would invest it to the best of their ability, and someday they would find a way to return it to the people, from whom it came.

For a time the brothers managed their own investments, and being casual and naive about it, they suffered some heavy losses. And sometimes they got into company they did not like.

One time Dr. Will put some money into a chain of banks a Rochester man was establishing to serve the new communities in the Dakotas. In due time the stockholders assembled for the annual meeting, and the banker with satisfaction reported a wonderfully successful year. He had earned them twenty-two per cent on their investment. Those westerners needed money so badly they were willing to pay any rate of interest to get it.

This had an unpleasantly familiar sound to Dr. Will. It had been true in Olmsted County when he was a boy, and he had seen the effects of it in the lives of the borrowers. Abruptly he announced to the meeting that he was turning in his stock and would take just six per cent on his investment for the year, not one penny more.

Before long the brothers admitted to themselves that they were not cut out to be businessmen and decided to ask Burt Eaton to handle their savings for them.

Eaton hesitated a little but finally agreed to take on the job. He never forgot how Dr. Will then walked over to the office safe, took out a bundle of papers, tossed them over to him, and said, "For God's sake, take them."

There was no inventory, no record of the interest paid or due, just the certificates, and it took Eaton a year to weed out the poor choices and assemble a list of gilt-edged securities. He made it his business from then on to watch the Mayos' personal account, and when it got up to twenty-five thousand dollars, he would "swipe it for the investment account" and buy more securities.

Dr. Will and Dr. Charlie never asked for an accounting but Eaton thought they ought to have one, so he sent them a copy of the inventory each year, until one time some clerk in the office opened the letter by mistake, and spread all over town the news of how much the Mayos were worth. After that Eaton merely jotted down the results of the inventory on a slip of paper and gave it to Dr. Will personally.

With a glance so indifferently brief as to exasperate the lawyer, who was proud of the job he was doing, Dr. Will would put the slip into his pocket and forget it. Mr. Eaton once saw him take it out again nearly a year later.

Not long after Mr. Eaton had taken over the financial affairs of the brothers the Old Doctor fell sick, seriously so, and though he recovered, the anxiety of the moment had given the lawyer cause for thought. If one of the partners should die, what would become of the partnership?

Eaton raised the question with Dr. Will, and made him see the possibility of an arbitrary distribution of the practice by the probate judge if the affairs of the partnership ever got into court. Drs. Stinchfield and Graham had entered the partnership on purely verbal terms, and though the men themselves might have complete confidence in each other's good faith, families and heirs are an uncertain quantity.

Together Will and Charlie worked out a general outline of their wishes. They did not want their practice to be disrupted by the death of any one of the partners; they wanted the survivors always to have unhampered control, so that the practice might continue intact; but they wanted some provision made for fair payment to a partner's heirs.

To put these intentions into legal terms Mr. Eaton drew up a contract limiting the partnership to participation in income. A retiring partner or a deceased partner's heirs should receive in liquidation of his full share in the partnership and its profits a sum equal to the amount of his income in the year preceding his retirement or death, and the survivors should continue the practice without further obligation to him or his estate.

Dr. Will and Dr. Charlie signed the document and then presented it to Dr. Stinchfield and Dr. Graham.

It was an arbitrary procedure, no matter how admirable its purpose. There could have been no objection had it been done when the men joined the firm, but they had understood that their share applied to properties and assets as well as to income. To ask them now to sign away this share in the ownership was too much, and they balked. For two years and more they refused to sign.

Then the steel in Dr. Will came out. Flatly he named the alternatives: Either you sign this contract or we dissolve the partnership now. You can then open separate offices for yourselves and we will send you what business we can.

There was no question who held the whip hand. Dr. Stinchfield signed first, and after a time Dr. Graham, protestingly. Thereafter each man joining the partnership signed the contract and understood that he was to have only a stipulated share in the income and not in the ownership.

This contract episode was an early instance in which Dr. W. J. Mayo showed the impersonality of action that later caused some people to call him ruthless. When a course of action seemed to him to be for the good of the practice and its patients, neither friendship nor family ties could turn him from it. Personal likes or dislikes had little effect on his decisions.

At the turn of the century the Mayos needed more room for their offices, and it occurred to Dr. Charlie that they could help the Masons finance a new building and in return secure the use of its first floor for their offices.

The lodge agreed to the proposal with alacrity, and within a month the plans had been drawn and the work of construction was under way. In January 1901 Drs Mayo, Stinchfield, and Graham moved into their new quarters, on the corner of Main and Zumbro streets, diagonally across from the Cook Block.

The name Masonic *Temple* and contemporary descriptions of the "handsome, three-story structure' make the new quarters sound de luxe, but pictures show an ordinary brick building, top-heavy with fire escapes on the second-story walls, surrounded by mud streets, and fronted by a row of horse-drawn hacks.

As a matter of fact, this very unpretentiousness, the unmistakable country-town surroundings, and the informality of the office methods helped to catch the fancy of the world, for it was in these Masonic Temple offices that the world made the acquaintance of the Drs Mayo.

The entrance led into a wide hallway lined with straight wooden chairs to make a waiting room, off which opened three rooms on each side. The first on the left was the library and general office, and the two behind it and the three across the hall were the examination rooms. Off to the right in an L-shaped extension were rooms for minor surgery and the laboratory work.

There was a homely bustle about the place and very little system in the way of doing things. When patients arrived they simply took chairs in the hallway and waited their turns to see one of the doctors, for there was as yet no formal receptionist to greet them, only Jay Neville sometimes, when he was not out driving Dr. Will's carriage or back in one of the offices helping Dr. Graham set a broken finger or down in the cellar firing the furnace.

Jay had begun working for the Old Doctor as a young man lately returned from the Civil War, and he had managed the Mayo farm for many years. When Dr. and Mrs. Will moved into their home on College Street they hired a Swedish immigrant to look after the place for them, but one day Jay appeared at the door and told them he had fired the Swede and was going to run things himself. He moved in and lived with Dr. Will for twenty-four years.

Pudgy and bald-headed, with a little fringe of hair around the edges, Jay was given to chewing tobacco, eating onions, and swearing, not offensively, just easily and constantly. He was fiercely loyal to Dr. Will and Dr. Charlie, but he still thought of them as the boys he had bossed on the farm. That he need take their orders seriously or fear their firing him was unthinkable.

Dr. Will did fire him, often, but Jay never paid any attention and Dr. Will did not enforce his hasty decisions.

One of Jay's many duties was to file the correspondence, and he was fabulous at the job. He simply pasted the letters end to end—as they came, alphabetically or chronologically only by chance—and rolled them into a cylinder. To find a letter he unrolled the cylinder like a scroll. Then someone showed him how druggists filed their prescriptions, and he began stringing the letters one atop another on a length of wire or heavy twine.

Shortly after moving to the Masonic Temple the Mayos decided they needed a business manager to take over the collecting, bookkeeping, banking, and payroll, and they named a layman to the post, William Graham, brother to Dr. Graham and Mrs. C. H. Mayo.

Mr. Graham's coming made little change in the method of collecting, which was highly informal. Each doctor set his own fees and took the money from those who paid on the spot, putting it in his pocket or in a table drawer to be turned over to Mr. Graham at the end of the day, together with the scrap of paper or old envelope on which he had jotted down the names of those who had not paid. Occasionally he also penciled a brief "no pay" or "could pay nothing" alongside the case history in his ledger.

Those old case ledgers are a mutely eloquent record. There they stand, shelves of them, tall, gray, cloth-bound volumes, rarely opened nowadays. The pages filled with a dimming script, much of it in pencil, evoke a picture of the busy offices with an endless stream of sick folk, worried, weary, querulous, moving through them, and the doctors listening, pondering, and deciding.

The ledgers cover the years from 1885 to 1907. There is a series for each doctor, because each man kept his own, writing four or five case histories to the page until the book was full and he called for a new one. At first a thinnish volume would last him two years or more; then it took a thicker one for a single year; and at last the thickest that could be bought was enough for only a few months, so much did the practice grow.

The records in these volumes are meager. There is a little description of physical findings, and half the time not even the diagnosis or treatment prescribed. Only rarely is there such a direct statement as "Goes to the hospital" or "Operated on next week"; more often the fact that the patient came to surgery is learned, if at all, from a note in the margin, "Died six months after operation" or "It was appendix."

For many cases the record includes only the name, date, age, place of residence, and phrases like "Complains of sciatic rheumatism," "Wants to know the cause of her sterility," "Gas on the stomach and poor sleep," or "Night terrors—wetting bed."

The comments that sometimes escaped the doctor's pencil lift the curtain briefly on comedy or near-tragedy. Dr. Graham, for instance, listed carefully the complaints detailed by a man from Sleepy Eye, then added, "Well as ever he was, so says his wife." A man from South Dakota "Thinks has been poisoned by his daughter-in-law. Bad in bowels and can't sleep. Diag.— Insane." And a patient from Canton "Feels weak, pain no particular place, some water trouble, constipated. Full of witchcraft nonsense."

Tragically numerous were the patients classed as neurasthenic or neurotic. A woman from Woodstock complained of spells of crying and screaming and "Gave me a sample of her scream," while another, from Le Sueur, was "Such a hopeless neurotic difficult to give her credit for any ailment." And a man from Lemond told a story of many fears: "Mind off— says can't tell good from bad. The cold weather makes him feel better."

To the brief account of a woman from Elkton, South Dakota, who was pregnant and so worried about it that she feared she was losing her mind, Dr. Graham added, "C. H. Mayo saw her with me."

This was an early instance of the way the Mayos' associates turned to Dr. Charlie for help with patients who needed reassurance more than medicine. For such persons his gentle, homely way eased tense nerves and distrait minds. Fully aware of the importance of emotional and mental factors in physical disease, he did not worry overmuch about scientific justification for his methods of dealing with them, preferring instead to follow the great Sydenham's rule of practice: "Whatever is useful is good."

From these years comes the story of a girl who insisted to Dr. Charlie that there was something wrong inside her head. He knew there was no physical lesion, but he knew too that it would do no good to tell her this. So he took her to the hospital, gave her some anesthetic, and wrapped a bandage around her head. When she "recovered" the quirk was gone and she was content.

The doctors' day began at seven-thirty in the morning and even then they found patients waiting, for the farmers rose early and the first train arrived in Rochester at six-thirty. Work went on without pause until seven or eight o'clock at night. The offices were open on Sunday forenoons too, for the convenience of the country folk who drove into town for church and liked to look after their souls and their bodies on the same trip.

The Mayo brothers could no longer share in the work of general diagnosing and prescribing; they had time now only for examining the patients their partners found in need of operations. Dr. Will and Dr. Charlie thus became wholly surgeons and surgical consultants.

And Drs. Stinchfield and Graham were becoming wholly diagnosticians. The medical side of the practice was decreasing fast. There was literally no room and no time for it. In the early years approximately one third of the hundreds of patients admitted to St. Mary's Hospital were medical cases; now only ten or twelve out of three or four thousand a year were medical.

This was partly because more ailments were treated surgically, but mostly because rooms at the hospital were too few for all who came and preference was naturally given to surgical cases. The others could more easily be taken care of at home if the patient was a resident or at one of the hotels or boardinghouses if he came from out of town.

But it was growing harder for the doctors to find time to visit such patients. Often they could go only after the office closed at night. Many a time Dr. Graham would get home from the office late, have a bite of supper, then hitch up the horse and go out to make some country calls. Frequently he would be summoned for a confinement and would have only an hour or two of sleep before returning to the office to begin another day.

This could not continue for long. Although no local call was ever refused, gradually most of the patients from a distance who were found to need only medical care were referred back to their home-town doctor with a report of the diagnosis made and the treatment recommended.

The medical men of the firm surrendered to this necessity reluctantly. They would have liked to follow up the diagnoses themselves, especially in unusual cases, and they knew the patient had come not just to be told what ailed him but to be cured of it. But the pressure of too many patients and too little time pushed them into concentration on diagnosis alone.

This specialization, unplanned though it was, brought excellent results. Spending all their time in interpreting the symptoms of various diseases, the Mayo partners naturally became more expert at differential diagnosis than practitioners who saw fewer patients and divided their time between examining and treating. As Dr. Graham put it, "How could we help being good in diagnosis, with all the cases we saw?"

The Mayo brothers, like Dr. Graham and Dr. Stinchfield themselves, saw this development only in its relation to better surgery. None of them yet thought of diagnosis as an independently worthwhile function; it was the handmaid of surgery. The primary function of the diagnosticians was to pick from the procession of patients passing before them those whom the Mayo brothers as surgeons could benefit.

Only young Dr. Plummer held out against this idea and its consequences. To him each patient presented a problem to be solved, and diagnosis was only the beginning; it merely unlocked the door to treatment, and treatment should be catholic, making use of *all* available methods, of which surgery was but one.

With these ideas Henry Plummer did not fit easily into the division of labor that developed in Rochester. Nor did he try to. He went his own way in his own time. And the Mayo brothers not only suffered him to do so; they encouraged him.

Dr. Charlie had good reason, for Henry Plummer's chief and most enduring interest was the thyroid gland. As a boy he had known Mr. Strain, the Mayos' first goiter patient, and the course of events in that case so impressed him that he had given particular attention to the thyroid in all his medical studies and experiments since. Now his interest coincided neatly with Dr. Charlie's, and together they were to make medical history.

The Mayo partnership and its patients had now become an inescapable feature of the Rochester scene. The practice had long been an invitation to druggists, and now that men and women were coming from farther afield it offered golden opportunities in other lines as well.

In transportation, for instance. The mile that lay between St. Mary's Hospital and downtown Rochester called for means of conveyance, and independent hackmen prospered in providing it. One of them had enough initiative to inaugurate an ambulance service in 1897.

Almost every patient who came to Rochester was accompanied by one or more relatives or friends to stand by him during the possible surgical ordeal. These people had to have places to eat and sleep, and the restaurant and hotel business boomed. Old hostelries took on new life and new ones appeared.

The Cook House, which had been such a white elephant for its owners in the seventies, was taken over in the late nineties by a Mr. Kahler and his son, formerly the managers of the Archer House in Northfield. Young John Kahler was an able hotel man, and aided by Rochester's prosperity he soon put the Cook House on its feet. Its original forty-five rooms grew to a hundred, with "the accommodations taxed every night."

The Cook House was entirely a hotel, but most of its smaller competitors became in part nursing or convalescent homes for those waiting to enter St. Mary's, those discharged from the hospital but not yet able to go home, and those receiving medical treatment only.

Hotels were too expensive for most of those whose stay must be long, and "Rooms for rent" signs began to dot the streets and boardinghouses flourished, especially in the vicinity of St. Mary's Hospital.

This growth of business possibilities in Rochester required a decision from the Mayo brothers. It was of vital concern to them that all necessary services be provided for their patients and those who came with them. And investments in such services promised good returns, which after all would accrue indirectly from their practice. Should they participate?

They decided not. "We felt that our position should be one above suspicion or selfish purpose and that neither directly nor indirectly ought we to profit from the sick who came to Rochester, except through professional fees."

In spite of indications to the contrary in this talk of restaurants and hotels, Rochester was still a small country town. Its population in 1900 stood between five and six thousand. The trade of the farmers was still its chief reason for being, and there was nothing of urban smartness about the place, either in manner or in appearance.

The best of its stores were small and cluttered, lamp-lighted and stove-heated. In any of them on almost any afternoon could be found two or three farmers' wives hanging forlornly about while their husbands topped off the trading trip to town with a spell of sociable drinking. Her shopping done, there was nothing for the wife to do but wait in some store, sitting on a packing case near the stove perhaps, trying to hush a crying baby or keep track of the restless older children, who roamed the store, poking dirty little fingers into open barrels of crackers or brown sugar.

When Rochester's newly organized women's club resolved to alleviate this situation and opened a women's rest room furnished with chairs, cradles, cots, and a cookstove, the number of visitors from the country who made use of it rose quickly to between five and six hundred a month.

Private enterprise had given Rochester the pure water supply the Old Doctor had worked for so long, and also a city telephone system. Electricity was available through a municipal plant, but only at night. The city fathers doubted there would be enough call for daytime service to justify the added expense.

In street-paving the progress was slow. Except for half a dozen blocks of the main business street, the thoroughfares were rutted lanes of dust or mud, Zumbro Street as well as the others. The need for improving the "execrable condition" of that important artery from town out to St. Mary's Hospital was often the subject of sharp comment from medical visitors. But paving waited while factions bickered about costs, the proper width, and the best wearing material.

The Mayo brothers shook their heads at such shortsightedness, for they had lately been looking at Rochester with critical eyes.

So far all their partners and assistants, with the exception of Dr. Herb, had come from southern Minnesota and like themselves were used to small towns and rural surroundings, but the Mayos knew that they would soon have to look farther afield for new men. Could they hope to persuade well-trained, capable men, able to practice successfully wherever they chose, to settle in Rochester? How would the town appear to them as a home?

A little thinking along these lines convinced Dr. Will and Dr. Charlie that it would be to their own advantage to provide for Rochester some of the improvements its citizens seemed unlikely to provide for themselves, and they decided they could afford to spend about one tenth of their income in this way.

They made their first gift to the city in 1904. One evening in July the Commercial Club sponsored a lecture by Charles

Loring of Minneapolis, a crusader for city beautification. He spoke enthusiastically of the possibilities he saw in Rochester—in the park site along Bear Creek, the lengths of riverbank winding through the town, and the hilltop behind St. Mary's Hospital.

At the close of the address it was announced that Drs. W. J. and C. H. Mayo had given five thousand dollars and John R. Cook one thousand "for the purpose of buying a park or otherwise improving or adorning the city."

At last the Old Doctor's dream was realized, for the money was used to buy the Bear Creek land. But it took the city two years and a long series of appeals to the courts to obtain title to it.

By that time the Mayos had decided on a second gift. They bought a tract two blocks long on the hilltop behind the hospital and presented it to the city, along with a thousand dollars, to which Mr. Cook again added a thousand, to be used in making it into another park. With a later addition or two this became the St. Mary's Park of today, Rochester's miniature "skyline drive."

This policy of systematic giving was the chief means of providing Rochester with facilities for recreation, education, music, and art that are unusual, perhaps unique, in American cities of its size. And the practical purpose was achieved—that good men should not be deterred from joining the Mayos by the disadvantages of Rochester as a home.

15. *Recognition Won*

IN THE mid-1890s Dr. Franklin H. Martin, professor of gynecology in the Chicago Postgraduate Medical School, attended a meeting of the Minnesota State Medical Society. As he recalled it:

A young man modestly stepped forward, was recognized by the presiding officer, and began his discussion of a paper that had been presented. His talk was very much to the point, and notwithstanding his boyish appearance, his words and manner were most impressive. He did not indulge in the usual complimentary references, and the wisdom he dispensed was too good to be true. The entire audience, including the older wheelhorses of the profession, listened with rapt attention, and applauded appreciatively as the speaker finished his terse, interesting, and definite discussion and took his seat.

A second young man, a boy in stature and appearance, addressed the audience. There was the same direct discussion with pertinent references to distinguished men whose operations he had watched, and to recent scientific articles he had perused. An occasional humorous observation brought smiles and chuckles from his attentive listeners. I was profoundly attracted to these young men, their simplicity, and their unconventional appearance.

"Who are these youngsters?" I asked of the doctor who was seated next to me. He looked surprised. "Don't you know the Mayo boys? They are two surgeons practicing in the little country town of Rochester."

My conversation with this man convinced me that the two country surgeons had already won the respect of their elder confrères in their state medical association.

The medical code of ethics does not sanction a doctor's reporting his achievements to the world at large, but it requires him to make them known to the profession, in order that "the experience of one may contribute to the instruction of all," and from the beginning the Mayo brothers gave serious attention to reporting their work in professional circles.

Writing and speaking were hard for both of them at first, and time for the preparation of papers had to be found at odd hours, which were few and mostly at night. But they forced themselves to write reports of their work in surgery for the state medical journals and societies.

Statewide recognition of their ability was swift. They were elected to one office after another in the state society, were appointed in turn to membership on the state board of health, where they served with men of their father's generation like Dr. Staples and Dr. Hewitt, and were elected to coveted memberships in the Minnesota Academy of Medicine, an exclusive fifty of the state's medical elite. And in 1892 Dr. Will was elected president of the state medical society, at thirty-one the youngest man to have held that office.

One has only to read the published *Transactions* of these medical groups to understand why the young Mayos made such an impression on their fellows. Time and again after a paper full of fumbling, rambling surmise, one of the brothers rose to explain simply and quietly, but with a barrage of names, facts, and figures, just where this procedure would work and where that, to what extent, and precisely why. Their own papers were chock-full of references to the work of other men, and of the details of anatomy, physiology, and pathology on which their opinions and conclusions rested.

They knew everything, it seemed, though they were still such boys!

They looked utterly unlike successful professional men, with their earnest, intent young faces above suits that were obviously from a small-town store and hung loose and ill-fitting on their slender frames. Dr. Will had a natural dignity of manner and an assured bearing that saved him from any appearance of naiveté, but Charlie always looked like the farmer's son come to town, uneasy in his dress-up suit and his attempts at dress-up deportment. His dark hair would not stay down, his tie was soon awry, and if his suit had a press when he left home it always lost it on the way.

Dr. Will was also the better speaker in those early years. Making the same determined effort to improve his speaking ability as to improve his surgery, he gradually evolved a formula for his papers: Begin with an arresting sentence; close with a strong summary; in between speak simply, clearly, and always to the point; and above all be brief. He heeded the maxim of the old minister to the effect that few souls are saved after the first fifteen minutes of the sermon, and he acquired a gift for compact sentences and a piquant turn of phrase well suited to his own dry humor.

The Rochester newspapers were soon happily reporting that Dr. Will Mayo was considered one of the best public speakers in the state, but even so, they showed more than a little surprise when he was invited to give the commencement address for the medical school of the University of Minnesota in 1895. That invitation usually went to some big name from the East, and it was a remarkable honor for a local man, one from downstate at that.

In giving the address, Dr. Will, in words at least, was a bit diffident. "It is customary to give some practical advice . . . but I fear that my age and limited experience do not qualify me for the task." He essayed it all the same, and the advice he gave would have point for the medical graduates of today.

> I wish to call your attention to . . . the necessity of a broad culture upon your part to enable you to sympathize with all classes and all people in the hour of their need. . . . Your study of exact methods and detail work, which has occupied your time until now, must be supplemented by a general knowledge of the lives and the work of peo-

ple in other walks of life, in order that you can meet them as patients with a certain degree of sympathy and understanding. . . . The whole tendency of modern life is toward the amplification of purely technical work. . . . It is incumbent upon you to develop a broad culture as the only means whereby you can obtain and maintain a proper appreciation of social conditions.

Dr. Will and Dr. Charlie had made their mark at home, but outside Minnesota the name of Mayo meant nothing except to a few who knew the two young doctors from the West as frequent and earnest observers in the nation's chief surgical clinics.

The brothers had been attending the conventions of the national societies regularly, but only once had either of them found courage to participate. Dr. Will loved to tell the story of that once. It was at a meeting of the American Medical Association, and the highlight of the program was a paper on the incidence of cancer presented by the surgeon general of the army. The speaker appeared, pompous and paunchy, stiff from head to toe in official regalia, with two assistants to handle his statistical charts.

The gist of his remarks was that cancer was increasing in the United States. Though it was growing more prevalent even in such a new state as Minnesota, the larger percentage was in the older communities, and there seemed to be more of it among residents in old houses than in new dwellings. The inevitable conclusion, he thought, was that cancer is an infectious disease.

The learned men of medicine who had been invited to discuss the paper agreed that it was an excellent contribution to its important subject.

In the intensity of his disagreement Dr. Will forgot his shyness and rose to his feet, protesting that there was another way of explaining those facts. When the audience became aware of what was happening—a beardless, unknown youth daring to challenge such eminent authorities—they were delighted and began to shout "Platform! Platform!" The president invited Dr. Will to the rostrum and, as he recalled it, he spoke to this effect:

> I am from Minnesota. It seems to me that this is the way it is. Cancer is preeminently a disease of forty and beyond. Only the young people who were in good enough health to struggle with the development of a new country came to Minnesota from the East, leaving the people of cancer age behind. There was therefore greater freedom from cancer in the new state. Now Minnesota is older. The young people are moving on, leaving behind a larger percentage of people in the cancer age, and we note an increase in cases of cancer just as happened in New England and the older states. As to the old houses, they are more likely to be inhabited by old people of cancer age. And anyway the question of coincidence must play a part. I am not a poker player, but I am told that a perfectly honest man may sometimes hold four aces.

The crowd laughed and applauded heartily, and for many years thereafter Dr. Will was told by men he met, "The first time I remember seeing you was when you challenged the surgeon general of the army on cancer."

That was an isolated instance, however. A biographical dictionary of the physicians and surgeons of the United States published in 1896 made no mention of either William or Charles Mayo.

It was wise of the Mayos not to rush their debut in the national arena. When the opportunity came they were ready with experience enough to take a place at once among the leaders, ready to rise, not slowly and therefore unimpressively, but like rockets.

The opportunity came in 1896, when Dr. Charles A. Wheaton of Minneapolis was chairman of the surgical section of the American Medical Association and invited Dr. W.

J. Mayo to appear on the program. Dr. Will chose his topic in the youngest field of surgery, the stomach, and with admirable restraint he stuck to his formula, even to the old minister's fifteen minutes.

Whatever the audience may have expected when it came time for Dr. Mayo to speak and they saw he was a mere youth—he looked much younger than his thirty-five years—what they got was obviously one of the best papers of the entire session. In frank wonder Dr. Alexander H. Ferguson of Chicago observed that the young man's talk was a really remarkable presentation of its subject. "I do not think that I have ever heard so much condensed into a paper occupying but fifteen minutes to read, and I congratulate the author upon the mature opinions expressed and the manner in which he states the case."

Each year thereafter Dr. Will gave a paper before the surgical section, usually on gallbladder or stomach surgery, and it was the story of the Minnesota state society all over again: The men who heard him were profoundly impressed by the extent of his knowledge and experience, in such contrast to his youthful appearance and modest manner.

Take the matter of gastroenterostomy. Probably not half the men attending the section meetings had yet seen that operation performed, and hardly more than a score had actually tried it for themselves. Yet here stood this youngster, talking with quiet authority about gastroenterostomy on the basis of *his personal experience* in twenty-five, fifty, one hundred cases —with results that not one of his listeners could equal.

Men listened in amazement and turned to ask their neighbors, Who *is* this Dr. Mayo?

Early in 1899 Dr. Will prepared a report of the one hundred and five operations he had done to date on the gallbladder and its ducts. Carefully he tabulated the statistics, computed the mortality rate in the several types of cases, and set down his observations and conclusions. Then he submitted the paper to the exclusive *American Journal of the Medical Sciences,* probably the best of the medical monthlies.

The manuscript came to the Philadelphia office of the editor, Dr. Alfred Stengel, and his eyebrows went up as he read it. One hundred and five gallbladder operations? Amazing, this Dr. Mayo. And just where is Rochester, Minnesota?

Dr. Stengel looked up the town and learned that it had fewer than six thousand inhabitants. Was it possible that a doctor in so small a western town had done so many operations in so new a field?

When Dr. Stengel inquired into the records of some of the leading Philadelphia surgeons, he found that not one of them had done anything like that amount of work on the gallbladder, and a survey made in Louisville the year before showed that all the surgeons of that outstanding southern center together had performed just one hundred and six gallbladder operations.

And this country doctor claimed he and his brother had done one hundred and five themselves! The man must be a knave. Without further ado Dr. Stengel put the manuscript in an envelope and addressed it back to the author, with "regrets."

Others too found the Mayo brothers' experience and results utterly incredible.

Dr. Carl Beck of Chicago was a Czech by birth and by training in medicine. After graduation from the German University of Prague, a period of postgraduate study at other European universities, and a turn at teaching on the Prague faculty of medicine, he moved to the United States in 1886. In the middle 1890s he began his long career as professor of surgical pathology at the University of Illinois College of Medicine and professor of surgery at the Chicago Postgraduate School.

One morning he was conducting a clinic for the benefit of practitioners attending the latter school. The principal case was a stricture of the common duct and Dr. Beck attempted to use a Murphy button to effect the union between the gallbladder and the intestines. He had such difficulty in placing the button that he finally had to give up and resort to suture anastomosis.

When the clinic was over, a short, stocky young man came up to discuss the case, and Dr. Beck soon saw that this fellow knew an uncommon lot about the operation he had been trying to do. A little sharply, Dr. Beck inquired who he was and how he came to know so much about it. Why—with an engaging smile—he was Charles Mayo. He and his brother were surgeons in Rochester, Minnesota, and they had had occasion several times to use the button in gallbladder surgery.

In Dr. Beck's own words: "I was naturally more than surprised that he should have ever attempted to operate on a gallbladder," let alone his having had "an experience much wider than my own."

Beck reported the incident to Nicholas Senn, whose assistant and protégé he had been. "Senn was astonished." He had just returned from a meeting of the American Medical Association at which this man's brother had reported cases and results "such as only very progressive surgeons with large practices could have." Senn did not believe the stories these chaps were telling; they must be stretching the truth, and it was high time someone checked up on their tales. He advised Dr. Beck to accept Dr. Charlie's invitation to visit Rochester, and investigate. Dr. Beck did so, within the week.

It took me about a day and a half to make the trip, and when I arrived I saw the most interesting conditions. I stopped at the Cook House, a very antiquated hotel in front of which was a large square with dozens of buggies and carts with their horses tied to the hitching posts. There was a large building in the square, in the basement [on the first floor?] of which were the offices of Doctors Mayo, Stinchfield, and Graham.

As I entered the office, I saw an old gentleman behind a desk covered with large books. I introduced myself to him, and with a smile he turned to a lady who was present (Mrs. Mayo) and said, "This is the man Charlie saw in Chicago."

The "boys" were not there at the moment but Dr. Beck was invited to meet them at supper at the Old Doctor's home.

The next day he made his investigation. He watched the brothers do several operations, with a skill the like of which he had seldom seen, was shown over the hospital, and met the partners in the office. The number of patients thronging the waiting rooms would have done credit to a Chicago outpatient clinic. By the end of the day Dr. Beck was a convert.

When he got back to Chicago he told Dr. Senn he was mistaken about the Mayo brothers; they were doing all they claimed and much more. They could teach a man many things and he intended to visit them often. He did so, became one of their good friends, and aided materially in spreading their reputation.

Believing waited upon seeing for many, but though they might doubt Dr. Will's figures they could hardly deny the excellence of his ideas. His papers drew the warmest kind of commendation from men whose opinions everyone respected, and tangible recognition followed.

In 1897 he was elected vice-president of the American Association of Railway Surgeons, in 1898 chairman of the surgical section of the American Medical Association, in 1899 vice-chairman of the section's executive council, and in 1900 chairman.

In 1899 he also received the accolade which above all else he had labored to deserve. Despite the high honors that came to him in later years, Dr. Will always said the proudest day of his life was the day he was elected to membership in the American Surgical Association. Only fourteen years before, as a youth just out of medical college, he had asked himself whether a small-town man could possibly achieve fellowship in that company of the surgical mighty. The small-town man

had done so, even in advance of big-town men like Drs.
Ochsner and Murphy.

Dr. Will was granted the honorary degree of master of arts
by his alma mater in 1900, "in recognition of his labors for
the advancement of the science and art of surgery," and he
was invited to address the Michigan medical school in the fall
of 1900. Other invitations to speak followed: from the surgical
section of the Suffolk District Medical Society in Boston in
February 1902, the Chicago Medical Society the next month,
the New York Surgical Association the following October, and
the New York Academy of Medicine in December.

Early in their travels to learn from others the Mayo brothers
had decided that when a man was called a liar for his reports
of success it might be worth their while to see his work. When
in their turn their word was questioned, they logically reversed
the process. They said to their doubting brethren, Come and
see.

Men who went to satisfy their curiosity returned again and
again to learn. Their enthusiasm for what they saw sent others
"to see what it was all about," and to the doctors of southern
Minnesota reported to be attending clinics at St. Mary's Hospital were added national names—and even some international.

Although American medicine was nearing the age of self-
reliance, Europe was still its great postgraduate school. Even
in surgery the universally acknowledged masters were Euro-
peans. But they were beginning to watch developments in
American surgery, reading its literature and marking its rising
stars, sometimes before Americans themselves had done so.

In the spring of 1901 Arthur Mayo Robson of England was
guest of honor at the convention of the American Surgical Association. Chief of staff at the Leeds General Infirmary, Robson was Great Britain's brightest surgical light, and his contributions in surgery of the gallbladder and the stomach were
known and acclaimed the world over. After attending the convention for which he had come, Mayo Robson took the train

west to spend a week with William and Charles Mayo before returning to England.

In May 1903 the Mayos played host also to Johann von Mikulicz-Radecki, the brilliant Pole who had been a pupil and assistant of the great Billroth and was now preeminent in visceral surgery on the Continent. He too had come to the United States by invitation, to be the featured speaker at the triennial assembly of the Congress of American Physicians and Surgeons in Washington, but he insisted on going first to Rochester to watch the Mayos at work.

American jaws dropped when these titans from abroad merely nodded to the Eastern centers and passed on across the continent to Rochester, and Robson and Mikulicz were only the first of a long procession.

The weeks immediately following Mikulicz's visit provide a good illustration of the way Dr. Will sometimes scuttled around the country when it was medical convention season.

On May 4 he went to New Orleans for the meeting of the American Medical Association, where he talked about the operation he had stumbled onto for the repair of umbilical hernia. The discussion of the paper was a contest in enthusiasm. This Mayo operation was a great boon to surgery, said Dr. Ferguson of Chicago. Yes, said Dr. Ochsner, it made such perfect use of anatomical structures that the more strain the patient put upon the repaired abdominal wall the more firmly it seemed to hold!

The enthusiasm of the surgeons communicated itself to the convention as a whole and Dr. Mayo was voted the association's crowning distinction in surgery; he was chosen to deliver the oration on surgery to the general convention the following year.

When Dr. Will was called on to speak briefly at the banquet that ended the session, Dr. Frank Billings, the great Chicago internist who was acting as toastmaster, said that Mayo was a miracle worker, and that not the least of the miracles he had worked was to make Chicago a stopping-off place on the way to Rochester, Minnesota!

That convention ended on May 8, and on May 11 Dr. Will gave "A Review of 303 Operations upon the Stomach and the First Portion of the Duodenum" before the Philadelphia Academy of Surgery. It was a real honor to be the speaker of the evening for that august body, especially when the men invited to discuss the paper included "Mr. B. G. A. Moynihan."

Plain Berkeley Moynihan he was then, not yet Lord Moynihan, "one of the greatest surgeons of this century," but he was already sufficiently challenging company to keep. He had recently succeeded to the position of Mayo Robson at the Leeds Infirmary and had been called across the Atlantic to address the convention of the American Surgical Association. He was a surgeon without a superior in craftsmanship, and a speaker whose poise, polish, and grace in diction were the despair of even John B. Murphy.

Mayo and Moynihan were to meet again in a few weeks when Moynihan in his turn made his way out to Rochester before returning to England. This was the first of many visits, and the two men became mutually admiring professional friends.

Next day the American Surgical Association and the Congress of American Physicians and Surgeons convened simultaneously in Washington, and at the congress Dr. Will scored a triumph. His version of it, given many years later, is a good story.

At this meeting the guest of honor was a German authority on gallbladder disease. He was to give a lecture on the gallbladder, and I was the American surgeon chosen to open the discussion.

While Mikulicz, Murphy and I were walking in a park before the meeting, we chanced to meet the lecturer. Mikulicz introduced me, said some nice things about me, and told the lecturer that I had done much work on the gallbladder. He snorted, "I never heard of him."

Mikulicz was embarrassed and very indignant. Murphy could hardly keep from laughing; he had to turn his face away. As we walked on, Mikulicz raged, "He is a boor, a peasant." The incident was amusing; it was not strange that he had not heard of me but it was strange that he should have said so.

In his paper the German authority reported a large number of cases with a mortality of sixteen per cent; I reported several hundred more cases, with a mortality of two per cent.

After my discussion, the lecturer was very disagreeable, said such a report could not be true. But I had another chance. In closing, I said, "We are greatly indebted to the Professor, for he has given us a knowledge of mortality in these cases which we, with our much smaller death rate in this field of surgery, could not obtain." He thought he was being complimented, looked friendly, and gave me his stiff German bow.

Unfortunately the published *Transactions* tell a more prosaic story.

Hans Kehr of Halberstadt, Germany, was the visiting authority. In his private clinic in Halberstadt he had confined his attention almost entirely to gallbladder surgery for several years and had amassed the largest series of cases on record. He was quite capable of the disagreeable deportment Dr. Will attributed to him, for even in cold print his every sentence oozes arrogance. He would not have taken kindly to any report of an achievement that surpassed his own. But Dr. Will's did not. Kehr's record was "some 800 cases," Mayo's a tabulated 547, and their mortality was about the same, three per cent in uncomplicated cases.

Kehr must have heard of Mayo previously, for he included him in the list of American surgeons to whom he paid perfunctory tribute. And the "discussion" as printed was all stodgily cut and dried, leaving no room for such a retort ideal as Dr. Will remembered.

Yet Dr. Will's story cannot be dismissed as mere wishful wit. More happened on that occasion than the published records reveal, something that caught the fancy of those present, because the episode was referred to in subsequent medical meetings and formed the core of the first layman's article on the Mayo brothers. Despite Dr. Will's previous reputation in the gallbladder field, the profession's full realization that the American Mayo could match experience and results with Europe's best dated from this occasion.

Thereafter Dr. Mayo's words on gallbladder surgery were accepted virtually as *ex cathedra* pronouncements. When Dr. Joseph C. Bloodgood, distinguished surgeon on the staff of the Johns Hopkins Hospital, was called on to discuss a paper on that subject the next year, he voiced the hope, a little petulantly, that in the future the chairman would allow him to speak before Dr. Mayo. "After him there is nothing left to say but ditto."

Returning from Washington, Dr. Mayo went to Milwaukee on June 4 to give the annual address on surgery for the State Medical Society of Wisconsin, and on June 17 he appeared as usual with a paper for his own Minnesota group.

His activity there had not slackened as his national labors developed, and the Minnesota men watched his rise with mingled surprise, pleasure, envy, and inevitably in some cases jealous resentment.

Men who had given up, or had never had, aspirations to more than local reputation gloried vicariously in their young neighbor's success. At this 1903 session Dr. A. W. Abbott of Minneapolis called attention to the honor the profession of the state shared in having Dr. Mayo named orator on surgery by the national association, and Dr. J. Warren Little said, to the accompaniment of "much laughter and applause":

It reminds me of what a Chinaman said to me in a chop

suey house a few days ago. . . . I saw on the bill of fare, "Best Dinner, $5.00." I said to the Chinaman, "What does the best dinner consist of?" He replied, "Everything better."

I was praising [Dr. Mayo's work] to a man the other day and he asked me what Mayo did that I did not do. I told him that I could tell him in no better way than to say what the Chinaman said to me, "Everything better."

Meanwhile Dr. Charlie was not just holding the fort at home; he was merely traveling in different directions. Though he would derive no less pleasure from recognition than Dr. Will, he was less impelled to strive for it. He was more easy-going, and alone would perhaps have been content with local acclaim.

He had willingly agreed that Dr. Will should represent the team before the national groups, because he knew he was not so good a speaker. Put him among a group of farmers, at the bedside of a patient, or in a small company of close friends and his tongue moved easily and well. But before a crowd he felt shy and awkward, and his low, soft voice was not good for platform talking. His natural way of speaking was a slow, comfortable drawl that seemed hesitant when stiffness before strangers deprived it of personal intimacy.

Dr. Charlie knew as many facts as Dr. Will, but he did not marshal them so well. His mind did not walk straight from this point to that, but proceeded by a kind of hippety-hop from side to side, turning off into picturesque bypaths, exploring this lane and that, covering a lot of extra territory before it reached its destination.

All in all, it was obviously best that Dr. Will give the important papers

But it soon became evident that this was going to work an injustice. The older brother got an unfair share of the traveling and of the recognition as well. He was careful to say "we" and not "I," and "my brother C. H. Mayo" has done this or that, but this was a poor substitute for Dr. Charlie's appearing personally. Also, it was a pity to waste the work of half the team. Dr. Charlie had contributions to report in fields of surgery that Dr. Will could not adequately cover.

So Dr. Charlie set doggedly to work to make himself a better speaker, with his wife's encouragement and active help. Together they worked over his speeches, pruning away the luxuriance of Charlie's ideas and straightening some of the crooked paths his mind persistently followed. Then Dr. Charlie practiced his delivery before his wife, giving the speech over and over until she knew it as well as he. Many an evening they worked till midnight and after.

Then Mrs. Mayo would go along to the meeting and take her place in a rear seat, to tell him how he was doing by signals they had agreed upon. If he must speak louder, she would hold her handkerchief so; if faster, then this way.

The signals worked all right, but poor Mrs. Mayo was always disconcerted. She never heard the speech they had so carefully prepared and rehearsed, because Dr. Charlie simply could not stick to his manuscript. He would think of something extra to say or some story he wanted to tell and would soon be so far from the prepared speech that there was no use trying to get back to it. So he would just talk.

It was much better that way of course, for then he spoke with the engaging spontaneity, the homely analogies, and rich humor that constituted his own peculiar gift. Once he had conquered his voice difficulties and got used to the platform spotlight, he became as good a speaker as Dr. Will, though in a very different way. His forte was not to impress but to win, not to enunciate fundamental principles but to describe what he called the "wrinkles and recipes" of surgery, the little details of technique that made the differences between good surgery and bad, within the framework of a few big principles.

Dr. Charlie's charm as a speaker was a byword with all who knew him. His chuckle-raising humor and his droll stories became legendary in Rochester and in medical circles the country over, but one looks for them in vain in his published papers—perhaps because the prepared speeches were printed, not those he actually delivered.

Dr. Charlie concentrated his speaking efforts on the two big regional societies, the Western and the Southern Surgical and Gynecological associations, of which he became a member in 1899 and 1902, respectively.

His papers for these groups covered a wide range of topics. One year he would talk about the surgical treatment of tic douloureux and the next describe his operation for the removal of bunions. Or he would speak to the southerners about the surgical physiology of the lymph glands and then tell the westerners about a procedure he had worked out for correcting deformities of the male urethra and penis.

And he was always a participant in all the discussions. From the society *Transactions* it would be hard to guess that Dr. Charlie had ever been loath to speak in public, for he talked on any and every subject. If he did not get up and talk of his own accord, someone was sure to ask him what the Mayos thought or did about the matter under consideration, and he always responded, usually at length and with such a wealth of technical detail that it is easy to understand why he was so often called upon.

Meeting everyone with a simple friendliness that inspired genuine liking in return, Dr. Charlie was soon personally popular with the men of the profession. Impulsively he would invite all and sundry to visit him and Will in Rochester, and in increasing numbers the men accepted the invitations. Doctors from widely scattered points were soon referring in medical discussions to their "annual pilgrimages to the mecca of surgeons the country over."

Before long these men were giving Dr. Charlie substantial assistance in reporting the Mayos' work. This speaker would describe C. H. Mayo's method of correcting harelip and cleft palate; that one would tell how C. H. Mayo performed prostatectomy. Dr. Bernays of St. Louis had seen the Mayos do excision of the rectum for cancer and marveled at the exhibition of perfect teamwork. Dr. Haggard of Nashville described the fishtail drainage tube he had seen the Mayos using; it was of their own invention and it worked like a charm.

Sometimes the comments took a wistful turn. Dr. Robert Carothers was much excited about the new method C. H. Mayo had devised for stripping out varicose veins. Yes, said Dr. Stuart McGuire of Richmond, Virginia, it is a tremendous improvement on the old ways; "I have never seen more brilliant results more quickly accomplished." But that was in the hands of Dr. Mayo. Dr. McGuire feared the operation was not for the likes of him; he would be afraid to try it.

Again, Dr. Hugh Young, genitourinary specialist at Johns Hopkins, complimented Dr. Mayo on his contribution to the surgery of tumors of the bladder, but Dr. Stone of Washington thought, sadly, that "the surgery he has described is so difficult that many of us would hardly undertake it."

So the tokens of recognition came to Dr. Charlie in his turn, usually four or five years after Dr. Will had received them. In 1900 he was invited to give the commencement address for the state university medical school, and in 1903 he was elected to the presidency of the Western Surgical and Gynecological Association and to membership in the American Surgical Association.

It had taken the Mayos twelve years to accumulate their first five hundred operations on the gallbladder and ducts, but their second five hundred came in eighteen months, and in December 1904 Dr. Charlie read to the Southern Surgical Association his and his brother's joint report of one thousand operations for gallbladder disease.

The listeners were overwhelmed. One after another rose to express his pleasure in being present to hear the report of such an achievement. Said Dr. Finney of Baltimore:

It gives me great pleasure to congratulate the Association on being the vehicle of giving to the world this report of the Mayo brothers, which, as Dr. Haggard has said, is surely unequalled in the annals of surgery. I am sure that we are all proud to have as members these two men who have done so much for surgery not only in this country, but in the world. We are all impressed with the special characteristic of their work—its honesty. . . . because of the limited experience I have had as compared with the Mayos I can only say that our experience at the Johns Hopkins Hospital has borne out every point that Dr. Mayo has made.

The paper was published in the *Transactions* of the association and was promptly reprinted in a number of medical periodicals, including the *American Journal of the Medical Sciences,* whose editor only five years before had found it impossible to believe Dr. Will's report of a hundred and five operations on the gallbladder.

There was reason for Dr. Finney's remark about the Mayos' honesty. Differing ideas of what constituted success in surgery were one of the stumbling blocks in evaluating printed reports. Since there were as yet no accepted standards for reckoning surgical mortality, how was one to decide whether in a given case death had resulted from the operation or from some coincident factor?

Many surgeons when using their own judgment in the matter did not resist the temptation to prejudice the figures in favor of whatever fact they were trying to establish. Some were suspected of forgetting to record their failures. That charge had been leveled against John B. Murphy in his campaign to put over the Murphy button, and he admitted that he did not report every death that followed the use of the button. Why blame the button for the death of a patient when the fool surgeon had not known any better than to leave the gangrenous portion of the bowel in the man's insides?

But no one ever charged the Mayos with concealing their

failures. They reported many of them. One of Dr. Will's addresses to the American Surgical Association was entirely an analysis of cases in which he had failed.

In this review of their one thousand gallbladder operations the Mayo brothers made an unequivocal statement of the basis on which they reckoned mortality from operation. They took the position of the layman: If the patient goes into the hospital alive and comes out dead, the death should be charged to the operation, no matter how many months have elapsed or what other disorders have developed to be the actual cause of death.

This standard was hard on the statistics. "A percentage of the deaths could be fairly excluded, but since our object is to show the relative curability of gall-stone disease rather than good statistics, we have adopted this method, as it is at least unprejudiced." Even so, their mortality for the entire series, including the operations done in the years of inexperience, was only five per cent, and for cases of simple gallstones it was just above two per cent.

To the early victories for gastric surgery too the Mayos' statistics contributed immeasurably.

At the 1905 session of the American Surgical Association Dr. Will read "A Review of Five Hundred Cases of Gastro-enterostomy," in which he described clearly, step by step, the evolution in his performance of the operation, announcing as the climax the method he and his brother had determined to be the most nearly ideal—the subsequently famous "no-loop" operation.

Once again the audience expressed their profound respect. Dr. Weir of New York said that Dr. Mayo's paper announced so big an advance that he could not digest it all at once; Dr. Munro of Boston wished to acknowledge publicly his "everlasting gratitude to the Mayos for what they have taught me in stomach surgery"; Dr. Ochsner thought "There is no doubt but what the advance in stomach surgery in this country today is largely due to Dr. Mayo's teachings"; and Dr. Moore of

Minneapolis pointed out that "the evolution of an operation . . . generally comes to us through the experience of a large number of men. Today we have had something which is almost anomalous in the history of surgery. We have been given the whole evolution of surgery within the experience of one man."

Although Dr. Will said explicitly that he and his brother had learned this step from Peterson, that from Mikulicz, and these from Moynihan, Americans were soon referring to the no-loop method as the "Mayo operation." But to this Dr. Will quickly called a halt. He said all he and Charlie had done was gather up good ideas from many men, assemble them as a whole, and tie a string around them, so that all they could claim credit for was the string.

Because they did so often make up the bundles and provide the string, the Mayos could have had their name attached to many operations, but they were scrupulous about giving credit where it was due—and as Dr. Will once said, "all this priority stuff is bosh anyway."

It was unquestionably gastroenterostomy that brought Dr. Will the most recognition during this period, but even as he announced his success with that operation he was moving on to the refinement and greater use of the more radical gastrectomy. Because with almost a crusader's zeal he was championing early operation as a possibility, and the only one, for curing cancer of the stomach.

It aroused his wrath to visit hospital after hospital and in all of them find the stomach cancer patients in the medical wards. The examiners in the outpatient clinics would send suspected cancer of the breast, the uterus, or the rectum straight to the surgeons, but cancer of the stomach they turned over to the physicians—in spite of the fact that in all medical history there was not a single instance of a medical cure of stomach cancer.

"It is worse than a blunder; it is a crime," declared Dr. Will with unwontedly strong feeling.

But to secure acceptance of operation for gastric cancer, the mortality of gastrectomy must be reduced. And here again Dr. Will was arranging the bundle and braiding the string, as some of his fellow surgeons were well aware. In the course of the discussion in 1905 Dr. Munro said, "We all owe a debt of gratitude to the Mayos for their gastrectomy operation. This operation, as they have perfected it, has robbed that procedure of almost all its terrors, and the results are, I think, almost phenomenal."

As yet none of the Rochester group other than the two brothers had ventured beyond the state either in speaking or in publication, though several of them were doing good service on the home front.

Because surgeons were awakening to an intense interest in the problem of anesthesia, the work of Alice Magaw won more widespread notice than that of any other member of the Rochester group apart from the brothers.

Early methods of administering anesthetics were dangerously crude. Ether was given by saturating a sponge and holding it over the patient's nose and mouth until he became unconscious. The stuff might burn his face, or, since little air could pass through the wet sponge, the patient, inhaling nearly pure ether vapor, might get "ether pneumonia" and die. In any case he was likely to fight violently against the suffocation.

Consequently most surgeons preferred to use chloroform. Its aftereffects were less unpleasant and it put the patient to sleep more quickly and easily. Just drench a cloth—a large handkerchief would do—and clap it over the man's nose for a few minutes; even the office boy could do it if necessary. Of course if the patient inhaled too deeply and got too big a whiff, his sleep might suddenly become eternal. But that was just one of the day's risks.

In 1885 Dr. James E. Moore of Minneapolis went abroad for a year's study. Accustomed to pouring chloroform "by the hatfuls" on the accident victims the patrol wagon brought to his office, he was impressed by the method practiced in the clinics of Berlin. The bottle of chloroform he would have used up in one busy morning lasted the German surgeons an entire week, because they poured the stuff drop by drop onto a few thicknesses of gauze laid over a piece of wire netting stretched on a frame above the patient's nose.

When Dr. Moore returned to the United States he brought with him an anesthetist from one of the German clinics to teach the open-drop method to him and any of his surgeon friends who wanted to learn it. Among these were the Old Doctor Mayo and his sons. They promptly applied the method in the use of ether too, and since slow administration with a generous admixture of air helped to overcome the most objectionable phases of ether anesthesia, this soon became the Mayos' favorite.

The drop method spread slowly, and the old ways were still in use at the Johns Hopkins Hospital in 1895. As late as 1906 a Massachusetts surgeon visiting the Mayos was surprised to find them using "the newest method" of giving ether.

In employing a permanent, full-time anesthetist, and that a nurse, the Mayos were unusual if not unique. In other hospitals anesthetizing was one of the duties of the interns.

The Mayos had given the job to Miss Graham and then to Miss Magaw in the first place through necessity; they had no interns. And when the interns came, the brothers decided that a nurse was better suited to the task because she was more likely to keep her mind on it, whereas the intern was naturally more interested in what the surgeon was doing.

In other hospitals the anesthetic was administered in an adjoining room and the patient was not taken into the operating room until he was unconscious, because it was thought that he would be less nervous and more manageable if he had not seen all the paraphernalia to be used in the operation. But the Mayos soon came to the conclusion that moving a person in a state of relaxation from one room to another of possibly differing temperature sometimes contributed to the development of a respiratory complication. So they inaugurated the practice of anesthetizing in the operating room.

To their pleasure they discovered that the psychological effect of this procedure was good. The patient was less disturbed by the actuality than by what he imagined, and he went to sleep more readily in the presence of the surgeon than in that of some strange assistant.

The Mayos emphasized such psychological factors. Miss Magaw maintained that an anesthetist's first job was to size up the patient's mental and emotional state and then "adjust her firmness of manner," as well as the anesthetic, to it. Dr. Charlie contributed the principle of positive suggestion. He noticed that when the anesthetist got rough and kept saying, "Don't do that" or "Hold still now," the patient just grew more obstreperous. It was like antagonizing a drunk man, Dr. Charlie decided. If the nurse gently explained what she was doing and said, "You're all right; your pulse is good; your breathing is fine," the patient was much more likely to go under easily and quietly.

This was the sort of thing Miss Magaw discussed in her papers, together with a hundred and one details as to signs of sufficient anesthesia and ways of recognizing and preventing impending disaster. Since she could not be a member of any medical society, she gave her first talks by invitation before the Olmsted County group and they were then accepted for publication in the state medical journals. In 1904 she was asked to address the state society and gave a review of what she had learned from *eleven thousand* anesthesias.

To such experience and knowledge they must all bow, commented Dr. Moore when she finished; if he could have Miss Magaw to give his anesthetics he would never worry about the patient. He could not agree, however, that ether was better than chloroform. Miss Magaw had said, "Ether kills slowly, giving plenty of warning, but with chloroform there is not even time to say good-bye." But Dr. Moore found chloroform so much quicker. Miss Magaw's reply was sharp. Time ought not to be a consideration. "The surgeon's time may be precious, but the patient's life is more so."

Often in medical meeting discussions of anesthesia doctors would refer to what they had heard or seen in Rochester. On one occasion an Iowa doctor, in reporting a decrease of anesthesia fatalities in that state, remarked that "Many of us have had the pleasure of seeing that peerless anesthetist, Alice Magaw . . . 'talk her patients to sleep'." And a few years later a German surgeon reported to his countrymen that anesthetists from all parts of the United States were going to Rochester to learn their craft from the Mayos' expert nurses.

In 1904 it was Dr. Charlie's turn to receive an honorary master of arts from his alma mater, Northwestern University, and shortly thereafter he made his first appearance before the American Surgical Association. He spoke on the removal of the thyroid gland as a treatment for exophthalmic goiter and was able to report forty cases in which he had performed the operation, a hint to those who heard it that the Mayos were pioneering in another field of surgery.

In the spring of 1905 Dr. Charlie was elected president of the Minnesota State Medical Society, shortly afterward Dr. Will was notified that he had been awarded fellowship in the Royal College of Surgeons of Edinburgh, and in July the elder brother was elected president of the American Medical Association.

Rochester was elated when it heard the news. To Will Mayo first among Minnesota's doctors had come "the highest honor within the power of the medical profession to bestow"! Nothing, not even the appearance of European masters of surgery on their streets, had made Rochester folks so aware of the heights to which these Mayo boys of theirs had climbed. At once the leading townsmen laid plans to greet the return of their triumphant son with the most impressive celebration they could arrange.

On the sultry evening of July 24 the guests, some hundred and fifty of them, gathered in the parlors of the Cook House. Among them were many state officials, come to bear witness that by this honor to Dr. Mayo Minnesota too was honored, and present also were a dozen or so doctors from as many states who had stopped off for a few clinics at St. Mary's on their way home from the convention.

At nine-thirty John Kahler threw open the doors to the dining room and the guests moved into a chamber transformed. The walls were screened with great banks of ferns and flowers; festoons of asparagus fronds and colored lights swung from the ceiling; the name of the honor guest was everywhere, spelled out by lighted letters among the leaves and by braided strands of sweet peas and smilax in the center of each table.

When the caviar, fried chicken, champagne, and ice cream had come and gone, the speechmaking began. Rochester men eulogized their famous neighbors: "Where in the history of the world do we find such a trinity as in this family—the father and his two sons—great doctors, great men, and the father the noblest Roman of them all." Visiting doctors told the home folks they really had little idea of the renown the Mayo brothers had won in the medical world. Yes, both brothers, said Dr. C. H. Rosser of Texas, for "We of the medical world find it hard to separate the two men, Will and Charlie. We wish that it could have been possible to have elected them both to the honored position which the elder brother now holds."

After Dr. Charlie had been presented with a "handsome cut glass vase" to assure him that his worth too was appreciated, Dr. Will was called to the toastmaster's side to receive a silver loving cup as a memento of the evening.

The emotional imperturbability William Mayo always showed the world cracked a little that night as he spoke his thanks. At the end he said he wanted everyone to understand that he felt the honor which had come to him was as much his brother's as his own. They had labored side by side and the achievements of one were the achievements of both.

Dr. Will was inducted into office at the 1906 convention in Boston, in a brief ceremony performed by the retiring president, Lewis S. McMurtry of Louisville—the man who almost fifteen years before had interfered to prevent Joseph Price from rudely dismissing the very young doctor from the West who had come to watch him operate.

As Dr. Mayo stepped forward the crowd broke into an unwontedly wild ovation. The entire five thousand rose to their feet, cheering, clapping, stamping, waving hats and papers in the air.

"It must be a psychological moment in any man's career to receive such honor and homage," remarked the *Northwestern Lancet*. "Yet in the face of this enthusiasm and in the presence of the governor of the state of Massachusetts, President Eliot of Harvard, Mayor Fitzgerald of Boston, and many prominent foreign physicians, Dr. Mayo maintained the calm, dignified, and unassuming manner that is so characteristic of him."

When quiet returned Dr. Mayo gave his presidential address, on "The Medical Profession and the Issues Which Confront It." Among other points, he urged the profession to educate the public to an understanding of the new spirit in medicine. How could laymen be expected to accept legislation for public health and the regulation of medical practice when most of the information they received about medical matters came to them from the advertisements of patent-medicine vendors and voluble charlatans? "The time has come for the public to be taken into our confidence; if we wish better results, we must enlighten the people, for with them lies the final word."

That evening Dr. Will was again the guest of honor at a social function, but this time at a brilliant and sophisticated affair, the association's formal reception for its president. "The costumes of the ladies, the enormous throng of dancers, and the music of a military band made a spectacle long to be remembered." If he had time to think as he moved through it, Dr. Will must have reflected that the "green Western boy" of medical school days had come a long, long way.

16.　*The Surgeons Club*

BY THIS time Rochester was unquestionably a place to be included on every traveling surgeon's itinerary. Early in 1906 there was published in Boston a description by Dr. George N. P. Mead of a trip he had just made to the little Minnesota town. On the train he found himself one of eight doctors bound for Rochester, from California, Texas, Iowa, Kentucky, New York, and Massachusetts.

Going directly to the hospital upon their arrival, they were conducted into a moderately large operating room, where Dr. W. J. Mayo was performing a resection of the stomach. When he had finished the major part of the procedure, he suggested that the visitors go into the next room where his brother was at work. They went reluctantly, feeling sure they could not possibly see anything as fine as what they had just witnessed.

But they were quickly disabused of this notion. The younger brother was doing a thyroidectomy for exophthalmic goiter and the men watched in fascination, for the patient was stirring so restlessly that most surgeons would have stopped operating, "and would have sworn too. Not so Dr. Charles Mayo. He went right on, where a single false cut might have meant a bad case of bleeding, or the severing of a nerve and possible paralysis; he cut true, with a marvelous sureness and dexterity of touch, and the job was soon done."

The visitors spent the morning passing back and forth between the two operating theaters. Dr. Will alone did ten operations, and Dr. Mead reported that together the two brothers were doing four thousand operations a year, "a total that is simply staggering."

At about the same time Dr. A. C. Bernays of St. Louis published in the *New York Medical Journal* an account of "A Visit to the Mayos at Rochester, Minnesota." In six days he had seen one hundred and four operations, ranging through all branches of surgery, and, he wrote, "Among the many physicians and surgeons who visit the Mayos are all kinds, from the most expert and renowned metropolitan surgeon to the plain country doctor who has brought in a case for operation. There were usually from twenty to thirty spectators every day."

In such accounts *by doctors* the anomaly of the "clinic in the cornfields" was first described, for in them the Rochester setup was first called a clinic—not yet, of course, the "Mayo Clinic" but the "Mayo clinic at St. Mary's Hospital." The name was natural, for the visitors saw in the Mayos' private practice a form of organization apparently similar to institutional groups like the Osler clinic and the Halsted clinic at the Johns Hopkins Hospital.

On June 7, 1906, seven of the visiting doctors in Rochester met in a room of the Cook House and organized the International Surgeons Club. Their purpose was to provide a means "whereby the many physicians who come here to see the work done at St. Mary's Hospital by the Mayo Brothers may be enabled to meet together and discuss the work of the day and other matters of mutual interest."

Any visiting physician could become a member of the club by paying a nominal registration fee (at first fifty cents, later a dollar, finally two dollars). Officers were to be elected each Monday afternoon, and two members were to be named reporters each day to take notes on the next morning's clinics and present them as an aid to discussion at the afternoon meeting of the club.

Amid the distractions of a large city such a club might have failed to take hold, but in Rochester, where the transient doctors lacked occupation for their late afternoon and evening hours, it filled a real social need. Within a month it had become an important part of the visitors' activity. A room had been rented and furnished to accommodate the group, the daily attendance had risen to an average of twenty-five, and the custom had developed of rounding off the discussion with an informal talk by some visitor of repute or one of the local staff.

All this was done by the visitors themselves. The Mayo brothers took no part in it. Although they were named honorary members of the club, they attended its meetings only when they were asked to speak, because they wanted the discussions to be frank and free from any possible embarrassment of their presence.

Only once did Dr. W. J. Mayo interfere. When it became evident that the club was to be a lasting thing, he informed the members through their secretary that he wished they would adopt some less pretentious name. To oblige him they voted to drop the *International* and become simply the Surgeons Club.

Actually the original name had not been unreasonable. When it was only three weeks old the Surgeons Club admitted to membership on one day Alexis Thompson of Edinburgh, Henry Stokes of Dublin, W. H. Parkes of New Zealand, and Baron Kamhiro Takaki, surgeon general of the Japanese navy. By the end of its first summer the group numbered more than three hundred members, the roster of whom reads like a medical roll call of the American states, the Canadian provinces, and many foreign lands.

Larger club quarters soon were a necessity and the entire second floor of the building next door to the Mayo offices was rented, redecorated, and furnished with tables, chairs, and a blackboard. Dr. J. E. Crewe, a Rochester physician, was hired to act as permanent secretary.

With the Mayos to teach surgery in the operating room, their associates to teach the several phases of scientific diagnosis, and some of the biggest figures in the world of surgery to add comment and different points of view, the Surgeons Club of Rochester became a postgraduate school of surgery without equal elsewhere in America.

Indeed, one Canadian doctor, writing about the Mayos for the *Canada Lancet,* called it "the greatest post-graduate centre of the century, with possibilities practically illimitable."

On their own visits to other clinics Dr. Will and Dr. Charlie were sometimes irritated because the surgeon gave no explanation of what he was doing and made no effort to be sure the visitor could see the operation. Early in their traveling experience they had vowed that if they ever had anything to show visitors they would make them welcome, arrange things so they could really see, and explain the operations to them.

They went far toward realizing this early vow by working with as few assistants as possible, and the visitors were grateful. Said one of them:

A phase of the work which is particularly gratifying . . . is the absence here of the vast horde of assistants that one sees in the majority of surgical clinics, both at home and abroad. The onlooker . . . has a beautiful view of the tops of the heads of the assistants and occasionally sees a bloody sponge or a gaping wound, but he seldom really sees the various steps of an operative procedure. Here at Rochester, however, things are different. Each brother has but one assistant or actual helper at the table. The other assistant or nurse stands back and only comes forward to exchange instruments, bring up suture material, etc. The Mayos have apparently found that one highly-trained assistant is better than a half dozen poorly-trained ones.

So "highly-trained" indeed was Sister Joseph that sometimes when Dr. Will turned to answer a question from the gallery she automatically went on with the operation!

As a further step toward accommodating the "gallery," the Mayos had built to their order—and Dr. Charlie's design—a number of metal platforms mounted on wheels and topped with handrails on which people could lean. These stands, each carrying a number of men, could be rolled into good positions for observation, and they were high enough to permit the spectators to look over the operator's shoulder without getting in his way. The brothers also had slanting mirrors installed above the operating tables in such a way as to make the work visible at a considerable distance from the table.

There was as much to be heard as seen in a Mayo clinic, for the brothers accompanied their operations with a running commentary, reviewing the case history and the diagnosis, describing the conditions they found, and explaining what they did and why. In these talks they illustrated with unforgettable object lessons the principles of differential diagnosis, antemortem pathology, and early surgery that filled their formal papers.

No man could attend Dr. Will's clinics very often without witnessing such a demonstration as this: The history, read by the assistant while the anesthetic was given, was a classic one of "stomach trouble"—years of treatment for indigestion without relief—yet when incision brought the stomach into view it looked perfectly normal.

"You have heard the history, gentlemen, but you see this stomach. In my opinion there is nothing wrong with it; the trouble is somewhere else. I will see if it is in the appendix." And he pulled into view a badly diseased appendix.

Then as he proceeded to remove the appendix and close the abdomen he told them how from many experiences like this he had learned that stomach pain might actually mean a bad appendix or gallbladder, but he was still undoing many a gastroenterostomy some other surgeon had lately done for stomach trouble that was not in the stomach. The next day the men might watch him undo just such a gastroenterostomy, or they might see him operate on a "dyspeptic" who had a normal stomach but a gallbladder full of stones.

Such lessons were effective as they could never be in public speaking without demonstration, so that soon a paper on stomach or gallbladder disease at any medical meeting was likely to call forth a flock of stories beginning, "The first time I understood . . . was when I saw Dr. Will Mayo in his clinic . . ."

Dr. Ernest Hall of British Columbia did not exaggerate when he wrote, "To-day catarrh of the stomach and chronic dyspepsia, through the genius of Dr. Will Mayo, are fast becoming matters of history. . . . What Lawson Tait was to the pelvis, Will Mayo is to the upper abdomen."

Dr. Charlie was working in too many fields to have yet attained such an outstanding position in any one, but he was fast rising to the fore in thyroid surgery, and visitors noted it. Dr. Will saw what was coming and once remarked to Dr. William D. Haggard, professor of surgery at Vanderbilt University in Nashville, "Charlie is going to be the Kocher of America."

As a clinical speaker Dr. Charlie was surely unique. He "kept his audience in a bubble of anticipation. During the morning's work of anything from ten to fifteen major cases he might discuss the number of nails and match-heads, the weight of charcoal and gunpowder which could be made from the constituents of the human body; he might philosophize about the gallbladder of the pocket gopher, the pineal eye of the tuatara lizard, the galls on his oak trees, the tuberculous lesions of turkey's livers, or a hundred other odd subjects, and between these divagations introduce sound clinical teaching drawn from the accumulated wisdom of his vast experience. Those who listened . . . fascinated by his extraordinary discourse never knew what curious information his wide reading and shrewd observation would bring to light."

Both brothers had a gift for phrasing things so they stuck in the hearer's mind and he went away quoting the "maxims" of the Mayos. Dr. Charlie's forte was description through homely analogy. "Don't remove the parathyroid. It looks like a piece of fat, somewhat harder, and is about the size of a lima bean," he would say. Or, "When the hatchet-sharp edge of the liver is gone, you had better take out the gallbladder." His listeners had looked at the normal liver many times, but they had never seen its edge as hatchet-sharp until Dr. Charlie saw it for them.

Dr. Will's gift was for an almost epigrammatic conciseness. "Don't monkey with the ovary; either remove it or leave it alone." "In obstruction a silent belly is a septic belly. The bowels are paralyzed and the case is inoperable." "Draw your conclusions before your experience is large. . . . Those of large experience are wary of conclusions."

Grateful as they were for this instruction, many visitors wondered how the surgeons stood the strain of giving it. A verbatim report of either brother's daily clinical commentary ran to fifteen or twenty printed pages, and all the while they talked they were "working placidly yet rapidly . . . cutting, sewing, ligating, and performing all the manipulations of surgical technique."

The Mayos were not brilliant surgeons in the earlier sense of that term; they did not dazzle their audience with a display of speed, daring, and flourish. But surgeons no longer asked to be thrilled by a spectacular performance; sureness, soundness, and thoroughness were now more generally respected than brilliance, and of these saner qualities the Mayos had a large share.

Their surgery was, in the words of one who studied it, "the essence of the techniques of all masters of surgery, enriched with the original ideas of the Mayo brothers." They did not claim to be original often; they were more concerned that they should know and practice the very best methods available, no matter who had discovered them.

Both men were entirely frank about their role, constantly telling visitors where they had picked up this good thing or that. Sometimes it was from their father, often from Joseph Price, Ochsner, Murphy, or Halsted. "I used to do this differently, but Moynihan showed me his method when he was here and it was better, so I use it now," Dr. Will would say. And Dr. Charlie, "The first time I tried this operation I got stuck at this point, but Dr. George Monk of Boston was here and he told me what to do."

Many of their listeners, more used to the kind of man who "invented" some good method or instrument he had seen, were humbled by the Mayos' simple honesty. But when they spoke to the brothers about it or complimented them on their constant efforts to keep on learning from other surgeons, the answer was merely an echo from the Old Doctor: "No man is big enough to be independent of others."

Or Dr. Charlie might cite the case of a European surgeon who was doing several hundred abdominal operations a year but who never bothered to see or read what others were doing, so that he was proud of a mortality of sixteen per cent long after others had reduced it to three.

Dr. Will and Dr. Charlie pretended to infallibility no more than they did to originality. In some American clinics the schedule would vaguely list "abdominal operations" so that the surgeon could make sure of his diagnosis while the assistant was reading the case history. But the Mayos always listed a specific diagnosis, or if they had been unable to reach one they admitted the operation was to be exploratory. If their diagnosis proved wrong they called for a rereading of the history and with the aid of their visitors tried to discover what had led them astray.

Some surgeons saved the difficult operations for doing in private, but every visitor was welcome to see any operation the Mayos did and learn from the hard luck as well as the good. Often the master was most fully revealed when things went wrong.

One day Dr. Will was removing a tumor of the kidney. As an upheaval of the ocean floor might render useless the navigator's charts, so the huge growth had pushed all the familiar surgical landmarks out of place and attached itself to the adjoining body parts. As Dr. Will lifted it to the surface, the largest vein in the body was ruptured; blood welled forth in a horrifying flow that would have ended the patient's life in a few minutes.

With one flash of his finger Dr. Mayo found and plugged the opening, entirely by his trained sense of touch, for the blood shut everything else from sight.

Then he said quietly to the tense watchers, "Gentlemen, I have torn the *vena cava* and it will be necessary to make another incision to repair the vein."

He stitched up the hole, made sure it was tight, and then went calmly on with the task of cutting the growth away from the tissues to which it was attached. Suddenly the tumor came loose, making a long tear in the bowel.

Dr. Mayo continued talking: "This, gentlemen, is a much more serious accident than the injury to the vein. I have torn a long rent in the duodenum and if it is not made intact, the contents will leak out and the patient will live but a few days." Then slowly and carefully he sutured the torn bowel before he went on to complete the work on the kidney.

The operation took three and a half hours. At the end the spectators were exhausted by the strain and stared in awe at the outwardly unperturbed man who had carried the responsibility.

Either accident would have meant death in the hands of the average surgeon, so the men watched the postoperative course of the case with great interest. There were no signs of shock, no complications, and the patient progressed smoothly to a complete recovery.

Asked one time to compare the two Mayos as surgeons, Dr. Haggard replied, "Dr. Will is a wonderful surgeon; Dr. Charlie is a surgical wonder."

The amazing characteristics in Dr. Charlie were his versatility and ingenuity. Other surgeons observed with wonder the ease with which he turned from removing a thyroid in one case to taking out a prostate or a varicose vein in the next. To him was due the range of work at Rochester, which made it possible for one man to say, "If you stay here long enough you can see every operation known to surgery."

His ingenuity in devising operative procedures for the unusual case became a byword in the profession. The fellows of the American Surgical Association met in Rochester one year and, wanting to see Dr. Charlie's peculiar talent in action, they asked Dr. Will to select some difficult case that Charlie had not examined and let them see what he did with it. As Dr. Will told the story:

> I chose the case of a woman who had been operated on seven times before coming here, and whose condition was apparently hopeless of surgical repair, and had the Fellows examine her. They all agreed that it was a case hopeless of relief, and so the whole crowd was prepared to see Charlie floored. The patient was placed before him, and when he looked at the ghastly postoperative results he whistled. Then, without apparent effort, he outlined an entirely new plan of operative treatment, which was successful, and the crowd of doctors was simply dazed.

The visitors were impressed too by the service that pathology was rendering to surgery in Rochester, as the result of an innovation that permitted immediate microscopic diagnosis during operation.

Yielding to Dr. Plummer's insistence that laboratory techniques be made something more than a stepchild in their practice, Dr. Will and Dr. Charlie had decided, when Dr. Herb's leaving made it necessary to hire a new pathologist, to add to the staff a well-trained man who would give his full time to the development of the laboratories.

They chose Dr. Louis B. Wilson, assistant director of the bacteriological laboratory of the Minnesota State Board of Health and assistant professor of bacteriology and pathology at the University of Minnesota, from which he had received his medical degree in 1896. The Mayos knew him to be a man of boundless intellectual curiosity who had repeatedly

demonstrated his scientific abilities in investigations undertaken for the state board of health.

When in the fall of 1904 Dr. Will invited Wilson to come
down and discuss the possibilities of the Rochester job, the
scientist was dubious. The Mayos were offering a bigger salary
than the state paid him, but independence in his work and
opportunities for research meant more to him than money.
Dr. Mayo's description of the job promised plenty of freedom,
but there must be a profit motive in private practice. Would
he have to account for every test tube and slide he used?

"What would be my budget?" he asked.

"You won't have any."

"Then that settles it. I won't come."

Dr. Will explained that he meant there would be no *fixed*
budget. "When you want something ask for it and we'll get
it for you."

One could hardly ask more than that—*if* the man kept his
word. So Dr. Wilson agreed to take the job, beginning January
1, 1905.

He was distressed to find that only a few of the Mayos'
thousands of surgical specimens had been saved for study.
The rest had been thrown away or lost except for a few that
had been sent to the university for examination. He soon had
equipped an empty room at St. Mary's and began the systematic examination, cataloguing, and preservation of all the
specimens removed at the operating and autopsy tables.

Autopsies were performed in twenty-two per cent of the
deaths that occurred at St. Mary's Hospital in 1904, a record
considerably above the average at that time, but in his first
year with the Mayos Dr. Wilson raised the percentage to seventy. He never requested permission from the relatives as a
favor; he put it squarely on the basis that the family and
descendants ought to know the exact cause of death and everything possible about the processes of disease in their dead.

Being an intensely sympathetic man, he often found it hard
to make his request of a family when their grief was fresh.

But on one occasion he found he was unnecessarily distressed, for his gentle, tactful sentences were suddenly interrupted by one of the relatives. "Of course we want you to do a post-mortem. We want everything we're paying for."

Thereafter Dr. Wilson included this idea among his arguments, though he phrased it in less sharply mercenary terms.

One day Dr. Will remarked to Wilson, "I wish you pathologists would find a way to tell us surgeons whether a growth is cancer or not while the patient is still on the table."

It was often impossible to tell from the gross appearance of a tumor whether it was malignant or benign, and by the methods then in use it took hours, sometimes days, to prepare the tissues for microscopic diagnosis. Meanwhile the surgeon, acting on his best judgment, might have done too much cutting or too little. Perhaps he had removed a breast where the lump itself would have been enough, or worse, perhaps he had taken just the lump and left an organ sprinkled with cancer cells.

The essence of the problem was to find a satisfactory method for handling fresh tissues. The early histologists had done their work on such tissues, but virtually all the later progress in microscopic pathology was based on the use of tissues hardened, or "fixed," in alcohol. Consequently, when methods of freezing instead of fixing the tissues began to appear pathologists were inclined to view them askance.

The chief objection to them was that they gave poor differential staining; the stains in general use for fixed tissues would not work for fresh tissues. A new one was needed.

As a boy dabbling in botany Dr. Wilson had used methylene blue, an aniline dye with a special affinity for living cells, to stain fresh sections of such things as May apple roots, and he had used it again in bacteriology to make the living organisms visible. Now he decided to see what methylene blue would do to microscopic sections of fresh tissue.

Drawing again upon his experience in botany, he fastened a piece of tissue between layers of elder pith, sliced off sections by hand with a razor, and—it was January in Minnesota—froze them by putting them outside the window for a few minutes. Then he dipped them into methylene blue, washed them in salt solution, and mounted them in a glucose mixture that he had also learned about in botany.

The result was a good clear microscopic picture with well-differentiated details. But it was a picture in red, purple, and dark blue instead of in the browns and pinks with which pathologists were accustomed to deal, and it was a picture of living cells, not dead ones.

For weeks Dr. Wilson examined every bit of fresh tissue he could get his hands on, normal and abnormal, so as to make himself familiar with the new microscopic patterns, and he checked every fresh-tissue diagnosis by later examinations of sections prepared in the usual way. Simultaneously he standardized each step of his staining method and bought a microtome to freeze and cut the sections automatically.

By the end of April 1905 he was able to give the Drs. Mayo his report within two to five minutes of the time they handed him a bit of tissue just removed from the patient!

The Mayos immediately recognized the revolutionary possibilities of this development, and fresh-tissue diagnosis quickly became the scientific mainstay of Mayo surgery and one of its distinctions.

For this new kind of microscopic diagnosis the pathologist must be constantly at the service of the surgeon, and Dr. Wilson soon needed help. A letter to Dr. William Welch brought his recommendation of William C. MacCarty, a graduate of Johns Hopkins in 1904, and within a few months Dr. MacCarty was sharing Wilson's labors and enthusiasm for the fresh-tissue cause.

A year or so later Dr. Wilson, on one of the study trips the Mayos financed for their associates, visited Halsted's operating room in Baltimore. He saw the surgeon take a specimen of tissue from his patient and then, leaving the woman on the table, work in the laboratory for more than an hour to determine the nature of the growth. Knowing his own procedure was much better for the patient, Dr. Wilson told Halsted about it and invited him to come to Rochester and see it in use. Halsted accepted, and his unwonted enthusiasm at the sight of Wilson's fresh-tissue preparations delighted the Mayos.

For surgeons to be impressed with the value of fresh-tissue diagnosis was one thing; for pathologists to adopt it was another. Even when they could be persuaded that it was reliable, few hospitals could afford the extra pathologist needed to practice it, and besides, in many cases the pathology laboratory was located far from the hospital, so that when the surgeon removed the specimen in the morning the pathologist did not get it until afternoon or the next day, much too late for fresh-tissue diagnosis.

The Mayo "system" of clinical diagnosis was one of the most discussed features of their work, and the visitors usually went to the offices in the afternoon with considerable anticipation.

There was certainly nothing impressive at first glance about the Masonic Temple and its dark hallway, furnished only with wooden benches and a framed copy of "The House By the Side of the Road" by Sam Walter Foss, but through that hallway and the examining rooms that flanked it passed some two hundred patients a day. While the Mayo brothers were busy at the hospital throughout the morning their associates carried on the work of diagnosis downtown, asking patients who seemed likely candidates for surgery to return in the afternoon for a final verdict by the Mayos themselves.

When a diagnostician had a patient for one of the brothers to see he stepped into the hall and stuck a piece of colored cardboard above the doorframe, a red card for Dr. Charlie, a green card for Dr. Will. All afternoon the Mayos went from one room to the next, pausing only to exchange a word of greeting with some new arrival waiting his turn in the hallway.

This procedure was a revelation to private practitioners. Most surgeons, working alone, were too busy to make a really thorough examination and unable to afford the facilities needed for it, and they looked with envy upon the division of labor that had developed through the Mayos' efforts to achieve the most accurate diagnosis possible without curtailing their own time for surgery.

"Specialization and cooperation, with the best that can be had in each department, is here the motto. Cannot these principles be tried elsewhere?" asked one of the guests from Canada.

Only Henry Plummer had anything unusual in the way of medical treatment to show the visitors. The work in esophageal stricture had been turned over to him as the sort of problem in clinical investigation he excelled in. He read, examined, reexamined, pondered, and soon he was able to treat with dramatic success many cases of stricture that previously would have required surgery.

A cousin of Dr. Wilson's was one such patient. He was a man of thirty-five, but puny and wizened because he had lived on a liquid diet ever since he swallowed lye as a child of three. After two weeks of treatment by Henry Plummer he was able to eat a steak dinner without difficulty.

Many of the instruments with which Dr. Plummer worked such wonders he made himself, turning them on a lathe in his office workshop, sometimes according to a design he had worked out to fit the needs of the individual.

It was of this work Plummer talked when it was his turn to address the Surgeons Club, and the members were impressed with its originality. Naturally when they were confronted at home with a difficult case of esophageal derangement they advised the patient to see what Henry Plummer could do for him.

So people from many states were soon going to Rochester for treatment by Dr. Plummer.

Here and there among them appeared a type of disorder

he had not yet solved. The patient was unable to eat anything but liquids, yet there was no stricture of the esophagus, for the probes could be passed readily into the stomach. Dr. Plummer could not help these patients, so they returned, disappointed, to their homes.

But he did not forget them. He knew their difficulty was caused by cardiospasm. For some unknown reason the cardiac muscle contracted to obstruct the passage of food into the stomach, and after a while the esophageal muscles, tired out by the extra effort necessary to force the food along, gave up the struggle and dilation of the lower esophagus occurred.

Attempts had been made to overcome this difficulty by introducing a rubber balloon and inflating it to stretch the cardiac muscle, but they had not been very successful and in some cases had caused rupture of the esophagus. The method seemed logical to Dr. Plummer, though, so he analyzed the reasons for its failure and then fashioned a dilator free of those defects.

The results were sensational. Even Dr. Plummer, given to understatement as he was, was moved to say, "The immediate results are most striking. The patients are almost invariably able to take any kind of food at the following meal."

Reporting this development at a meeting of the Surgeons Club, he took one of his patients along as a demonstration. In the midst of his unemotional, scientific presentation of the case, the patient, unable to restrain himself, interrupted.

"I was dying, and he saved my life," he shouted.

Embarrassed by the outburst, Dr. Plummer hustled the man from the room, but some in the audience knew how truly he had spoken, for two weeks before they had seen him carried from the train on a cot, comatose and seemingly within a few hours of death from starvation.

Now that he had solved the problem of those patients he had been unable to help, Dr. Plummer could not rest until he got them all back and cured them. One by one they came until finally there was only one left, a washerwoman from a small town in Ohio. She had paid the costs of her first trip with the lodge insurance she had received upon the death of her husband, but she had no way of financing a return trip. Although the treatment would cost her nothing, there were the expenses of transportation and lodging to be met.

Dr. Plummer's associates had been following his work with great interest, so he told them about this case. "Men, we've just *got* to get that woman back and fix her up." They agreed, and all chipped in to pay the woman's way to and from Rochester.

The story of Henry Plummer's work provides a good illustration of one highly important by-product of the Surgeons Club. Men who had visited Rochester and seen for themselves what the brothers and their associates could do thought of the Mayos when they were faced with a case beyond their own skill. It was cases referred by other doctors that first extended the scope of the Mayo practice beyond the Upper Midwest, to include American states from Maine to California and all the Canadian provinces as well, and boosted the number of operations in Rochester at the rate of about one thousand annually.

Not only did the doctors send their patients to the Mayos; when they themselves required surgical treatment they too took the train for Rochester—so many of them in time that Dr. Will and Dr. Charlie came to be called the "surgeons' surgeons" and the following anecdote gained wide currency.

A story is told of a Southern practitioner of some note who, finding himself compelled to undergo a serious abdominal operation, went to New Orleans to put himself in the hands of a celebrated specialist. He found the specialist's office closed on account of illness. There was a fine operator at Memphis. Thither the patient went only to be confronted with the announcement: "Away for a month." Cincinnati was his next stop. The man he wanted to see there was in Europe. He telegraphed to the Mayos and took a train for Rochester.

"You've come quite a distance, Doctor," said the super-intendent of the hospital, who greeted him.

"Yes, but not direct," replied the Southerner. "Frankly, I intended to go to Dr. M . . . of New Orleans, but failed to find him."

"Yes," said the superintendent. "He's been here for ten days and is convalescent now."

"Then," pursued the patient, "I tried Dr. S . . . of Memphis, but . . ."

"He'll be able to see you by the time you're able to see him," said the smiling superintendent. "He's in the second room down the hall."

"You haven't got Dr. L . . . of Cincinnati here, have you?" asked the other, looking at her suspiciously. "They told me he was in Europe."

"He is by this time. We shipped him off last week to recuperate after a gastrotomy operation."

Although fiction has undoubtedly enhanced fact there, many American surgeons did become patients of the Mayos. In less than two years Dr. Will operated on three nationally known professors of surgery in three Philadelphia medical colleges, J. William White, Charles H. Frazier, and William W. Keen.

When Dr. White arrived he was so sure he had cancer of the bowel that he told Dr. Will he almost hoped he wouldn't recover from the operation. He didn't want to live "with that thing inside of me." As incision brought the sigmoid flexure of the colon into view, the pathologist who had accompanied Dr. White took one look at the hard nodular mass and turned away. Yes, it was cancer.

But Dr. Mayo and Dr. Wilson were not so sure. A few months before, they had had a patient whose colon presented a very similar appearance, but Dr. Wilson had been unable to find any evidences of cancer. The mass had proved to be an intestinal diverticulum, a protrusion of the inner lining through the outer wall of the bowel.

In Dr. White's case too Dr. Wilson reported the condition

to be diverticulitis and not cancer. White's pathologist friend and the watching surgeons were strongly inclined to doubt Wilson's diagnosis, but when they examined fixed-tissue preparations later they were forced to admit that he had been right. Within two weeks Dr. White was serving as president of the Surgeons Club, and he lived for some thirty years longer.

Discussing the incident with Dr. Wilson, Dr. Will remarked that a few years before he had operated on a Rochester man for what he was sure then was cancer of the bowel, and he had been wondering ever since why the man was not dead. Now he thought maybe the "cancer" had been a case of this diverticulitis.

Shaking his head to think that the specimen had gone so long unstudied, Dr. Wilson dug into the old records and discovered it was one of those that had been sent to the state university. He had it returned to Rochester and found that it *was* a mass of diverticula.

Thereafter the Rochester men were on the lookout for clinical signs by which they could make a differential diagnosis between diverticulitis and cancer, and they felt a sense of triumph the first time Henry Plummer suggested the possibility of diverticulitis and operation proved him right.

When they had accumulated enough cases to suggest that the condition was fairly common, they made a joint report of their experience to the American Surgical Association. Dr. Reginald Fitz, the pathologist who had named appendicitis, was present at the meeting and congratulated the Rochester men on their report of "what must be recognized as a new disease of the lower abdomen." Such diverticula of the bowel had often been observed at postmortem, he said, but so far as he knew, the fact that they gave rise to symptoms simulating malignant tumors was altogether new.

In the earlier days, when visitors from a distance were an event, the Mayos celebrated their presence by serving refreshments at the conclusion of the clinic. They had long since outgrown this custom, but newcomers in the gallery were quite likely to be invited to the home of one of the brothers for lunch.

The demands thus made upon Mrs. Will and Mrs. Charlie would have tried the good nature of angels. Their larders must always be stocked, their kitchens staffed, and their menus arranged to accommodate from two to ten extra guests at a moment's notice, but they rose nobly to the task, and the simple but gracious hospitality they dispensed became legendary in medical circles the world over.

Hattie Damon had not bargained for renown when she married Will Mayo, and she would have preferred a quiet life and simple good times with the home-town folks. But she adjusted herself without complaint to the way of life her husband's position required, seeking satisfaction in achieving a smooth-running, efficient household.

One day she planned to serve at the evening meal two wild ducks a friend had given her, and when Dr. Will arrived with two unannounced guests just at dinnertime, there was not an oversupply of fowl. During the task of carving, which Mrs. Mayo had assumed to relieve her husband, one of the ducks slid to the floor. Calmly she rang for the maid and, with a barely perceptible lowering of one eyelid, said, "Bring in another duck, Bessie." So Bessie took the fallen duck to the kitchen, wiped it off, and brought it back to the table.

To converse with the men of medicine who were her husband's guests was hard for Mrs. Mayo, yet the burden of conversation at the noontime meal fell upon her shoulders, for Dr. Will took that occasion to deal with his voluminous correspondence. His secretary sat at a table near by and he dictated the answers to his letters while he ate.

There was no chance for any such occupation at mealtime in Dr. Charlie's home, for his house was filling with children who adored their father. They greeted his arrival with squeals of delight and after lunch they struggled noisily for the best position on his knee.

Watching this contest one day, Dr. Haggard remarked to Mrs. Mayo, "Charlie has done a day's work this morning, and will do another this afternoon. He ought to be resting now, but how can he with those children clambering all over him?"

Smiling Mrs. Mayo advised him to look a little closer, and he saw that Dr. Charlie was asleep! It was his habit to nap for fifteen or twenty minutes after lunch each day, and he had trained himself to do so in spite of the children's bedlam.

Visitors to the "red house" did not always take the full measure of its informality. On one occasion a visitor from England was entertained overnight and in the British fashion left his boots standing outside the door when he retired. Finding them there when they went up to bed, Dr. and Mrs. Mayo knew the Englishman expected the servants to polish them before morning, but the Mayos' help were not of that kind, and besides they had all gone to bed. Chuckling softly at his wife's dismay, Dr. Charlie carried the boots to the kitchen and polished them himself.

Sooner or later conversation at Dr. Charlie's would turn to automobiles, the host's favorite hobby. Mrs. Mayo was sure she knew every hill in the vicinity of Rochester, for she had at some time or other walked up each one, taking the children out of the car at successive levels to make it lighter so it could get to the top.

Since there were as yet no automobile dealers, Dr. Charlie took on the agencies for several of the various makes, to be sure of getting all the new models. They were shipped to him in pieces, and it was relaxation for him after a hard day of surgery to take the parts from their crates and assemble them into a car. He made the process seem so simple that some of his doctor friends were persuaded to buy an auto for themselves, but they seldom found a mechanic at home who could put the thing together and make it go.

Inner tubes had not yet been invented, so the whole tire was inflated with air. Characteristically Dr. Charlie attempted an improvement: he filled the tires on one of his cars with a mix-

ture of molasses and glue and in wintertime it stayed hard as
rubber. When he sold the car to an Olmsted County farmer
early in the spring he forgot about this stuff in the tires.

On Easter Sunday the farmer and his wife started for church
in their new finery, the wife bright and beribboned in stiff
taffeta. Presently the air was full of floating threads of gluey
molasses that spun from the tires at every revolution of the
wheels, and the farmer and his wife were beating madly about,
trying to keep the sticky stuff away from their faces and
clothes.

Dr. Charlie had to buy them a new set of tires, a new suit,
and a new taffeta dress, but it was well worth the cost for the
many hearty laughs he got and gave as he told the story on
himself.

Dr. Will was slower than his brother to succumb to the fascination of the motor car, but at last he got one too, "a handsome machine of the Pierce make, styled the 'Great Arrow'."

Dr. Carl Beck arrived in Rochester for one of his periodic
visits while the car was still new, and the Old Doctor showed
him Will's Pierce Arrow with pride. Warming to Beck's admiration, he impulsively suggested they take a ride. The guest
agreed, they got in, and Dr. Mayo started the motor. But at
this point Dr. Will came running from the office calling to
his father to stop. Breathlessly he explained to Dr. Beck that
his father had never driven a car.

The visiting surgeons found the Old Doctor very entertain-
ing, and they often asked him to talk to the club about the
early days. Some of them liked to chat with him in his little
office at the hospital, and to one of them it seemed that "a
visit to Rochester is not complete without making the acquaintance of this most interesting man."

One afternoon when the Old Doctor took some visitors for
an automobile ride—with a chauffeur this time—the car broke
down on the outskirts and the men had to hire a team to
take them back to the office. This was a humiliation the Old
Doctor could not endure, and there was determination in his

eye as he walked into the office, rapped the table with his cane, and told one of the assistants he wanted to see Will.

When Dr. Will sent the young man back to say he would come as soon as he got through with his patient, the Old Doctor struck the table again with his cane. "I want to see Will *now*." The assistant reported this to Dr. Will, who said quietly, "I guess father means *now*," and excused himself to his patient.

The Old Doctor declared emphatically that he wanted a new car. All right, they would see about getting him one, said Dr. Will.

"Damn it," cried the old man with another blow at the table, "I want a new car *now*."

That was the Old Doctor as the associates of the Mayo brothers knew him—sometimes amusingly, sometimes irritatingly headstrong, irascible, past his days of active participation in the work. Consequently they were never able to appreciate the extent of his contribution to the origins of the development in Rochester.

Yet there were many indications still of the remarkable man he was. In a note to the Sisters of St. Francis thanking them for a gift they had sent him he wrote,

The gracious privilege is not often accorded mortal man to live to witness the accomplishment, the culmination of his best wishes, his ideals. That this happiness has come to me after many days, fills my heart with deepest gratitude and peace. Of me it can be truly said:

Every yesterday was a vision of hope,
Every today is a dream of content.

But the content did not efface the hope. When the Methodist Episcopal Church of Rochester celebrated its semicentennial he was invited to give one of the addresses, and the subject assigned him was one on which he at eighty-seven was well qualified to speak, "The Changes of Half a Century." But Dr.

Mayo brushed the topic impatiently aside and chose instead to describe the marvels of three industrial plants he had recently visited, concluding with the hope that Rochester would soon make use of its water power instead of coal for operating its electric light plant.

Despite his more than eighty years, the Doctor had become a veritable vagabond—off to Florida, Cuba, and the Bahamas one year, the Atlantic Coast another, the American Southwest and Mexico the next, and the American Northwest and Canada the year following. Reports of his travels written back to the newspapers while he was away and told to audiences in church and lodge when he returned kept Rochester entertained.

The letters Dr. Mayo wrote while on a tour of Europe breathe his delight in new sights and sounds. "I wish you could get from my letters what I feel and dream," he wrote. "I am in the land and sea of fable and strange myths. . . . This trip to me is fairy land and sea." He described the "procession of beauty" at a fancy dress ball on the boat, and immediately thereafter the homely details of how the crew swabbed down the decks, the awful beauty of the towering Rock of Gibraltar, the motley of human kinds in the Spanish market places, and the lot of the poor peasants who had to pay taxes on everything they took to or from Gibraltar.

The old gentleman, so dapper and precise, inclined to get choleric when crossed but so alive and eager about everything, was the darling of the party. "Have no fear for me," he told his friends. "Everyone wants to take care of me." And again, "I am well, perfectly. The ladies all look after my interests."

When James J. Hill learned that his old friend, "the little doctor coming up the river," wanted to visit China and Japan, he invited him to make the journey as a guest on one of Hill's boats. Dr. Mayo sailed from Seattle in March 1907, and for more than five months his family heard nothing from him. Then he returned in good health and full of tales, proud because he had gone on around the world and had celebrated his eighty-eighth birthday on board the ship with a party and cake provided by the officers.

But when people questioned him about the Orient he referred them to his wife. Mrs. Mayo had refused Mr. Hill's invitation to accompany the Doctor on his journey, but she had sent for all the books on China and Japan she could get and knew more about those countries than her husband by the time he returned.

When he was past ninety Dr. Mayo began experimenting with a process for extracting alcohol from animal and vegetable wastes. While he was supervising an experiment one day the mechanism got stuck, and he impatiently thrust his hand in to see what was wrong. It had only seemed to stick, and his hand and lower forearm were badly crushed.

Not liking the way his sons dressed the injured limb he got the hired man to help him rearrange the bandages and splints to his own satisfaction!

The injury was so severe that within the next year three operations were necessary, the last to amputate the hand and forearm. The nerves had been so bruised that Dr. Mayo suffered intense pain much of the time, and his general health failed rapidly under the strain. His life closed on March 6, 1911, just a few months before his ninety-second birthday.

The funeral was held next day, and by proclamation of the mayor flags were flown at half-mast, the schools closed, and all business suspended in Rochester during the service, which was a simple one without eulogy and without music, as Dr. Mayo had requested.

An epitaph was pronounced privately by Sister Joseph, who was not given to loose praise of men: "He was an alert, able, earnest humanitarian, worthy of all the glory his sons have added to his name."

A few months later the William Worrall Mayo Memorial Association was organized to raise funds for erecting a monument to Rochester's foremost pioneer. Although at the Mayos' request contributions were limited to one dollar each, five thousand dollars poured in, and Leonard Grunelle of Chicago, assistant to Lorado Taft, was commissioned to execute in bronze the statue of the Old Doctor that stands in Mayo Park.

It was Dr. Will who, in providing the inscription for the base of the statue, hit squarely upon his father's salient characteristic: "A man of hope and forward-looking mind."

Mrs. Mayo was present at the ceremony of unveiling, but in a wheel chair. Going to the door one night to call in her cat before going to bed, she had slipped off the step and broken her hip. The long confinement to bed while the bones knit sapped her strength, and less than two months after this last public appearance she passed quietly away, on July 15, 1915.

The true memorial to Dr. and Mrs. Mayo was a living one, the minds and characters of their famous sons.

For a number of years Dr. Will and his wife entertained summertime guests at Lake Allis near Oronoco, but after a while Dr. Will got bored with the lake cottage; it afforded too little variety to give him recreation. So he exchanged it for an old river towboat, which he had remodeled into a comfortable pleasure craft that he named the *Oronoco*. A week-end cruise down the Mississippi with a party of professional friends refreshed him as nothing else could do.

Dr. Charlie shared in the ownership and use of the *Oronoco*, but he was beginning to find his principal recreation in farming. Mrs. Mayo, feeling that the two boys, Charles William and Joseph Graham, were getting too old to spend all their summer vacations at play, one day suggested a farm home for the summertime. The idea met with Dr. Charlie's approval, and within a month he had found a place and bought it.

The site he chose was in the midst of rolling hills, still wooded and wild, and he wanted to keep it that way, so whenever he heard that the owner of some view or walk he particularly liked was about to cut down the trees, he bought the plot to preserve them. As his interest in various phases of practical farming grew he acquired other acres for fields and pasture lands, and almost before he knew it the little farm had become an estate of two thousand, then three thousand acres. He named it Mayowood.

An Australian surgeon who enjoyed the hospitality of Mayowood in 1914 has left a pleasant little account of the house and the host and hostess.

Charles Mayo . . . called for me in his car, with a doctor from China, and another from some other distant part. . . . It was a lovely frosty moonlight night. We drove up to a fine "cement" house in the centre of two thousand acres . . . on the side of a hill overlooking a valley, in which there is a winding river looking very beautiful in the moonlight. We entered the house by steps leading up to a porch and a "cloak room," up some more steps to a large hall with a tremendous old-fashioned fireplace, in which logs were burning, surrounded by seats. The floor of wood, covered with rugs. Under the house was the garage. In the side of the hill a garbage destructor, fuel house, ice house, and engine for generating his own electricity; several living rooms and bathrooms, a billiard room; and on top a large ballroom for the children, of whom he has seven.

His wife is a charming lady. We had an old-fashioned tea-dinner . . . all very plain and homely; no "frills" and no "side."

His wife joked him about the farm, especially about a flock of geese, of which he was proud, but which had— so she said—that day flown away. So he told us about his farm experiences.

He got trout and put them in the stream. As soon as they were doing well, a cloudburst was sure to come and sweep them all high and dry. . . . He bought a fine herd of Guernseys, and claimed to have the finest dairy in the State. . . . They all became tubercular, or rather, were so when he bought them. He could, of course, have taken action against the man who sold them, but he did not "squeak," as he did not wish to proclaim to the whole State that he was a "sucker."

His poultry was the talk of the neighborhood—all the best broods—but they would not lay. One day one did, and all the countryside came to see the egg.

His pet desire—his wife told me this tale—was to have at the farm some Chinese pheasants, but he did not know how to get them. However, a friend sent him a pair from Portland, and he was very anxious that they should breed. While at dinner one night, a servant came in and whispered quietly to him. He said, "All right; I'll see after dinner." His family asked him what it was, but he only gave a self-satisfied chuckle and went on with his meal. . . . At last his son burst out laughing, and his father asked him what *he* was laughing at, and he replied . . . "That egg under the pheasant is an 'Easter egg'."

"And now to cap everything . . . my wife tells me of that flock of geese. I was right proud of those geese; raised them myself; they were doing well; fed themselves on the bank of the river and cost nothing; and now they have followed a flock of wild geese and left.

"Farming is the finest thing for a busy professional man. I guess when I leave town and get in the car all thought of work goes and I concentrate on this farm."

His wife joked him about being a farmer, but he said: "I am not a farmer. . . . I am an agriculturist." "And what's the difference?" says she. . . . "In the first place an agriculturist makes his money in town and spends it on the farm; while a farmer makes his money on the farm, and spends some of it in town. Also, a farmer eats all he can't sell, while an agriculturist sells all he can't eat." . . .

His is a charmingly simple home and household—he a delightful personality.

Dr. Will felt not a prickle of his brother's interest in farming. He had had all of farm life he wanted when he was a boy. Ironically enough, he inherited the old farm homestead, but an occasional visit to look over the premises was quite enough to satisfy him.

When Dr. and Mrs. Charlie decided to make their home permanently at Mayowood and gave the old "red house" to the Rochester YWCA, Dr. Will and his wife built a new house too. They chose a lot a few blocks farther up College Street and erected a large, impressive residence of cut stone, and it was of this house that Dr. Will asked only that it have a tower like the one from which he had watched the stars with his mother.

In that tower, on the fourth floor, he established a "hide-out" to which he could retire from the guests and distractions downstairs. The little room was simply furnished, with books and pictures, a large flat-topped desk, and the view from the windows. There in the few hours he could spare to be alone Dr. Will made his plans and decisions and dreamed his dreams.

Behind the dairy and the tubercular cows of which Dr. Charlie spoke so jokingly to his guests lay an earnest purpose and a new professional interest.

Neither brother ever showed any inclination to imitate his father in political activity. When an earnest citizen proposed to an assembly of Rochester's businessmen that they start to clean up the city government by nominating Charles H. Mayo for mayor, Dr. Charlie rose to protest, and as soon as he could make himself heard above the cries of "Mayo for mayor! Mayo for mayor!" he said, "I will do anything I can for the good of Rochester. It is the place I was born in; it's the place I want to live in and die in. I thank you for this apparent appreciation, but I want to stay out of politics."

Four years later, in 1912, scarlet fever appeared in Rochester. After reporting the first twenty-nine cases the newspapers applied voluntary censorship lest they frighten away prospective customers and patients, but the disease rapidly assumed epidemic proportions and several visiting surgeons contracted it, much to the Mayos' chagrin. As Dr. Charlie said, "That's a fine report about Rochester to have spread all over the country."

A short while before, the Civic League, which was the Rochester women's club, had offered to contribute two thousand dollars toward the salary of a full-time health officer to be appointed by the state board, but the city fathers refused the offer and elected a local physician, Dr. A. S. Adams, as part-time officer at a salary of one hundred and fifty dollars a year. Now Dr. Charlie rounded up the angry members of the Civic League and appeared with them before a joint meeting of the city council and the Commercial Club to demand that something be done about the public health administration.

The session was long and stormy. Dr. Adams defended himself by saying that whenever he tried to enforce any regulations about milk or meat the dairymen and the butchers threatened to have him fired. To which Dr. Charlie replied, "Then give me the job. They won't try to fire me."

At midnight Dr. Charlie withdrew and went home to bed. But about one-thirty he was awakened by a loud knocking at the door downstairs. "Who's there?" he called out the window.

"The city council," was the reply. "Dr. Adams says he'll resign if you'll take the job and take it tonight."

So Dr. Charlie went downstairs in his nightshirt and dressing gown to be sworn in as health officer. He asked one of his associates to act as his deputy for a few weeks, and together they soon put an end to the epidemic by enforcing strict measures of quarantine.

It was obviously impossible for Dr. Charlie to perform the duties of the new office himself, so he and Dr. Will decided to pay the salary of a competent deputy. To what better use could they put a share of their yearly contribution to Rochester?

Dr. Charlie had long been convinced that many of the humped backs, crippled limbs, and scarred necks he saw were due to the drinking of infected milk, and a state inspector had declared Rochester's milk to be the dirtiest in the state for a town of its size, so the milk supply was the first problem he tackled. He persuaded the city council to pass, over the mayor's veto, an ordinance providing for the inspection of dairies to secure at least elementary cleanliness. More than this was impossible in the face of the dairymen's protest that they could not afford to institute a lot of falderal.

It was to see for himself exactly what they could afford that Dr. Charlie established a dairy farm at Mayowood. Step by step he made it into one of the model dairies of the state, producing pure, clean milk that could be sold at a reasonable price.

But experience taught him that the most scientific precautions could not guarantee a herd of cattle free from tuberculosis, that only compulsory pasteurization could assure the consumer safe milk, so he set out to secure a city ordinance requiring Rochester dairymen to pasteurize their milk.

The bill he proposed was sensationally advanced for the time. Imagine it, commented the Twin City newspapers, Dr. Mayo wants to make Rochester dairy farms observe rules almost as strict as those in force in his own operating room. He wants the milkmen to wash their hands with antiseptic soap before entering their cow barns, to wear spotless clothing, handle the milk in specially equipped cooling rooms, and pasteurize every drop of it!

The inevitable battle took place at a meeting of the city council, where twenty milk distributors led by the one woman among them fought Dr. Charlie's bill, insisting that its provisions would drive them out of business. Dr. Charlie cited the statistics of his own farm to prove that the measures of the bill were not financially impossible.

The debate dragged on until Dr. Charlie's patience was exhausted. In a burst of heated eloquence he told the aldermen their primary job was to safeguard the health of the city, not the pocketbooks of the dairymen, and dared them to defeat the ordinance. When the count was finally taken, long after midnight, the bill passed by one vote.

Dr. Charlie promptly astonished everyone by naming as milk inspector the woman who had led the opposition—and she did a good job of enforcing the new regulations.

When Dr. Charlie took charge of the health office there was no provision for garbage collection in Rochester. About twenty families in the town were paying a dollar a week each to have their kitchen waste hauled away, and the same man performed a like service for the hotels and hospitals, but throughout the rest of the city the garbage lay scattered about in the back yards and alleys until it was hauled away with ashes and rubbish at irregular intervals.

Dr. Charlie was sure that feeding the garbage to pigs would be a profitable enterprise. So, prodding the city council into requiring immediate disposal of garbage, he rented from John R. Cook thirty acres of sandy land and turned it into a feeding farm stocked with purebred hogs. The garbage was collected from each house three times a week, scientifically treated to eliminate any possible source of infection, and then fed to the pigs.

Meat packers refused to buy Dr. Charlie's garbage-fed pigs until they had been inveigled into visiting the farm and seeing the methods in use, and then some of them refused to buy anything else. The farmers of the neighborhood complained of the competition and went so far as to institute court action, declaring the hog farm to be a public nuisance. But Dr. Charlie went serenely on his way.

When the income from the farm had repaid the investment in it, John R. Cook deeded the land to Dr. Mayo, who then turned the enterprise over to the city on condition that the proceeds thereafter be used to finance public health activities. By that time the farm with its equipment was valued at more than ten thousand dollars, was stocked with hogs worth five thousand dollars, and had more than two thousand dollars cash on hand. During the preceding year it had shown a profit of more than seven thousand dollars. Dr. Charlie had proved his point.

17. *Target and Magnet*

IT WAS a source of wonder to members of the Surgeons Club that the Drs. Mayo with a world-wide reputation in medical circles should be so little known outside of them. As late as 1905 a *Minnesota* newspaperman could report that "Dr. C. H. Mayo of *Duluth*" had been elected president of the state medical society!

But early that year Samuel Hopkins Adams published in *McClure's Magazine* a popular account of contemporary surgery in which he told how medical men had awakened to the competence of American surgeons when a country doctor from Minnesota was able to match the figures of Hans Kehr, the greatest European authority on gallbladder surgery. Then briefly but dramatically he recounted the story of that country doctor and his brother, and of St. Mary's Hospital, which handled more surgical cases annually than any other hospital in the United States, more even than the great Johns Hopkins.

McClure's Magazine was then at the peak of its popularity and influence because of such coups as Ida Tarbell's exposé of the Standard Oil Company and Lincoln Steffens' unmasking of the "shame of the cities," and Adams' article introduced the Mayos to thousands of Americans who had never heard of them.

Then when Dr. Will was elected president of the American Medical Association, the seemingly sudden elevation of a young man from an unknown western town to that position caught the attention of journalists. The *Boston Transcript* skimmed the cream from Adams' article and from the accounts written by members of the Surgeons Club for a feature story, which was reprinted in several other papers. And a few months later a newspaper syndicate supplied its clients with a Sunday-supplement feature about the two "mischievous country lads" who had been "swift to rise" to the pinnacle of success.

Whereupon the doctors who had never been persuaded that the Mayos were anything but liars began to mutter about their resort to unethical advertising.

The boy-wonder tone of the newspaper accounts was offensive to the Mayos, and also, they were alarmed by the possibility that such publicity might lose them the respect and support of the medical profession. So they issued a brief statement, which was published in both state and national medical journals, disclaiming any responsibility for the newspaper articles, and they sought the advice of their lawyers as to possible legal redress. Somewhat amused, the lawyers informed them that such laudatory accounts could not be considered libel by any stretch of the imagination.

The Mayos' next appearance in the lay press was written by Wilfred T. Grenfell, "the Labrador doctor," who paid a long visit to Rochester in February 1907 and then told the story of what he had seen and heard there for publication in the *Outlook* four months later.

The humanity of the two brothers interested Grenfell quite as much as their astonishing surgical skill, and he added another appealing story to the already familiar tale of the southern doctor who finally found in Rochester all the great specialists he had tried to consult.

> A patient, after a most successful operation, was asked if he could afford to pay. He replied in the affirmative.
> "What is the source of your income?"
> "I mortgaged my farm to raise the money."

The check was accepted and the good faith thereby proved. But on returning home the man received a letter which contained not only his returned check, but one of a similar amount, as "a trifling help" towards the losses that had accrued to him and his family through his unfortunate illness.

Grenfell was well known in America, and the *Outlook* was a popular weekly magazine among the educated classes. So the effect of the article was in nowise lessened by the editor's prefatory statement that "neither of the famous surgeons whose work and spirit it interprets had any knowledge that it was in preparation. . . . They are distinguished by their avoidance of public distinction."

The publisher of *Human Life*, a ten-cent monthly devoted to American success stories, was less thoughtful. His issue for April 1909 carried the stories of " 'Bill White' of Kansas," "James Stillman, Banker," "Samuel Gompers, Labor Leader" —and "The Mayos, Father and Sons, America's Most Remarkable Surgeons." The Mayo story began:

How would you feel if you were a millionaire, one of the richest men in the world, with an income almost too big to estimate, and with this great wealth you had a disease that baffled the physicians of this country; if in despair you had sought relief from the surgeons and physicians of France and England; if failing to find it you had finally gone to the greatest medical men in Germany, only to be told, after a thorough investigation, that your only chance of living for even a few months was to return to your own country and travel out into the West to the little town of Rochester, Minnesota.

You would be surprised, wouldn't you? . . .

And you would hasten homeward and speed across the country to that little town, and offer your fortune to those wonderful men, plural it is, who could save you when all other earthly beings could not, wouldn't you?

Well, this was the recent experience of one of America's financial masters, and it has been the fortune of a number of other famous men who have sought abroad in vain for cures for their ills, and returned to find the remedy here.

For several pages more the author raved about "those wonderful men." Not a single patient had ever died under their knife, he said. They had been offered alluring titles and untold wealth from every quarter, the German government, even the Kaiser himself, having sought strenuously to persuade them to take up residence in Germany. They were the court of last appeal for the sick of all the world. And yet they gave as freely of their services to the poor who could pay nothing as to the rich who could pay well.

This was quite enough to raise a howl from the Mayos' critics, but to make matters still worse the publisher mailed marked copies to many of the nation's doctors and followed them up with letters soliciting subscriptions. Undoubtedly he meant only to suggest that *Human Life* carried items of interest to the medical profession, but many doctors interpreted the free copies to mean that the Mayo brothers had authorized the story, and for weeks thereafter every mail brought to the Masonic Temple offices a batch of accusing letters that quoted from the medical code about the bad ethics of advertising.

Once again the Mayos sought advice from their lawyers, but to no avail. The law could not help them. One of the attorneys said to them, "Do you suppose for a moment that the wizards of oil and finance would allow themselves to be commented on by the press in the way they are if they could prevent it? If they with all their money and influence cannot stop it, how can you expect to do so?"

So Dr. Will and Dr. Charlie did what they could. They prepared a statement of their case, including the written opinion of the lawyers verbatim, for publication in the *Journal of the American Medical Association* and sent reprints of it to as many doctors as they could. After denying any responsibility whatever for the disgusting exaggerations and untruths of the article in *Human Life,* they said:

> It seems incredible that any fair-minded man in the medical profession could read this article and believe that we had anything to do with its production. . . . It is incomprehensible how anyone could suppose that two men over forty years of age and one at the age of ninety would deliberately take measures to discredit the work of a lifetime.

A dispassionate view of the matter finds sufficient explanation for the publicity without resorting to the belief that the Mayos had suddenly lost all regard for professional ethics. No magazine or newspaper editor could be expected to forgo the use of such a Horatio Alger story in the flesh—a story full of human drama enhanced by the intriguing paradox of a country town that had become a world capital in medicine.

Reasonable men in the medical profession understood and sympathized. In the midst of the furor over the article in *Human Life* Dr. Maurice Richardson expressed his understanding in striking fashion by sending the Mayos a copy of a Boston newspaper with his picture and a eulogy of his work sprawled full across the front page. But many men who could not make page one would not understand, and the Mayos became a bone of contention in medical circles.

Those who had grown hostile sneered that the brothers were not great surgeons; there was nothing original in their work. They were just two more quacks out to get all the business they could. By adding so many partners and employees and hiring a layman as business manager they were commercializing the practice of medicine. Their adjustment of fees to income was nothing but cutting rates, and the provisions they made for the visiting surgeons, such as the mirrors above their operating tables, were only instances of their cheap showmanship.

According to these critics the Mayos padded their figures or got them by soliciting patients. Whenever they wanted to impress the profession by the number of their cases in some new field of surgery, they offered low rates in that field to entice patients away from "the country surgeons who were just as able to operate on them."

One indignant Minnesota physician told a story about a railroad porter he was treating for kidney trouble. Deciding the kidney was tuberculous, he told the man he must have an operation, which would cost him one hundred dollars. The porter went away to think it over, and the next time the doctor saw him was when he came to report how fine he was feeling since he had had the kidney removed—in Rochester.

"You see what happened," said the doctor. "He met Charlie Mayo on the train and Mayo told him if he would come to Rochester for the operation they would do it for fifty dollars."

A more plausible explanation is that when the porter told his fellow trainmen he must have an operation *they* advised him to go to Rochester for it. The critics admitted that railwaymen were enthusiastic boosters for the Mayos, but said this was because the brothers had conducted a deliberate campaign to make them so.

To all these charges the brothers' admiring friends simply answered, Go and see. The Mayos carry on their work with about as much privacy as goldfish in an aquarium, and if there is anything off-color in their practice members of the Surgeons Club ought to have found it out long since.

Naturally, criticism of the Mayos increased in intensity in inverse proportion to the doctors' distance from them. It was most bitter in Minnesota, where the competition of Rochester was still strongest. It was humiliating for a St. Paul doctor, say, in introducing himself to some European surgeon to be met invariably with the question, "St. Paul, Minnesota. Is that anywhere near Rochester?" And it was irritating to watch one's patients take the train for Rochester the instant they were told they needed an operation. Resentment was only human.

After several years of worried efforts to prevent the publication of articles in newspapers and magazines and to counteract their untoward effects among doctors—to which Dr. Will once attributed his first gray hairs—the Mayo brothers decided to ignore it all. They would walk as circumspectly as possible, keep everything they did open for inspection, and let men say what they pleased. After all, as Dr. Will once said, "A target must arrest attention to be a target."

Two episodes for which the Mayos were clearly not to blame gave momentum to the rolling ball of publicity.

The first derived its effects largely from a political situation of the moment. John A. Johnson, Minnesota's highly popular Democratic governor, had been persuaded to try for the presidential nomination in 1908, and though the Bryan machine proved too strong for him, he inspired such a demonstration of personal popularity that it was generally believed he would be the Democratic candidate in 1912.

During the 1908 campaign the Republicans had promised a downward revision of the tariff, but the Payne-Aldrich Act of 1909 was in effect just the opposite. In a speech at Seattle in September Governor Johnson charged President Taft with violation of his campaign pledges in supporting the objectionable act, and the President, even then on a speaking tour to defend himself for his vastly unpopular action, replied with an attack on Johnson.

In the midst of this exchange, which aroused unusual interest because the two men might be opponents in the next election, the nation was surprised to learn that Governor Johnson was undergoing a major operation at St. Mary's Hospital in Rochester, Minnesota.

Several attacks of severe pain had warned him that no matter how crucial the political moment he dared no longer postpone a fourth resort to surgery. Dr. Will had already operated on him three times for a chronic intestinal disorder, and he and the Mayos were such warm friends that he was considered "one of the family" in Rochester.

The governor anticipated no trouble in this fourth operation and confidently assured his associates that he would be back at his desk in the capitol in four weeks' time.

Dr. Will and Dr. Charlie joined forces to perform the operation, but they encountered unsuspected complications and were apprehensive about the outcome. So were those who witnessed the operation. Said Raffaele Bastianelli, personal physician to the king of Italy, "It was one of the most difficult and dangerous operations I have ever seen . . . a brilliant success, but I did not believe that the patient would recover."

For several days the issue hung in the balance and the eyes of the nation were on Rochester. The case was front-page material for newspapers everywhere, for President Taft had reached Minnesota and was paying tactful tribute to Governor Johnson every time he spoke. And the people of the state were clamoring for news so constantly that the twenty telephone lines of the *St. Paul Pioneer Press* were busy all day long answering the inquiries.

Twin City and Chicago newspapers sent special reporters, their "brightest and brainiest," to Rochester, and these worthies hounded everyone for news, the Drs. Mayo, their associates, their friends and Governor Johnson's, even Mrs. Johnson herself. They sought out the members of the Surgeons Club who had watched the operation and sent back to their papers a succession of professional opinions, always including that of Signor Bastianelli. When they lacked news of Governor Johnson, they filled in with stories of the town, the hospital, the Mayos, and their other patients.

All this was a new experience for Rochester, and the residents gaped at the tactics of the big-time gentlemen of the press, who paid the hackmen fancy prices to speed the tiniest bit of news from the hospital to the telegraph office and fought among themselves for control of the long-distance telephone connections, even paying some local man a dollar an hour to talk nonsense or read the Bible over the line so it would be open whenever they had news to report.

For four days the doctors hoped for the governor's recovery, but on the afternoon of the fifth day he suddenly collapsed, and although Dr. Will, Dr. Charlie, and Dr. Judd worked desperately to rally his strength he sank rapidly to a point past hope.

At two o'clock in the morning Dr. Charlie withdrew and went home. Mrs. Mayo was waiting for him, and in her words:

> Charlie came home in an awful state, saying that Governor Johnson couldn't live more than an hour longer. We were both just sick. I tried to tell Charlie he had done his best, all that he could, but that didn't help when the best hadn't been good enough. We had had an awful time with the newspapermen too; there were lots of them here and they would climb trees to look in the windows, and other annoying things like that. It was our first experience with them, and it was terrible.
>
> While we sat talking the bell downtown began to toll. We both shook with a nervous chill. That was one of our bad times.

The Mayo brothers themselves were the central figures in the second episode. Late in 1911 Dr. Charlie was taken suddenly and acutely ill in New York. He diagnosed his own trouble as gallstones, but the doctors called in to attend him said it was appendicitis and operated to remove the appendix.

The idea of the great surgeon himself in need of an operation caught the public fancy, and throughout the nation newspapers carried the story in detail. For a few days after the operation they printed the brief daily bulletins from the hospital announcing that Dr. Mayo's convalescence was progressing nicely.

Then came a flurry of headlines: "Famous Surgeon Takes Turn for the Worse." "Condition of Dr. Mayo Alarming." "Dr. Charles Mayo Dying in the East."

When the relapse occurred the New York doctors decided that Dr. Charlie did have gallstones after all and that he must undergo a second operation.

The news reached Dr. Will about four o'clock one morning and he decided to go to New York at once and take a nurse with him. They left Rochester at four-thirty, riding a locomotive engine to Winona to catch the morning train for Chicago.

Word of their journey preceded them and when they reached Winona a special train was waiting. The railroad men set themselves the task of breaking all existing records to get Dr. Will to his brother's bedside, and freight cars were shunted onto sidings and other passengers were made to wait while "Dr. Mayo's train" sped through on a cleared track.

The story had everything—irony, drama, sentiment, suspense—and the newspapers made the most of it. Dramatic headlines pictured the great surgeon lying at death's door, his anxious wife waiting in the next room, his loving brother racing with a nurse to his bedside. They traced the record-breaking journey mile by mile, even the last wild ride from the station to the hospital in the car of Dr. Raymond P. Sullivan, a New York surgeon.

The only thing they missed was Dr. Will's wry comment that during the train trip he was afraid Dr. Charlie would not live until he arrived, but after Ray Sullivan began that mad dash to the hospital he feared *he* would not live to get there.

The journalists took this occasion to tell once more the whole story of the Mayos and their hospital. They repeated the anecdotes made familiar by writers like Adams and Grenfell, said the Rochester clinic was the biggest in the country, and compared the crowds in its waiting rooms to those standing in line to get football tickets at a university stadium. They told their great lay audience that surgeons crossed oceans and continents to consult the Mayo brothers "about operations they had not the skill or courage to perform themselves."

When daily bulletins had traced Dr. Charlie's second convalescence, his removal from the hospital to a hotel, and finally his journey back to Rochester, the newspapers concluded the incident by voicing the thanks to Providence of "thousands and thousands who owe their lives and health to Charles Mayo."

All this publicity which made the Mayo brothers a target for the darts of resentful doctors made them also a magnet drawing patients to Rochester from all over the nation. To this the brothers' many professional papers contributed, for now that they were becoming known to laymen the newspapers found it worth while to report what they said to medical societies.

Here the subject of most interest to laymen was Dr. Charlie's surgery of the thyroid.

By the end of 1908 he was able to report the results of one thousand operations for goiter. The period of trial and error in the field was over, and the major problems of surgical technique had been solved. Surgeons had learned how to control hemorrhage, how to avoid myxedema, how to escape tetany by leaving the parathyroid bodies intact—in short what to do and what not to do. Operation for simple goiter was now relatively safe in competent hands.

But nearly half of Dr. Mayo's thousand cases were operations for *exophthalmic* goiter, with a mortality of about five per cent. Only Kocher of Switzerland had a better record in this disease, and the usual record in the United States was a score or two of cases with a death rate often as high as twenty-five per cent.

Exophthalmic goiter was one of the most treacherous and perplexing maladies the surgeon had to deal with. No matter how flawless the operation, within a few hours an acute postoperative crisis might develop marked by high fever, vomiting, prostration, delirium, or coma. The patient might die in the crisis, or if not he was likely to be extraordinarily susceptible to complicating infections.

This tendency to postoperative crisis was the principal cause of surgical mortality in exophthalmic goiter, and there seemed to be no way of telling which patients would develop it; a rosy-cheeked, healthy-looking girl might die while a thin, sickly woman pulled through safely.

Because of this uncertainty a surgeon with a limited local practice did not dare to operate for exophthalmic goiter. He could not risk his reputation on an operation in which the death rate was so high.

To improve his own results Dr. Charlie in 1908 adopted Kocher's graduated, or multiple-stage, operation, in which the removal of the gland was accomplished by degrees. The surgeon might begin by injecting hot water into the gland. If this produced too violent a reaction nothing more would be attempted, but if the patient responded fairly well the surgeon might in a day or two tie off the vessels on one side or both and then send the patient home. Or he might perform the ligation and a week later remove both lobes of the gland, or remove one lobe and later the second.

The extent of each installment and the length of the interval between were determined by the condition of the individual patient. Feeling their way carefully, Dr. Mayo and Dr. Plummer slowly learned to recognize little warning signs in the patient's appearance that told them how far it was safe to go at the moment, and gradually their mortality of operation dropped to about three per cent.

Reports of these results brought other surgeons to Rochester to see how Charles Mayo did it, but they were bewildered by the array of procedures he used. Why did he do this in one case and that in the next? Dr. Charlie and Dr. Plummer could not tell them. There was just something about the look of the patient they had learned to recognize, but what it was not even Dr. Plummer could put into words. Consequently the method seemed mysterious, and instead of trying it for themselves most surgeons simply sent their patients to Rochester.

Because of these developments Dr. Charlie was invited to

address many state medical societies, particularly in the South and the Middle West, on the subject of the thyroid, and the local newspapers reported the substance of his remarks, always adding the fact of his remarkable record in the removal of goiter.

Although family doctors no longer told a woman with goiter that she would die if she was operated on or would be "foolish" (myxedema) if she recovered, these ideas still lingered among laymen and they were desperately afraid of operations for goiter. Consequently the newspaper reports of Dr. Charlie's work and the increasing number of living examples of his skill intensified the magnetic properties of the Mayo name. "Mayo Brothers" and safety in a goiter operation become synonymous in the public mind.

For example: The adolescent daughter of a middle-class family in Fort Wayne, Indiana, began to display symptoms of an abnormal physical condition and her mother took her to see a doctor one afternoon. When they returned and the father asked, "Well, what did the doctor say?" the mother began to cry.

"He says it's goiter. What will we do? The operation is so dangerous."

"Yes, but we'll see some other doctors and if they agree the girl has goiter we'll put her right on the train and take her out to the Mayo brothers."

The mother's tears stopped short. "Oh, *could* we do that? Could we *afford* it?"

"If our girl has goiter we *will* afford it."

That was the sentiment which sent such a stream of goiter patients to the Mayo brothers that pregnant women in Rochester were afraid to go downtown lest they "mark" their babies by their repugnance at the sight of the many big necks and protruding eyeballs.

Operations on the thyroid mounted from a total of one thousand to five thousand in four years and took the place of appendectomy as the most frequent operation in Rochester. Be-

ginning in 1911 and for ten years thereafter thyroidectomies
made up more than one tenth of the total number of operations performed by the Mayos and their associates.

The ripeness of time that is a leitmotiv in the story of the
Mayos appeared in this spread of their reputation among
laymen, for it coincided with a period of national prosperity.
The rising values of farm lands, still a broad jump ahead of
rising taxes, and the expansion of industry and commerce
in the cities provided money for improving the comforts and
conveniences of homes, for multiplying churches, colleges, and
public libraries, for beautifying cities with parks and playgrounds—*and* money for journeying halfway across the continent to see the doctor of one's choice.

Equally important was the increasing mobility of the population. The automobile was beginning to carry men's minds
and bodies beyond their own back yards, even though low-
powered models and unspeakably bad roads still made a hundred miles a good day's journey. The railroads were adding
to their established trunk lines a vast system of feeder rails
and were improving their roadbeds and rolling stock to make
train travel more comfortable and safe. Long-distance travel
by rail was becoming commonplace.

So the people and the money came. The number of persons registering annually at the Mayo offices rose steadily to
fifteen thousand in 1912 and then more than doubled in the
next two years—the beginning of what those who experienced
it could describe only as "an avalanche of patients." The office
force found it exciting, never knowing what wealth or fame
or far-distant place might be represented in the rush that followed each train's arrival.

It was no thrill for Jay Neville, though. While Dr. Will was
away one time his wife and Mrs. C. H. Mayo persuaded Dr.
Charlie to discontinue the Sunday morning office hours, and
when Dr. Will returned they talked him into approving the
accomplished fact. Only Jay refused to be reconciled to the

change. While the rest of the staff scattered for the Sunday holiday he remained gloomily at his post in the office, and so one time received an eminent personage who arrived in a private railway car to consult the Drs. Mayo.

Jay told him grumpily that "Will and Charlie" had gone to the country for the day, whereupon the personage declared that if one of them was not called back to attend to him he would return immediately to Chicago.

This was too much for Jay. He poured a torrent of wrath into the ears of the astonished would-be patient, ending with, "Take your goddamned private car and go to hell if you want to; we've got more patients now than we want."

The influx turned Rochester into a camp whose transient population annually exceeded by many thousands the number of its permanent residents. More and more the life of the town came to reflect the dominance of the Mayo practice. Cab drivers greeted new arrivals with the query, "Are you a patient or a doctor?" Restaurants put up signs requesting their patrons not to talk about their ailments at table. And wags made jokes like the one about a visitor who stopped to pet a kitten on the street. "Who do you belong to, kitty?" he asked. And kitty in true Rochester fashion replied, "May-ow, May-ow."

The flood of registrations meant more work at St. Mary's than the sisters could cope with alone. Also, the direction of developments was toward professional standards and licensing for nurses, and, foreseeing a day when a staff of formally trained and registered nurses would be necessary to maintain the standing of the hospital, Sister Joseph decided it was time to institute a school for nurses.

The Drs. Mayo did not welcome the idea. They had great confidence in the sisters as nurses, and they doubted that others, lacking their devotion, could be trained to do the work as well.

Some of the sisters had acquired a truly astonishing facility in their work. Sister Joseph was the outstanding example, but Sister Fabian, who was in charge of postoperative dressings in the hospital, had developed an inexplicable sixth sense that told her better than the doctors' ordinary senses whether a patient was going to get well or not. Her wizardry at prognosis was a kind of last hope to which the Drs. Mayo and Judd clung when things were going wrong.

Sometimes Dr. Charlie would go home much worried about a patient and say to his wife, "Things look bad for him, but Sister Fabian says he'll pull through all right and she's not often wrong."

Sister Joseph did not share the doctors' doubts about nursing care by lay women students; she thought the results would depend on the kind of person selected to superintend the school.

One day, favorably impressed by the appearance and manner of a young woman in the gallery at Dr. Will's clinic, she was pleased to learn that the visitor was a Catholic and a nurse. Anna C. Jammé was her name, and she was a graduate of the Johns Hopkins Training School for Nurses. Sister Joseph thought she had found the proper head for a St. Mary's school of nursing, and Miss Jammé was not long on the job before the Mayos and their associates thought so too.

The school opened with a class of two, chosen from five applicants, on November 19, 1906. Three others were admitted four months later and eleven the following year, and applications were already coming from states as distant as New York and Oregon.

The next problem the sisters had to solve was the need for more space. Often several of the operations scheduled for a given morning had to be postponed simply because there were no beds available. The sisters were reluctant, though, to incur again the debt necessary to build another addition.

Discussing the matter with the Drs. Mayo one day, someone suggested that a percentage of the fees received by the surgeons might properly be allocated to the hospital.

Under the circumstances the idea was not unreasonable. St. Mary's was the institution to which the brothers' fame attached. Many tributes directed to the Mayos were given publicly in terms of St. Mary's Hospital, and when any member of the Rochester group, including the Drs. Mayo themselves, published a paper, the author was always identified as "surgeon [or physician] to St. Mary's Hospital." It was natural, therefore, that some of the sisters should have an exaggerated notion of the part played by the hospital, important as that was.

But whoever made the suggestion was certainly not aware of the Mayos' views on fee-splitting. Dr. Will rejected the idea peremptorily and nothing more was heard of it.

It had given the Mayos food for thought, however. Although it was largely their work that had given St. Mary's its world-wide reputation, there was nothing but a sense of moral obligation to keep the sisters from capitalizing on that reputation through the medium of other surgeons imported for the purpose. Dr. Will and Dr. Charlie did not anticipate any such eventuality, but they thought it might be wise to add another string to their bow.

They had just passed through a season marked by such a rush of tonsillectomies that neither offices nor hospital could furnish facilities for them. In the emergency Dr. Will appealed to his friend John Kahler, and one floor of the Cook House was turned into temporary hospital quarters, including a small operating room. The rooms were restored to hotel uses when the emergency passed, but the idea of a downtown hospital had been born.

It was nourished by the urgent need for additional hotel accommodations. A member of the Surgeons Club observed that every second house in Rochester had two or three of its rooms occupied by convalescent patients, their friends, or visiting surgeons. Even so there were not rooms enough, and the newspapers got anxious inquiries every day from persons unable to find suitable lodgings.

Knowing this state of affairs could not be allowed to persist, Dr. Will suggested to John Kahler that he build a high-class convalescent hotel that could be turned into a hospital if the need arose. Kahler agreed and announced his intention of doing so, but he backed out when he learned that the building would cost much more than the forty thousand dollars he was willing to invest.

Unwilling to give up the idea of a big hotel-hospital downtown, the Mayos decided to break their rule of not participating in Rochester business developments and invested ten thousand dollars in the venture to demonstrate their faith in it. E. A. Knowlton, the local drygoods merchant, then put in his residence on the corner across from the old Mayo home on Franklin Street and other Rochester businessmen contributed additional capital. The Rochester Sanatorium Company was organized and plans for the Kahler House went forward.

Meanwhile Mr. and Mrs. Charles Chute, finding their boardinghouse filled to overflowing all the time, tore it down and built a sanatorium twice the size, but within six months this too was so overcrowded that the rooms were engaged as much as a week in advance. So the proprietors again doubled the size of the Chute Sanatorium, and in the new wing set apart a small "operating room" for the postoperative care of their patrons. Dr. Judd entered into residence as the house physician.

The Kahler House was opened two months later, in May 1907. Sixty of its beds were set aside for hospital purposes and Dr. J. E. Crewe, the secretary of the Surgeons Club, and Dr. E. H. Beckman of the Mayo staff became the resident house physicians.

Although the facilities of the hotel included a completely equipped operating room, for the time being this was used only for dressing wounds; the Mayos continued to do all their operating at St. Mary's and their relations with the sisters remained unruffled.

But Sister Joseph did not miss the meaning of the operating rooms provided in the new buildings, and plans were immediately prepared for a new wing to St. Mary's, which was opened the following year. It increased the capacity by a hundred beds, added several new laboratory rooms, and made available a third operating room to be used by Dr. Judd. The stringency in space was relieved—for the moment.

18. *The Mayo Clinic*

THE outstanding result of the tremendous increase in patients was the swift expansion of personnel in every phase of the practice. There was little of plan or fixed policy about it; the group just grew, as one man after another was added to keep pace with the work to be done.

Dr. Stinchfield was forced by ill health to retire in July 1906, and Dr. Herbert Z. Griffin, a graduate of the Johns Hopkins Medical School who had served an internship at the Children's Hospital in Philadelphia, was the Mayos' choice to replace him. At the same time Drs. Plummer, Millet, and Judd were taken into the firm as "participating partners," but for Dr. Millet the participation was not long. He died from Bright's disease early in 1907, and the Mayos brought Dr. William F. Braasch down from Minneapolis to carry forward the work Millet had begun in urology.

Some three years later Dr. Arch H. Logan, who had taught medicine at the University of Pittsburgh, set up the fourth diagnostic office, and the fifth was opened another three years later by Dr. Walter D. Shelden, who had been practicing medicine in Minneapolis.

Around these senior diagnosticians moved a growing group of clinical associates and assistants, some like the hospital interns on annual appointments and others in lesser positions on the permanent staff. By 1914 the permanent diagnostic staff numbered seventeen, and the clinical assistants were eleven.

These staff members were all engaged in general diagnosis, each of them seeing all kinds of cases in whatever order they chanced to come. But a measure of specialization developed among them as each found a field of special appeal to him. Although there was as yet little system for referring patients from one clinician to another, those with ailments in any of the special fields tended to gravitate into the care of the clinician whose major interest it was.

And with numbers in any one field came exceptional expertness. Dr. Plummer's facility in diagnosing exophthalmic goiter was uncanny, and Dr. Graham had become one of the world's best at the difficult task of differential diagnosis among diseases of the upper abdomen. Dr. Will used to say he thought Kit Graham could *smell* a diseased gallbladder, but when asked how he knew the trouble was gallstones, Dr. Graham could not tell; he had just developed the sixth sense that comes with accumulated experience.

In other disorders frequent repetition made the signs so clear that an experienced nurse could guess the diagnosis. This was notably true of duodenal ulcer, which the Rochester men were diagnosing readily before many in the medical world had come to appreciate the commonness of the malady, let alone recognize its symptoms.

A member of the Surgeons Club told the story of a South American dignitary who arrived in Rochester accompanied by a large retinue of subordinates. He had sought the aid of several European specialists without benefit and on the recommendation of a German surgeon had come to try the Mayos.

While Dr. Graham's assistant was taking the case history a nurse standing by remarked, "Why, it sounds like duodenal ulcer," and the young doctor agreed. Whereupon the mogul stalked from the office in a rage, saying he had not come halfway around the world to have his case diagnosed by a nurse when it had baffled the foremost surgeons of Europe. Members of his retinue managed to pacify him, however, and his personal physician was able to see for himself at operation that the nurse's guess was correct.

The surgeons too needed more help, especially Dr. Charlie, who sometimes feared he would have time for nothing but removing goiters. In quick succession the brothers employed Dr. Justus Matthews and Dr. Gordon B. New to do the ear, nose, and throat work, Dr. Carl Fisher to take over the surgery in diseases of the eye, and Dr. Emil H. Beckman, city physician and the chief internist of the city hospital in Minneapolis, to be trained like Dr. Judd in general surgery.

Dressing the wounds of the convalescent patients in the smaller hotels and boardinghouses of Rochester was now enough to occupy the full time of one man, and Dr. Beckman was given that job for a few months. Then after a period of apprenticeship with the Mayos he became a full-fledged associate, first sharing Judd's operating room and later in a room of his own.

When Beckman moved into the operating room the work of postoperative dressings was taken over by Dr. Melvin S. Henderson, a graduate of the University of Toronto who was just concluding his internship at the City and County Hospital in St. Paul.

"Beckman met me at the train," Dr. Henderson recalled, "and I thought he would fall on my neck, he was so glad to have someone take over the dressings." Dr. Henderson soon learned why; some days he dressed the wounds of one hundred and fifty patients. Unable to afford a horse and carriage, he made his rounds on a bicycle, lighting his way with an electric torch after the Rochester street lights were turned off. As he said, "The going was hard sometimes," and he was glad to transfer to an assistantship in surgery.

A second man came from Toronto in 1907, Dr. Donald C. Balfour, a classmate of Dr. Henderson's. After a year as an assistant pathologist Dr. Balfour was transferred to a clinical assistantship in the offices downtown, to take charge of the postoperative dressings of ambulatory patients. He had only an annual appointment and expected to leave at the end of the year. But one day Dr. Will walked into his little office.

"We'd like to have you stay with us, Balfour. We think you're the kind of man we want here. We've noticed that patients like you; they come back to say good-bye to you when they're ready to leave." Dr. Balfour was quite willing to stay and soon joined Dr. Henderson as an assistant in surgery.

They performed some of the simpler operations, tonsillectomies and an occasional appendectomy, but for the most part they served as first assistants to the attending surgeons, including Dr. Will with increasing frequency as Sister Joseph began gradually to retire from her operating-room post.

Then one summer, about 1911, while Drs. C. H. Mayo and Judd were out of town Dr. Beckman suddenly fell ill and Dr. Will had to have independent help immediately. Knowing his man, he unhesitatingly called Dr. Balfour into the breach, and in the words of one of Balfour's associates, "He turned out to be a wonder. He performed a series of more than two hundred operations without a single death." The following year he was made an attending surgeon and in 1914 he became a participating partner.

The Mayos had never been satisfied with the work they were doing in orthopedic surgery. Dr. Will used to say orthopedists were not surgeons at all, just "saddlers and harness-makers" who covered up with contrivances of leather and steel the deformities they could not correct. After seeing Robert Jones of Liverpool applying real surgical principles to the treatment of deformities, Dr. Will was eager to have Jones's methods used in Rochester, and when Dr. Henderson declared his desire to specialize in orthopedics the Mayos were delighted.

They sent him abroad for six months' study under Robert Jones, Harold Stiles of Edinburgh, and Arbuthnot Lane of London. When he returned, all the work in orthopedics was turned over to him and he began the development of a new surgical specialty in Rochester.

Once these men, and those who came after them, had been given equal standing with the Mayos as attending surgeons, their cases became entirely their own. Neither of the brothers ever interfered to dictate the operative procedure or aftercare, though they were willing to give advice when it was asked for. And of course their associates asked for their advice all the more willingly on that account.

The chance to observe at close hand over an extended period the work that experienced surgeons traveled far to watch for a few days made the surgical assistantships at Rochester worth much more than the hundred dollars a month they paid, and the Mayo brothers never lacked applications from able, well-trained young men.

Apart from the daily clinical lectures, the brothers gave their assistants little instruction by precept; they chose to let association do its own teaching. They might give a word of advice or mild criticism sometimes, but they never scolded about mistakes. Dr. Will believed that any man worth his salt would recognize his own errors and learn from them, and if he could not it was of little use to point them out to him.

Neither brother had the prima donna temperament. "No surgeon should allow himself to be irritated," said Dr. Will. "When I feel irritated I always tell a funny story, anything that will take my mind from the irritating incident." So in the Mayos' operating rooms there was none of the profanity and tantrums that were the rule with many operators. In pleasant contrast to the German surgeon notorious for his habit of throwing knives at his assistants when they displeased him is this picture of Dr. Charlie given by one of his assistants:

I can vividly remember my first nervous clumsiness as his assistant when he suddenly interrupted the curious mixture of half-scientific and half-popular medical lore with which he delighted his crowded theater to whisper in my

ear: "You're doing fine; so long as you don't drop the
bits on the floor I don't mind."

And of Dr. Will another assistant wrote:

> To me he is the greatest personality I have ever known
> or ever expect to know. I have felt that it was worthwhile
> studying medicine merely for the sake of having the op-
> portunity of standing across an operating table from him
> as his assistant. Even as I write . . . I can see his grave,
> yet kindly face, and those keen blue eyes as he used to
> look quizzically into mine from time to time while we
> were struggling with some difficult problem of surgical
> technique. . . . He was the soul of kindness always. He
> never spoke an unkind word to me in the operating room,
> yet the provocation was on occasion surely great.

Growth in the laboratories paralleled the expansion in surgery and diagnosis. The number of young women at work as
technicians in the clinical laboratory, which was still under
Dr. Plummer's supervision, rose from one to five; Dr. Russell
D. Carman, a St. Louis physician who had published several
contributions to roentgenology, was engaged to take full
charge of the x-ray laboratory; Dr. Frank Smithies, demon-
strator of clinical medicine at the University of Michigan, was
employed to centralize and manage the gastric analysis laboratory at St. Mary's Hospital.

For several years Drs. Wilson and MacCarty performed all
the varied duties of general pathologists, and in spite of their
best efforts they could not keep up with the possibilities in the
rapidly maturing fields of bacteriology and biochemistry. They
hopefully bought a new bacteria incubator, for instance, but
they could find no time to use it, except as a convenient storage space for record blanks.

"We couldn't do everything and pick the chickens too,"
quoted Dr. Wilson to describe their plight.

Obviously another pathologist was needed. Two extra rooms

were rented above a storeroom near the Masonic Temple offices, and there in August 1911 Dr. Arthur H. Sanford, who had been teaching physiology at Marquette University, opened a second clinical laboratory, for work in bacteriology and two of its budding branches, serology and parasitology.

These various laboratories were set up for the sole purpose of aiding in diagnosis, but research was an inevitable by-product of their work because of its volume. Findings from thousands of blood counts or thyroid specimens invite, indeed demand, analysis and induction. And to research of this sort the Mayos gave wholehearted encouragement from the beginning, because it was merely an extension of their own habit of reviewing cases to learn from them.

The development of independent research based on experimentation came more slowly because Dr. Will was of two minds about it. His intellect forced him to recognize the truth of Dr. Plummer's and Dr. Wilson's contentions that a research program was necessary to the vitality of the group, that it would keep the practice from sinking to routine on the dead level of present knowledge. But, like many practicing physicians, in his heart Dr. Will resented the collective arrogance of the "pure research" men in assuming that the pursuit of knowledge which may bear fruit in some distant future is necessarily more commendable than efforts to relieve pain and disability in the present.

Nevertheless he came step by step to support an extensive development of experimental laboratories staffed by full-time research men.

Dr. Wilson had begun work in experimental pathology and surgery shortly after going to Rochester, keeping his animals in the basement of St. Mary's Hospital. But he could never be sure of the state of his subjects there, for the kindhearted sisters would slip them extra bits of food and sometimes even let them out of their cages. So when he was making plans to build a new barn at his farm home in 1908 he offered to include space there for the animals if the Mayos would contribute five hundred dollars to the cost of the structure. They did, and Dr. Wilson fitted up an operating room, a small laboratory, and quarters for the monkeys, rabbits, rats, and guinea pigs on the second floor of the barn.

All too soon, though, the experimental work became one of the chickens Dr. Wilson couldn't pick.

Then one day he received a letter from the professor of pathology at Indiana University. Was there an assistantship in pathology available for an exceptionally able Indiana graduate? There was, replied Dr. Wilson; tell the young man to come right on.

It took no more than two months to convince Dr. Wilson that keeping Frank C. Mann on an assistantship was a waste of time and talent, so despite his youth Dr. Mann was put in charge of the work at Wilson's barn, and experimental medicine in Rochester was really on its way.

Almost in the same mail Dr. Wilson received a letter from Edward C. Kendall of New York City, a young research chemist looking for a new position. First in a job with a pharmaceutical manufacturing concern and later in a minor post at a New York hospital, he had been trying to isolate the active hormone of the thyroid gland. He had made considerable progress on the problem, and it had been suggested to him that the Mayos might have a place for him. Did they?

Isolation of the active product of the thyroid gland was just what Dr. Charlie and Dr. Plummer were waiting for.

Dr. Plummer had gradually come to a pregnant conclusion: The group of cases generally labeled exophthalmic goiter actually included two distinct diseases. One was an advanced stage of simple goiter, in which the thyroid was secreting too much of its normal product, and the other was true exophthalmic goiter, in which there was present not only too much thyroid secretion but in addition some abnormal product which by its toxic action produced the tendency to postoperative crises that complicated the surgical problem.

Dr. Plummer had become able to distinguish these two

kinds of disorder correctly in ninety per cent of the cases. But there he stuck for the moment. To verify and expand his two-product theory he had to know what the normal product of the thyroid is and be able to measure it. Perhaps young Kendall could help. So Dr. Wilson wrote him to come out for an interview.

He arrived carrying in his pocket a test tube full of a whitish substance that he had obtained by treating thyroid glands with sodium hydroxide. This residue exhibited all the physiological properties of thyroid extract, and he felt sure that with further refinement it would yield the essential constituent.

Dr. Plummer was all for putting him to work at once, but Dr. Will demurred; he was not sure they were ready to undertake a program of biochemical research in Rochester. Then Dr. Charlie added his voice to Plummer's: Kendall had a big job half done and he would like to see him get on with it without delay—in Rochester. Dr. Will capitulated and Dr. Kendall was hired.

That was in February 1914. Within a very short time Dr. Kendall discovered that barium hydroxide was the proper agent for purifying his material and raising the iodine content of the residue, and by December he had obtained a compound containing forty-seven per cent of iodine. There was now such a small fraction of his material left that another treatment with barium hydroxide would dissipate it entirely. So he decided he had better try to crystallize something from the fraction he had.

Being a true research man, Dr. Kendall could think of no pleasanter occupation for Christmas Eve than this experiment. He dissolved his pinch of material in alcohol and put it in a crystallizing dish over a steam bath. Then while waiting for the liquid to diminish to a small volume he fell asleep.

When he woke up he went into action in a hurry, for the alcohol had entirely evaporated. He added more at once, but a marked change had occurred; a crust of white material had formed that would not dissolve in alcohol. Before throwing it away Dr. Kendall analyzed it—and found it contained sixty per cent of iodine!

Christmas Day or not, the next morning found him in his laboratory early. He dissolved the precious little crust in a mixture of alcohol, acetic acid, and sodium hydroxide, and the crystalline substance that resulted proved to be the active hormone of the thyroid gland. He later named it thyroxin.

Excitement rose high in Rochester then. It was decided to repeat the experiment on a larger scale in order to secure enough thyroxin to test its properties thoroughly, and Dr. Kendall was moved into a larger room and provided with the necessary vats and supplies of glandular material.

But try as he would he could not repeat his experiment successfully. For more than a year he worked at it, so entirely in vain that he sometimes wondered whether he had dreamed that Christmastime success. Then he discovered, again by accident, that carbon dioxide was the agent needed to cut the bond fastening thyroxin into the protein molecule.

The problem was solved, but where had the necessary carbon dioxide come from in his first success? The question nagged at Dr. Kendall until he finally remembered that there had been an automatic microtome in the room he was working in. Unbeknown to him the freezing chamber of that instrument had provided the dash of carbon dioxide needed to release the thyroxin.

In later years Dr. Kendall admitted that though he was not superstitious he frequently dropped into his laboratory on Christmas and other holidays after 1914, "just to see whether anything might turn up."

The isolation of thyroxin was of tremendous importance, quite apart from the therapeutic possibilities of the compound. In Rochester it provided the basis for the next big step in the treatment of exophthalmic goiter, and it won the support of all concerned for the development of research activities as an integral phase of the group's program. In the world of medical science generally it served as an impetus to advance in endocrinology, for it demonstrated the possibility that the ductless glands could be made to yield the secret of their functions.

Along with the expansion of the professional group went the steady development of accessory services. While Dr. W. W. Keen of Philadelphia was convalescing from his abdominal operation, Dr. Will asked him one day, "Now that you've seen what we're doing here, what improvements would you suggest for us?"

"You ought to write more, make more reports to the profession, all of you," was Keen's recommendation.

Write more! Although each member of the staff had a day a week off for reading and study, it was all he could manage in that time to keep up with the outpouring of medical literature.

Soon after joining the staff Dr. Giffin had suggested that it would help if the men shared their reading through reports at a weekly meeting. The Mayos immediately approved the idea and opened their homes turnabout for the gatherings. At each meeting several members of the group summarized for discussion the current periodical articles they had read, and their abstracts were filed for future reference.

These sessions revealed the ineptness of some members of the group in extracting the essence of an article and reporting it without distortion. If they were to write more, and of a kind it would not be a disservice to the group to publish, they must have assistance and supervision of an expert sort. The question was where to find it.

Dr. Will took the problem to his friend Ochsner, who immediately recommended Mrs. Maud H. Mellish. She was just concluding a year's work for him, cataloguing the Augustana Hospital library and helping him prepare a book for publication. Recognizing her intelligence and ability, Dr. Mayo invited Mrs. Mellish to take on the job at Rochester at his first meeting with her.

The offer came at a psychological moment in her life. A trained nurse, she had for sixteen years put her interest in and knowledge of medicine to use in assisting her husband, Dr. Ernest J. Mellish. When he died in 1905 Mrs. Mellish was forty-three. She did not want to return to nursing, and she felt it was too late to take a formal course in medicine. Accepting temporary employment with Dr. Ochsner, she resolved to take the first real offer that came to her in any line connected with medicine. That offer was the one from the Mayos.

Mrs. Mellish arrived in Rochester on March 1, 1907. Her introductory tour of the offices included the "library," which contained an easy chair, a table, a few straight chairs, and one revolving bookrack on which were arranged a miscellany of medical books and magazines.

Was that the extent of the book collection? she asked. Why yes, it was. Of course each member of the staff had his own library, and there were probably some reprints and back numbers of periodicals around somewhere.

Mrs. Mellish's quick imagination saw the room *lined* with books and in use as a real library workroom for the staff, and she suggested that her first task be to assemble and centralize a collection of essential reference materials. The Mayos agreed enthusiastically and offered their personal libraries as a nucleus.

The next morning Mrs. Mellish set out to find the old reprints and journal numbers. The care of these had been entrusted to Jay Neville, and when Mrs. Mellish asked him where they were, he led her to the coalbin in the cellar.

Maud Mellish was a tall, handsome woman, regal in appearance and in manner, but she never hesitated to do anything that had to be done. She went right to work in the coalbin. With Jay's grumbling help, she separated the papers from the coal, stacked them, and carried them to the room upstairs, where she cleaned and sorted them. She ordered missing numbers to complete the periodical sets and had them bound in annual volumes; she bought book shelves, books to fill them, and more tables and chairs.

Then she was ready to give the group editorial assistance in their writing and publishing. Her view of this task did not stop with checking grammar and punctuation. Medical writing at the time was uniformly bad, and medical literature was almost entirely lacking in distinction of style and often in coherence and accuracy. Mrs. Mellish set herself the task of seeing to it that the Rochester men said what they meant to say, that they were accurate in their facts and, as far as she could ensure it, straight in their thinking.

She was a severe critic and inclined to be highhanded in correcting and revising, and like most authors, the Rochester men did not welcome such interference. But the Drs. Mayo, seeing the improvement she worked in their own papers, backed her loyally. In time it became accepted policy to refer all papers to Mrs. Mellish for revision before submitting them for publication, and then the editors and readers of medical journals began to remark upon the uniform technical excellence and the clarity and readability of papers emanating from the staff of St. Mary's Hospital.

In 1909 Mrs. Mellish undertook to issue a volume of the papers written by the group from 1905 to 1909, including some of the reprints she had rescued from oblivion in the coalbin. The problem of a title was discussed at length. It could hardly be "The Collected Papers of Drs. Mayo, Graham, Plummer, and Judd." In the end it was decided to adopt the name given the group by members of the Surgeons Club and the book was called *Collected Papers by the Staff of St. Mary's Hospital Mayo Clinic.*

Another step in the evolution of the group's name took place about 1912. Although the Mayos and their partners inaugurated their various assistantships solely as a means of securing additional help, Henry Plummer insisted that the effective training of these assistants was part of the professional and social responsibility the development at Rochester entailed.

One morning after a trip east Dr. Will wandered into the pathology laboratory to talk this problem over with Dr. Wilson. He said he had been impressed anew with the undesirable status of interns, residents, and house physicians in most eastern hospitals. They seemed to spend their days in subservient yessir-ing, in being flunkies for the permanent staff. He did not want any such attitude to prevail at Rochester, and he thought it might help if they called the men something other than interns or assistants.

Dr. Wilson suggested the term in use at Oxford University, *fellow* from the Middle English *felawe* meaning comrade or companion. This appealed to Dr. Will. But fellows of what? Certainly not of Drs. Mayo, Graham, Plummer, and Judd. And "fellows of St. Mary's Hospital Mayo Clinic" was not much better. Well, why not just "fellows of the Mayo Clinic?" So that is what they became.

The increase in number of patients and size of staff made the old ledger system of keeping records intolerably cumbersome. When a patient returned for a second examination, the doctor had to leaf through several volumes to find the earlier records, and then the findings of the return visit had to be scribbled in like a marginal wreath around the original case history.

Worse still, the records were not complete in one place; the clinical history was set down in Dr. Graham's book perhaps, the laboratory and x-ray findings in several others, the surgical record out at St. Mary's. To make a study of case records on any given subject required a time-consuming and irritating search in many places.

The great volume of the practice and the brothers' tremendous reputation were making St. Mary's Hospital a kind of national proving ground for hospital and surgical procedures. Other practitioners seeking to determine the worth of some technique or instrument would write to ask how it had worked out in Rochester. This being so, the Mayos owed it to the profession and to society to make their records as complete, accurate, and readily accessible as possible.

Henry Plummer, painfully aware of this social responsibility, finally persuaded the Mayos to let him devise a new system of records. For more than a year he studied the problem, went traveling to see what others were doing, and getting no help from medical men, turned to business and industry for ideas.

The dossier system he subsequently evolved became a model for medical records. Each patient is registered upon arrival and assigned a serial number. An envelope bearing that number is set up in a central file, and in that envelope is placed all information about that patient: the diagnostician's clinical history, the surgical and hospital records, and the findings of all laboratory examinations, each set down on a standardized record form that Dr. Plummer drew up in conference with his colleagues.

All subsequent correspondence with the patient is filed in the same envelope, and if he returns for a second, third, or fourth visit, he is always given the same number and the records are put into the same envelope. Thus is accumulated in one place a full history of each patient's physical condition as far as it is known to the Rochester doctors.

This history is immediately available to any member of the group upon request, but whenever an envelope is removed from the file a charge card bearing the exact date, hour, and destination is put in its place, so that the whereabouts of any history not in the file can be known at a glance.

When the patient has been discharged and before his history goes into the permanent file, the records are cross-indexed according to disease, surgical technique, surgical results, and pathological findings. Thus whenever one of the group wishes to study a series of cases of any one kind, he has only to get

the list of case numbers from the index and ask the file clerk
to pull out the envelopes bearing those numbers.

Patient number one was registered under the new system
on July 19, 1907. To some of the doctors the new way seemed
at first a lot of unnecessary red tape and they just forgot
about the record blanks and used their ledgers when they
were especially busy, but in time the new system became a
routine followed without question.

Improvement of the business procedures came next. When
the needs of the business office outgrew the help that Jay
Neville and a few girl clerks could give, Dr. Will asked the
president of the bank to suggest a good man to assist Mr.
Graham, and the banker recommended one of his tellers, a
tall, handsome young man of twenty-one years, a native of
Minnesota and a graduate of the Winona high school. His
name was Harry J. Harwick.

When he began his work for the Mayos in 1908 the bookkeeping was still done in the old-style ledgers, but he soon
persuaded Mr. Graham that a card and loose-leaf system
would be more convenient. The doctors were still making their
own collections and coming in at the end of the day to empty
their pockets onto "Daddy" Graham's desk, and this Mr. Harwick could not immediately change, but in 1910 he took over
the duties of purchasing agent for the group.

Until then all and sundry had had a finger in the buying,
each man ordering whatever he needed with little regard for
cost or duplication. Jay Neville was the only one who took
time to bother about economy. If he thought the clerks or
even the doctors were using too many towels, for instance, he
reminded them sharply that it cost money to have towels
laundered.

Jay was growing more eccentric with age, and his antics
often relieved the tedium for the patients in the hallway. He
could not endure seeing the benches out of order, so whenever
he heard the screech of wood on wood that meant one had
been moved he darted out to set it straight again. Sometimes

the hackmen waiting outside for fares would peer in through the doorway to see whether anyone was getting ready to leave, and Jay, outraged by such open eagerness for customers, periodically dashed through the hallway and out the door to send them scurrying back to their hacks.

One Saturday in July 1914 the Mayos' *Oronoco* remained at the dock in Winona. Informed that the scheduled trip had been postponed because somebody was sick, a Winona reporter called Rochester to find out who it was. Jay Neville, the caretaker of the offices, had been stricken with apoplexy and was near death, Dr. W. J. Mayo told him.

When the reporter implied his surprise that this should interfere with the Mayos' plans, Dr. Will answered curtly. "We wouldn't think of leaving. Jay has been like one of our family. He worked for my father for twenty years and he has lived in my home for twenty-four. He was an exceptional employee."

Jay was buried from Dr. Will's home. To the "boys," Will and Charlie, he bequeathed his most prized possession, the automobile they had given him.

Because additions to the group were always a step or two behind the growth in the number of patients, everybody was working very hard. Some who joined the group found the hours too long and the pressure too much, and they soon left. When those who stayed were asked why they did so, their answers were astonishingly similar, in general tenor this:

The variety and volume of the work was fascinating and the opportunities for professional growth unequaled. The Mayos worked just as hard as we did, and they made us feel important to their success. They never bossed us; we didn't have to call at the office each morning to get an outline of our duties for the day. They allowed us plenty of time off for vacations and for the kind of study trips they took themselves. They even paid our way and often added enough money for us to take our wives along. We each had a day every week free for reading and writing in the library. Those were luxuries a doctor practicing alone could not afford. When he took a vacation his income stopped, and if he was away too long his patients went to other doctors. But when one of us stopped to catch his breath, the group went on. We all worked a little harder when one man was gone because we knew our turn to go would come.

The Mayo brothers had by this time arranged their schedule so they operated on alternate days, Dr. Will on Tuesday, Thursday, and Saturday and Dr. Charlie on the other three. To fill up his Friday schedule Dr. Charlie had to use a little blarney, telling his patients that far from being an unlucky day Friday was his very luckiest.

The afternoons in the office were often hectic, especially for Dr. Charlie. An extra measure of the consultation fell to his lot because he had trained most of the younger surgeons and the younger clinicians too usually turned to him when they were in difficulty. They found it easier to confess their perplexity to him than to Dr. Will, and they knew he would always find a graceful way out of an awkward situation involving a patient.

Because of these many demands upon his time Dr. Charlie was often so worn out by late afternoon that he slipped quietly away and went home. But this usually complicated matters in the office, so the staff took to hiding his hat and coat. The strategy worked sometimes, but if Dr. Charlie was very tired he just went home without them.

There was fun as well as work, though. The number of young men in the group made for high spirits and gay times. On warm summer evenings Dr. Will and Dr. Charlie would send their drivers to pick up any of the staff who wanted to go for a ride, and there were many picnics, hay rides, and sleigh rides on which romances budded and bloomed.

Dr. Will's elder daughter Carrie became Mrs. Donald Balfour, the two Berkman girls, Daisy and Helen, married Henry Plummer and Starr Judd respectively, Nellie Stinchfield was soon Mrs. William Braasch, and Harry Harwick married Margaret Graham, the daughter of his chief in the business office.

These friendships and relationships contributed to congeniality in office hours. Dr. Graham lived on a farm, and sometimes when he came back to the office at noon he brought along a big basket of apples and put them on a table in the laboratory. Then during the afternoon the doctors would slip out to eat an apple and talk for a few minutes. On such occasions Dr. Will proved himself a tease, often tossing off some remark that would start a political argument. He never took any further part in it; he just "liked to hear them rave."

The rapidly accelerating growth kept making the problem of more space continually acute. The surgeons took over the operating rooms at both the Kahler House and the Chute Sanatorium, and new additions were built to both. Then in 1912 Mr. Kahler and his associates ventured to construct a larger and more pretentious hotel, the Zumbro, thus relieving pressure on the Cook House enough so that one of its floors could be turned into quarters for the orthopedic surgeons. In the same year still another addition was built to St. Mary's Hospital, raising its capacity to three hundred beds and six operating rooms.

Expansion at the offices was not so easily managed. Because it occurred only as forced by need, what resulted was a collection of offices and laboratories sprawled helter-skelter along the block and mixed honeycomb-fashion with shoe stores, drugstores, and restaurants. When the partners needed another room or two they rented them wherever they could find them, then boarded up the street fronts and built a passageway at the rear to connect them with the other offices.

When there were no more rooms of this sort available, the partners built a two-story structure on the lot behind their offices and moved into it the library and the editorial office, the general correspondence office, and the medical art studio. Needing still more space the next year, they built an annex connecting the library with the offices to house the x-ray department. Then they began to crowd other services into these new buildings. Room was made in the library for the diagnostic work in orthopedics, and the x-ray technicians were squeezed together to make room for the department of postoperative dressings.

Special personnel had to be provided to direct patients through the maze, and Kate Fitzgerald, transferred from Dr. Sanford's laboratory to serve as the first "routing clerk," soon found herself in charge of a small corps of desk girls scattered about the various corridors.

Such conditions made close cooperation difficult. Surgical consultation was taken for granted, and the red and green cardboard signals for Dr. Will and Dr. Charlie had given way to devices like railroad semaphores above each examining-room door. The color of the light indicated which surgeon was wanted in that room. But consultation among the clinicians was only by individual impulse, and it was not encouraged by the lack of quick means of communication.

Dr. Plummer tried to remedy this lack by installing a cable carrier system like those then used in department stores, to circulate correspondence, case histories, and memorandums. But in damp weather the cotton cables would swell and the baskets get stuck between offices.

The crowding finally became intolerable, and it seemed clear that the only way out of the difficulty was the one Henry Plummer was urging: the construction of a separate building large enough to meet the needs of the group and adapted to its peculiar purposes.

Dr. Will hesitated to take this step; he was afraid it was too ambitious. But finally one Saturday night when the group after a particularly hectic day voted in favor of the move, the Mayos gave their consent. Dr. Plummer was named chairman of the building committee, which included Mr. Harwick to look after the business arrangements and Dr. Wilson to supervise provisions for the laboratories. By ten o'clock the next morning Plummer had called an architect down from St. Paul and was outlining the problem to him.

The site selected was that of the old Mayo home across from the Central School. Moved in part by a sentimental wish to locate their clinic building on the spot where they had spent their childhood, Dr. Will and Dr. Charlie arranged to buy the property from their sister Mrs. Berkman, to whom the Old Doctor had deeded it several years before his death.

The cornerstone was laid on October 9, 1912, but it was nearly two years before the building was ready for use. Working without a precedent to guide them, the architects had to rely upon Henry Plummer for knowledge of the exact purposes to be served and the problems to be met, and Dr. Plummer proved as much of a perfectionist in this as in everything else he undertook. No detail of mechanics or materials was too small to receive his personal scrutiny and decision.

But what principally took the time was Plummer's efforts to formulate a plan of organization that would coordinate and integrate the activities of the group.

The Mayos had long since been persuaded to his view that the advantages of specialization in medicine could be achieved and its dangers avoided only if the group of specialists functioned as a unit in relation to the patient. Dr. Will said repeatedly that a sick man is not like a wagon, to be taken apart and repaired in pieces; he must be examined and treated as a whole. As early as 1910 he told the graduating class of Rush Medical College:

> As we men of medicine grow in learning we more justly appreciate our dependence upon each other. The sum total of medical knowledge is now so great and widespreading that it would be futile for any one man . . . to assume that he has even a working knowledge of any large part of the whole. The very necessities of the case are driving practitioners into cooperation. The best interest of the patient is the only interest to be considered,

and in order that the sick may have the benefit of advancing knowledge, union of forces is necessary. . . . It has become necessary to develop medicine as a cooperative science; the clinician, the specialist, and the laboratory workers uniting for the good of the patient. . . . The people will demand, the medical profession must supply, adequate means for the proper care of patients, which means that individualism in medicine can no longer exist.

Dr. Will could look far forward into the future and lay out broad policies, but neither he nor Dr. Charlie had much flair for arranging the fine points of organization and method. It was up to Dr. Plummer to work out the details of integration that would achieve the cooperation among specialists they sought, and this he was trying to do in designing the new structure.

The building was formally opened on March 6, 1914, and during that afternoon and evening the rooms were shown and their intended uses described to some sixteen hundred persons. They saw the spacious first-floor lobby, cheerful and restful with walls of soft-colored ceramic finish, wicker furniture, and a fountain banked with palms—so different from the old hallway waiting room! Around it were ranged the business offices, registration desks, and principal examining rooms.

An impressive double stairway led to the second floor, where there were more examining rooms, the x-ray cubicles and darkrooms, and some of the clinical laboratories. On the third floor were the handsome library, an assembly hall, and more laboratories, on the fourth the pathology museum, art studio, and the workshops of the instrument-makers, and on the fifth the experimental laboratories with adjacent roof-top runways for the animals.

All the research and diagnosis had been gathered into the one building and organized into divisions and sections. Each senior clinician was now the head of a section in the division of medicine; each attending surgeon was the head of a section in the division of surgery. With the exception of the sections in ophthalmology, otolaryngology (ear, nose, and throat), and orthopedic surgery, these were all sections in general medicine and surgery, for Dr. Will insisted that specialization should go no farther than the *addition* of a "major interest" to general practice in each section.

The scattered clinical laboratories were at last brought together in a section of clinical pathology under the direction of Dr. Sanford. Dr. MacCarty was named head of the section of surgical pathology, Dr. Mann of the section of experimental medicine, and Dr. Kendall of the section of experimental biochemistry. Together these made up the division of laboratories, of which Dr. Wilson was the director.

The library, editorial office, and art studio were joined in a division of publications, with Mrs. Mellish its general director. Into the division of records and statistics, headed by Mabel Root under the supervision of Dr. Plummer, were gathered the registration clerks, desk girls, and filing clerks. And finally, to the business office, from which Mr. Graham had retired, leaving it in the highly capable hands of Harry Harwick, was allocated full responsibility for investigating the financial status of the patients, assessing their fees accordingly, and collecting them.

These were the various members of the body. Its veins and arteries were the ingenious system Dr. Plummer had devised for the prompt circulation of the case histories, and its central nervous system was the means of ready communication by telephone, signal lights, and telegraph ticker.

Each floor was connected with the main file desk in the basement by a constantly moving conveyor belt. When a history was wanted on floor three, say, the desk girl there had only to pencil the number on a request card and put it on the carrier. In the file room below, the desk girl pulled the history from its drawer and put it into the proper compartment of the carrier, from which it was automatically tripped off at desk three above—in two or three minutes, with no more trouble for the doctor than the speaking of a number.

A flat panel with room for many signal lights had taken the place of the ungainly semaphores above each examining-room doorway, and to each doctor had been assigned a specific call on the new ticker. When his tick sounded, no matter where he was in the building he had only to lift the receiver of the nearest telephone to learn from the operator what was wanted of him and where.

When Henry Plummer appeared at the offices of the telephone company to ask them to install a system that would enable the doctors to talk to each other directly, to the operator, or to an outside person at will, the officials stared at him. That was impossible, they said.

"No, it isn't," replied Plummer calmly. "Call in your engineer and I'll show him how to do it."

The engineer came, Dr. Plummer explained with diagrams, and the first intercommunicating telephone in the country was installed in the new building.

As far as mechanical aids could contribute to effective co-operation, Henry Plummer had provided them.

At his suggestion too the custom of making definite appointments for each patient was now adopted, to eliminate many hours of tedium for the patients and to encourage the reference of patients from one doctor to another.

But here Dr. Will stepped in with a warning. The sick person was not to become the patient of the group in the sense that he was to be referred from one man to another with no one in charge of his case. He must remain the private patient of the examining clinician, who should have full responsibility for the case, making use of the special knowledge of his colleagues as he thought best.

It is not possible to assign a date for the founding of the Mayo Clinic; it came into being too gradually. The germ of one phase of it existed in the Old Doctor's clinics at Mrs.

Carpenter's; the outpatient aspect appeared when the brothers began trying to persuade their patients to come in to them instead of calling them out to the homes; adding the first partners and adopting a program of laboratory development initiated other phases. But with the reorganization and the new building of 1914 the Mayo Clinic emerged as a distinct institution, "a complete clinic, including laboratories, housed under one roof, and *independent of any hospital.*"

It has grown to many times its size then, its building has climbed fourteen stories farther into the sky, its sections have multiplied and its activities expanded, to take in medical treatment and put surgery in something like its proper place in the whole of medicine. But the central idea and the fundamental organization had been achieved by 1914.

That central idea, of cooperative group practice, has been called by some doctors the most important practical achievement in modern medicine. In a discussion of medical practice some years later Dr. Will remarked that he and his brother had been called the fathers of group medicine, but "if we were we did not know it." They had not proceeded according to a blueprint drafted in advance; they had merely tried to solve the problems of their overwhelming practice in the way that seemed at the moment most likely to improve their surgery. The actual result was a new kind of private medical practice.

For to be precise, the Mayos were not the fathers of group practice, but of *private* group practice. Cooperation of a sort among clinicians, surgeons, and laboratory men was taken for granted in municipal, state, and university hospitals; it was something quite new in private practice. And the more centralized control in the latter made it possible to develop greater integration than was possible with the loose-knit, constantly shifting, and part-time staffs of public institutions.

Given the state of medicine that demanded specialization and the volume of patients that permitted it, what made the Mayo Clinic possible was the brothers' attitude toward their associates.

They did not merely mouth the Old Doctor's dictum, No man is big enough to be independent of others; they really believed it. And so they did not consider their employees hirelings but fellow workers, who must also travel to other centers to learn, have time for research and writing, and be granted independence in opinion and action. The ability and reputation of these associates would not dim the glory of the Mayos, but would enhance it. Feeling so, Dr. Will and Dr. Charlie actually managed to retain, in cooperative form, the individualism Dr. Will had said could no longer exist in medicine.

19. *The Mayo Foundation*

SHORTLY after George E. Vincent became president of the University of Minnesota in 1911, he went down to Rochester to see the Mayo brothers of whom he had heard so much.

Not the least impressive aspect of their work, he found, was the well-rounded training they were giving to their thirty-six fellows. The unfortunate thing, he told Dr. Will, was that there was no recognized way of distinguishing doctors who had this kind of advanced training from those who merely held certificates from a proprietary postgraduate school.

The early polyclinic schools had served a much-needed purpose in repairing the glaring deficiencies of the undergraduate schools, but as they multiplied, their quality declined and now most of them were staffed with second-rate doctors whose sole interest in teaching was the profit and prestige it brought them in their personal practice.

Real graduate education in clinical medicine simply did not exist. Nowhere could a doctor of medicine take an organized course leading to an advanced degree in surgery, internal medicine, pediatrics, or any other branch of clinical medicine.

Much had been done to raise the standards in undergraduate training, and more improvement was in prospect as the result of the stinging, plain-speaking report on medical education prepared by Abraham Flexner in 1910 for the Carnegie Foundation for the Advancement of Teaching. State licensing had also helped to improve the quality of general practitioners and certify competent ones to the public. But on the level of specialization the door still stood wide open to quackery and incompetence. Specialists were designated solely by self-proclamation, so that there was nothing to prevent a man fresh from medical school setting himself up as a surgeon in Oregon or Maine one month and as an obstetrician in Iowa the next.

The preferred form of advanced training was still a period of study in Europe, but for the few who became true specialists through extended and concentrated work in European clinics and laboratories there were many who blossomed as experts after one summer's junket to the Old World, and there was no way for the public to know which group a man belonged to.

In any case, when the coming of the First World War put a sudden end to trips abroad, the development of opportunities for special training in the United States became imperative.

By this time the Mayo brothers' personal savings under Burt Eaton's management had piled up to a seven-figure sum. Believing that "it is a disgrace to die rich," as Dr. Will once said, and that it is unwise of parents to leave their children so well off that they feel no compulsion to join in the world's work, Dr. Will and Dr. Charlie decided to establish a moderately substantial trust fund for their families and with the remainder, a million and a half dollars, to realize the trusteeship they had declared to themselves some fifteen years earlier.

They had come to think they could best give the money back to the people by using it to endow medical education and research, and they were inclined to do so through the agency of the state university. Dr. Will had been a regent of the university since 1907, and he was convinced that a state-perpetuated group like the board of regents would be more likely than a group of bankers and businessmen to achieve the social purposes of such a public trust as he and Charlie intended to establish.

The university medical school had come into being in 1888 when representatives of two Twin City proprietary colleges offered to surrender their charters and tender the temporary use of their buildings to the university if the regents would establish a school of medicine.

The beginning was not impressive, just a three-year course in surgery, internal medicine, and obstetrics, but more subjects were added as the space and equipment became financially possible, and the required course was gradually lengthened until during Dr. Mayo's second year as a regent a six-year course was made compulsory and rewarded with both the B.S. and the M.D.

In that year too the last private medical college in the state merged with the university school, thus centralizing all medical education in the state institution.

Thus when Flexner made his survey in 1910 he was able to report that Minnesota was "perhaps the first state . . . that may fairly be considered to have solved the most perplexing problems connected with medical education and practice."

But the university officials were painfully aware of a problem that Flexner may have missed: The various consolidations had accumulated a preposterously large faculty of part-time teachers; at one time there were at least eight full professors of "mental and nervous diseases." Everyone agreed that the staff ought to be drastically deflated, but each of several personal factions thought the others ought to be the ones to go.

Finally the regents decided they must act and Dr. Will helped to formulate their plan. All members of the medical faculty were asked to resign, and then a committee of distinguished doctors nominated a compact staff which the regents appointed, along with a new dean from outside the state, Elias P. Lyon, a physiologist from St. Louis University.

This reorganization was necessary and ultimately of great benefit, but it left behind resentment and rancor that plagued the school for many years.

Early in 1914 the medical faculty began to make plans for instituting graduate work in clinical medicine. Left to themselves they would probably have set up another short "refresher" course such as several universities were offering in futile imitation of the proprietary postgraduate schools. But part of President Vincent's plan for a closer integration of the university's various colleges was to centralize the control of all advanced work in one graduate school, and he would not willingly let another shoot of separatism come to bud.

Guy Stanton Ford, newly appointed dean of the graduate school, was in wholehearted agreement with this idea. Possessing a firm conviction that it was the university's obligation to train specialists and mark them out so the public could tell them from brazen imitations, Dean Ford felt that graduate work in medicine could best be pulled up to the proper level in association with graduate work in other branches of learning and art. Fortunately Dean Lyon was also a man with the university idea, unlike many other members of the medical faculty whose every thought was for the glorification of the medical school irrespective of the rest of the university.

So in September 1914 eleven students began graduate work with selected members of the medical faculty under the supervision of the graduate school. They were to take a three-year course combining study, practice, and research, pass an oral examination, prepare an acceptable thesis, and receive a "degree with designation," that is, a Ph.D. in Surgery, or an M.S. in Pediatrics, for example.

Here was something truly new under the sun.

Almost from the beginning the idea of a possible affiliation with the Mayo Clinic had been considered, but the first formal step toward it was taken in October 1914 when the medical administrative board appointed a committee to confer with the medical alumni and with the Drs. Mayo.

An obstacle to affiliation appeared early in the negotiations: The Mayo Clinic was not a corporate body with which the university could readily make a contract. President Vincent suggested that to remove this hurdle the Mayos form a corporate foundation to handle the educational and research phases of their work, and Dr. Will immediately agreed.

So on February 8, 1915, Drs. Mayo, Graham, Plummer, Judd, and Balfour executed articles incorporating the Mayo Foundation for Medical Education and Research, and the next day Dr. Will and Dr. Charlie endowed it by transferring to three trustees, Burt W. Eaton, George W. Granger, and Harry J. Harwick, securities amounting to a million and a half dollars.

Meanwhile a series of conferences had produced tentative terms of affiliation to be submitted to the university regents. The university would conduct a part of its graduate education in medicine at Rochester for an indefinite period of trial, during which the Foundation would make available free of charge all the facilities of the Mayo Clinic and the Rochester hospitals and the Mayos would personally pay all expenses, so the interest on the endowment could be added to the principal until the fund reached a total of two million dollars.

The work at Rochester was to be carried on by a board of "scientific directors" and a selected faculty, both appointed by the university regents on nomination by the Foundation and approval by the administrative board of the medical school. All details as to courses and requirements were to be under the supervision of the dean of the graduate school, in which school all the students would be registered and from which they would receive their degrees.

The trial affiliation could be terminated by either party on one year's notice, but if and when the affiliation became permanent the Mayos would transfer the endowment fund from their trustees to the university regents, subject to the condition that the income be used to maintain the graduate work at Rochester.

Barely had the regents received this proposal for consideration when intense opposition to the whole idea appeared.

The Hennepin and Ramsey county (Minneapolis and St. Paul) medical societies passed resolutions of emphatic protest and persuaded downstate county and district groups to do likewise. Pamphlets picturing the evils of the plan in lurid light were distributed, one of them entitled "A Phantom Gift and a Trial Marriage," in which the university medical school was described as an unwilling bride. And a bill forbidding the regents to effect any such affiliation was introduced into the state legislature, then in session.

The objections on which this opposition was based were many but the ones most often repeated were these:

Since it would be impossible in practice to separate the activities of the Foundation from those of the Clinic, the university would actually be affiliating itself with a private partnership. Because the partners as incorporators of the Foundation were, through the scientific directors, to control the appointment of teachers and expenditure of funds, the regents would in effect be granting to a private enterprise scholastic rank equal to that of the medical school. If they gave such privileges to one group they must grant them to any other that asked, and medical education in the state, so lately centralized at great cost, would again be dispersed, more widely and weakly than before.

Also, the objections went on, the entire income of the endowment was to be spent in Rochester; the university was not to have a cent of it for its own medical school. This was a "phantom gift." Advanced medical education would overshadow undergraduate work and check the development of the medical school. And then in the future, when the Mayo Clinic deteriorated to mediocrity, as the critics said it surely would when the Mayo brothers died, the university would be saddled with the responsibility for maintaining it and would have to divert to it legislative appropriations intended for the medical school.

Some of these objections were valid criticisms of the plan as it stood, and some of the objectors were unquestionably sincere. Among them were lifelong friends of the Drs. Mayo, four of whom made a special trip to Rochester to tell Dr. Will and Dr. Charlie they must oppose the affiliation because they thought it unwise, though they did not at all doubt the nobility of the Mayos' motives.

Dr. Will replied as honestly, telling them to go ahead because if there was anything wrong with the idea he and Charlie wanted to find it out before they put their lifetime's savings into it.

Other men used the same arguments but for reasons less worthy. The bitterness left smoldering by the reorganization of the medical school flared into blaze against the affiliation, presumably because it promised advantages to the hated school. Yet the most active agitators were half a dozen or so of the medical faculty who could see *no* advantages for the school that was their life and love, because the Foundation was to be affiliated with the graduate school, not with the medical school.

But none of these elements in the opposition can account for the spite and malice, the misrepresentation and abuse, that accompanied the respectable arguments. For this there seems but one explanation: Anxiety for the welfare of the medical school and zealous concern over the precious powers of the university regents were a convenient screen for attacks by jealous competitors upon the men whose success infuriated them. The bile that had been accumulating for years overflowed in action now that it could appear in the guise of lofty intent.

Personal antagonism toward the Mayos was implicit in charges that the real object of the affiliation was to perpetuate the Mayo Clinic, that it was just another effort to increase the Mayos' dominance of Minnesota medicine, that contact with the Mayo Clinic would commercialize the standards of medical students, that the Foundation fellowships would provide the Clinic with good help cheap, and so on.

Pure venom inspired the articles that appeared in a Minneapolis newssheet of the kind that exists without paid subscribers. After promising its readers to investigate the proposed affiliation, the paper published a list of questions which the Mayos were invited to answer. They were many and some of them were columns long, but paraphrases of a few will sufficiently illustrate them.

Isn't it true that the Mayos have made many appearances before state and county medical societies for advertising purposes, making absurd statements about cures, "such as claiming to cure cancer of the stomach with a knife"?

Didn't the Mayos advertise in an Iowa paper with a long write-up of the Clinic and then say it was done by the Rochester Commercial Club? "You are just as responsible for it as though you had done it yourselves and . . . you were advertisers and . . . you are sneaking under the cloak of ethics of the American Medical Association and have put up a howl with them for medical ethics."

Isn't it true that the Mayos split fees with doctors who bring them patients?

Won't it benefit the Mayos' hotels and banks to have students at Rochester, though it will add to the students' expenses to have to go that far?

Why did Charles Mayo go East to have his operation? Didn't the Mayo Clinic recognize the cause of his trouble? If so, why didn't they operate at Rochester? Didn't they feel the Clinic surgeons were capable of operating?

The Mayo brothers did not stoop to reply. Dr. Will often remarked that if you fight with a polecat you'll smell like a polecat.

So the paper published a series of abusive editorials calling the Mayos "the highest classed team of advertising grafters in the medical profession," and saying that since they suggested the deal with the university they must be getting something out of it.

"Did you ever see a fellow with a million who didn't want more millions?" This deal is a good bet for the Mayos. Through it they will get a lot of advertising, turn the charity patients over to students, and grab off fat fees on private cases that can pay. "Who gets the advertising? The Mayos. Who pays the freight? The People. Who grabs the profits? The Mayos."

Despite such attacks and all kinds of form letters and post-cards, petitions and hearings, the public refused to believe in the bogeys the medical men were so exercised about. When the opposition leaders appeared at a meeting of the St. Paul Civic and Commerce Association with prepared resolutions for the group to adopt, the association members instead voted overwhelmingly their approval of the affiliation.

The press of the state was preponderantly in favor of the plan. The *St. Paul Pioneer Press* remained neutral at first but finally ran an editorial urging the regents to accept the affiliation, adding that it was impelled to this action "by the line of argument advanced in opposition, which seems to be founded in selfishness, adorned with commercialism, and capped with a touch of envy."

Downstate papers came to the same conclusion. "It will be hard for the doctors of the Twin Cities to convince us that their protests are not inspired by a selfish, self-grasping spirit," said one of them. "They are not thinking of the benefit it might bring to the state, but rather they are afraid that it might bring a little more business to the Mayo Institution."

The controversy had one effect the Mayos' critics did not intend and did not enjoy. As the *Pontiac* (Michigan) *Press* stated it: "The Mayo brothers of Rochester, Minn., are undoubtedly having the most wretched time of their lives. For if there is anything in the world that these famous surgeons hate and fear, it is publicity, and the giving of $2,000,000 to . . . the University of Minnesota has brought them such a flood of fame as they have never faced before in their lives."

Papers from coast to coast told the story of the proposed affiliation and took the occasion to recount once again the Mayo story with all its staple anecdotes. The writers all wondered what could conceivably be the matter with the University of Minnesota that it should hesitate to accept such a magnificent contribution to the welfare of mankind the world over, in this generation and those to come.

The *Boston Herald* considered the Foundation "a fitting climax to what has been a distinctively American career. The country has few stories to match that of these scientists, who are still so young." And the staid *Commerce and Finance* was moved to exclamation: "Of all the wonder stories of America there is hardly one to surpass that of the Mayo brothers. . . . What an inspiration their lives must be!"

The bill forbidding the affiliation passed the state senate by a vote of thirty-six to thirty-one, but not until too late in the session for the lower house to act on it.

Burt Eaton was astonished, then thoroughly angry, when he saw that the senator from Olmsted County, who had avowed his hearty approval of the affiliation, had voted for the bill against it. His explanation when Eaton taxed him with his perfidy did not soothe the lawyer's temper.

"Oh, I knew it wouldn't get through the house," he said airily, "so I swapped my vote on that one for a couple of votes for the boxing bill I was interested in."

Now that the opposition had lost in the legislature, the question was left to the university regents, and, recognizing the validity of some of the objections, the Mayos offered new terms for consideration:

The proposed board of scientific directors should be dropped and the regents should have full control of all appointments and rules of procedure; the trial period should be set definitely at six years and if the affiliation was in effect at the end of that time the original endowment and the accrued interest should pass automatically into the regents' control; the major part of the income was to be used for maintaining the work at Rochester but some of it could be spent for research elsewhere, inside or outside the state.

When an executive committee charged with analyzing the terms of this proposal recommended its acceptance, the board of regents voted unanimously to accept the proposed affiliation for a trial period of six years.

The response of medical educators and students all over the world was immediate. Two hundred and fifty applications for fellowships were received and the sixty-odd fellows chosen from among these represented thirty different undergraduate schools in places as widely separated as Italy and India, Louisiana and Canada.

The eyes of the university medical faculty were opened when a young East Indian arrived to take his undergraduate training at Minnesota because of the graduate work he could look forward to there, and when the possibilities of the affiliation led one important man from outside the state to accept a position on the faculty and persuaded two of the most able local men to exchange part-time private practice for full-time teaching.

So gradually harmony was restored and everybody settled down to work out the very real problems presented by the new experiment, serene in the belief that they had six years in which to solve them.

Then almost as from the blue all the fuss and fury broke out again. When the legislature reconvened in 1917 the old opposition crowd appeared with a bill instructing the regents to dissolve the affiliation with the Foundation at once.

To the familiar charges they now added the ugly suggestion that the whole Foundation idea was just a huge publicity stunt on the part of the Mayos, who had no intention of making the affiliation permanent or of surrendering the endowment to the regents. As soon as they had squeezed all possible advertising out of the scheme, they would give notice to terminate the affiliation. The medical faculty was said to be torn with dissension and the school to be deteriorating so rapidly that even a casual visitor could see it.

This outrageous untruth aroused the friendly members of the medical faculty to action. They immediately issued a flat denial of the charges, asserting that the medical school had never been in a more flourishing condition, and one of them gave to the newspapers a scorching indictment of the disgruntled doctors who were conducting this campaign of deliberate misrepresentation.

The Mayos acted promptly to scotch the new accusation in the most effective way possible. They agreed to give the regents absolute possession of the endowment immediately and to relinquish their right to terminate the agreement, leaving it solely to the regents whether or not the affiliation became permanent.

About the only solid leg this left for the opposition to stand on was the stipulation that the major part of the income be spent to maintain the work at Rochester.

When a public committee hearing on the pending bill was announced, some of the university officials considered the situation serious enough that they asked Dr. W. J. Mayo to appear for the Foundation. It was an amazing request to make —to ask a man to defend himself for being magnificently generous! But after a minute's thought Dr. Will replied, "If you gentlemen think it's necessary, I'll do it."

The chamber was crowded the night of the hearing. The backers of the bill presented their arguments at length and with vehemence, President Vincent and Regent Fred B. Snyder replied, and then Dr. Mayo took the floor. The chairman had asked the audience not to applaud the speakers, but now, forgetting his own injunction, he led the crowd in a resounding tribute to the state's most famous son.

Then the people hushed as Dr. Mayo began to speak. He

talked without notes or manuscript, simply, earnestly, colloquially.

"Every man has some inspiration for good in his life," he began. "With my brother and I it came from our father. He taught us that any man who has physical strength, intellectual capacity, or unusual opportunity holds such endowments in trust to do with them for others in proportion to his gifts."

He went on to describe the unusual opportunity that had been his and his brother's and what they had sought to do with it. He told how as their income grew with their practice they had come to feel a sense of trusteeship for the money. He explained the ideals they had sought to apply in their practice and the purpose they wished to achieve with this gift of money and service.

As he continued, his voice rose. "I can't understand why all this opposition should have been aroused over the affiliation with the university. It seems to be the idea of some persons that no one can want to do anything for anybody without having some sinister or selfish motive back of it. If we wanted money, we have it. That can't be the reason for our offer. We want the money to go back to the people, from whom it came, and we think we can best give it back to them through medical education."

He paused a minute and his voice was quiet again as he resumed. " 'That these dead shall not have died in vain.' That line explains why we want to do this thing. What better could we do than help young men to become proficient in the profession so as to prevent needless deaths?"

Except for those few lines reported by the newspapermen present, no record of Dr. Mayo's talk survives. It is a "lost oration." But twenty-five years later men from varied walks of life who had heard it were still referring to it as the greatest, most eloquent speech they had ever listened to.

The bill died. It was reported out of committee and given a second reading but that was the last heard of it. And once again the opposition subsided to a rumbling growl.

That was in March 1917. America declared war against Germany on April 6. Dr. Will and Dr. Charlie had already joined the Medical Reserve Corps and it seemed likely that one or the other of them would shortly be going overseas with the troops. So they decided to put their house in order.

Suggesting to the regents that the affiliation be made permanent at once, they agreed to waive most of their one remaining stipulation as to the use of the endowment income. The graduate work should remain at Rochester for twenty-five years, but then the regents could move it elsewhere if they thought best. Ten per cent of the income was to be spent outside the state, investigating disease in India or Argentina or wherever, so as to keep the Foundation's work world-wide in scope, and another ten per cent was to be earmarked for meeting emergencies within the state.

The regents agreed to the proposal, and articles making the affiliation permanent were signed on September 17, 1917. As Dr. Will emerged from the room after the signing he was met by representatives of the Twin City press, all primed with the questions he had steadfastly refused to answer for them, and he gave in.

What we want to do is to make the medical experience of the past generation available for the coming one and so on indefinitely, so that each new generation shall not have to work out its problems independently, but may begin where its predecessors left off. This foundation, its fund, and all that goes with it are the contribution of the sick of this generation to prevent sickness and suffering in the next and following generations. . . .

Why do we do this now? . . . My brother and I are at a time of life when we see things as clearly as we may ever be able to see them. As one gets older one's horizon becomes more limited. We are in our fifties, and we don't want to take a chance on what the future may bring.

We are at war. My brother and I expect that next year when the recruits go over one or the other will go too.

. . . War is serious business, especially to men of our years. . . . If I should not come back, I shall be satisfied. I have done the thing in life that I wanted to do.

For at least four years longer opposition to the affiliation flared up in attacks on the Mayos or the university administration. Once Dr. Will was publicly charged with malfeasance in office and his removal from the board of regents was demanded "for carrying out a corrupt combination of a state institution with his private business." Dr. Will offered to resign from the board, but his fellow regents would not permit it.

On another occasion it was charged that the "Mayo faction" was disrupting the entire university and that Marion LeRoy Burton, short-term successor to President Vincent, had resigned his position because he was unacceptable to this group. From his new post as president of the University of Michigan, Burton sent an emphatic denial of the charge and declared there was no such thing as a Mayo faction in the university.

Dr. Will took it all with good grace. When one of the most persistent of the opponents seized the occasion at a gridiron banquet to deliver in his presence a venomous attack on the Foundation, Dr. Will merely said to him when he had finished, "That's the best speech I ever heard you give on that subject, Soren." But those who were close to Dr. Will said he was deeply hurt by the misrepresentation of his and Dr. Charlie's motives.

Minnesota men might carp and heckle but others took the gift at its face value, and when the affiliation was made permanent another wave of articles about the Mayos rolled over the land. The *New York Post* thought their story "one of the most stirring in the annals of medicine"; the *New York Sun* said, "The world can scarcely ask more from the fund than that it will develop more Mayos"; and the editor of a Colorado newspaper concluded his account with a burst of feeling, "God, but it's good to live in a generation of such men!"

20. *Wartime and After*

WHEN the days of American neutrality in the war with Germany appeared to be numbered, the General Medical Board of the Council for National Defense was organized, and Dr. Will was made a member of its executive committee, with Dr. Charlie as his alternate.

In the fall of 1916 the board decided to organize, through the medium of the Red Cross, fifty base-hospital units to serve overseas if the need came. Each unit was to include medical officers, nurses, and enlisted men enough to manage a hospital of five hundred beds, and each was to be recruited from the staff of a large hospital or medical school, which would also be responsible for outfitting the base hospital with necessary medical supplies.

The Mayo Clinic was asked to sponsor such a base hospital from Minnesota, but the affiliation with the University of Minnesota was then on trial and Dr. Will tactfully said he thought the university would be a more proper sponsor. But he and Dr. Charlie contributed fifteen thousand dollars toward the expenses of the unit and enlisted approximately a third of its personnel from Rochester. And throughout its service Base Hospital No. 26 was always referred to informally as "the Mayo unit."

By early June 1917 the unit was reported ready, but it was not mobilized until December 13. Then after spending two weeks in makeshift quarters on the university campus it was ordered to camp in Atlanta, Georgia, for a period of intensive training, and the following June set sail for Europe.

When the company, minus its nurses, who had been detached for service elsewhere, reached its station at Allerey, Saône-et-Loire, it found barracks under construction to house ten base hospitals and a convalescent camp for five thousand. The Minnesota unit was the first of the ten on the scene, and all its members pitched in to help finish the plumbing and wiring and dig the sewers.

The wounded were coming in from the front long before the supplies arrived from Minneapolis, so the staff contrived a hundred and one ingenious makeshifts—tubs and sinks and laboratory receptacles out of biscuit tins, bathing slabs out of lumber and roofing materials, sterilizers out of empty barrels, and refrigerators from gunny sacking stretched over frames and kept wet by dripping water. The doctors scoured the surrounding villages for whatever drugs, dressings, and suture materials they could find, to serve until their own supplies arrived a month or so later.

As the great summer offensive of 1918 continued, Base Hospital No. 26 received hundreds of wounded a day, and when its sister units arrived it became solely a surgical hospital, while they took over other specialties such as contagious, venereal, and nervous diseases. By the time the unit was ordered home and disbanded, it had treated seven thousand two hundred men.

Although the Mayo brothers had supposed that of course they would serve with the medical forces at the front in France, the authorities in Washington saw other uses for their abilities. They were asked to act as general advisers to Surgeon General William C. Gorgas, and they agreed to do so, each serving three weeks at a time while the other carried on at home.

Their principal task was "to insure and maintain, as far as possible, the proper standard of character and professional ability in the medical men taken into the medical service [about 40,000 of them], and to plan ways and means for their special training." It was their job too, until a special committee (with Henry Plummer as one of its members) was appointed for the purpose, to judge the worth of the scores of devices and methods recommended by would-be inventors for use in the army medical services.

In addition to their general advisory work, "Dr. W. J. Mayo *or* Dr. C. H. Mayo" was appointed to several special committees of the medical board, and Dr. Will was named medical aide to the governor of Minnesota to supervise the administration of the selective service law.

The brothers also managed to give a good many wartime pep talks before various medical groups, and what Dr. Charlie said about the beneficial effects of sacrifice and discipline on the nation's character and the contributions of war to medicine was widely reported because he was president of the American Medical Association. He was elected and was in his turn tendered a banquet and loving cup by Rochester citizens in 1916, and he took office in 1917.

The strain of their war service, added to the extra efforts needed to keep the Clinic going and continued for more than two years without a pause, finally took its toll in the health of both men. Dr. Charlie came down with pneumonia during one of his turns in Washington and Dr. Will was forced home in the fall of 1918 by a severe case of jaundice.

He said to Harry Harwick, "This is either a benign condition that will clear up in sixty days or it is cancer of the liver. I must assume that it is cancer of the liver."

He had chosen the young business manager as the one among their associates he considered most capable of carrying the Clinic forward in the event of his own death, and for the greater part of the next two months Harry Harwick virtually lived with him, riding for hours through the countryside, listening to his hopes and fears, his plans, his dreams for the Clinic.

The jaundice cleared away and Dr. Will returned to the helm himself, but from that time onward, in his mind at least, Harry Harwick was his heir apparent as executive head of the Clinic.

The Clinic staff found the wartime days rushed and upset. As one man after another volunteered or was called (at one time the number of staff members in the armed services was sixty-three), the load doubled and tripled for those who stayed, because a simultaneous increase in registrations carried the annual total from thirty thousand in 1914 to sixty thousand in 1919. The publicity attending the setting up of the Mayo Foundation, followed almost immediately by the boomingly prosperous "silk-shirt era" of the war, sent people in droves to Rochester, more of them than the attenuated staff could readily handle.

In addition there were draftees to examine and the war training school to keep going. Dr. Will and Dr. Charlie had agreed to provide short courses for incoming members of the medical corps, to bring them quickly abreast of the latest developments in medicine and surgery.

The Clinic men also gave courses for noncommissioned officers and privates who were to serve in the ambulance corps or as hospital orderlies or laboratory assistants, and St. Mary's Hospital took charge of the nurses who were sent, fifteen or twenty at a time, to brush up on anesthesia and operating-room procedure.

All told, there were always between sixty and seventy persons—in addition to the Foundation fellows—in training at Rochester throughout the war years, and the responsibility for supervising their work was heavy on the time and shoulders of Dr. Judd, who directed it all.

Under these conditions patients sometimes had to wait days or even weeks for examination, and the well-known Clinic rule, "First come first served," was changed to "The needy first." St. Mary's nurses long remembered how Dr. Graham, white-haired, weary, overworked, would say to someone clamoring insistently for his attention, "Here on my list are the names of two hundred people whom I must see first because they are poor and cannot stand the expense of waiting for medical help."

"And then came the flu epidemic!"

So sooner or later said anyone who talked about the war years at the Clinic. The staff had only *thought* they were busy before, for now the people literally poured into the Clinic from the immediate community. Assigned duties and stations were forgotten, and every doctor, nurse, technician, and secretary worked wherever he was needed most at the moment, often until late at night.

The doctors usually worked on the Clinic floor until four or four-thirty and then started out on drives through the countryside, sending the worst cases they found to the isolation unit at St. Mary's.

This new addition to the facilities of the hospital was a small hotel building next door which the Sisters of St. Francis had bought to get rid of the growing congestion on their very doorstep. It was remodeled and opened for use in June 1918 and so was ready when the influenza arrived in September.

The disease broke out in a mild form in the town first, then suddenly and virulently in the hospital itself. On one day in early October twenty persons, eighteen of them nurses, had to be moved to the isolation house. The next day patients began arriving from all over the county, and within a week the new unit was packed, even to cots in the hallways.

The St. Mary's staff also had been greatly reduced by summons to war service, and with the influenza victims absent too it was woefully inadequate to handle the influx, though everyone worked to the limit of her strength. Sometimes the nurses and even the superintendent went down to help in the kitchens and laundries. And on top of everything else, the sisters were driven to distraction by the constant phone calls from anxious friends and relatives of the patients.

The panic induced by the high mortality of that season's influenza was general throughout the country, and to the Clinic's burden of local victims were added hundreds of telegrams a day asking for advice as to treatment and for supplies of any possibly useful vaccine. The signing of the armistice went almost unheeded in the hectic rush.

"Medicine is the only victor in war."

When Dr. Louis B. Wilson went overseas early in 1918 as assistant director of the A.E.F. division of laboratories and infectious diseases, he found the entire scientific setup in a feeble state. Laboratories were few, competent personnel fewer, and clinical pathology was only something to play with when "more important" business was slow.

Dr. Wilson and his chief, Col. Joseph F. Siler, worked wonders. By early fall 1918 there were nearly three hundred laboratories in use in the A.E.F. and the internists and surgeons were beginning to view the laboratory doctor as a fully worthy member of the medical team.

Thousands of doctors who first experienced the regular use of a diagnostic laboratory in their war service returned home to demand similar facilities in their community hospitals, and clinical pathology came of age during the next decade. In 1926 the American College of Surgeons included in its list of minimum requirements for accredited hospitals a complete laboratory service headed by "a graduate of medicine, *especially trained in clinical pathology.*"

War service gave many a doctor his first taste also of organized cooperation among specialists—teamwork in practice. When Dr. A. L. Lockwood, a young Canadian surgeon who spent four years in service at the front in France, received his discharge he was reluctant to return to the private practice he had left, because he was convinced that the future of medicine lay in the kind of coordinated effort he had been sharing in. Stopping off in London for a few days on his way home, he found himself next to Sir Berkeley Moynihan at a public dinner one night and discussed the problem with him.

Finally Moynihan said to him, "If I were your age, my boy, I would try to attach myself to the Mayo Clinic, because there in my opinion is the most outstanding center for surgical and medical advance in the world today."

Dr. Lockwood took the older man's advice and three months later arrived in Rochester to begin work with the Mayos. "My first reaction was unutterable amazement," he wrote later, "amazement that increased month by month." For he found in Rochester a degree of integration and cooperation that the army medical corps had not approached.

Not all doctors shared Lockwood's reaction to their war experience with medical teamwork—those who must solo to be happy did not like it—but many were impressed with its advantages and scores of private group clinics were organized immediately following the war.

A desire to improve the quality of medical care was not the only motive at work; new methods were also bringing to the fore the corollary problem of increasing costs.

As the medical course lengthened from two years to six and more, as the family doctor's little black bag grew into a battery of expensive equipment, as laboratory diagnosis was added to physical examination by the clinician—in short, as the horse-and-buggy era yielded to modern scientific medicine —the doctor's investment multiplied many times.

The increasing costs meant fewer patients, more unpaid bills, and an overhead out of all proportion to returns. Some doctors attempted to solve the problem by renting offices in a "physicians and surgeons" or a "medical arts" building, where they might share the use of common laboratories, and others banded together in frank imitation of the Mayo Clinic, now so well and widely known.

The tremendous publicity given the story of the Foundation had finished the process of making the Mayos national celebrities. Everything they said or did now was news the public wanted, and newspapers everywhere carried all sorts of items about the brothers and their Clinic.

In a St. Paul hotel reporters came upon an English airman who was on his way to Rochester because the surgeons at home had told him that was the only place he could get effective treatment for his eyes, injured in a plane crash at the front.

Down in Tulsa a man was found paralyzed and unconscious in the street, apparently the victim of thieves, and a wealthy benefactress took him to the Mayo Clinic and then, in the hope of locating his relatives, advertised his story, including the miracle of repair worked by Clinic surgeons.

Over in Marinette, Wisconsin, the relief committee of the Lloyd Manufacturing Company, investigating the case of a young man and his wife, both ill and without means of support, discovered that they owed the Mayo Clinic two hundred dollars for services in a previous illness. Having written to inform the Clinic of the circumstances, the committee were so impressed when they got an immediate reply canceling the bill that they thought the story ought to be made public.

The national news services picked up such stories as these and spread them through the country, and reporters, assigned to get material for feature stories, nosed out more anecdotes that became perennials.

There was one about the business tycoon who sent the Clinic a check for a thousand dollars to pay for an operation on a member of his family and promptly got a courteous letter returning his check, informing him that the Clinic set its own fees, and enclosing a bill for five thousand dollars. And another about the pompous millionaire who, seeing Dr. Will cross the Clinic lobby, bustled up to ask importantly, "Are you the head doctor here?"

"No," Dr. Will replied soberly. "My brother is the head doctor. I'm the belly doctor."

On top of all this came a succession of famous patients who carried the Mayos with them into the newspapers. Dr. Will and Dr. Charlie were called to St. Paul to perform an emergency operation on James J. Hill, the railroad magnate; Dr. Charlie was summoned to Washington in consultation on Mrs. Harding, wife of the President; and Franklin K. Lane, secretary of the interior under Woodrow Wilson, was sent to Rochester by his New York doctor, "to see if it is true that my stomach and my gallbladder have become too intimate," he said. "Rochester is the Reno where such divorces are granted."

The verdict was a diseased appendix and gallbladder; "the latter was a stone quarry and the former a cesspool," said Lane. But he had a bad heart too, and Dr. Will advised him against operation, since with care he could live for some time without it.

But Lane was tired of his invalidism, and after a few months in California he returned to Rochester determined to run the risk of surgery. He came through the operation well and everyone was jubilant, but an attack of angina carried him off suddenly ten days later.

Then some of the many letters he had written from Rochester, colorful accounts of his reflections on life and death and politics, were widely published and made the subject of much editorial and pulpit comment. And these letters were full of bits about the Mayos and their Clinic.

Thus it was that *Mayo* became a household name in America, so generally familiar that a Michigan newspaper could print the following business notice: "Goodfellows' Barber Shop Closed for Two Weeks, On Account of Having to Go to Mayo Brothers."

Attempts to exploit this reputation were many and varied. Scarcely a month passed without some new report that the Mayos intended to establish a branch of their famous clinic here, there, everywhere—in Red Wing, in Winona, in Manitoba, on the Salton Sea! Where the rumors came from was a mystery, and Dr. Will's emphatic denials did not always put a stop to them.

The story that the Mayos planned to move to southern California persisted for months, and when it was denied in one town it sprang up in another. Finally it settled on the Ambassador Hotel in Los Angeles; the Mayos had bought it and would turn it into a sanatorium. Angrily the manager of the hotel denied the story; the Ambassador was having the best season in its history, he said, and no part of it had been sold or was for sale. But his statement was discounted on the grounds that the Mayo brothers wanted to discourage the real estate promotion the rumor had started.

At last Dr. Will wrote to his old friend, John Willis Baer, now president of Occidental College, asking him to do anything he could to squelch the story. There had never been the slightest foundation for it, he said; he and Charlie did not have and never had had any intention of starting a branch clinic anywhere. Baer gave the letter to the newspapers and the story died.

More annoying were the many fakers who proclaimed themselves representatives of the Mayo Clinic or exhibited testimonials from the Mayos for the nostrums they were selling. One scoundrel in Winnipeg called himself Dr. Gordon Mayo, opened a luxurious suite of offices, and was the busiest doctor in town until the municipal authorities, suspecting he was performing abortions, uncovered his identity as Russell Dumas, an ex-convict.

The impostors in Canada got so numerous that the Clinic, as a warning, threatened to prosecute two doctors who established "a branch of the Mayo Clinic" in a Manitoba town, saying the Mayos' large Canadian clientele had made it necessary to do so. The threat was enough to force a public apology from the doctors and the closing of their clinic.

It was not so easy to deal with those who clung to the edge of truth and artfully *implied* their connection with the Rochester institution. A practitioner in Brazil, Indiana, managed this by saying that such clinics as his were approved by the Drs. Mayo because they had more patients than they could handle and that his surgeons and anesthetists had spent years at the operating table with the Mayo brothers—all on the basis of one former Clinic fellow who was on his staff for a few months.

The American College of Surgeons, organized in 1913 on the model of the royal colleges of England and Scotland to establish such qualifications for election to its fellowship that the designation *F.A.C.S.* would signify to profession and public alike a competent practitioner of surgery, elected Dr. W. J. Mayo its president from 1918 to 1920.

Wearied by all the postwar debate over the proper role of the United States in the affairs of Europe, Dr. Will revived the plan, dropped during the war, to extend the College fellowships to worthy Latin American surgeons. Pan-American cooperation, he thought, would be a less controversial and more fruitful possibility than entanglements in Europe.

With the approval of the board of regents of the College, Dr. Will and Dr. Franklin Martin, secretary of the College, decided to visit the southern continent, and with their wives sailed from New York early in January 1920.

Dr. Will as usual had planned an occupation for the interval on board ship. Professional and lay friends had been urging him and Charlie to publish their own version of how the Clinic and Foundation came to be, and they had finally decided to do so through the Clinic division of publications. So Dr. Will asked Mrs. Mellish to go with him to South America, and he spent much of his time on the way dictating to her an outline of the story she was to write.

When at the proper place in the narrative he paid tribute to Dr. Wilson's work in organizing the laboratories, Mrs. Mellish was moved to interpolate some sentences of her own. "L. Wilson is tremendously brilliant," she wrote. "I have met few men his intellectual equal. In addition to his scientific abilities he has a most pleasing personality."

Her admiration for Dr. Wilson was fully reciprocated, and shortly afterward they were married. Together they wrote the *Sketch of the History of the Mayo Clinic and the Mayo*

Foundation that was published anonymously in 1926. As they worked on it they discovered they were too close to the story and its characters to see it in proper perspective, so with Dr. Will's approval they deliberately stripped their sketch to a skeleton of statistics, names, and dates, leaving it for someone with more temerity to flesh the facts.

The gracious Latin Americans turned the Mayo-Martin tour of the major cities of Peru, Chile, Argentina, and Uruguay into a triumphal procession. Wherever their boat docked or their train stopped, a reception committee was waiting to whirl them into a round of luncheons and dinners on the lushly beautiful estates of medical men, government officials, and wealthy civilians. In between times they attended clinics, toured hospitals, and addressed many gatherings of medical students and practitioners.

In impressively formal ceremonies Dr. Mayo and Dr. Martin were both declared members of the Society of Surgery of Peru, and Dr. Will was awarded an honorary degree by the University of San Marcos in Lima, the oldest university in the western hemisphere.

Everywhere the two men were impressed by the wealth and social influence of their surgeon hosts, and even more by their learning in literature and art, their fine private libraries and art collections.

The spaciousness of the hospital and medical school buildings and the elaborately landscaped gardens surrounding them amazed the visitors from the United States. Nor could they find any fault with the instruction offered. Throughout South America the medical course was seven years in length and the examinations were so exacting that few North American or European surgeons could have passed them.

In Santiago, Chile, Mayo and Martin were taken to see a new dental college that was entirely equipped and staffed by North Americans. When they asked how this happened they were told a story worthy of Dr. Watson.

Some years earlier a fire broke out one night in the German

embassy, and amid the debris in the basement afterward was found a charred body that was identified from a ring, a watch, and bits of clothing as that of the German consul. A fortune in negotiable securities had been taken from the embassy vault, and the janitor of the building was missing. The authorities promptly issued a warrant charging the missing man with murder, theft, and arson.

Germany displayed great diplomatic indignation about the crime, and the Chilean government tried to make amends with fulsome eulogies of the dead consul and plans for elaborate obsequies. But it did not suspend the law requiring that in all cases of death by violence the corpse must be examined by a member of the jurisprudence faculty of the medical school, and the body in the basement came under the eye of Dr. Germán Valenzuela, who found it furnished with a perfect set of teeth except for one missing molar.

This was so unusual for a man of the consul's age that the curious Valenzuela sought an interview with the bereaved widow. Her husband had had a great deal of work done on his teeth, she said, and she gave the good doctor the name of the dentist who had done it. When the dentist's records showed a long list of bridges and fillings that should have graced the consul's mouth, Dr. Valenzuela went to see the wife of the missing janitor. As far as she knew her husband's teeth were quite sound, except for one he had had pulled.

A new warrant was immediately issued, and the German consul was caught at the Argentine border, where his escape had been delayed by a landslide that blocked the Trans-Andean railroad. The stolen securities were found in a money belt he was wearing, and he was tried and executed for the murder of the janitor.

When the grateful Chilean government told Dr. Valenzuela to name his own reward, he asked for money to build and equip a dental college on the American plan. The school Drs. Mayo and Martin were visiting was the result.

The two doctors had left home with a measure of the North

American's condescension toward Latin Americans, certain that the requirements for fellowship in the American College of Surgeons would work highly beneficial reforms in Latin American medicine; they returned with a wholesome respect for the southerners' ability to manage their own progress.

Both Dr. Martin and Dr. Will published long accounts of their trip, stressing the excellence of Latin American hospitals and surgeons, and when other surgeons were unbelieving, Dr. Will urged them to make the trip themselves, assuring them they would find it profitable, if only in an access of humility and modesty, which the United States so sadly needed in its relations with the southern nations.

Others did go, a few at first and then hundreds as the American College of Surgeons began organizing large clinical cruises of the sort Mayo and Martin had made. When the Pan-American Medical Association was organized in 1926 the cruises, or "floating congresses," were continued under its sponsorship, and either Dr. Will or Dr. Charlie was usually among those enrolled, often as an officer of the group.

In his account of their trip in 1920 Dr. Martin insisted that the enthusiastic welcome they received was in part a personal tribute to Dr. Mayo, whose work, he found, was widely known and admired below the border. The Latin American nations had contributed their share of members to the Rochester Surgeons Club, and Mexico was already sending occasional patients to the Clinic, among them relatives of both Obregón and Calles.

Then one day early in 1921 Dr. Howard Hartman, one of the younger clinicians, answered his phone to hear Dr. Will ask, "How would you like to go to Mexico City?" Very much, of course. Dr. Will told him the train was leaving in twenty minutes and that Dr. Lockwood the surgeon was going too. A telegram had just come from President Obregón asking for someone to attend General Benjamín Hill, his trusted companion in the many political rough-and-tumbles that marked his rise to power.

Drs. Hartman and Lockwood caught the train all right, but before they got across Iowa they received a wire telling them to return to Rochester; word had come from Obregón that Hill was dead.

Two weeks later Dr. Hartman got another call from Dr. Will asking how he would like to go to Mexico City. "Wolf, wolf," laughed Hartman, but Dr. Will said there had been some mistake two weeks before, because another telegram had come from Obregón calling for Clinic men to take care of Hill. So once again Drs. Lockwood and Hartman started for Mexico City.

The trip was a thriller. First they were stopped at the border because a railroad strike was in progress in Mexico and train travel was risky, and when they did get across, in a train that started secretly at night, they were delayed several times by the strikers. Once these men drained the feed tanks and once they made off with the engine, stranding the train in the middle of the desert with nothing for the passengers to eat but some unappetizing goatflesh the Mexican peasant women in the boxcar ahead cooked over an open fire. After a day and a night the ragged, unarmed soldiers sent along to guard the train got the engine back, and the doctors eventually arrived in Mexico City.

As they stepped off the train they were mobbed by Mexican newspapermen who had somehow got the idea that the two doctors were emissaries of President Harding bringing word of official United States recognition for the Obregón government.

And when at last the two men got away from the reporters and reached the president's palace, they learned that they had come in vain. The Clinic translator, a fellowship man of dubious attainments in Spanish, had gone astray; Hill *had* died three weeks before, and Obregón's second telegram was merely to ask the amount of his bill for the doctors' previous start.

Nonetheless, Obregón kept Lockwood and Hartman in

Mexico for ten days and gave them a good time. He supplied them with a car and an interpreter and they saw the sights in royal fashion. They returned to Rochester singing the praises of Mexican scenery and Mexican hospitality.

The next spring Dr. Ochsner invited several of the Clinic staff and their wives to vacation on his ranch-estate in Mexico. While the party were in Mexico City Dr. Will called on Obregón and was invited to attend a bullfight as the president's guest the next Sunday afternoon.

It was a benefit performance for the widow of a famous Mexican matador lately killed in Spain, and several of his most popular fellows were to appear. The huge crowd cheered wildly as the first fighter presented himself before the president's box and with a flourish of oratory dedicated his bull to the chief guest of the nation, Dr. Mayo.

The second fighter was the youngest of the lot, Luis Freg, the idol of the moment. His bull was Obregón's and he sought to dazzle the crowd by a display of extra daring, but his luck slipped and the bull gored him. He was carried from the field bleeding badly, and word soon went round that he was dying. Feeling an extra measure of responsibility since Freg's dedication was to him, President Obregón asked Dr. Mayo to see whether he could do anything to save the young man.

The little hospital in the rear of the ring was full of noise and confusion, crowded with the weeping friends and relatives of the injured matador, and the doctors, unable to check the hemorrhage by external pressure, gladly stepped aside for Dr. Mayo. After a quick glance he called for scissors, gloves, and gown. Then by the simple expedient of splitting the skin above the bleeding artery he was able to catch hold of the vessel and tie it.

The ease and speed with which he stopped the hemorrhage made a tremendous impression on the watching group, and word somehow got back to the crowd in the ring, so that when Dr. Will returned to his seat he was given a prolonged ovation.

The effect was as if a visiting Canadian doctor were to save the life of Joe Louis or Babe Ruth when American doctors could not. Everybody in Mexico heard the story and learned the name of Dr. Mayo.

A consequence of these incidental activities was a noticeable spurt in the number of Clinic patients from Latin America. Some were so obviously poverty-stricken that the Clinic men wondered how on earth they had managed to scrape together the money for the trip, but of course it was mostly the wealthy who came. The car of the Mexican secretary of war was virtually an ambulance carrying ministers and generals to and from the Clinic, and its driver became so familiar to the Rochester residents that they exchanged greetings with him on the street.

One satisfied patient brought half a dozen others, and the numbers coming from south of the border increased steadily to a thousand and more a year. This was the principal factor in the inauguration of a special airline from Minneapolis through Rochester to San Antonio, Texas, where the Latin American passengers fanned out by plane or train to their respective countries.

Among the earliest of the regular patients was the wealthy and cultured Larco Herrera of Peru. On one of his first visits he noticed how little there was for his compatriots to do in their free time, and shortly after he returned to Peru he sent the Clinic several hundred books in Spanish and French for the use of his people. He and others added to the collection from time to time until the Clinic possessed a Spanish library of well over a thousand volumes, shelved in a room set aside for Latin American patients.

In 1924 Beatriz Montes, an English-speaking teacher of Spanish literature and history in Havana, came to the Clinic for an operation, and during her convalescence she was so helpful in smoothing the way for Spanish-speaking patients that the Clinic asked her to stay on as a full-time Spanish secretary and librarian. And there were soon so many to be entertained and advised that she had to have an assistant.

It was the reputation of the Mayos that attracted the early patients from Latin America, but since by no means all of them were in need of surgery Dr. Will began referring them to Dr. Hartman. They learned to trust the internist and to feel at ease with him, because he made every effort to understand their way of thinking and feeling. Eventually they came to think of the Mayo Clinic in terms of Dr. Hartman, and many a letter from Latin America was addressed to "Dr. Howard Hartman, Director of the Mayo Clinic."

The growth of the Clinic's Latin American practice led the residents of Rochester to take an unusual interest in things Spanish. When Dr. and Mrs. Hartman returned from their journeys to Central and South America, they talked to many local groups about the lands and peoples they had seen, and soon other Rochester folk, inside and outside the Clinic group, were spending their vacations below the border.

Clinic secretaries bought Spanish dictionaries and registered for correspondence courses in the language, Spanish-speaking nurses were imported for the hospitals, and when WPA came along the citizens persuaded its director to give them a night class in Spanish. The first time the class met, the teacher got the surprise of her life, because she was expecting to meet ten or twelve persons and instead faced a crowd of nearly two hundred—barbers, waitresses, and clerks who felt a need for Spanish in their daily duties.

21. *Toward the Future*

THROUGH all the strain and disorganization of the war years, the future of the Clinic was never far from Dr. Will's mind. He knew that something less ephemeral than a personal partnership was necessary to guarantee the contract with the university and to fulfill the Clinic's obligations to its younger staff members and to the Sisters of St. Francis.

Endowing the Foundation had wiped out the brothers' personal savings, but as the "principal partners" they still retained ownership of the properties and capital of the partnership, and they wanted now to turn these into a permanent endowment for the Clinic.

After much thought and discussion, they decided to define only their general intentions in making the gift and to leave it for able men of future generations to realize these intentions in accordance with changing conditions. One thing above all they wanted to ensure: that the trust would contribute to the advancement of medicine and not to the enrichment of any individual or group.

As the first step toward these ends, on the advice of their lawyers they incorporated the Mayo Properties Association, a self-perpetuating charitable organization without capital stock, made up of nine trustees. The trustees were to serve without compensation and were to be responsible before the law for administering the trust in accord with the purposes outlined in the deed of gift—

> to aid and advance the study and investigation of human ailments and injuries, and the causes, prevention, relief and cure thereof, and the study and investigation of prob-

lems of hygiene, health and public welfare, and the promotion of medical, surgical, and scientific learning, skill,
education and investigation, and to engage in the conduct
and to aid and assist in medical, surgical, and scientific
research in the broadest sense. . . . No part of the net
income of this corporation, or of its property or assets
upon dissolution or liquidation shall ever inure to the
benefit of any of its members, or of any private individual.

The first trustees were Dr. Will and Dr. Charlie and their
partners, Drs. Plummer, Judd, and Balfour, together with
Harry Harwick, and Lawyers Eaton, George Granger, and
L. L. Brown of Winona. To them the Drs. Mayo in October
1919 transferred the ownership of all the properties of the
Mayo Clinic from the building itself down to the last test
tube, case record, and pathological specimen in it, along with
all accumulated cash and securities.

By 1925 the properties were valued at five million dollars
and the securities amounted to five and a half millions more.

This transfer of ownership was marred by one outstanding
unpleasantness. Dr. Graham was too wholeheartedly a clinician to favor making research and education auxiliary functions of the Clinic. He had disapproved of the Foundation and
its affiliation with the university, and when it came to under-
writing that affiliation by assigning the assets of the partnership to the Mayo Properties Association, he refused to give his
consent.

Since Dr. Will was determined to carry the plan through,
the two were at an impasse for some time. Mr. Harwick tried
to work out a compromise settlement but could find none that
both men would accept, and in the end Dr. Graham resigned
from the Clinic, receiving the one year's income allowed him
by the agreement he and Dr. Stinchfield had signed some
twenty years earlier.

Dr. Will was sincerely sorry to see Graham go, because, he

said, "I would rather have his opinion on the medical aspects of a surgical case than that of any other man I have ever had the privilege of working with."

But it was Dr. Charlie whose position was least happy. As Graham's brother-in-law, he was caught between two loyalties, but in the test the bond between him and Will did not fail. Gently but unequivocally he backed his brother's decision.

Retiring to his farm, Dr. Graham gave his whole time to the stock-raising that had been his hobby for several years. He had more time to think than his Clinic job had ever left him, and as he watched the growth of the Foundation and its effect on the Clinic he came finally to see that he had been wrong. When he did, he was big enough to go to Dr. Will and tell him so, and the day of their reconciliation was a happy one for both of them.

The second step toward the brothers' goal was the reorganization of the Clinic itself, and in 1923 the personal partnership was replaced with a "voluntary association," a kind of cross between a group partnership and a corporation. At that time all proprietary and participating interests in the Clinic income ceased, and the former partners, including Dr. Will and Dr. Charlie, joined the rest of the staff on a fixed salary.

Then by a formal contract the Properties Association leased its building and all its equipment to the Clinic, the annual rental being the total net income of the Clinic, which was to be added to the endowment funds of the Association. So that the Clinic should not at some future date raise the salaries of its staff to eat up the gross income and reduce the rental, thus defeating the purpose of the arrangement, the contract stipulated that all Clinic salaries must be approved by the Association.

As Dr. Will explained, he and Charlie wanted to provide their staff members with a reasonably good living and a guarantee of security in their old age, but they did not want anyone to receive enough wealth from the Clinic "to keep his children on the beach at Miami when they ought to be working."

The administration of the Clinic was vested in a board of governors made up of the former partners, Mr. Harwick, and two members chosen from the staff. The supervision of professional activities was entrusted to an executive committee of five members appointed by the board of governors from a list of fifteen nominated by the staff, and all matters of general policy were to be determined by a council made up of the board of governors, the executive committee, and the president of the staff.

Despite the new degree of representation thus accorded to the staff, Dr. Will was not satisfied. Looking toward the future, when he and Dr. Charlie and their partners would be gone, he felt that a wider distribution of administrative responsibilities was necessary to educate more members of the group to an understanding of its problems and policies. So he proposed entrusting various phases of the administration to standing committees appointed from the staff.

Dr. Charlie approved, and in spite of strong opposition from other members of the board of governors the committee system was gradually put into effect throughout 1923 and 1924. There the brothers let the reorganization rest for the moment, to allow time for consolidation and testing before further steps were taken.

In his look toward the future Dr. Will saw clearly that it was as necessary for the hotel and hospital facilities to be secure from dispersion on the owners' death as for the Clinic itself to be so. On his urgent recommendation John Kahler and his friends, who had built the big Colonial Hospital in 1915, organized the Kahler Corporation and began in earnest to provide hospitals and hotels for the Clinic patients.

They opened three new hospitals in as many years, the Stanley, the Worrall, and the Curie, with a combined capacity of just under three hundred beds and five operating rooms. When these were still not enough and the addition of a large annex to the Zumbro Hotel did not fill the pressing need in that direction, the Kahler Corporation plunged. They bought the site across the corner from the Clinic and began building a huge new hotel-hospital, a truly remarkable structure to rise almost in the midst of cornfields.

Then came the postwar agricultural depression. Registration at the Clinic dropped swiftly back from sixty thousand in 1919 to just above forty-nine thousand in 1922, and the proportion of nonpaying patients rose sharply. Under these conditions neither the Clinic nor the Properties Association was in any condition to help the Corporation out of a serious situation, and for the first time the investment of outside capital was sought; Kahler Corporation stock was put on the open market and sold throughout the country.

For a while the prospects were dark indeed, but by the middle 1920s conditions had greatly improved, registrations were climbing fast again, and Kahler stock rose to two hundred dollars a share.

The new Kahler provided two hundred and ten hospital beds, one hundred and fifty more for convalescent patients, and two hundred and twenty for hotel purposes. When it was opened in September 1921 the old Kahler House across the street was renamed the Damon in honor of Mrs. W. J. Mayo and turned into a hospital for a few years. Then it was changed back into a hotel, which it has remained.

While the Kahler was under construction Henry Plummer, seeing the possibility of a further convenience for Clinic patients, suggested that it be connected with the Clinic by an underground passage. Recognizing a good idea, the Corporation and the Properties Association joined forces to build the first subway tunnel, between the Kahler Hotel and the Clinic building. With the years this grew into an extensive system of subways connecting the Clinic with all the Kahler hospitals and hotels, a convenience that both patients and staff greatly appreciate, especially in wintertime.

The Mayo organizations and the Kahler Corporation were

mutually independent in financing and management, though a number of individuals in the Clinic group owned Kahler stock and Harry Harwick was a director of the Corporation as well as an administrative officer of the Clinic. The Properties Association owned Corporation stock only to the amount of the Mayos' investment in the old Kahler House, which the brothers had turned over to the Association along with their other securities. But a formal contract gave the Clinic control of medical policies in all Kahler hospitals, stipulated that none but Clinic surgeons should operate in them, and provided that the Properties Association could buy them on one year's notice should this ever seem expedient.

Dr. Will and Dr. Charlie made no move to transfer their operating from St. Mary's, but as the beds provided by the Kahler hospitals pulled ahead of St. Mary's three hundred, the threat of being superseded in their preferred position was enough to spur the sisters to action. And they decided to have done with building additions that were full again almost before the carpenters left. They borrowed two million dollars and ordered the construction of a big surgical pavilion that would double the capacity of the hospital at a single stroke.

The pavilion, opened in the spring of 1922, provided spacious quarters for the surgeons on its fifth floor: ten new operating rooms grouped in pairs with a small sterilizing room between each two. Everything was the latest in design and equipment, providing, by its striking contrast to that first St. Mary's operating room, a measure of the astounding progress of surgery.

Amid all this clean, gleaming tile, in this bare, bright world of white, so sterile and stripped, there was no place for the old makeshifts of handrail platforms and slanting mirrors; here members of the Surgeons Club were accommodated on two rows of concrete benches railed off above the table on two sides of each operating room. And across the corridor a comfortable lounge was set aside for them, furnished with an electrically operated bulletin board that told them at a glance what operation was in progress in each room at any moment.

The Clinic building, which had seemed so spacious, was now totally inadequate and resort to all kinds of expedients was again necessary. The old annex and library and even some of the storerooms previously used were reoccupied; one floor after another of the adjoining Zumbro Annex was rented from the Kahler Corporation, connected with the Clinic by a covered bridge, and filled with the overflow of offices and laboratories; and finally several whole sections were transferred to an upper floor in the Kahler Hotel.

Thus the close integration so happily achieved in 1914 was physically shattered by 1925, but the attitudes and habits it had developed in the group survived and intersectional cooperation and consultation were maintained in spite of the difficulties.

The multiplication of diagnostic sections went on as before, though at an even faster pace, through a process of reproduction by cell division. Each section swelled in number of associates and of major interests till the limit of practicability was reached and somebody split off to start a new one.

For example, Dr. Plummer's section eventually gave rise to a second section in diseases of the thyroid, to one in diseases of the esophagus and bronchi, and to one in cardiology, or heart disease, as well as to an electrocardiograph laboratory.

By this time diagnosis had come of age as an independent function of the Clinic, and during the 1920s it matured rapidly to a point near equality with the surgery that had brought it into being. More and more general practitioners were acquiring the habit of referring their uncertain cases to the Clinic, or to some similar institution, just for diagnosis, so they could proceed with greater confidence in their own treatment of the case. Also, some doctors had begun to see that their proper job was *Keeping* people well and the medical profession was awakening to the need for taking the public into its confidence instead of shrouding its work in ignorance-breeding mystery. The consequence was a noticeable increase in what may be called preventive examination, a periodic physical checkup designed to catch incipient disorders before they produce actual illness.

All these developments contributed greatly to the growth of the diagnostic function at the Clinic.

The most sweeping development of the postwar period was the addition, at long last, of internal medicine and medical specialties to the Clinic practice. Thanks to Henry Plummer, medical treatment had never been entirely lacking, but it was too incidental and too meager in volume to be taken much into account.

When the 1912 addition to St. Mary's was built its fourth floor was set aside for medical patients, and the Colonial Hospital was intended to be largely a medical unit. But each time, before the internists could gather sufficient momentum to fill their beds with patients, the busy surgeons, needing more room than they had, took over the empty medical beds and literally crowded the incipient development off the scene.

It was the organization of the Foundation that finally made action imperative. No matter how fine the Clinic provisions for training young doctors in diagnosis and surgery, it could not pretend to true graduate school status without facilities and staff for teaching internal medicine. As soon as the affiliation with the University of Minnesota became permanent, Dr. Will and Dr. Charlie ordered a section of beds in the Stanley Hospital set aside and kept free for medical patients.

There were not yet many qualified internists with the investigative turn of mind, but in the course of their war duty the Mayos and Dr. Wilson made the acquaintance of some good ones who, left foot-loose when the war ended, were persuaded to join the Mayo Clinic and develop the new medical unit.

The Kahler Corporation provided temporary quarters for them in an old hotel, which was renamed the Olmsted Hospital, the Clinic furnished them with laboratories and assistants, and they began treatment and research in pediatrics and certain diseases of metabolism. Eighteen months later, when the surgeons moved into the new St. Mary's pavilion, the medical men took over the beds of the old building and set up their laboratories in the old operating rooms.

One diagnostic section after another was assigned its own group of hospital beds for the treatment of patients in its special field of interest, and with surprising speed the medical practice passed surgery in the volume of patients handled.

Then the day when the internist and laboratory members of the group served solely to pyramid the usefulness of the surgeons was gone, and far across the sea, from his post as professor of medicine at Oxford University, William Osler noted the change and hailed it with joy: "The surgeons have had their day—and they know it! The American St. Cosmas and St. Damian—the Mayo brothers—have made their Clinic today as important in medicine as it ever was in surgery. Wise men! They saw how the pendulum was swinging."

But surgery did not slacken in its progress or decline in its usefulness for the patient. True, in their advance the internists took back the treatment of some maladies they had surrendered to the surgeon, such as duodenal ulcer, but in more instances they made discoveries and originated methods of pre- and postoperative treatment that brought within reach of the scalpel a host of cases which earlier would have been unlikely subjects for operation.

The postwar surgical development at the Clinic was a matter of multiplying and expanding the sections in general surgery and marking out a number of new surgical specialties.

Operations on the brain and nervous system had gravitated almost entirely into Dr. Beckman's section, and by 1916 his work in that field was one of the most promising phases of Clinic surgery. It was a severe loss to the group when he contracted an infection during an operation on a septic case and died from it.

After his death the neurological cases were assigned to Dr. Alfred W. Adson, a young man of thirty who had been Dr. Beckman's associate. Adson was not proud of his first efforts, and he determined to "beat this thing." So he went to Boston to study with Harvey Cushing, one of the world's foremost neurosurgeons, and returned to carry on Beckman's work with gratifying success.

One morning shortly after he returned from Boston he was preparing to operate on a case he had diagnosed as a tumor of the spinal cord when in walked Dr. Will, Dr. Charlie, and a guest, the great Moynihan of Leeds.

Exact diagnosis of spinal cord tumor was a difficult matter, and young Adson standing beside his patient under the eyes of those three felt he was on the spot. His hands began to perspire. Sensing his predicament, Dr. Charlie considerately suggested that they might move on since it was nearly time for lunch.

"No," said Moynihan, "I want to see this."

He pulled a chair close to the table and sat down. He was the Mayos' guest, so there was nothing they could do but stand by, and Dr. Adson had to proceed.

"Well, the tumor showed up where I had believed it to be," he said in telling the story, "and after that I relaxed again because the operation itself was not difficult."

When Moynihan returned home and was asked what he had seen at Rochester on this trip, he replied, "A high school boy operating for spine tumor!" But the "high school boy" did so well that three years later a special section on neurological surgery was established with him in charge, and it rapidly developed into one of the distinctions of the Clinic.

Plastic surgery on the face and neck became another Clinic specialty by virtue of volume. Through the removal of malignant lesions many of the patients in the ear, nose, and throat section lost some part of their face or throat. Their postoperative state was often sad indeed, and agreeing with Dr. Will that "every human being has a divine right to look human,"

Dr. Gordon B. New, an associate in the section, concentrated on the problem of restoring these patients to something like a normal appearance.

As his work grew to include the correction of deformities like harelip and cleft palate and the repair of facial injuries received in automobile accidents, it proved necessary to establish a separate section on "laryngology, oral and plastic" under his direction. By the end of the 1930s the section had grown to a staff of four full-time surgeons, using three operating rooms in the Kahler and performing more than two thousand operations a year.

Although only a minor part of the section's work was what the layman calls plastic surgery—face lifting and the like, more specifically named "cosmetic surgery"—Dr. New and his associates learned that they must exercise special care in selecting the patients for operation. They had to weed out those who came with a dream of sudden transformation from ugly ducklings into glamorous swans, for however amazing the results achieved, such persons were likely to be disappointed in their exaggerated expectations and so their end, psychologically, would be worse than their beginning.

For many years diagnosis by use of the proctoscope, an instrument that permits the doctor to make a direct examination of the rectum, was one of the incidental duties of the urologists. Then one day Dr. Will remarked casually to young Dr. Louis A. Buie that there was a big opportunity waiting for someone enterprising enough to concentrate on proctology. Because no one liked the idea of spending his days examining and treating rectums, a great many persons were suffering from uncorrected deformities or diseases of that body part, and they would seek relief if it were available.

Dr. Buie took the hint and within a few years he was doing so much work in his new field that a separate section on proctology was formed with him as its head. By the end of the 1930s his section was one of the busiest at the Clinic—another demonstration of Dr. Will's genius for seeing opportunities.

These few examples must illustrate the many others like them that carried surgery far beyond its state in the days when the Mayo brothers made their phenomenal reputations. The Clinic pioneered in its share of new techniques, but in most it continued the role of the Mayo brothers by adopting the best discoveries of others and through intelligent use of them in its huge practice refining them and extending their scope.

The development of laboratory medicine was, as in diagnosis and surgery, a matter of continuing differentiation of function due to the amount of work. The one clinical laboratory of early days became a whole cluster, one each for serology (serum tests and therapy), hematology (blood counts and smears), bacteriology, parasitology, urinalysis, and gastric analysis. These constituted the division of clinical pathology under the joint directorship of Dr. Sanford and Dr. Thomas B. Magath, who joined the group in 1919.

The work in clinical chemistry became so extensive that it was made a separate division entirely. In addition to the tremendous job of doing all the chemical analyses of blood, urine, and spinal fluid, this section was charged with the manufacture of all therapeutic solutions and compounds that were not yet widely enough used to be put on the market by a commercial company.

In surgical pathology Dr. MacCarty's work grew with St. Mary's Hospital until in the new pavilion his laboratory across the hall from the operating rooms was considerably larger than the whole of the surgical floor in the first building. A similar laboratory was established in each downtown hospital as it was opened, and these were placed in the charge of Dr. Albert C. Broders, who as assistant and then associate had been trained by Dr. MacCarty.

The sheer volume of the work passing through the laboratory sections forced the staff members in many instances to make important technical improvements.

For instance, the x-ray section simply could not handle a

thousand and more films a day in the usual way—that is, immersing each film in the developing bath for a few minutes, drawing it out to see whether it was ready, then putting it back for a minute or so longer. So with the help of experts from the film company the staff worked out an exact time-table: exposure so long and immersion so long for perfect results. Then they could develop the films in units of eight or ten at a time. They also devised an apparatus for controlling the heat and humidity in the drying room, so they could finish the drying of a film in twenty minutes instead of the usual hour.

As a result of these improvements they could make their report to the clinician the same day he called for the x-ray, thus saving many a patient a day or more of idle waiting.

Virtually no research is done in the clinical laboratories. The volume of purely clinical work leaves the staff no time for research, and none of their specimens are taken or their tests made for research purposes. But their findings are filed with the case histories and so contribute to the investigation that is an important by-product of all the clinical processes.

Few problems arise for which the vast accumulation of Clinic records and specimens cannot provide a series of cases that yield valuable statistical information, and most of the Clinic internists and surgeons are continually engaged in some piece of investigation, reviewing their own experience and that of the group as the Mayo brothers and their pioneer associates had always done.

And the patient benefits from the attitude this scientific curiosity engenders in his clinician. As Thomas Huxley said, "He who does not go beyond the facts will seldom get as far as the facts," and the practitioner who is content with wrapping up a swollen ankle or cutting out a peptic ulcer will soon be falling short in even these processes. But the questing spirit of honest research is likely to set him asking why the ankle swelled or the ulcer developed, and this attitude lifts his horizon beyond the immediate case to possibilities for improvement.

The Clinic man who best demonstrated this approach to medical practice and its great possibilities for progress was, of course, Henry Plummer.

With the years Dr. Plummer had developed into a real eccentric—tall, thin, stooped, with a long, lean face, and the eyes and mouth of an eager dreamer. A mention of his name to anyone who knew him will start a stream of stories, most of them illustrating a degree of abstraction that makes the absent-minded professor a practical man of affairs by comparison.

He always ate his lunch at the same restaurant and always ordered the same meal, so that sometimes when he sat talking overlong his waitress would clear away the table and a second girl coming by would bring him his order all over again. And he usually ate it, forgetting he had already eaten. His table companions never knew whether their conversation would end up on a Cook's tour or on the fine points of Italian marbles. But they could be fairly sure they would have to pay the check, for Plummer never remembered it.

One day he sold his car to one of his young assistants, and the next morning he listened with great interest to the young man's excited tale of its disappearance the night before. Suddenly Dr. Plummer started for the door with a queer look on his face and in half an hour came back to explain sheepishly that the car was in his garage. He had driven home in it the previous night, forgetting that he had sold it.

A favorite tale told again and again by his former associates is that one morning Mrs. Plummer arrived at the Clinic all out of breath with a pair of her husband's trousers over her arm. When she saw that Henry was fully clothed she sighed with relief, and at his reproachful glance said, "Well, dear, the coat to these was gone and you know you might . . ."

Mrs. Plummer denied that this ever happened but admitted that it easily could have!

Often Dr. Plummer would wander into the office of one of

the administrative officers to discuss something he had on his mind, then suddenly break off in the midst of a sentence, stand lost in thought for a few minutes, turn and walk out. In half an hour or an hour perhaps, he would come back and take up his sentence exactly where he had left off, seemingly quite unaware that in the meantime the other man had started a conference with someone else.

Sometimes Plummer would disappear from his office on the Clinic floor and was nowhere to be found when he was needed. Finally one of the assistants would be sent to hunt him up, in the Clinic or out of it. And many times the young man found him in the basement, sitting in an old wooden chair, its back tilted against the furnace—just sitting there thinking and smoking, the ash long on the end of his cigar and the part that had fallen scattered over the front of his vest.

One man who worked closely with Plummer for many years as his student, assistant, and associate insisted that all this so-called absentmindedness was really a superb power of detachment that Plummer developed as a defense. Someone was always hunting him to ask about this or that or to have him see a patient or take a look at a laboratory process, and if he was to have the time to think that was so important to him he had to protect himself somehow. So he learned to hear, see, and remember what he wanted to and ignored the rest.

Whatever the reason for Plummer's behavior, all but a few who disliked him intensely are agreed that he was a great thinker and a superb clinician. He was "the best brain the Clinic ever had" in Dr. Will's opinion, and "the only genius on the Clinic staff" according to Dr. Mann. If genius is, as someone has defined it, "the ability to deduce correctly from observation without the benefit of previous experience," Dr. Plummer undeniably possessed it. His ability to reason straight, forward and backward, from a few data was phenomenal.

Among his many medical interests the thyroid gland remained his most enduring preoccupation, and his power to diagnose disease of the thyroid from the patient's appearance was at once the wonder and the despair of his associates.

One of them has told about a patient of his whose symptoms were confusing, some of them pointing to one trouble and some to another. He concentrated on the case, determined to arrive at the solution before he called Dr. Plummer in consultation. But before he was quite ready, Plummer walked through the waiting room one morning while the woman was sitting there. He gave her no more than a glance, but when he got back to the examining rooms he asked whose patient she was and said he wanted to see her. Then he described her exactly and outlined her case more completely than the younger man could after many hours of examination and thought.

Once a week all the men especially interested in the goiter problem, the clinicians, surgeons, chemists, and pathologists, met at the Kahler Hotel for a "goiter lunch," at which they discussed the problems in the field and the progress of their current cases. Plummer led these discussions, and some of the younger men later admitted that often they understood about ten per cent of what he said; the rest was over their heads. Plummer thought so fast and looked down so many alleys in order to pick the right one that other men were likely to get lost and left behind.

Once thyroxin had been isolated, the next step in the thyroid problem was to determine the normal rate of metabolism, the rate at which the human motor burns its gasoline, which is determined by the efficiency of the thyroid gland.

Physiologists knew how to find the rate in each individual, and they had a set of standard rates based on a series of studies of a small number of cases each, but a single study of a great number of individuals was necessary to answer with reliable exactness the question, What is the normal rate of metabolism and at what point does pathological variation begin?

The Mayo Clinic offered a peerless opportunity for such a

study, and Dr. Walter Boothby accepted the invitation to move from Harvard to Rochester to conduct it.

Over a period of years he and his associates in the new metabolism laboratory measured the rates of thousands of persons—patients, doctors, nurses, Rochester citizens, everyone they could persuade to submit to the simple procedure that is now a common diagnostic practice. On the basis of their findings in this vast series they set up new standards, which were generally adopted because nowhere else in the world had so many metabolism tests been made.

The Boothby standards made the rate of metabolism a reliable aid in diagnosing thyroid disorders, but they did not advance the *treatment* of exophthalmic goiter.

That had remained virtually at a standstill since 1913. There was still no sure way of determining the need for the multiple-stage operation and no way of eliminating the postoperative crisis that caused most of the mortality. Consequently most surgeons were still referring their patients to more experienced operators like Dr. Charlie and his associates. This was the situation in 1922.

Dr. Plummer meanwhile had been elaborating his two-product theory to explain the mechanism that produced the disease. When thyroxin proved to be sixty-five per cent iodine, he posed the possibility that the extra toxic substance which he postulated as the cause of the crises in exophthalmic goiter was a noniodized molecule of thyroxin.

He reasoned this way: Some stimulus causes the thyroid gland to work too fast, and if there is not enough iodine readily available in the blood, the gland turns out a half-finished product, a molecule of thyroxin with the essential iodine left out.

On the basis of this hypothesis it would be logical to give the patient iodine to increase the amount of raw material for the gland's production process.

The importance of iodine in the prevention of *simple* goiter was already well established, but no one had given it a real trial in exophthalmic goiter because everyone was certain it was dangerous in that disease. The great Kocher of Switzerland had found that it aggravated the symptoms in some cases, and he had so emphasized the dangers of the "improper" use of iodine that members of the medical profession had come to believe it was malpractice to give iodine in any form to a patient with exophthalmic goiter.

Apparently Dr. Plummer succumbed to this general idea, because for years he made no attempt to try out in practice his own reasoning about iodine.

Then early in 1922 he settled to the task of writing an account of thyroid disease for a new edition of *Oxford Medicine*. This in itself was unusual, for Dr. Plummer's major defect, in the opinion of his Clinic colleagues, was that he seldom carried any of his work to the conclusion of publication. But when he was persuaded to undertake a piece of writing he spent months on it and turned out a gem of a job.

It was so with this article; he did not write it from what he knew but insisted on reviewing all the literature first. And as he mulled over the reports on the use of iodine, he suddenly saw that Kocher might have gone wrong by not distinguishing between true exophthalmic goiter and simple goiter accompanied by hyperthyroidism. Plummer at once decided that iodine should have a thorough trial on his goiter service at St. Mary's.

The results were spectacular. Patients in the coma of a crisis were rational within a few hours after the first dose of iodine solution, and some who had been in crisis for days or weeks were able to take food the next day without vomiting. One normally athletic traveling salesman who was tossing about in bed, a nervous wreck with all sorts of things wrong with his heart, was in the best of health ten days later, exercising on the horizontal bars in his gymnasium.

The multiple-stage operation was no longer necessary because most patients, no matter how bad they were when they arrived, could be made ready for a complete thyroidectomy in from ten days to three weeks. The dreaded postoperative crisis was gone too, and mortality dropped to less than one per cent, in spite of the fact that many of the previously hopeless cases had entered the operable class.

After testing the iodine treatment thoroughly for a year Plummer announced to the profession at a meeting of the Association of American Physicians in May 1923 that the administration of iodine would prevent the crises that caused death in exophthalmic goiter.

The experience of others quickly confirmed this fact and a new era began in thyroid surgery. For Plummer's iodine treatment turned the most treacherous operation known to surgery into one of the safest, in the hands of any competent operator. It was hailed as one of medicine's greatest gifts to surgery, and the Germans coined a fitting word for it: *Plummerung*.

Although Plummer's role stands out in the solution of the thyroid problem, he did not achieve it alone. Dr. Charlie the surgeon, Dr. Kendall the biochemist, Dr. Boothby the physiologist, and several of the pathologists all contributed mightily to the successful outcome. In that respect the thyroid story typifies what is perhaps the outstanding characteristic of research in Rochester: the variety of skills available and the teamwork that brings them all to bear on a given problem.

As one of the Clinic men enthusiastically expressed it, "Here we have a gang working together in grand fashion. There is a problem relating to the body to be solved; it takes the knowledge of the physicist, the chemist, and the doctor. Here we have them all, and they all work together to solve the problem, each contributing his part and each criticizing the work of the others as far as he is able."

Teamwork has been forced upon modern science everywhere by the expansion of knowledge beyond the power of any one man to be expert in all its phases, but close collaboration is naturally more difficult to attain in the loosely cohesive groups attached to university schools and research institutes than in an organization in which cooperation in everything is the cornerstone of executive policy.

Almost certain to share in any major research undertaking at the Clinic will be one or another of the four full-time research divisions of the Foundation: animal experimentation, experimental bacteriology, biochemistry, and biophysics.

Animal experimentation remained under the supervision of Dr. Frank Mann. He did not like the quarters provided for his subjects on the roof of the Clinic building. With the space and isolation of the countryside so near at hand Dr. Mann did not see the reason for keeping the animals at the Clinic building, where they would be a constant incentive to opposition from sentimentalists.

So the animals were never moved into their intended quarters. Instead Dr. Charlie offered space for them on his farm and told Dr. Mann to pick his own site. He chose forty acres in a lovely little valley, and Dr. Charlie later bought an adjoining forty acres to give the unit ample space to grow in.

The Institute of Experimental Medicine, as it was thereafter called, grew steadily to a staff of nine and a crew of more than twenty expert technicians, with a budget of some hundred thousand dollars a year. It provided excellent facilities for experimental surgery, pathology, biochemistry, biophysics, bacteriology, and physiology, as well as first-class accommodations for fifteen kinds of animals.

The Institute serves the Clinic group like any other laboratory, except that it works with problems instead of with patients. Any clinician may use its facilities for his research, or if he does not have time to do the experiments himself, some member of the Institute staff will do them for him. Institute teams have made especially outstanding contributions to knowledge of the cause and processes of surgical shock and the pathology and physiology of the liver.

Dr. Kendall the biochemist tends to be more of a lone wolf in his research. Finding himself at a dead end once thyroxin had been isolated and synthesized, he turned to approach the thyroid from the angle of its relation to the other endocrine glands, hoping to find the key to the intricate gearing of the whole endocrine system. Concentrating on the cortex, or capsule covering, of the adrenal glands, he piled up a probable world record for the purchase of these glands, for he used tons of them in his experiments.

The cost was a tremendous gamble, but it paid off handsomely when Kendall, working with Dr. Philip S. Hench, head of the Clinic section on rheumatic diseases, discovered cortisone, an achievement important enough to win for the two men the Nobel Prize in Medicine in 1950.

It was the x-ray and radium that first introduced the physicist into medical practice, and it was the need for a radium plant to permit radium therapy that led to the establishment of a physics laboratory at the Clinic. When such radium plants were still new the Mayos sent to Harvard for a man to install one for them and to Dartmouth for an engineer to operate it, but nothing more was attempted until about 1923, when Dr. Charles Sheard, professor of physics at Ohio State University, became the head of a Foundation division of biophysical research.

Dr. Sheard and his associates have contributed to most of the group's major research problems by devising the necessary apparatus and techniques for accurate physical measurement of body functions. They have also helped in solving some of the practical problems of the clinical laboratories.

For instance, when the hematology laboratory was swamped by its job of performing two or three hundred hemoglobin tests a day, Dr. Sanford called on Dr. Sheard to help him devise a mechanical way of doing the work. The result was the Sanford-Sheard photolometer that performs some fifty kinds of chemical tests mechanically, without the human propensity to occasional error.

Since the research men seldom come into direct contact with patients and therefore seldom witness the effect of their work on human well-being, they find it peculiarly satisfying when they do. Dr. Sheard had the experience when Dr. New, the plastic surgeon, asked him to try his hand at contriving a device for restoring the power of speech to a man who lost his voice through removal of the larynx. Dr. Sheard fashioned a "voice box" that did the trick.

As he described his subsequent experience, "You can't explain electric potentials to the man in the street, but John Jones doesn't have any trouble understanding a little tube and box that makes him able to talk. There is a real thrill in seeing a man hopeless, discouraged, unable to speak, turned into a whole human being again by a simple contraption that lets him speak as well as we can, from Alaska, Arizona, or anywhere as clear as a bell."

The voice boxes have to be custom tailored to fit the individual, and Dr. Sheard has made and fitted many hundreds of them.

For all medicine's remarkable progress there are still many diseases for which no effective treatment is known, and some of these send a thousand and more patients to the Clinic every year. The entire research program is aimed more or less directly at reducing the number of these unconquered ills, but most specifically charged with the task are the clinical investigators—clinical because they study the disease in the patient himself.

Although the unit is called the clinical investigation *laboratory,* the layman would not recognize it as such, for it is not a place of benches, sinks, and Bunsen burners. It consists of a section of hospital beds, a group of rooms equipped with the special apparatus needed for whatever study is under way at the moment, and quarters for a sizable out-patient department.

No patient is referred to this unit without a careful explanation of its purposes and procedures, because the Clinic, being engaged in the private practice of medicine, cannot make any patient the subject of investigative study without his knowledge and consent. But when medicine knows no remedy for an ailment, few sufferers from it refuse the chance to have one found by intensive study.

The patients referred to the clinical investigators are of two types. For the first: Suppose a clinician at work on the Clinic floor gets a patient whose difficulty he cannot diagnose. He cannot spend half a day or more studying that case; he simply does not have the time. But the patient is not to be turned away on that account; instead he is offered the service of the clinical investigation unit. Sometimes its staff can solve his problem and sometimes they cannot, but at least they have given him the benefit of special study.

An interesting illustration is the case of a woman who came to the Clinic complaining of spells of sudden collapse. She was so upset that the clinician could not get enough information to warrant a diagnosis. He suspected that her trouble might be caused by an abnormal sensitivity to cold, but he could not be certain of this from the few facts he was able to coax from her in an hour or so of questioning. So he called on the investigation service for help.

The patient was made comfortable in bed for a few days while one of its staff doctors, a friendly, personable young woman, worked to put her at ease and win her confidence. Then by conversational questioning the doctor was able to get the facts, all of which bore out the clinician's guess that the woman was hypersensitive to cold—all of them, that is, but one: Her worst spell had occurred in the midst of a heat wave the preceding July, and she could recall no circumstance of unusual cold attending it.

As the doctor tried to think what to do next, she turned through the pages of a magazine on the table and, passing an advertisement for electric refrigerators, aimlessly commented on their usefulness.

"Yes," agreed the patient, "they're wonderful. My husband bought me one last summer, and for the first time in my life I had all the frozen desserts and iced drinks I wanted. I just about lived on them the first few days after we got it."

Immediately alert, the doctor asked casually whether she had got it early in the summer.

"Yes, in July. Why, it was just a few days before I had that bad spell!"

The problem was solved, the diagnosis made, and treatment instituted. Never could the clinician in his office have elicited from the patient the fact of that simple domestic experience.

Good luck plays a part too in solving the problem of the other kind of patient referred to the service, the one for whose ailment no successful treatment is known.

"Parasites of diagnostic obscurity" Dr. Will used to call the vague abdominal miseries that were lumped together under the term *dyspepsia,* and in the same category are the undifferentiated headaches similarly grouped in the modern catchall, migraine. The clinical investigators learned to distinguish one of these headaches and were having gratifying success in treating it with histamine. So the clinicians referred to them all patients with headaches of obscure cause, and if the person's headache was of this particular kind treatment was given.

One day a patient was sent to them who had not only this kind of headache but also a severe case of Ménière's disease, a fairly common malady named for the Frenchman who first described its symptoms in 1861. Neither its cause nor any treatment for it was known. But to everyone's immense surprise, when the patient was given the histamine treatment for the headache the Ménière's disease vanished too.

Could it be that histamine was a remedy for this malady?

The investigators sent word of the possibility to the clinicians, who now instead of sending the victims of Ménière's disease home without hope began telling them of the possibility of relief, carefully explaining that they did not know whether the treatment would benefit them or not, but it would do them no harm and they could try it if they wished.

Within a month the clinical investigators had treated fifteen cases of Ménière's disease with histamine. These were too few to permit a definite conclusion but the immediate success was so striking that the doctors felt it warranted a preliminary report announcing to the profession the possibility that histamine would cure the supposedly incurable Ménière's disease.

The Clinic story provides many such instances of extensive developments from chance occurrences, made possible by the size of the group and the tradition of ready collaboration among its members and sections. One other will illustrate how a single idea may grow into a vast program of investigation involving many Clinic units.

Dr. Will and Dr. Charlie never relaxed their custom of bringing back some specific contribution from every trip they took, and Dr. Will's journey to Australia in 1924 yielded a peculiarly fruitful one. He found the whole medical community talking about the work of two young men at the University of Sydney. Dr. John Hunter the anatomist was making a study of the effects of the sympathetic nervous system on muscle tone, and on the basis of his findings, Dr. N. D. Royle the orthopedic surgeon had achieved extraordinary results in treating spastic paralysis by severing certain branches of the nervous system.

Dr. Will spent an entire afternoon with the young men, looking over their case records, watching a demonstration of Royle's operation on a goat, and examining some of the patients he had operated on.

When he returned to Rochester, Dr. Will gave a detailed description of Royle's operation to Dr. Adson, the Clinic neurosurgeon, who promptly used it in his next case of spastic paralysis. Watching the patient's postoperative course carefully, he observed that the temperature of the skin on the man's feet was much higher than it had been before the operation.

This curious fact suggested to Adson that severing the proper nerves in the sympathetic system might prove an effective treatment for diseases of the peripheral vascular system, the veins and arteries of the hands and feet. This was another field in which relatively little was known. Its various diseases had not been differentiated, and there was no treatment for them except amputation when they were so advanced that circulation failed entirely and gangrene developed.

Dr. Adson promptly reported his observation to Dr. Brown, the clinical investigator, who began to study the patients on whom Adson performed sympathectomy for spastic paralysis. In every case the skin temperature of the feet increased markedly.

The significance of this rests on a fact of physiology. The human body has a hot-water heating system, in which the blood is the circulating medium, the heart is the pump, the stomach the boiler, and food the fuel. Somewhere there is also a thermostat that keeps the mouth temperature always the same in a normal body. Extra heat, like that produced by eating a meal, is carried to the hands and feet by the blood and there eliminated. But if something goes wrong with the circulatory system at these exit points they fail to perform this function.

It seemed logical therefore to deduce from the increased temperature of the feet that Dr. Adson's operation improved the peripheral circulation. Consequently he tried sympathectomy in a case of peripheral vascular disease in March 1925, and cured it.

Then the clinical investigators and the neurosurgeons concentrated on vascular diseases. Dr. Brown examined, compared, correlated, and classified till he was finally able to differentiate the various diseases and describe ways of making a differential diagnosis among them. He and his associates studied the effect of every promising treatment from drugs to postural exercises, including baths, rest, diet, and massage, in order both to learn more about the mechanism of the vascular system and to find some effective treatment less radical than surgery.

Often their methods were successful in milder cases, but for the severer types the neurosurgeons had to provide the treatment. Sometimes, however, the operation did not work, so some means had to be found for telling *before* operation whether or not surgery would help in that particular case.

Dr. Brown finally found a way. He gave the patient typhoid vaccine to induce fever, and if the rise in the skin temperature of the foot was proportionately much greater than the rise in mouth temperature, the patient would benefit from the operation.

Fundamental in all this work was the measurement of variations in skin temperature, and finding early that the devices available were not adequate, the clinical investigators sought assistance from Dr. Sheard the biophysicist. He contrived an electrothermometer to do the job. As the patient lies on the bed with thermocouples on his hands and feet, a pencil of light from an electric eye automatically registers the temperature on a numerical scale across the top of the room, and as the temperature changes the light shifts along the scale.

Thereafter Dr. Sheard participated actively in the study, contributing techniques and apparatus for many of the mechanical treatment methods that were tried. When it became evident that more rigidly controlled room conditions were needed to make sure that the changes in skin temperature were produced by the patient's own heating plant and not by that of St. Mary's Hospital, Dr. Sheard devised and installed equipment for keeping the room temperature and humidity absolutely constant.

As the investigators dug deeper into the physiological aspects of their problem, they undertook a study of the rate and volume of the blood flow and the factors that speed it up or slow it down, and for parts of this study experiments on animals were necessary. So the services of the Institute of Experimental Medicine were requested. There the work was done by a team that included a physiologist to direct and interpret the whole, a biophysicist to arrange and supervise the intricate physical technique the experiment required, and a surgeon to handle the animals.

Thus did Dr. Will's trip to Australia and Dr. Adson's close observation of his patient's condition grow into an investigative study that in fifteen years produced nearly eight hundred published reports of progress, some of them containing findings of great general significance. Such an accomplishment, involving many special skills and fields of science, would be quite beyond the power of an individual, even if he gave a lifetime to it.

22. *Training Young Doctors*

AFTER 1917 the work of the Mayo Foundation was a vital factor in every phase of activity at Rochester, for the alliance with the university imposed new obligations and set new standards that took some striving to meet.

The experiment in graduate medical education was administered by a committee of five from the Minneapolis faculty headed by Dean Lyon of the medical school and a committee of five from the Rochester faculty with Dr. Louis B. Wilson, who was named director of the Foundation, as chairman. Each group was in full charge on its own campus, but in deciding matters of general policy they acted as a joint committee under the chairmanship of Dean Ford of the graduate school, who felt, he said, "like a land lubber presiding over the navy department."

It was something new, this putting a layman in charge of a project in medical education, but it proved wise. Dean Ford was a man of broad social and educational vision, alive to the need for raising professional education of all kinds above the mere teaching of techniques, the mere learning of a trade.

But could it be done? Could clinicians with a training and tradition wholly practical be turned into scientists imbued with the spirit of inquiry and the methods of scholarship? Men in the basic medical sciences, long since become a true graduate discipline, doubted it, and Dean Ford himself sometimes wondered.

The clinical men, for instance, had no idea what a thesis or an examination at the graduate level meant. The first theses their candidates presented were nothing more than ordinary case reports, and when these were rejected they turned to the Clinic files, pulled out a stack of histories, and came up with a statistical study of how many red-haired women had developed cancer of the left breast, or something equally futile.

Finally terms of description were found that meant something to them: The subject should be important enough and the work sound and original enough to warrant publication in the best professional journal in the candidate's specialty.

Then the oral examinations! The clinicians made them little classroom quizzes or turned them into clinical conferences and spent the time arguing a point among themselves while the candidate sat quietly by, doing nothing. It was also hard to persuade them to give an adverse vote on each other's candidates. When one of them presented a student, saying in effect, This is my man and I know he's good, he expected the others to take his word for it. That was his diagnosis, and to have it publicly challenged was a personal affront to him.

For a while Dean Ford loaded the examining committees with faculty members in the basic sciences, because they had gone through the graduate mill themselves and were used to putting others through it, and gradually the idea of academic detachment took hold, so that a professor of the clinical branches "no longer roared, he only grumbled subterraneously" when his candidate went down before the questioning of his colleagues.

It was not only the Rochester men who experienced these difficulties; clinicians on both campuses faced them, for they were the result of the newness of the experiment, not of personal inadequacy.

With understanding came pride that the Clinic group was functioning as a part of the state university, and this was attended with a conscientious concern about meeting its standards. For fear the mortality of Rochester fellows in the final examinations would disgrace the Foundation faculty, its members began giving their candidates a stiff preliminary examination at home before they let them appear before the joint examining committee at Minneapolis.

From the beginning the requirements for a fellowship either at the university or in the Foundation were put on the high level of a bachelor's degree plus the medical degree and one year's internship. During the war years it was hard to hold to these requirements, for there were scarcely enough qualified applicants to fill the vacancies. And even after the war, applications continued to come from dissatisfied, middle-aged practitioners who wanted to become surgeons in six months.

But as time went on the idea sank in that the Minnesota plan was not an easy short cut to specialization, and the number and quality of the applicants rose until the eighty-odd annual vacancies in the Foundation were being filled from some two thousand applications. Then the stated requirements faded to an almost forgotten minimum; a goodly number of those chosen had a master's degree, some had teaching experience, and the majority had served more than one year's internship.

The applications came from all over the world. By 1940 the fellows of the Foundation represented seventy-three medical schools in the United States and Canada and sixty universities in twenty-six foreign countries.

In the traditional manner of graduate students the Foundation fellows choose major and minor subjects. The major may be internal medicine or general surgery or any one of the recognized medical and surgical specialties, and the minor must be in some basic science related to the major field. Two years of the fellowship are to be spent in various aspects of the major, six months in the minor, and six months in either or neither, as the fellow may elect. Within these broad general limits the arrangement of the specific program is determined by the fellow in consultation with his major adviser.

During the first five years sixty-six per cent of the Foundation fellows elected general surgery for their major, but this proportion decreased to thirty-one per cent in the five years from 1935 to 1940, whereas the proportion choosing internal medicine rose from nine per cent to twenty-eight per cent in the same period, much to the satisfaction of the Foundation officers.

Fellows in the surgical sections live in the hospital and are responsible for the pre- and postoperative care of the patients in the surgical wards. In the mornings all are on duty in the operating rooms. There a first-year fellow performs general duties or merely watches. During his second year he acts as a second assistant in a surgical team, and if he shows the necessary ability he may stay on as a first assistant for a third year.

The first assistant makes the incision and closes the wound, but the remainder of each operation is performed by the surgeon himself, because all Clinic patients, whether paying or nonpaying, are private patients and none of them can be turned over to the assistants.

Because the surgical fellows perform no complete operations on their own responsibility, the opportunities for practical experience in operating are said to be better in university fellowships or hospital residencies where the private-patient restriction is not in effect. But the Foundation men maintain that by mastering the routine motions till they are second nature and watching an experienced operator meet the problems of many major cases, the fellow becomes a more competent surgeon than he would by performing a limited number of less important operations himself.

In internal medicine and the medical specialties the young doctor takes the case history, makes the preliminary examination, and prepares a résumé of the case stating his opinion as to the diagnosis and the treatment indicated. Then the staff internist takes over, and as the case progresses both he and the fellow can see where the latter was right, where wrong, and why.

When the Foundation's work began, the university graduate school recognized only nine legitimate major subjects in clinical fields, but as the Clinic developed more specialty sections these were also accepted for degrees, and by 1940 the number was twenty-one.

The faculty in these newer fields, self-conscious about their youth and determined to prove them worthy of recognition, select their fellows with special care. In this class are anesthesia, now called anesthesiology, to which fellowships were allowed in 1929, and physical medicine and plastic surgery, both accepted into the family in 1937.

The Foundation setup offers no such peculiar advantages in the basic sciences as it does in the clinical subjects, so the major development on that side of the Minnesota program has been left to the university, where the laboratory fields are well developed in connection with the undergraduate medical school.

More than half of the science fellowships at Rochester are in pathology, and many fellows in medicine or surgery also choose to spend six months or a year in the postmortem service, because this is fundamental to so many phases of practice.

A postmortem does not tell the doctor merely what caused the patient's death; his state of health throughout his lifetime is recorded in the lesions of his body, and from the organs of a man who has died of pneumonia the pathologist may learn a great deal about the workings of an operation for gastric ulcer twenty years before or about the effects on the liver of removing the gallbladder ten years ago.

Whenever a death occurs in any of the hospitals, boarding-houses, or hotels of Rochester the manager or superintendent immediately notifies the Clinic telegraph operator, who relays the message to the pathology fellow on call. He goes at once to interview the relatives and secure permission for an autopsy, then notifies the consultant and the patient's doctors if they were not present.

When the autopsy has been completed the fellow and the consultant hold another conference with the relatives to report the findings and to offer all possible assistance in making arrangements for shipping the body, filling out insurance blanks, and the like. This is a courtesy service given without charge. The fellow is also responsible for notifying the business office of the death and of any changes it may have caused in the family's financial condition, so that proper allowances may be made in computing the Clinic's bill.

Although there are seldom more than two or three majoring in any one of the other sciences at Rochester, the laboratories are full of fellows most of the time, because of the required minor in a basic science and because much of the research for theses is done in the various laboratories. There are always from fifteen to twenty-five fellowship men at work at the Institute of Experimental Medicine.

With research of all kinds as pervasive as it has become in Rochester, the fellows take in its spirit with the air they breathe. If a man has any capability for this phase of medicine, he can hardly fail to be caught up in one of the many projects under way, and frequently he contributes appreciably to it. At least he is likely somewhere along the way to assist some staff member in working up the materials in files and museums for a paper or two.

In doing this, as well as in the work on his own thesis, the fellow makes the acquaintance of the wonderfully rich resources that have resulted from the decisions taken and the policies instituted in years past. There is first the library, grown with the years to more than forty thousand volumes, rich in the periodical sets that are essential tools of research in any field. And the bound periodical volumes are supplemented by subscriptions to more than six hundred medical journals, about one third of them American and the rest representing all the major countries of the world from Africa to Norway and Japan to Ireland.

In finding their way through this material both Clinic staff and Foundation fellows have the assistance of a corps of trained medical librarians. Here as elsewhere in the organization everything practicable is done to help the staff members accomplish as much as possible in the time at their command by relieving them of work that is as easily done by others. The librarians, and the secretaries too, are expected to give an unusual amount of assistance in the preliminary task of finding references and preparing bibliographies.

As the library opens to the fellows the heritage of their profession, the division of records and statistics makes available to them the accumulated experience of the Clinic. Now at the command of the Foundation fellows as well as of Clinic staff members are the complete health histories of more than a million patients, thoroughly indexed and immediately accessible. And at hand are highly trained statisticians to teach the fellows how to do statistical research—how to collect significant numerical data and interpret them properly.

The Foundation fellowship program includes no formal classroom work or lecture courses, and in this respect it is more truly of graduate stature than many academic programs. Yet the practical service of the fellows is supplemented at many points by conferences, lectures, and seminars.

Perhaps the most important of these is the weekly staff meeting on Wednesday night. Tacitly limited to an hour each, the meeting programs are an index to the range of Clinic activities, for the topics at one week's session may range from an internist's report on a study of vitamin deficiency to a statistician's report of population trends since Malthus. These reports not only serve to keep all staff members informed of new developments in every section but they constitute the finest kind of seminar for the Foundation fellows.

The interest and scope of the meetings are greatly increased by full use of modern methods of rapid and vivid presentation. Statistical charts and tables, before-and-after shots of illustrative cases, microscopic slides, and x-ray pictures, all are flashed on the screen, and surgical techniques are demonstrated by colored motion pictures made in the operating rooms.

The photographic studio's collection of more than seven hundred films on all kinds of medical matters serves the Clinic's staff and patients well, and items from it are borrowed by medical colleges, schools of nursing, and professional societies in the United States, Canada, and South America.

Dr. Will's last gift to the Foundation was his own home, which as Mayo Foundation House has become a center for the fellows' activities, both social and professional. There every Tuesday night some two hundred young doctors meet with their teachers to discuss medical problems. They assemble in ten or a dozen different groups, each in a room equipped with blackboards, a stereopticon, tables, and chairs.

Suppose the group is the senior surgical seminar and the topic is "Surgical Risk in Renal Disease."

The evening starts off with a formal paper by one of the fellows who has been making a special study of the topic. Then a staff member from the section on cardiology talks about the things a bad heart can do to wreck a kidney operation, and the head of the division of medicine, whose specialty is the study of diabetes, cites some examples of the surgical trouble this disease can cause and adds some figures the statistician has gathered for him that show the surgical mortality of diabetic patients is rising.

He is worried about the reason for the rise and lists some of the possible explanations he has considered. Perhaps the trouble is a slackened rate of circulation, he suggests, whereupon someone reminds the group of recent findings in the clinical investigators' study of blood flow and someone else adds that if the circulation proves to be at fault, the metabolism laboratory's new treatment with high concentrations of oxygen may solve the difficulty.

After a while the head of the postmortem service reports cases that have come to his division because some risk was overlooked in a seemingly simple operation. The surgeon may be operating for nothing more than an ingrowing toenail, he says, but if he has failed to take into account a leaky heart and the patient dies during operation, the death is charged to the ingrowing toenail, because that's the only way to keep the mortality figures straight.

Finally one of the staff surgeons brings the seminar to a close with a brief review of his own experience in deciding whether or not to operate for kidney disease.

Except for the first paper the discussion has all been informal and free, with questions and comments from all sides. It continues here and there as the group breaks up and moves into the dining room next door to join the members of the other seminars for doughnuts and cider and perhaps to take part in a hot argument left over from another meeting.

These Tuesday night seminars are said to be unique in the world of medicine, and this is not hard to believe, because even the academic world offers few such examples of consistent cooperation among specialists in teaching and in learning with their students.

Three years of such training, in some cases four or five, and the fellow becomes a candidate for the degree. His thesis accepted and a successful oral examination behind him, he receives from the University of Minnesota the advanced degree he has earned, a degree that the public has come to understand is a sign of the trained specialist. The master's degree is granted to those who have given evidence of scientific proficiency in practice; the doctor's degree is reserved for those who have shown marked ability to advance medical science by original investigation.

By no means all the fellows receive a degree. Some drop

out before they have completed the three years, others go through the term in residence but do not fulfill the other requirements, still others try and fail. But the proportion receiving the final stamp of approval from the university has risen steadily. Only eleven out of forty-three who began their fellowships in 1915 took degrees; fifty-three of eighty-six who began their work in 1935 did so. The Foundation gives no certificate of any kind to those who do not run the full course.

These fellowships are not salaried positions but subsidized opportunities for graduate education; the fellow is considered a graduate student, not an employee on salary. In other branches of learning the student pays a tuition fee for such work. But knowing what a long period of training the young doctor has already passed through and wanting to select fellows according to their ability, not the size of their fathers' bank accounts, the Foundation and the university both prefer to pay a stipend—without, however, making the fellowship so desirable financially that it would attract men for that reason alone.

The medical graduate committee sets the amount of the stipends, and university members have insisted that the Foundation payments be kept within reach of those the university budget can support.

Sensitive to the charge, made when the affiliation of the Foundation with the university was under fire, that the Mayos' purpose was to provide the Clinic with good help at the tax-free Foundation's expense, the Clinic has from the beginning paid the stipends of all fellows in the clinical branches, that is, all those whose work could be considered "help" for the Clinic.

Until the Foundation endowment reached the sum of two million dollars the Mayos through the Properties Association paid all its expenses, and in 1935 they added another half million dollars to its endowment. But the yearly income from the entire sum by 1940 was not more than a hundred and twenty-five thousand dollars, whereas the annual budget of the Foundation was about five hundred thousand. The Mayo Properties Association paid the difference.

At the end of its first twenty-five years the Foundation had reason to be proud of its accomplishments. Its influence, on the Clinic, on the university, and on progress in medical education, had been incalculable.

Many of the younger staff members and department heads in the university medical school were university or Foundation alumni, and one hundred and five members of the Clinic staff were former Foundation fellows. Other alumni, numbering more than two thousand, were scattered all over the world, literally from Kalamazoo to Timbuktu.

Many of them, enthusiastic about Rochester methods and spirit, were trying to achieve a measure of these in their own practice, and small group clinics on the model of the Mayo Clinic had been established in many cities of the United States and Canada. There was even a good-sized one in Brussels, Belgium. And in far-off India a former fellow was the director of the University Medical College of Mysore, from which he sent a succession of able men to take advanced training at Rochester and at the University of Minnesota and then return to practice and teach in India.

Two hundred and forty-two of the Foundation alumni were holding responsible teaching positions in the United States and abroad, to the deep gratification of the Foundation's early leaders.

When the experiment began, the clinical faculties of medical colleges were not recruited from a pool of trained teachers regardless of geography, as are academic faculties and those in the basic sciences. The professor of economics might come from Kansas, the associate professor of English from Vermont, but all the teachers of clinical medicine were sure to be from the local community, chosen solely because of propinquity and home-town influence.

Progress in medical education depended on correcting this

situation, and it was a major achievement of the Foundation that it had made the University of Minnesota a recognized source for trained teachers in the clinical branches.

To such extent as the prohibitions of the medical code would allow, the Foundation added the medical education of the public to its functions. This was always a pet idea of both Mayo brothers. As Dr. Will once observed, "The quacks 'educate' the public. Why shouldn't we?"

A feature of the Foundation's exhibit at the Chicago Century of Progress Exposition was a "transparent man," a life-size figure of transparent material through which the internal structures of the body can be seen as the lighted form revolves on its platform. Another very popular exhibit, probably because about a fourth of the adult population have lost their appendixes, was a series of life-sized, colored wax models showing the various steps in the technique of appendectomy.

When the exposition closed, these exhibits became the nucleus for a museum of hygiene and medicine in Rochester, set up in the old Central School building across the street from the Clinic. Dr. Arthur H. Bulbulian, formerly with the natural history museum at the University of Minnesota, was named its director and he and his associates have done much pioneering in methods of designing and displaying medical exhibits for the instruction of both profession and public.

The technical exhibits are sent to conventions all over the country, carrying graphic information on many medical matters to thousands of doctors. They have been received so enthusiastically that each year one section of the Clinic is assigned the task of developing a detailed exhibit for the annual meeting of the American Medical Association.

Requests from visitors have served as a guide in selecting topics for popular museum treatment—among them cancer of the breast, the development of the human embryo, and gallbladder disease. From charts, photographs, and lifelike wax models the patient with idle hours on his hands—or perhaps more often his friends and relatives—can see what this operation or that is like, why it is necessary, what it does, and in some cases how the need for it may be avoided.

The local community, however, contributes almost half the annual museum attendance of about one hundred thousand visitors. On a fine Sunday afternoon the crowded rooms look as though the whole countryside had driven in to pore over the exhibit cases, study the captions, and listen to the hourly lecture illustrated by the transparent man. Idle curiosity doubtless brings many of them, but some deeper drive to pierce the mysteries of health and disease is apparent in the earnestness of others. And even the most thoughtless can scarcely fail to take away some new idea or have a mistaken one corrected.

23. *My Brother and I*

FOR many a Foundation graduate his diploma from the University of Minnesota had only half its meaning until he had had it countersigned by Dr. Will and Dr. Charlie. Not alone because of the prestige of their names, but because of the deep respect and admiration they inspired. Few of the fellows who won the coveted assignments to their sections did not come out with an abiding affection for Dr. Charlie and something close to reverence for Dr. Will.

The fellows in other sections knew the brothers from their appearances at one or another of the group conferences. They seldom missed the weekly staff meetings if they were in town, for they appreciated their value and knew the younger men would argue that meetings worth Dr. Will's and Dr. Charlie's time were certainly worth theirs.

Often after the meeting one of the section heads would get a telephone call from Dr. Will. "That was an excellent piece of work your fellow reported tonight. He's a good man, isn't he? Well, see that he has everything he wants to work with. He's the kind we want to encourage."

He gave direct encouragement too. As one young doctor told it, "You'd read a paper at staff meeting and afterwards he'd see you in the elevator or the hall, would shake hands, or put his hand on your shoulder with a quiet 'Good work' and a straight, warm look that made you think he meant it. Or perhaps a day or two later you'd get a note from him, just a short one, saying something like 'Dear ——, I learned more about —— from that paper of yours the other night than I ever knew before. It was a good job.' Believe me, a fellow prized those notes. I have two or three and I wouldn't take anything for them."

Dr. Will sent such notes of personal appreciation to the permanent staff members as well, when they published an exceptionally worthwhile article, received some professional recognition, or when the fifth, tenth, or twenty-fifth anniversary of their joining the Clinic came around.

"An ounce of taffy is worth a pound of epitaphy," he used to say.

He also on occasion called some man's attention to an error in his ways. Once when a young man on the staff got into a fracas with his older colleagues he went to talk it over with Dr. Will. He was upset about the incident, but Dr. Will told him, "This business won't do you any harm, son. A man needs a knock every once in a while. One knock to every two pats is about the right ratio." And one knock to every two pats was about what he gave.

As long as the brothers were serving as active surgeons, they carried their full share of the duties in the operating rooms. They still alternated, each operating at St. Mary's in the mornings and acting as surgical consultant at the Clinic in the afternoons three days a week.

Their days on duty began at seven-thirty in the morning

with a round of visits to those patients on whom they were to operate that day. Then came the morning's schedule of operations, lunch at home with a brief nap afterward—for both of them now, because Dr. Will had got a secretary who could handle the correspondence without his dictating letters at lunch—and a busy afternoon in the examining rooms.

Neither of them nor any of their surgical colleagues ever operated on a patient he had not personally examined beforehand; the division of labor between diagnosticians and surgeons was not allowed to go so far that the patient became just one body in a series passing across the operating table.

For the brothers to look after all the Clinic staff—in round numbers two hundred professional members, a thousand nonprofessional, and three hundred Foundation fellows—personally and individually as they once did became impossible. So they inaugurated elaborate insurance and pension plans and provided for generous vacations and sick leaves.

Knowing, however, that some men must recharge their batteries more often than others, Dr. Will continued to finance privately many an unofficial trip for rest or study. If a valued man was wearing noticeably thin or his wife was acting bored he would receive a check from Dr. Will and a note telling him to go off to Florida or to Europe and take Mary along to make the trip more pleasant.

Provision for needy patients now was formalized through the section on social service, which was organized early in the 1920s to help patients whose personal problems prevented proper treatment.

Perhaps a man from some distant state is found to have tuberculosis; he needs to enter a sanatorium, and the members of his family ought to be examined to make sure that they have not contracted the disease. Or a patient in the orthopedics section has lost an arm or a leg; he needs help in rehabilitating his life, perhaps even to the extent of learning a new occupation and finding a new job. Or a diabetic child is brought in in a coma; obviously she is not following the prescribed diet, and her parents show a strange indifference to helping her readjust her life to the demands of the disease; somehow the reason for their apathy must be discovered and corrected if the girl is to live.

In all such cases the section on social service takes over the job and tries to overcome the obstacle that is hampering the doctor's program for the patient.

But for the majority of patients referred to the section the problem is wholly or chiefly financial. Some arrive without money for hospitalization or for maintenance, others are stranded without transportation home, still others need supervision to make the amount they have cover the costs of their residence. All these patients are referred to social service for help.

Yet Dr. Will could never bring himself to leave financial aid entirely to the section. He usually asked his secretary to get him some cash from the business office before he started his rounds for the day, and she knew that he would probably return from them without a cent in his pocket. Nor did he hesitate to make his own arrangements about the payment of bills.

He was called in consultation one afternoon on the case of a boy just out of high school. When he decided the lad needed an operation, the boy exclaimed, "But I haven't any money to pay for an operation!"

Dr. Will looked at him soberly. "Do you think you could earn some after you get well?"

The boy was sure he could.

"All right, you see if you can send me ten dollars a month till you've paid a hundred dollars."

Two five-dollar bills came to his desk regularly each month, and when the tenth pair arrived he sent the boy a check for a hundred dollars plus generous interest, with a note: "You've shown yourself and me you could do it. Now you can put this in the bank and make it grow."

For the most part, however, setting and collecting the fees

was left entirely to the business office. The Clinic operated on strictly business principles, but the policies adopted by the brothers in their early years as partners were still in force. No note was taken, no mortgage allowed, for the payment of a Clinic bill, and no lawsuit was ever instituted to collect one. The bills were set in accordance with the size of the patient's income, and for many years the percentage of paying patients varied little. Twenty-five per cent paid nothing for the Clinic's services, thirty per cent paid the bare costs of their treatment, and the other forty-five per cent defrayed the expenses of the institution and its program.

Consequently some fees were high, and Dr. Will was sometimes disturbed to learn just how high. A Seattle doctor told the story of a multimillionaire friend of his who was charged ten thousand dollars for a major operation on his wife and paid the bill willingly. But Dr. Mayo happened to see the amount of this fee on the books and ordered four thousand of it returned, with the comment that the patient had been overcharged. Indignantly the millionaire returned the refund, saying his wife's life was well worth ten thousand dollars.

Many stories were told of bills reduced or canceled for patients who, because of the loss of a job or the death of a husband or parents, found themselves unable to pay them. When asked if these stories were true the Clinic business officers said, Yes, but don't give us undue credit on that account. Every doctor in the country does the same thing. And it's only good business practice. If a person's financial condition makes it unlikely that you will be paid anyway, you might as well cancel the bill, save the expense of carrying the account, and gain good will at least.

No phrase was so often on Dr. Will's lips as "my brother and I." Every honor that came to him he accepted "on behalf of my brother and myself." He did this so consistently that one of his friends remarked, "I believe if Dr. Will were elected

best-selling paperbacks

Compiled by
National Bestsellers Institute, Phila. ★ MONTHS ON LIST

1 JAWS (Bantam, $1.95)
Peter Benchley

2 THE OTHER SIDE OF MIDNIGHT
(Dell, $1.75) Sidney Sheldon

3 ALIVE (Avon, $1.95)
Piers Paul Read

4 THE FAN CLUB (Bantam, $1.95)
Irving Wallace

5 FEAR OF FLYING (N.A.L., Signet, $1.95) Erica Jong

6 WATERSHIP DOWN (Avon, $2.25)
Richard Adams

7 THE DEVIL'S DESIRE (Avon, $1.75)
Laurie McBain

8 THIRTY-FOUR EAST (Popular Library, $1.95)
Alfred Coppel

9 THE REINCARNATION OF PETER PROUD (Bantam, $1.75)
Max Ehrlich

10 JANE (Avon, $1.75)
Dee Wells

11 CASHELMARA (Fawcett, $1.95)
Susan Howatch

12 THE DEVIL'S TRIANGLE (Bantam, $1.50)
Richard Winer

☆ ☆ ☆ best bets ☆ ☆ ☆

☆ THE PIRATE (Pocket Books, $1.95)
Harold Robbins

☆ THE MEMORY BOOK (Ballantine, $1.95)
Harry Lorayne and Jerry Lucas

☆ THE BERMUDA TRIANGLE (Warner Books, $1.75)
Adi-Kent Thomas Jeffrey

☆ THE PLANTATION (Bantam, $1.75)
George McNeil

☆ CHIEF (Avon, $1.95)
Albert A. Seedman and Peter Hellman

☆ THE MILLIONAIRE'S DAUGHTER (Fawcett, $1.50)
Dorothy Eden

☆ THE WAR BETWEEN THE TATES (Warner Books, $1.95)
Alison Lurie

☆ IF BEALE STREET COULD TALK (N.A.L., Signet, $1.95)
James Baldwin

☆ ENDGAME (Avon, $1.75)
Harvey Ardman

☆ THE HOLLYWOOD ZOO (Pinnacle, $1.75)
Jackie Collins

☆ FORBIDDEN FLOWERS (Pocket Books, $1.75) Nancy Friday

☆ FRENCH CONNECTION II (Dell, $1.50) Robin Moore and Milton Machlin

LITTLE PROFESSOR BOOK CENTER
1456 Sheldon Rd.
Plymouth Township, Mich. 48170

President of the United States he would accept the office in the name of his brother and himself."

In so many phases of the story, however, Dr. Will is the dominant figure, the man who acts and speaks, the Chief, that one must wonder whether "my brother and I" was a legend he deliberately fostered for the good of the Clinic. He was perfectly capable of doing precisely this, but his friends and associates were vehemently sure that he did not, that he was honestly pointing up Dr. Charlie's contribution to their joint achievement.

True, Dr. Charlie alone could never have built the Clinic, but then neither could Dr. Will. It took the two of them to do the job, each complementing the other. But the task of administration fell mainly to Dr. Will's lot. He had the decisiveness and single-mindedness of the successful executive; Dr. Charlie did not. He lived in the present, savoring it to the full; Dr. Will lived in the future, not planning for tomorrow or next week but for ten or fifteen years ahead.

The two brothers did not always agree by any means, and when they did not they scrapped it out. In the early years Dr. Plummer and Mr. Harwick sometimes tried to referee these differences, but they soon learned that it was best to keep out. Dr. Will and Dr. Charlie might disagree themselves, but they instantly joined forces against an outsider.

If Dr. Will could not convince Dr. Charlie at such times, the plan was laid aside or modified until Charlie did approve. Dr. Will never rode roughshod over him. "When Charlie says no, it means no for me," he declared.

All accounts agree that Dr. Charlie never felt resentment about the greater glory that was Dr. Will's. Families, friends, and employees might split into camps and be jealous for the due honor of their favorite, but they could not drive a chisel between the brothers. They might start one, but as soon as the two men realized what was happening, they stopped it short and for a few days overwhelmed each other with special kindnesses.

There can be no doubt that the affection between them was real and strong; no sham could have withstood the strains put upon it. And it was cause for frequent remark among their many professional friends. "Your great success was not as surgeons," Dr. Haggard once told them. "It was as brothers. There has never been anything like it."

The two men were utterly unlike. Dr. Charlie's supreme gift was for human contacts. He had a way about him that won the liking of everyone he met, grumpy patient or hard-boiled doctor, and to the end of his active service the men on the Clinic floor called on him to pull their chestnuts out of the fire when they were in trouble with an obstreperous patient.

His daily visits to his own patients were like those of a wise, gay-spirited friend. If the patient was discouraged, per-haps at the prospect of a life handicapped by ill health or the loss of a limb, Dr. Charlie would sit down on the edge of the bed and talk for ten minutes or half an hour if neces-sary, till he had made the future seem less dreary.

"Even his smile would make you want to get better, just to show the world you could," wrote one patient in after years. "Because he always made me feel so much better I asked for him often," wrote another. "And he always came."

Dr. Will's visits to patients were likely to be rather impres-sive ceremonies, conducted in the presence of a group of assistants. He was as kindly as his brother and even wiser, but his cheer was studied, his jokes deliberate. He had to take thought to appear friendly.

One day as he was leaving St. Mary's a patient who was also leaving spoke to him, to say good-bye. Dr. Will had his hat in one hand and his coat in the other, so he just bade the man a cordial good-bye and wished him health. But later that afternoon he told his secretary about it, saying he had failed in that case, that he should have dropped his coat on the floor or something, anything to shake hands with that man. He spoke of it several times in the next day or two, wishing he had shaken hands with that patient.

Dr. Charlie always had "a tickle at the end of his tongue for a pleasantry." Many of those who knew him likened him to his friend Will Rogers, both in the slow nasal drawl with which he spoke and in his ability to put a common-sense truth in homely, salty phrases that gave it added punch.

Dr. Will was more austere always. Some of his staff and associates, even some members of the family, were awed by him. One of the younger sisters at St. Mary's who worked closely with both men expressed the reaction to them this way: "We all loved Dr. Charlie; he was so easy and approachable, so democratic. Whereas we were all scared to death of Dr. Will; he was so dignified and reserved."

Part of his reserve was the schooled aloofness of every executive, condemned to impartiality regardless of his personal feelings. But in the main Dr. Will's reserve was a trait he could not help. Although intellectually he sympathized with the reactions of the common man, he was an aristocrat in disposition.

Sitting on the lawn at Mayowood one afternoon, Dr. Will watched Dr. Charlie walk away with a trio of friends and in a rare moment of self-revelation remarked to Mrs. Charlie, "Everybody likes Charlie, don't they? They aren't afraid of him. No one ever claps me on the back the way they all do him." And then after a minute, "But I guess I wouldn't like it if they did."

When that story was repeated to one of the Clinic executives he exclaimed, "That's it. That was the difference between them. Many a time when Dr. Charlie came in to talk to me I helped him on with his overcoat and then with my arm around his shoulders walked out into the hall with him. But I would never have thought of touching Dr. Will in any way."

Another of the staff members put it succinctly: "You could visit for hours with Dr. Charlie, but when Dr. Will came in you got right to the point."

Even in appearance the two men were opposites—Dr. Will blond, Dr. Charlie dark in skin and hair; Dr. Will's eyes keen and direct of glance, Dr. Charlie's deep-set and somewhat sad; Dr. Will erect, compact, commanding, "he couldn't slouch"; Dr. Charlie more homey and comfortable looking, never so precise or neat.

With Dr. Will professional dignity, even in appearance, was almost a religion. If he saw one of the fellows in soiled linen, or unshaved, without his shoes shined, or acting flippant on the Clinic floor, he would call him in and talk to him, tell him he must look and act like a doctor as well as be one. Feeling so, he found Charlie's indifference to appearance something of a trial. When they went to have pictures taken he could snap into position in an instant, but he always had to fuss with Dr. Charlie to get him primped and posed properly for an official photograph.

One of the staff found him in his office one day poring over proofs, trying to select the one of Dr. Charlie to be finished. "That's the best, isn't it?" he asked. But the other man thought this one looked more like Dr. Charlie. "No, that makes Charlie look like a groceryman," objected Dr. Will.

His emphasis on dignity was all for the sake of the Clinic and its reputation; personally he was no more filled with self-importance than Dr. Charlie. Men from the world of finance and industry having business with one of the brothers were surprised by the ease with which they could reach the inner sanctum and fairly gasped when desk girls, secretaries, and even old-timers among the patients referred habitually to "Dr. Will" and "Dr. Charlie" and only a little less generally to "Mrs. Will" and "Mrs. Charlie."

Their simplicity and kindliness were unfailing. When the American Medical Library Association held its annual convention in Rochester, Dr. Charlie learned that the group were going out to visit the Institute of Experimental Medicine and said they might as well stop at Mayowood on their way, then called his wife to say they were coming and she should see they didn't miss anything.

Mrs. Charlie met the invasion with perfect composure and showed the hundred-odd librarians around the estate. Then they returned to the Clinic library for a late afternoon tea, and Dr. Charlie and Dr. Will both joined them.

"It never occurred to us that they wouldn't," said the Clinic librarian. "They always came to our little parties when they were in town." But the visitors were amazed. They seized the opportunity to ask the brothers to autograph Clinic bookplates for them and went home completely won, as visitors always were, by the unpretentiousness of the famous Mayo brothers.

Dr. Will was almost too successful in impressing his idea of dignity for the Clinic's sake on the rest of the staff. It was hammered into them for years on end that they must not talk for publication and must be careful what they told to friends and acquaintances outside the group, lest it find its way into print and reflect adversely upon the Clinic. As a result most of the writing about the institution was done by outsiders after a brief visit, and it almost invariably stressed externals like size and system, so that many laymen, and doctors too, came to think of the Mayo Clinic as a huge, efficient machine staffed by a race of cold-blooded supermen.

The efficiency is there, and the systematic precision by which hundreds of patients a day are moved from section to section through the diagnostic process. And of course it is hard to introduce much friendliness into the mechanical process of venapuncture or an x-ray. But within the examining rooms the degree of human warmth and personal interest in the patient varies with the individual doctor precisely as it does elsewhere.

To the end of their lives Dr. Will and Dr. Charlie struggled to keep the sheer size of the organization from making it an impersonal machine, and their attitude eventually permeated the service staff from the doormen up.

Though there are many hundreds of numbers on the Clinic

telephone exchange the operators know every one of them, and the names and voices of all the staff members and half their wives to boot. A visitor can pick up the receiver and ask for any man in the group and they will have him on the line in no time, or report where he is if he is not in the building. And if the visitor gives them his name half a dozen times, thereafter their pleasant voices will be calling him by name too.

The Clinic doctors themselves enjoy hugely the joke on their "machine" when occasionally it slips a cog. Even Dr. Will liked to tell this story:

The doctors use their examining rooms in rotation, seeing one patient while another is getting undressed, and carefully trained desk girls are responsible for getting the patients into the rooms and ready for examination. Then they snap on the doctor's light above the door to tell him as he passes that a patient is waiting for him in that room.

Answering such a light one day, the doctor found a man sitting on the table, partially undressed, with the usual cape over his shoulders to cover the nakedness beneath, and on a chair in the corner a woman, presumably his wife. After exchanging the time of day with them, the doctor read through the case history, laid out for him on the desk, and then looked sharply at the patient. "You've lost weight, haven't you?" he asked.

"Why no, I don't think so," said the man.

The doctor walked over, took off the cape, and felt of his arms and shoulders. "You must have lost some weight." Then turning to the woman in the corner, "Haven't you noticed it? Isn't he thinner than he was?"

Wide-eyed, the woman answered, "Why, doctor, I don't know. I never saw him before."

The doctor got the woman into another room in a hurry, with profuse apologies.

Many encounters with the vagaries of minds upset and confused by illness gave even the men in the administration a sympathetic understanding of the ways of sick folks. Once half the staff engaged in a hunt for a patient's overcoat and hat. Nobody could find them anywhere, and finally one of the executives told the desk girl to call the man's hotel and see whether he had left them there.

"But he couldn't have come over without them today," she remonstrated. "It's freezing cold and snowing hard."

"You call and see just the same," he told her. "That man is half out of his mind with worry about this operation he's got to have and it's hard telling what he might have done."

The girl called the hotel and the bellhop found the missing coat and hat lying on the man's bed.

"Will Mayo was the most imperious of autocrats," a few outsiders have said, and some within the Clinic found him ruthless in enforcing his decisions. His close associates said yes, he could be an autocrat, as every executive must be at times, but he was always amenable to argument if one's ideas were good and his reasons sound. Dr. Will himself once told Burt Eaton, "I may be wrong, but I decide things around here. Somebody has to, you know."

Sometimes he lost patience with negative attitudes and acted arbitrarily on that account. When the question arose of what to do with the pathological specimens that were overflowing the space allotted to them, he proposed that some of them be arranged in cases around the walls of the main library reading room. Everybody protested loudly, especially the librarians, who did not want their lovely room spoiled by a lot of ugly old gallbladders and appendixes.

Dr. Will waited for countersuggestions, and when none was forthcoming he gave orders for the specimens to be placed in the library. "Let them howl," he told his secretary. "I don't give a cuss. They haven't any constructive ideas; they just don't like this one."

He did care, however, and when it became possible to move the specimens to the museum across the street, he mollified everyone by a gift of new furniture for a browsing room in the library.

He was capable of complete detachment in his decisions. No matter who was involved or how much he liked him personally, if the man was disrupting the Clinic he had to leave. Ordinary frictions did not bother the Chief; a good scrap once in a while hurt nobody. It was when a man wanted to run things all his own way and began to form a faction within the group that the danger point was reached and Dr. Will firmly arranged for him and the Clinic to part. "We part on a friendly basis, *but we part.*"

Dr. Will was always ready himself to conform to rules, and he rarely asked for special favors. One Sunday morning he called the Clinic library to ask whether they had a copy of the current issue of *Fortune*. They did, and he drove down to get it. Would she rather he used it in the library? he asked the assistant on duty at the desk, or could he take it home for the day? The librarians did not soon get over that.

There was little conceit evident in Dr. Will. While everybody was showering plaudits upon him and Dr. Charlie for the miracle they had wrought in building a world center of medicine on the Minnesota prairies, Dr. Will alone kept insisting, in private as well as in public, that their accomplishment was due "to the transformation in medical conditions rather than to personal attributes."

Though they were in their sixties now and at the top of their profession Dr. Will and Dr. Charlie did not consider themselves beyond the need of further learning. By the end of the 1920s Dr. Will could say he had studied surgery in every town in America and Canada of one hundred thousand population or more, and had crossed the Atlantic thirty times—not to mention the side trips to Alaska, Cuba, the Antipodes, and South America. And Dr. Charlie was not much less traveled. Their friend Dr. Haggard dubbed them "the surgical travelers of the world."

The brothers also continued their activity in medical societies, rounding out their service till they had held the presidencies of all the major ones in turn. They did an amount of speaking and writing that is almost incredible, even when the help of their secretaries, the Clinic librarians, and other staff members is taken into account. Their bibliographies mounted toward six hundred items each—with less repetition than one might expect.

Among technical subjects Dr. Will's favorites were surgery of the spleen and the problem of stomach cancer, and in the latter he continued to rank first, so that on one occasion the doctor who was asked to discuss his paper began with the question, "What is he to say that cometh after the king?"

But their technical papers were outnumbered now by those on more general topics—usually medical education and the general progress of medicine for Dr. Will and public health and preventive examination for Dr. Charlie. Both talked increasingly often about the relationship of science to medicine, and though neither of them was a scientist in any sense of the term, their support of science was judged sufficient contribution to the cause to win them election to Sigma Xi.

Dr. Charlie's speeches were still the despair of the medical editors, who had to cut them apart and paste them together again sentence by sentence to secure anything approaching coherence. But they were the delight of audiences who heard them with the tickling overtones of Dr. Charlie's personality.

Mr. Harwick recalled an occasion when he was with Dr. and Mrs. Charlie on a trip to Florida. In St. Petersburg the local medical society, learning that Dr. Charlie was in town, asked him to address them and he, amiable as always, agreed to do so. But he wondered what he should wear. He had a dress suit with him but he had forgotten to bring the vest along.

In a hilarious half hour before they left the hotel he and Mr. Harwick agreed that if Dr. Charlie started to open his coat while he spoke, as was his habit, Mr. Harwick would pull on his coattails to remind him that the vest was missing.

But before the speech was far along Mr. Harwick forgot all about the coat. He and the audience both sat "with open mouths" as Dr. Charlie talked to them extemporaneously for an hour and a half about the likeness of plant to animal life. He spun the analogy to such lengths that Mr. Harwick, fascinated, wondered how he would ever get back to the proposition he started with. But for once in his life Dr. Charlie managed to round his circle and tuck in the ends before he finished, to the great applause of the crowd.

On another occasion he was less successful in this respect. Alfred Owre, dean of the University of Minnesota school of dentistry and a great reformer in dental education, became a good friend of both brothers, and when he left Minnesota to take a position at Columbia, Dr. Charlie was asked to represent the Foundation at the farewell dinner.

He began his speech well enough, with an appreciation of Dean Owre's work in raising the level of dental education at Minnesota, but then he started telling jokes and the rest of his address was simply a string of funny stories that, quite without pertinence to the occasion, kept the crowd in an uproar.

As he resumed his seat, he half turned to Dean Ford of the graduate school, who was seated next to him, and drawled in disgust, "I guess I've made a damned fool of myself again." But Dean Ford and the audience did not think so. Dr. Charlie had brought life into a dull affair.

It has been said that the recognition of merit accorded the Mayo brothers has never been equaled in extent anywhere in modern times, and if the length of entries in *Who's Who* is a valid criterion the statement is true.

The walls of the board of governors room at the Clinic were fast filling with diplomas, medals, and plaques of all kinds bestowed upon Dr. Will and Dr. Charlie in recognition of their services to surgery, to science, and to society. The awards came from a wide variety of sources and agencies—medical associations, learned societies, great universities, and governments, at home and abroad.

Both brothers were decorated by the king of Italy and Dr. Will by the king of Sweden. Dr. Will received the second and Dr. Charlie the third honorary degree to be granted by the University of Cuba in its four hundred years of existence.

Their popularity among laymen was so extensive that on at least two occasions the politicians tried to exploit it. While Dr. Will was in South America in 1920 Frank Day of Fairmont, the Minnesota newspaperman who had started John A. Johnson on his gubernatorial career, ran an editorial suggesting that William J. Mayo be named the Democratic candidate for governor.

Dr. Mayo was at the zenith of his career, said Day. He could win no more laurels as a doctor, but with his splendid executive ability he would make a great governor, certainly the most famous in America.

Other Democratic papers took up the idea at once, asking only, Will he run?

Day's suggestion had become a good-sized movement by the time Dr. Will returned from his trip, but he put an end to the "balloon ascension" immediately by a public refusal that was too unequivocal to be doubted. The Democrats reported it with disappointment, the Republicans with relief, admitting that if Dr. Mayo had said yes, their opponents would have had a sure-fire winner.

Four years later Minnesota politicians started a movement to make Dr. Charlie the Democratic candidate for the presidency. It never passed beyond the stage of talk, but the idea persisted for weeks and brought him many letters from fellow doctors, old patients, even governors of other states, predicting that he would be elected by a landslide. Even Republicans would abandon their party to vote for "my doctor," they promised.

Dr. Charlie said no too, but "he is not so vehement as one

would like him to be," remarked the *New York Times*, calling for an end to these attempts to seduce one of the famous Mayos into politics.

Everywhere Dr. Will and Dr. Charlie traveled they were met by newspapermen. They tried refusing to talk to them, but the reporters had been told to get a story and when the Drs. Mayo would not give them one they went back to the files, pulled out the old tales, and refurbished them to suit themselves, sometimes with fantastic results. And of course the effect on already hostile doctors was precisely the same as if Dr. Will and Dr. Charlie had given an interview.

So the brothers decided to talk to reporters if they must but agreed that they would say nothing about themselves or their work and nothing about the Clinic or Rochester; they would talk about the problems and progress of medicine in general. For the most part they kept to this resolve remarkably well, Dr. Will somewhat more religiously than the impulsive, amiable Dr. Charlie.

But it helped very little. Newspapermen admitted to medical gatherings did strange things to the brothers' remarks. When Dr. Will addressed the Wisconsin Society of Chicago in behalf of the Ochsner Foundation for Clinical Research, he talked about the growing specialization in surgery. Whereas the best surgeons of the old school were able to perform successfully all the operations then known, he said, no one man could do so now.

"I can count on the fingers of one hand the men I would trust to operate on myself or members of my family for any sort of surgical condition," he said, adding that he himself was not one of them, because there were many operations he would not attempt except in a dire emergency.

The newspapers reported his words accurately enough, but they ran the story under such headlines as "Dr. Mayo Limits Capable Surgeons in America to Five," and doctors as well as laymen seemingly read only the headlines. Medical skies clouded and it was thundery for a time. And from laymen came letters like this:

> Dear Dr. Mayo,
>   I read . . . where you said . . . there was about five good surgeons in America. . . .
>   I have doctored for gall-bladder trouble and find after fighting to keep from the knife I will have to have it out and would appreciate your kindness if you would tell me if one of the five is in Chicago and how close I could go to one. I am so scared of the knife and want the *Best*.

That is a good expression, not greatly exaggerated, of the feeling of fear and helplessness that made laymen turn, in the absence of other guidance, to well-known figures like the Mayos, especially when they read about this or that movie star, or sports idol, or government official heading for Rochester when he needed an operation.

About this same time the *Pictorial Review* decided to publish some articles about the shortage of nurses, and the editor sent a writer to Rochester to ask Dr. Charlie what he thought about it. It happened to be a matter on which he and Will had strong convictions, and he stated them.

He said the training course for nurses had been made too long, with the result that nursing fees were so high the man of moderate means could not afford proper nursing care. He was quite sure that he had never asked anything from a nurse she could not learn in two years, *providing* she did not have to spend her time in making beds, bathing patients, and other duties a hospital maid could learn to do in six months or less.

This statement merely anticipated the coming a decade or so later of the nurses' aide, but at the time it awoke reverberations that echoed for weeks throughout the country.

A few years later when Dr. Will was asked to talk on "Nursing and Hospital Costs for Individuals in Moderate Circumstances" at a symposium sponsored by the American College of Surgeons, he touched briefly on the same problem, adding *in part of one sentence* that the hospital "often shows too much salesmanship and too little humanity."

Of course this was the phrase that was chosen for quoting, to the great displeasure of hospital managers, one of whom, in Maine, dismissed it with the statement that Dr. Mayo had merely been talking "to get on the front page."

This was bad tactics. Reporters and magazine writers were continually grumbling in print about the Mayos' reluctance to talk for publication, calling them "publicity-shy" and "about as garrulous as sphinxes," and now a number of editors challenged the statement of the Maine medico. The controversy over hospital management was not for laymen to decide, they said, but, to quote one of them,

> The first page charge is another thing.
>
> It is a matter in which Dr. Mayo is without recourse. Most people who get on first pages have nothing to say about it. . . .
>
> The first page . . . is reserved for men who do things. That is the reason Dr. Mayo's name is found there so often. He was never a publicity seeker. None know this better than Minnesota newspaper men called upon to report his varied activities.
>
> If you would get on the front page do something worth while. Then try and keep off it if you can. It has never been done, even by such uncanny wizards in their profession as Dr. W. J. Mayo.

The editors might have spared their ink, for many doctors remained convinced that all the publicity the Mayos got was deliberate advertising, and every new article brought to Dr. Will's desk a bagful of letters ranging in tone from mild expostulation to vituperation. He answered them all patiently and courteously, denying responsibility for the offending item and assuring the writer that for every such piece that appeared in print he managed to head off three or four.

He knew that all his denials were futile, however, and he

no longer made any attempt to publish general disclaimers, having come to believe that the least said the soonest forgotten. But on the several occasions when individual doctors or local medical societies demanded that the Mayos be disciplined for unethical conduct, he and the Clinic officers themselves laid their case before the judicial councils of the Minnesota State Medical Society and the American Medical Association. They were always exonerated.

Members of the profession themselves have called those who caused the Mayos all this trouble over publicity "a jealous and ignorant minority," and certainly Dr. Will and Dr. Charlie could record on the other side of the ledger many pleasant relations with members of the profession.

With the addition of internal medicine to the Clinic practice the Surgeons Club became in name and in fact the Physicians and Surgeons Club, larger and more active than ever, and its members continued to publish accounts of their experiences in Rochester in the professional journals. Many doctors were numbered among Clinic patients, and Dr. Will was always proud of the fact that he and Charlie together had operated on almost fifty fellows of the American Surgical Association or members of their families.

River cruising was still Dr. Will's chief relaxation. The *Oronoco* gave way to the *Minnesota* and that in turn to a trim little yacht, the *North Star,* which he had built to his order. Many a summer weekend he spent with Mrs. Mayo on the river, and in spring and fall vacations they cruised slowly down to the Gulf or up the Ohio to Cincinnati.

But not even on the boat could Dr. Will forget his responsibilities. His itinerary was always carefully planned beforehand and rigidly adhered to, so that at any time the men left in charge at the Clinic could telephone him for advice or to ask him to return immediately if he was needed. Sometimes his chauffeur followed the boat's course along the shore, so that the car would be at hand if it became necessary for Dr. Will to return to Rochester in a hurry.

Dr. and Mrs. Will were generosity itself with the *North Star*. They always took with them a large group of guests, including anyone, friend, employee, or even patient, who Dr. Will thought needed a respite or an outing to recuperate. And when they were not using the craft themselves they lent it to clubs and groups of all sorts—medical societies, school-teachers, nurses, commercial clubs.

But when the depression came Dr. Will's pleasure in the boat was spoiled by the signs of distress he saw along the water front. After 1931 he made no more long trips and only occasionally went for a week-end's rest on the *North Star*. On such a trip in May 1938 the boat arrived at St. Paul during some kind of demonstration that had assembled a large crowd of ragged and shabby men on the dock. The contrast between their poverty and the luxury of his yacht was more than Dr. Will could stand, and when he returned to Rochester he ordered the boat sold and the money received for it added to the funds of the Clinic section on social service.

Next to the boat he got his greatest pleasure from motoring, because it too kept him in motion. "I can rest if what I'm sitting in is moving," he once said. When he left the Clinic in the late afternoon, Mrs. Mayo and the chauffeur were usually waiting to take him for a ride through the countryside before dinner.

For Dr. Charlie the pleasures of Mayowood still held first place. A pair of Japanese deer had succeeded to the place of the Chinese pheasants that laid an "Easter egg." Someone told him that when the first doe was born he could be sure the deer were happy in their new home, so with great anxiety he waited for the event and greeted it with chuckling satisfaction. Knowing his fondness for birds and animals, his friends sent him all kinds as gifts—so many that he was soon able to start a small zoo in Mayo Park.

He turned from animals to flowers finally and began raising

chrysanthemums, with such success that the annual chrysanthemum show at Mayowood, with its more than sixty thousand blossoms, came to rank among the largest and finest in the country.

For eight years, from 1915 to 1923, Dr. Charlie was a member of the school board in Rochester, and, like his father many years before, he sparked the board to ambitious projects. Within five years a building program that cost nearly a million dollars transformed the Rochester schools from the wooden buildings of a country village into urban structures of brick and stone.

Dr. Will and Dr. Charlie personally donated the instruments and paid the salary of a teacher so the high school could have a band and an orchestra. They gave the school its first motion picture machine too, and Dr. Charlie urged forward the program of visual education. Also on his motion the school system was extended upward to include a junior college, which was soon offering something unique in the United States —a special course for medical secretaries, most of whose graduates were absorbed into the Clinic offices.

Dr. Charlie was still Rochester's health officer. He tried to resign the post when he had completed his major program, but the women of the town persuaded him to stay on the job. As he once said, his deputy did most of the field work but it kept him busy fixing things up with the public and the city council so the deputy could do his job without interference.

Until about the middle twenties the two brothers financed most of the city health program; then they convinced the municipality that it ought to shoulder the responsibility, though the Clinic continued to give all the necessary laboratory service free of charge and its staff provided much of the professional service on the program.

Through the years the brothers' policy of contributing to the improvement of the city financed in whole or in part more parks, a baseball diamond, a large outdoor swimming pool, a new public library, and a civic auditorium that includes an art gallery, a handsome little theater, and an "arena" that can be adapted to any kind of show from a symphony concert to a prize fight.

Dr. Will did not miss the importance of adequate transportation facilities for the success of the Clinic. As soon as automobile travel became general, he saw its possibilities for widening the area of the local practice and entered actively into the movement for good roads throughout Olmsted County. And he was always ready with suggestions and encouragement for the efforts of the local businessmen to secure state and federal routes through Rochester. The network of roads converging on Rochester was not an accident.

Similarly through the years his suggestions effected a succession of improvements in railroad service from Chicago, especially in accommodations for handling the sick, all the way from the first couch placed at the end of the train to the modern Joseph Lister coach that opens wide at the side to give easy entrance and exit for stretchers and wheel chairs.

The Mayo Properties Association carried this policy on from where the brothers left off and by providing Rochester with one of the finest airports in the state put the capstone on a development that began in the Old Doctor's day and was vital in the Clinic's growth.

24. A Living Memorial

IN 1928 a new Clinic building was dedicated and occupied. Complete with all its equipment it cost the Mayo Properties Association three million dollars and was more than two years under construction. Fifteen stories tall it is, crowned with a bell tower of four stories more, all built of rich-toned Siena stone. Many who come to its massive bronze doors, fresh from farms on the Dakota prairies or cabins in the Canadian wilds, gape at its size and splendor and move in wonder through its marble halls.

In the tower that tops the building hangs a carillon of twenty-three bells cast in the famous foundry of Croydon, England. For years Dr. Will had wanted for Rochester a set of bells such as he had heard in other cities, and the new building gave him the chance to gratify this wish.

Day in and day out the bells ring the hours, and for half an hour three times a week Rochester seems to hush while the carillonneur sends hymns and folk songs singing through the sky into the farthest hotel and hospital room in town.

This Clinic building, like the first, was the work of Henry Plummer, who was in charge of its design and construction, and the well-nigh perfect fitting of its plan to its purpose is a monument to his genius. Once again as he planned the building he reviewed the entire Clinic organization and system—refining, extending, and integrating it till he had shaped the whole to his conception of needs to come.

In this process he had the assistance of Dr. Thomas B. Magath of the division of clinical pathology, and Dr. Magath's patience was sorely tried at times by Plummer's exacting and eccentric habits. Whenever Plummer got an idea he would send for Dr. Magath and goad him into picking it to pieces; then in the light of the arguments against it he would accept or reject it as seemed best. But he was more than likely to get his idea about midnight and the argument to last till nearly dawn.

When the new building was opened Dr. Will was sixty-seven years old, alert and active as ever. But on July 1, 1928, he went to the Clinic from St. Mary's in a mood of deep depression. His secretary asked him what was the matter.

"I've just done my last operation."

"But you don't have to quit yet," she protested.

"Yes, I want to stop while I'm still good. I don't want to go on like some others I've seen, past my prime, doing the surgery that younger, surer men ought to be doing."

He never spoke of the matter, and never operated, again—so little outward fuss did he make over a decision that must have been bitterly difficult for him.

Dr. Charlie's retirement came a year and a half later, suddenly and unexpectedly, as the result of a retinal hemorrhage that occurred one morning while he was operating—and while his elder son was getting ready in the next room for his first operation as his father's assistant!

Dr. Charlie was up and about after a few weeks' rest, but he was never really well again. A series of strokes, some so severe that death seemed likely, sapped his physical strength and to a degree his mental powers.

For years medical men argued about which of the Mayo brothers was the greater surgeon. Some in Europe as well as in the United States considered William Mayo the greatest surgeon of his time; others were certain that Dr. Charlie was the abler, more versatile, and more ingenious operator. The point does not matter; they were both masters of their craft, and by reason of their differences the complementary parts of a great team.

But not for their surgery will they be remembered in medical history. Their contribution in disseminating the new surgery was not of the nailable, datable kind that historians readily record, and even their original techniques have been superseded by the refinements that enable many surgeons to do today what the brothers were unique in doing in their time.

As Dr. Will once observed, "What a man may do with his own hands is small compared with what he may do to implant ideals and scientific spirit in many men who in endless chains will carry on the same endeavor." The length and strength of the chain the Mayos started by building a cooperative group clinic upon their surgical partnership will determine the niche finally accorded them in medical history.

The brothers' release from active surgical duties carried its

own consolation. One had always remained on duty while the
other was away, but now they could travel together.

They made their first joint trip to Europe in 1929, for the
purpose of dedicating a stained-glass window they had ordered
placed to their father's memory in the parish church in his
birthplace. Their many English friends made much of their
presence, and the University of Manchester took the occasion
to confer upon them its highest degree, the first they had received together.

The severe cold of Minnesota winters was hard on Dr.
Charlie now, and for his sake the two families built adjoining
houses in Tucson, Arizona, where he seemed to feel best.
There they spent the winter months in pleasant relaxation
from the hectic, hurried life they had lived so long.

But Dr. Will did not overnight drop the habits of a lifetime. Early one morning he struck across lots to visit the
Tucson hospital. It was a Janus-faced building and, not being
able to tell the front from the back, Dr. Will simply entered
the first door he came to, which led him into the kitchen.

A woman in uniform asked him sharply what he wanted
and he replied mildly, "I'm Dr. W. J. Mayo of Rochester,
Minnesota, and I'd like to visit your hospital."

The superintendent—for the woman was she—was startled
into a flurry of embarrassment. The great Dr. Mayo coming
unannounced and by way of the kitchen!

But Dr. Will soon put her at ease. When she led him into
the dining room where a shift of nurses were at breakfast and
introduced him with a flustered reference to his coming
through the kitchen, he spoke whimsically of the many times
he and his father in their pioneer practice had eaten breakfast
in the kitchen after a night on duty.

Seeing the humor of the incident in retrospect the hospital
staff told the story on themselves, and it won the heart of
Tucson when it appeared in the newspaper under the heading
"Mayo of Rochester Entertained in the Kitchen."

While the brothers were in Tucson they received periodic

reports on the state of affairs at the Clinic, and when the first one arrived Dr. Charlie read it over, then looked up at his brother with a grin, "Well, well, this is quite a comedown for us, Will. They're doing better now we're away than they did when we were there."

It is not easy for a man to accept the fact that he is not indispensable, especially in an institution he has built, and in nothing was William Mayo greater than in the grace with which he accepted age and yielded place to others. In 1931 when he attended the convention of the American Surgical Association in San Francisco, his friends, learning that the day was a milestone for him, made it the occasion for a public tribute, and he responded:

> Your greetings on this seventieth birthday of mine repay me for living long enough to have it. . . . The years have come upon me so easily and so rapidly that I can look back on each and every one of them without regret, and I feel no older now than I did when I came into this Association. As I have watched older men come down the ladder, as down they must come, with younger men passing them, as they must pass to go up, it so often has been an unhappy time for both. The older man is not always able to see the necessity or perhaps the justice of his descent and resents his slipping from the position that he has held, instead of gently and peacefully helping this passing by assisting the younger man. What pleasure and comfort I have had from my hours with younger men! They still have their imagination, their vision; the future is bright before them. Each day as I go through the hospitals surrounded by younger men, they give me of their dreams and I give them of my experience, and I get the better of the exchange. . . .
>
> There are many recompenses in a seventieth birthday. I look through a half-opened door into the future, full of interest, intriguing beyond my power to describe, but with a full understanding that it is for each generation to solve

its own problems and that no man has the wisdom to guide or control the next generation. It is a comfortable feeling, to be interested in what is to happen, but in bringing it about to be in no way responsible.

Again and again he rang the changes on the idea that it is both the duty and the privilege of the passing generation to hand on the torch for younger men to carry it in the time of their greatest physical and intellectual strength.

When he and Mrs. Mayo gave their house and gardens with sufficient endowment for their maintenance to the Mayo Foundation, Dr. Will made the presentation with these words:

"We have no desire in any way to dictate or control the manner in which this adventure in education shall be carried out. It is for the younger people to meet the conditions of their generation in the way that appears to them to be wise and best. We only hope that Mayo Foundation House will be a meeting place where men of medicine may exchange ideas for the good of mankind."

Nor did he stop with words. One night in November 1932 he rose to talk at staff meeting. He began with reminiscence and history, tracing briefly the steps in the development of the Clinic, beginning with his father's work in laying the foundation. That was the first period in the story, he said. The second had begun with the building of St. Mary's in 1889; and now a third was at the door. On December 31 he and Dr. Charlie and Dr. Plummer would withdraw from the board of governors of the Clinic in favor of three younger men from the staff.

The brothers had decided to take this step because the apparatus of self-government instituted a decade earlier was working well. More and more of the administration had been transferred to the standing committees, and those who had opposed the committee system when Dr. Will established it were now among its most enthusiastic supporters. For it had turned out as Dr. Will expected; committee service was an excellent way of educating staff members in the ramifications of Clinic problems and policies.

When any member got so full of his own and his specialty's importance that he could not see the rights of the other sections in the organization, the board of governors had only to appoint him to some important committee. Dealing there with the problems of the whole group, he soon had a better understanding of the relationship of his own block to the whole structure and was ever afterward more amenable.

Yet as long as the Mayo brothers held positions of authority the degree of self-government would be incomplete and the full strength or weakness of the machinery undisclosed. To put the Clinic wholly on its own while the Mayos were still alive to advise in moments of doubt was supremely wise.

There was another factor in the situation. As long as Dr. Will and Dr. Charlie retained their authority there would linger within the institution, outside it, and within their families the idea that the Clinic belonged to the Mayos—although legally they had been out of control since the reorganization effected in the 1920s.

It had been difficult for Dr. Will to give up the idea of perpetuating the institution through the family; but once he was convinced that its future would be jeopardized by saddling it with all Mayos to come whether they could carry their own weight in it or not, he acted with his customary impersonality and moved to sever the family control actually as well as legally.

True, Dr. Charlie's elder son and Dr. Will's two sons-in-law held life memberships in the Properties Association and on the Clinic board of governors, but in neither case is three a controlling vote, and the Clinic is under neither legal nor moral obligation to place the Mayos of future generations on its staff or its governing body unless they are worthy of the place in their own right.

The brothers were as good as their word. After 1932 neither of them ever attended a meeting of the board of governors or cast a vote in its decisions. Dr. Will's influence was still considerable, but it was exercised solely through the power of his prestige and the value of his advice, and he was proud that it was so.

He sought thereafter to further the transfer of public confidence from the Mayo brothers to the Mayo Clinic—as the Old Doctor had once transferred it to his sons. The process had already begun, of course; for years people had been going to the Mayo Clinic instead of to the Drs. Mayo. But it was still Dr. Will and Dr. Charlie who held the public eye and the public affection, and to change this as much as he could, Dr. Will deliberately began to withdraw from public activity. He refused more and more of the calls that came to him to speak or to serve on professional committees.

Ever since the war the Mayos had given their services and the Clinic's free of charge to disabled veterans for whom the American Legion arranged residence and hospitalization in Rochester. In 1934 the Legion recognized this service by a citation read in an impressive ceremony attended by many of the country's medical and civilian great, including President Franklin D. Roosevelt.

That the President of the United States should come to Rochester to join in honoring the beloved brothers seemed to many the culminating triumph of their career.

Later in the year, when the medical advisory committee to the Committee on Economic Security was being organized in Washington, President Roosevelt had only one suggestion to make as to its personnel: Dr. W. J. Mayo should be its chairman. But when the invitation to act in this capacity was transmitted to Dr. Will by Secretary of Labor Perkins, he declined the honor and would not be coaxed into reconsidering his decision.

"I think each generation must settle its own problems," he said, "and that men along in years who try to project such wisdom as they may have or think they have onto the problems of the future are more likely to do harm than good. I think that such a committee, to do the most good, should be made up of medical men in the active part of their lives, should contain few men over 60, and that at least half of the members should be men of 50. I have passed 70."

Dr. Will himself took little part publicly in the controversy that churned in medical circles when socialized medicine became an issue after the depression, but one of the leaders in the minority group of doctors who advocated this kind of public medicine was Dr. Hugh Cabot, a distinguished urologist then on the Clinic staff. Cabot was very active in writing and speaking about "the doctor's bill" and "the patient's dilemma," and in reporting his activities the newspapers invariably referred to him as a Mayo Clinic physician.

This upset Cabot's opponents, who feared the lay public would think he spoke for the Mayos. Accordingly some of them wrote to Dr. Will, strongly hinting that he ought to muzzle Cabot. To them his answer was unequivocal:

> We have always stood for freedom of speech and thought by the members of the staff of the Clinic, and never in any way have interfered with their religious, political, or social opinions. . . . It must be distinctly understood that Dr. Cabot is entirely within his rights in expressing his opinion on a social question, even though that opinion is exactly opposite to that held by the general staff of the Clinic.

Dr. Will did express himself in the debate over group medicine that grew out of the general review of medical practice induced by New Deal charges that large sections of the population were receiving inadequate medical care. In this debate the advocates of group practice based their arguments on the Mayo Clinic's methods and achievements, but the opponents insisted that the Mayo Clinic was unique and therefore not a fair example of group practice.

To Dr. Will's way of thinking, entirely too much of the

argument turned on the financial aspects of the matter—whether or not group practice reduces the cost of medical care to the patient and raises the return to the practitioner, whether or not a fixed salary destroys the initiative of the doctor, and so on. In one of many utterances on the subject he said:

Properly considered, group medicine is not a financial arrangement, except for minor details, but a *scientific co-operation for the welfare of the sick*. . . . The internist, the surgeon, and the specialist must join with the physiologist, pathologist, and the laboratory workers to form the clinical group, which must also include men learned in the abstract sciences, since physics and biochemistry are leading medicine to greater heights. Union of all these forces will lengthen by many years the span of human life, and as a by-product will do much to improve professional ethics by overcoming some of the evils of competitive medicine.

"The most amazing thing of all about the Mayo Clinic [is] the fact that five hundred members of the most highly individualistic profession in the world could be induced to live and work together in a small town on the edge of nowhere, and like it!" So said an English surgeon who spent several years in Rochester as a Foundation fellow. More usual is the attitude of a doctor who said to one Clinic member, "I wouldn't work at the Clinic for any amount of money. I'd be just a cog in a machine there."

If Clinic men are just cogs, they do not know it. The research men will tell you they are there because they have everything they want to work with and complete independence to follow where their interest and their results lead them. And the clinicians will rhapsodize about the opportunity and facilities they have to practice medicine in the best way they know how without any financial restrictions. The salary question is settled and the business office takes care of the fees; all they have to think about is getting the patient well.

They all agree that the size of their salaries is not what keeps them, and the administration says there is not a research man in the group who has not been offered more money elsewhere and not a single clinician who could not make more money as a specialist in individual practice.

As for regimentation, the sole complaint seems to be that there is not enough of it.

"The trouble with the system here is that you can't get a decision out of anybody," said one section head. "The board of governors have the authority supposedly, but they won't use it. They'll send you to this committee or that to talk it over, and they in turn send you to talk it over with somebody else. So you have to see half a dozen persons for a decision one could make.

"Of course," he admitted ruefully, "by the time you're through, you know the majority approve your plan and you can go ahead with it with full support, or else you've been talked out of it yourself." Which, of course, is precisely the purpose of the system.

Another section head once asked one of the Clinic officials whether he had the authority to discipline an employee. "Yes, you have the authority," was the answer. "But if I were you I wouldn't use it."

This is not to say that disagreement is not permitted. "We have a lot of friction here," said one of the Clinic laboratory men. "But ninety-five per cent of us can argue about the *thing* without getting sore at the *man*. So we scrap out our differences. The other five per cent leave sooner or later. There's a kind of natural selective process going on here all the time."

Such is the flower the Mayo brothers brought to bloom. How fragile it is no one knew better than Dr. Will, and he spent much of his time in his last years describing the conditions necessary for its continued blossoming.

These three things he considered to be of vital importance: an active ideal of service instead of personal profit, a primary and sincere concern for the care of the sick, that is, for the individual patient, and an unselfish interest of every member of the group in the professional progress of every other member.

If the Clinic failed, he said over and over again, it would do so because of dissension and jealousies within, not attacks from without. He urged the Clinic men to remember that a boost for a colleague was a boost for the group and so for every member in it, and that taking a dig at a colleague was just cutting a nick out of one's own nose.

Whether attitudes and qualities seemingly so rare in mankind can be perpetuated in an organization beyond the generation of the founders is a social question of the first magnitude. As an experiment in cooperative individualism the Mayo Clinic deserves watching—and not by doctors alone.

The 1930s brought the deaths, one after another, of many of the early members of the group.

Mrs. Mellish Wilson was the first to go, in 1933. A pioneer in medical editing, she made "of the Mayo Clinic" on a medical paper synonymous with good form and clear, readable English. The authors might grumble at her slashing of their sentences and complain that she made them all sound alike, but without her services their annual volume of *Collected Papers* would not have become the "surgeons' Bible" it is called. Dr. Will ranked her second after Charlie and himself in influence on the development of the Clinic.

First after them, of course, was Henry Plummer. Without him the Mayo Clinic would not exist in the form it does today nor in the house it inhabits. He put rather too much of himself into the second Clinic building, and the spark never burned so brightly thereafter. When he was stricken with bulbar paralysis in 1936 he knew it for what it was, sent for his family and his colleagues, and as long as he was conscious traced the progress of the disease in his own body—the clinical investigator to the last.

Dr. Judd was the master surgeon first, last, and always. In

his own realm he did a prodigious amount of work, but he took little active part in the affairs of the Clinic outside the operating room, although he was one of the early partners and later a member of the board of governors. He became head of the surgical staff upon the retirement of the Mayos, and in 1931 he was president of the American Medical Association. Four years later he was stricken with pneumonia while in Chicago attending a football game, and he died there a few days later.

Although Sister Joseph had long since retired from her operating-room post as Dr. Will's assistant, she continued as the superintendent of St. Mary's until her death on March 29, 1939.

When she began her work, the Sisters of St. Francis considered nursing a kind of glorified maid service, and curious pupils in their day school in Rochester, asking why Sister So-and-So was not sent to the hospital, were told in accents of horror, "Why, she is educated!" But before Sister Joseph died, members of the sisterhood with advanced degrees from Columbia or Minnesota in dietetics, hospital administration, and nursing education had taken back from lay women the management of the hospital and the school of nursing and were recognized as national leaders in their profession.

Dr. Will and Dr. Charlie, Drs. Graham, Judd, and Plummer, and Sister Joseph, all born and reared within a few miles of Rochester! How, some have asked, can one explain this incidence of exceptional abilities in medicine?

The question assumes that the air of southern Minnesota somehow produced unusual medical skill, but it seems more likely that because of the presence of a flourishing medical practice, an unusual number of those with talent were attracted into medicine instead of into something else.

The Mayos returned early from Tucson in the spring of 1939. Dr. Will was not feeling well and decided to go home for a checkup at the Clinic. The physical examination revealed nothing, but the x-ray showed—irony of ironies!—cancer of the stomach.

He was operated on at once and rallied nicely. He was soon so much better that Dr. Charlie decided to make a trip to Chicago for a fitting of some suits he had ordered months before. While there he was taken ill with pneumonia, and on May 26 the newspapers and radio flashed the words across the country, "Dr. Charlie is dead."

The first thought of thousands was for the loving and beloved brother. Would this great loss prove too much for him in his own feeble health? But for Dr. Will the shock was lessened by the greater sorrow he had suffered several years earlier when illness took away the real Charlie whose strength had supported his own.

Slowly Dr. Will recovered sufficiently to spend an hour or two a day in his office in the Clinic, but the improvement was only temporary, and soon after his seventy-eighth birthday he retired to his bed, where he slept quietly away on July 28, 1939.

It seemed fitting somehow that the famous brothers who had worked so closely and wrought so mightily together should die within two months of each other.

Their deaths produced eulogies in every major medical journal of America and in many across the seas. "Like Lincoln the Mayo brothers now belong to the ages," said one. "Two more names are enrolled among the immortals," said another. And another, "With their passing the curtain falls on an era in American medicine."

More impressive still is the flood—no other word is adequate—of letters and telegrams that came to their families and the Clinic during their illnesses and after their deaths. These fill many thick, thick folders in the files, and reading through them one wonders whether any other two men in history have ever evoked such a tribute either in volume or in range.

Few countries of the world are unrepresented in the collection, and messages of condolence from the wealthy and the well-born lie side by side with almost illiterate scrawls full of personal grief in the loss of "my doctor." There are notes from both President and Mrs. Roosevelt and literally next is a penciled letter, the handwriting cramped, the words misspelled, from an old woman in Texas who had sent a potted flower and wanted to tell Mrs. Mayo how much Dr. Charlie's kindness twenty years before had meant to her.

Then a little farther on lies the most moving expression of them all, a copy of the resolutions adopted by the surgical society of the Clinic:

Those who in years to come peruse these minutes may justly question what manner of men were we who, experiencing bereavement such as ours in recent months, yet inadequately expressed it. Let them remember, then, that those whose greatness they strive to recreate from graven names and printed pages were living men with whom we walked and talked and laughed; our preceptors, our colleagues, and our friends. We are too close to this grief to describe it: "True sorrow makes a silence in the heart."

. . . There is left for us their precedent—that immortal part of them—to cherish and hand on.

Portions of that precedent seem particularly left in trust to us, the surgeons of the institution which our great preceptors founded. They worked for something even greater than themselves, which lies in the future and which must be effected by their successors. Very gradually at first, then more definitely, as old age approached, they withdrew from the affairs of this society and of the clinic, encouraging their successors to plant their feet firmly in the way. They kept to themselves no knowledge or skill which they could impart to younger men. Always available for consultation and advice, yet they did not assume authority in another surgeon's case. They insisted that each surgeon have a full hand on his own service and that he shoulder the responsibility thereof. Guidance without pampering; help without meddling; these are the principles by which we were trained. Let us then train others thereby and as we close ranks for the months and years ahead as our great mentors would have had us do, let it be said of us: "They helped everyone his neighbor."

Men may raise shafts of stone and piles of brick to the memory of William James and Charles Horace Mayo, but so long as that spirit endures in the Clinic they created they will have a monument more fitting, a living memorial in their own image.

Index

Index